SHIFTING LEGAL VISIONS

What explains the success of criminal prosecutions against former Latin American officials accused of human rights violations? Why did some judiciaries evolve from unresponsive bureaucracies into protectors of victim rights? Using a theory of judicial action inspired by sociological institutionalism, this book argues that this was the result of deep transformations in the legal preferences of judges and prosecutors. Judicial actors discarded long-standing positivist legal criteria, historically protective of conservative interests, and embraced doctrines grounded in international human rights law, which made possible innovative readings of constitutions and criminal codes. Litigants were responsible for this shift in legal visions by activating informal mechanisms of ideational change and providing the skills necessary to deal with complex and unusual cases. Through an in-depth exploration of the interactions among judges, prosecutors, and human rights lawyers in three countries, the book asks how changing ideas about the law and standards of adjudication condition the exercise of judicial power.

EZEQUIEL A. GONZÁLEZ-OCANTOS is Associate Professor in the Department of Politics and International Relations and Professorial Fellow of Nuffield College, at the University of Oxford. He received his B.A. in Social and Political Sciences from the University of Cambridge in 2005, and his Ph.D. in Political Science from the University of Notre Dame in 2012. González-Ocantos won the American Political Science Association's Edward S. Corwin Award for the best doctoral dissertation in the field of public law. His work has appeared in the *American Journal of Political Science*, *Comparative Politics*, *Comparative Political Studies*, and *The International Journal of Human Rights*.

CAMBRIDGE STUDIES IN LAW AND SOCIETY

Cambridge Studies in Law and Society aims to publish the best scholarly work on legal discourse and practice in its social and institutional contexts, combining theoretical insights and empirical research.

The fields that it covers are: studies of law in action; the sociology of law; the anthropology of law; cultural studies of law, including the role of legal discourses in social formations; law and economics; law and politics; and studies of governance. The books consider all forms of legal discourse across societies, rather than being limited to lawyers' discourses alone.

The series editors come from a range of disciplines: academic law; socio-legal studies; sociology; and anthropology. All have been actively involved in teaching and writing about law in context.

A list of books in the series can be found at the back of this book.

SHIFTING LEGAL VISIONS

Judicial Change and Human Rights Trials in Latin America

EZEQUIEL A. GONZÁLEZ-OCANTOS
University of Oxford

CAMBRIDGE
UNIVERSITY PRESS

CAMBRIDGE
UNIVERSITY PRESS

One Liberty Plaza, 20th Floor, New York NY 10006, USA

Cambridge University Press is part of the University of Cambridge.

It furthers the University's mission by disseminating knowledge in the pursuit of education, learning, and research at the highest international levels of excellence.

www.cambridge.org
Information on this title: www.cambridge.org/9781107145238

First published 2016

A catalog record for this publication is available from the British Library.

Library of Congress Cataloging in Publication Data
Names: González-Ocantos, Ezequiel A., author.
Title: Shifting legal visions : judicial change and human rights trials in Latin America / Ezequiel A. González-Ocantos.
Description: New York : Cambridge University Press, 2016. | Includes bibliographical references and index.
Identifiers: LCCN 2016010902 | ISBN 9781107145238 (hardback)
Subjects: Comparative Politics | LCSH: Human rights – Latin America. | Criminal justice, Administration of – Latin America. | Due process of law – Latin America. | Court congestion and delay – Latin America. | Trials – Latin America.
Classification: LCC KG574.G67 2016 | DDC 345.8/02322–dc23
LC record available at http://lccn.loc.gov/2016010902

ISBN 978-1-107-14523-8 Hardback

Para mamá y la abuela Esther, en eterno agradecimiento.

Law is conservative in the same way in which language is conservative.... It seeks to assimilate everything that happens to that which has already happened.... Thus the lawyer's virtually instinctive intellectual response when he is confronted with a situation is to look for the respects in which that situation is like something that is familiar and that has a place within the realm of the understood.

Richard Wasserstorm (1968)

A rigorous science of the law is distinguished from what is normally called jurisprudence in that the former takes the latter as its object of study. In doing so, it immediately frees itself from the dominant jurisprudential debate concerning law, between formalism, which asserts the absolute autonomy of the juridical form in relation to the social world, and instrumentalism, which conceives of law as a reflection, or a tool in the service of dominant groups.

Pierre Bourdieu (1984)

CONTENTS

FIGURES

TABLES

ACKNOWLEDGMENTS

This book grew out of a conversation I had as a graduate student with my dear friend Ximena Medellín, during a coffee break outside the Hesburgh Library at the University of Notre Dame. It is certainly not common for a lawyer and a political scientist to be interested in the same questions, but there we were, braving the cold, cigarette in hand, equally puzzled by a phenomenon that we had both recently come across: Judges in Latin American countries with different histories of violence and state repression were beginning to respond in very similar ways to victims' demands for criminal accountability. In the process, judicial actors were reconfiguring the region's legal tradition by making an unprecedented use of international human rights law. Looking back at that conversation, it is remarkable how a few minutes came to shape my long-term obsessions, revolutionize my social networks, and lead me to incur many debts. Let me begin repaying some of them.

During my time at Notre Dame, Daniel Brinks, Michael Coppedge, Frances Hagopian, Scott Mainwaring, Monika Nalepa, David Nickerson, and Guillermo O'Donnell were wonderful advisers. They all cared deeply about my intellectual growth, well-being, and professional success. I will always be grateful for the time that they shared with me, and for their words of wisdom along the way. When this book was still an unwritten dissertation my graduate school friends were also an invaluable source of support. Juan Abarracín, Sandra Botero, Rodrigo Castro, Laura Gamboa, Craig García, Lucrecia García Iommi, Víctor Hernández, Chad Kiewiet de Jonge, Esteban Manteca, Ximena Medellín, Carlos Meléndez, Javier Osorio, and Nara Pavao all offered constructive feedback on this and other projects, and generally made my time in South Bend unforgettable.

The Center for Research and Teaching in Economics (CIDE) in Mexico City offered the perfect environment to begin the challenging process of turning the dissertation into a book. I was lucky to have the opportunity to start my professional journey in such a supportive and stimulating community. I completed the manuscript after I moved to Oxford, where my colleagues in the Department of Politics and International Relations and Nuffield College were incredibly welcoming. Ben Ansell, Nancy Bermeo, Des King, Leigh Payne, and Laurence Whitehead deserve special thanks for guiding me through the intricacies of the publishing world.

Over the years I benefited immensely from the feedback I received at seminars at the Due Process of Law Foundation in Washington, D.C., FLACSO Mexico, the University of Chicago, the University of Wisconsin-Madison, the University of Buenos Aires, and the University Torcuato Di Tella. Karina Ansolabehere, Sandra Botero, Eduardo Dargent, Matthew Ingram, Ximena Medellín, Paula Muñoz, Virginia Oliveros, Julio Ríos Figueroa, and Mariela Szwarcberg read parts of the manuscript, sometimes more than once, and gave me thoughtful and constructive comments.

Funding for this project was provided by the Kellogg Institute for International Studies at the University of Notre Dame. Doing fieldwork can be a frustrating and confusing experience, but I was fortunate to come across generous and effective gatekeepers, including Mariclaire Acosta, Milagros Campos, Martín Costanzo, Eduardo Dargent, Sol Déboli, María Amparo Hernández, Juan Pablo Iriarte, Francesca Lessa, Vladimir León, Ximena Medellín, Carlos Meléndez, Paula Muñoz, Leigh Payne, Xisca Pou, José Carlos Requena, Julio Ríos Figueroa, Juan Pedro Rosolén, Fabián Sánchez, Milagros Sanz, Lucrecia Servini, Jessica Sircovich, María Sirvent, Catalina Smulovitz, Karina Tchrian, and Sofía Tiscornia. I am also grateful to everyone at the Instituto de Democracia y Derechos Humanos of the Pontificia Universidad Católica del Perú, especially to Víctor Quinteros, José Alejandro Godoy, and Orieta Pérez Barreto, who gave me the institutional support I needed to infiltrate the Peruvian judiciary. Vanesa Baldino, Itzel de Haro, Marco de la O, Tomás Quesada, and Esteban Valle Riestra were excellent research assistants both in the field and back in the office. A special thank you goes to the Argentine, Brazilian, Peruvian, Mexican, and Uruguayan judges, prosecutors, and clerks who made room for me in their incredibly busy schedules. After learning about the conditions in which some of them work, and the pressures to which they are often subject, I cannot but express admiration for what they do.

At Cambridge University Press John Berger was immensely supportive of this project from the very start. Helen Francis and Susan Thornton provided helpful editorial assistance. The comments I received from two anonymous reviewers were simply outstanding, and greatly improved the quality of the final product. At Oxford, Fay Clarke and Claire Peacock did a wonderful job proofreading the entire manuscript.

Some of the material in Chapter 3 was originally published in "Persuade Them or Oust Them: Crafting Judicial Change and Transitional Justice in Argentina," in *Comparative Politics*, and is reprinted here with kind permission from the editors.

I met Matt when we were both struggling to finish our first books. He revolutionized my world, often guiding chaos into order, and generally making me laugh. I am very lucky to have him by my side, and hope this is just the first of many dedications. My brother Pedro and the two amazing women who raised me, my grandmother Esther and my mom, María Ester, are the three most important people in my life. My mother deserves more than just a few lines of acknowledgment. Her courage and self-respect will always be an inspiration. For my family, letting me go at the age of eighteen, when I decided to embark on a still ongoing academic adventure that took me away from Argentina, first to the University of Cambridge, then to the United States, and then back to Britain via Mexico, was indeed difficult. It was especially tough for my aging grandmother, whose eyes in every farewell concealed the doubt of whether that would be the last one. But their incommensurable love led them to support me every step of the way. I will be eternally grateful because without their encouragement it would have been much harder to pursue my dreams. For these and many other reasons, this book is dedicated to the memory of my grandmother, who passed away when I began working on this project, and to my mother, who always has my back.

1

From Unresponsive to Responsive Judiciaries

The dictatorships and armed conflicts that ravaged Latin America in the second half of the twentieth century led to the torture, exile, murder, and forced disappearance of thousands of individuals. Victims' relatives, in many cases unaware of the fate of their loved ones, knocked on the doors of military barracks, filed habeas corpus petitions, risked their lives denouncing these crimes in the press, and endlessly navigated the complex world of courts in order to seek punishment for those responsible. The quest for truth and justice evolved into a tortuous and protracted battle, but these efforts sometimes paid off.

In July 1992, military officers raided a university outside Peru's capital city in one of their many attempts to disband illegal armed organizations. Gisela Ortíz never again saw her brother, who thus became one of the seventy thousand victims of the internal armed conflict. The authorities turned a blind eye to her requests for information, to the point that they even denied her brother's existence. Luis Enrique had not only disappeared; for the Peruvian state he had never been born. In April 2009, seventeen years later, the Peruvian Supreme Court found former President Fujimori responsible for mounting a repressive apparatus that carried out this and other crimes. Similarly, after Peru's democratic transition in 2000 dozens of other high-ranking military and police commanders were prosecuted and punished in a wave of trials that is still ongoing. According to Gisela, courts "made official a series of facts that everyone denied. Before that day I felt like a mad lady with a story that no one believed in. The judiciary finally validated our story.... Today we can declare mission accomplished."[1]

In April 2011, former police officer Luis Patti was found guilty of planning and executing the kidnapping and forced disappearance of several activists during Argentina's last military dictatorship. Until his arrest, Patti benefited from the amnesty laws passed in the late 1980s, and, as a

[1] Interview, Lima, 27 April 2010.

member of parliament, used his congressional immunity to escape prosecution. After the judges announced their decision, Manuel Gonçalves, the son of a victim, appeared outside the courtroom and declared: "This is the product of many efforts and struggles.... Our objective was to get to the day in which a court handed down this ruling. Patti ... used our country's institutions to preserve his impunity."[2] This ruling is just one of more than four hundred prison sentences that have been handed down since the mid-2000s in what constitutes an unprecedented wave of prosecutions and trials.

The situation in Mexico is very different. Tita Radilla still sheds tears as she recalls the 1974 morning when army officers abducted her father, an activist from the state of Guerrero. She never heard from him again. For almost three decades Tita has been part of an organization that represents hundreds of victims of the dirty war, assisting them in their efforts to give testimony of the forced disappearances, torture, and sexual assaults perpetrated by the armed forces during the 1970s. In 2005, a special prosecutor appointed by President Fox filed her father's case in the federal courts. The case moved back and forth between civilian and military jurisdictions, but like all the other cases investigated by the special prosecutor it was eventually shut down. As she put it, "We have no faith in state institutions. There is a total lack of will to investigate what happened to our victims."[3] After forty years, Tita and many others are still waiting for justice.

Despite the enduring suffering of people like Tita, over the last decade and a half, judges and prosecutors across Latin America have become central actors in efforts at strengthening democracy by punishing the brutality of past regimes (Olsen et al.; Sikkink 2011). Figure 1.1 shows the explosion of antiimpunity rulings handed down by Supreme and Constitutional Courts after the year 2000, which paved the way for justice by overturning amnesty laws and pardons, declaring the nonapplicability of statutory limitations, recognizing victims' right to truth, or limiting the scope of military jurisdiction. As a result of these decisions, which relied heavily on international human rights law, courts throughout the region began to investigate – and in some notable cases, prosecute and punish – state agents responsible for human rights violations, thus putting an end to decades of judicial acquiescence. The magnitude of this shift in jurisprudential trends is remarkable not only because it took place years after the onset of the so-called third wave of democratization, but also because

[2] *Página 12*, 15 April 2011.

[3] Tita Radilla, Interview, Mexico City, 23 July 2010.

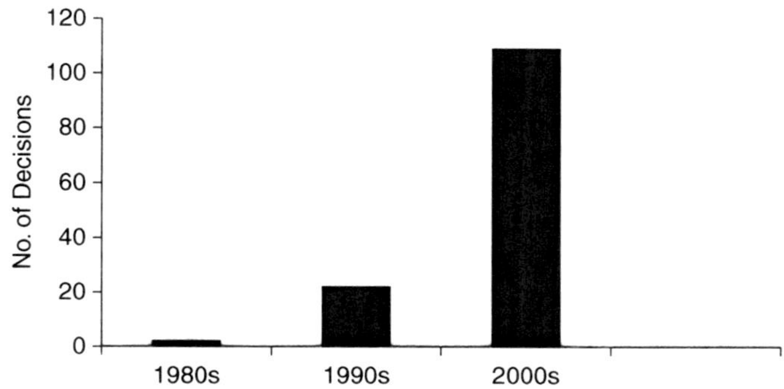

Figure 1.1. Number of Antiimpunity Rulings Handed Down by Latin American High Courts (1980–2010).

Source: DPLF (2010) and author's data set. The figure includes rulings on cases of human rights violations by Supreme and Constitutional Courts. The rulings use international human rights law and humanitarian law to limit the application of amnesty laws or declare their unconstitutionality; modify procedural and substantive aspects of criminal legislation to meet international standards; recognize victims' right to truth; and limit the jurisdiction of military courts. The data set was constructed using online public information systems, consulting with country experts, and reading the relevant legal literature. I am grateful to Ximena Medellín for facilitating some of the rulings.

prior to this explosion of judicial activism Latin American democracies put in place seemingly impenetrable impunity regimes.

During the 1980s democratic transition, Argentina took the first step in the direction of transitional justice by creating a truth commission and filing criminal charges against the leaders of the military juntas (Nino 1996). As a result of the civil-military tensions engendered by these initiatives, in the late 1980s and early 1990s there were important backlashes against transitional justice in the form of amnesty laws, presidential pardons, and the termination of all criminal procedures against perpetrators (Pion Berlin 1994, 1995, 1997; Acuña and Smulovitz 1997). Following the Argentine example, sixteen Latin American countries adopted amnesty laws to prevent criminal investigations that could potentially destabilize the political system (Sikkink and Walling 2007).[4] Moreover, as the years

[4] Some, like the one passed by the Peruvian congress in 1995, were blanket amnesties. Others contemplated exceptions. In Argentina the crimes of illegal abduction and trafficking of babies born in detention centers were excluded. In Guatemala, crimes against humanity were also excluded (Cassel 1996; Lessa and Payne 2012). For an analysis of amnesties around the world see Mallinder (2009).

passed, statutes of limitations began to run out for most of the crimes in question, barring criminal prosecutions. Consequently, even though the policies of transitional justice that had taken effect immediately after the waning of authoritarian regimes showed some degree of cross-country variation, by the mid-1990s there was a regionwide convergence toward impunity (Sikkink 2005).

As victims and their lawyers insisted on seeking redress for the violations in domestic and international courts, the institutionalization and legalization of impunity gave rise to heated legal debates (Teitel 1997; Lessa and Payne 2012). On one side were those who argued that international customary law, treaties signed and ratified by Latin American states before and after these violent episodes, and the jurisprudence of the Inter-American Court of Human Rights demanded that states treat human rights violations as serious international crimes subject to special judicial rules and procedures. According to this camp, when domestic actors invoke statutes of limitations or apply amnesties, they incur a violation of states' international duty to investigate and punish crimes against humanity. On the other side were those influenced by formalistic legal philosophies who argued that the passage of amnesty laws or pardons was a sovereign prerogative of presidents and congresses, and therefore courts had no place in questioning them. Moreover, invoking unwritten principles of customary international law or treaties signed after the perpetration of the crimes in order to apply special legal standards to these cases or define the crimes using extemporaneous criminal definitions would amount to a grave violation of due process.

The formalistic position was for decades the dominant one in Latin American judicial branches, generally leading courts to behave more as arbiters of procedure than as architects of fundamental rights (López Medina 2004; Couso 2010; Guzmán Dálbora 2010; Pásara 2010). Today the situation is very different, as judicial actors are more predisposed to make creative readings of the legal framework that afford citizens greater protections vis-à-vis the state (Nunes 2010; Rodríguez Garavito 2009). This is clearly seen in cases of organized state repression, in which customary and positive international law are recurrently invoked to define the crimes in ways that capture their historical significance, declare the unconstitutionality of amnesties and pardons, and limit the application of statutes of limitations, thus expanding the sphere of victims' rights. Moreover, innovative theories of criminal liability and investigative protocols first developed to address international crimes have been applied domestically to ascribe criminal responsibility to direct and indirect perpetrators (Roht-Arriaza

2015). Beginning in the late 1990s and especially in the 2000s, some Latin American judiciaries thus became a beacon of progress in the area of transitional justice.

Why did some judicial corporations evolve from unresponsive bureaucracies into suitable arenas for the advancement of rights claims, while others did not? In this book I compare the surge in prosecutions and prison sentences in Argentina and Peru with the failure of investigations and judicial proceedings in Mexico. I study the process that led judges and prosecutors in some countries to leave behind a formalistic legal orthodoxy strongly influenced by positivism, and embrace a new legal worldview grounded in the values of international human rights law. I show that this shift in the judicial imagination away from formalistic instincts and a narrow focus on domestic law constituted a necessary condition for the explosion of trials and convictions in the 2000s. In particular, my argument indicates that these bold and unprecedented jurisprudential steps became possible after litigants activated informal mechanisms of legal-ideational change inside judiciaries, and enhanced the technical capabilities of judges and prosecutors. These transformations in the norms, knowledge, and routines that underpin judicial decision making triggered effective judicial action in cases that were complex and idiosyncratic. By manufacturing a new logic of appropriate legal interpretation, litigants invested judges and prosecutors in investigations that required highly specialized knowledge and involved an unusual degree of juridical experimentation and numerous professional risks. Changes in legal preferences were also instrumental in motivating resistance against the pressures exerted by powerful presidents and soldiers adamantly opposed to the trials. In the absence of these shifts in legal visions, the impact of projustice pressures by local politicians, international institutions, and foreign governments was limited.

By exploring the microdynamics of norm and capabilities diffusion during the interactions among judges, prosecutors, and human rights lawyers, this book engages a series of theoretical questions about the nature of judicial power. In particular, I analyze the role that ideas about the law and received standards of legal praxis have in constraining or empowering judicial actors to become involved in thorny political territory. I emphasize that in order to understand changes in patterns of judicial decision making it is important to look beyond the degrees of freedom for action afforded by the surrounding political environment. We ought to recognize the role of internal norms of conduct and legal preferences, which can act as catalysts of bold and assertive judicial action in defiance of external political constraints. In so doing, the following pages explore the conditions under which judicial branches acquire the technical capabilities and the political will to become powerful and effective players in salient political struggles.

The Argument in Brief

Understanding how judicial actors think about their professional duties and how they perceive the solutions available for the cases they receive is crucial to explain the wave of trials and prison sentences observed in some Latin American countries. To this end, this book uses insights derived from sociological institutionalism to develop a theory that emphasizes the bureaucratically embedded nature of judicial decision making (Hall and Taylor 1996). I argue that judicial behavior is processed within a complex organizational environment that instills among its members profession-specific norms and identities. These in turn lead to jurisprudential outcomes that reflect the institutionalization of "sticky" ideas about the law in courts' routine practices (Smith 2008; Clayton and Gillman 1999; Hilbink 2007a; Couso 2010). These ideas or legal preferences bias judicial actors' knowledge of the legal corpus at their disposal, trace the landscape of values underpinning their decisions, and define their understanding of their role in the political system, motivating them to take a more or less critical approach to decisions made by politicians. Qua norms governing professional praxis, legal preferences are accompanied by expectations about acceptable courses of action within the organization, and stable behavioral patterns (e.g., recurrent use of certain precedents, doctrines, evidentiary standards). Responses to external requests, threats, and incentives are filtered through this thick cultural lens, leading behavior to result less from individual judges' opportunistic calculations regarding specific cases than from a shared understanding of what is the appropriate thing to do as members of the bench (March and Olsen 1984).

When confronted with the question of whether or not to investigate and prosecute human rights violations perpetrated in the distant past, most Latin American judges and prosecutors had to grapple with legal arguments that were out of sync with established legal preferences. For example, instead of dismissing these cases because of the expiration of statutes of limitations or the presence of laws barring prosecutions, as they would have normally done, judicial actors were asked to challenge the legal status quo by invoking international norms. Most of them were unfamiliar with these norms, as they had never featured prominently in judges and prosecutors' decision making routines. To complicate matters further, once the cases were opened, judicial actors were put in charge of unprecedented investigations. Although the bureaucratic instinct was to proceed as in regular criminal cases, many soon discovered the inadequacies of standard techniques to gather and evaluate the evidence. In the absence of knowledge about the whereabouts of victims or lacking access to documentation certifying the existence of clandestine repressive structures, judicial actors had to find the motivation to look for innovative ways to obtain information, weaving circumstantial evidence into convincing stories of individual criminal responsibility.

Overcoming these challenges required breaking with deeply ingrained institutional inertias. This was no small feat. Gaps in legal knowledge had to be filled and templates of juridical reasoning modified. In addition, judicial actors had to become invested in these cases in order to be willing to experiment with unorthodox legal arguments, go an extra mile when gathering evidence against soldiers and politicians, and risk their personal and professional integrity when handing down condemnatory rulings. In other words, the professional lens through which they perceived both the legal possibilities afforded by these cases and their institutional responsibility in transitional justice had to change. To the extent that this happened, judges and prosecutors became more willing and able to see viable legal pathways for truth and justice. This process involved the deinstitutionalization of historically dominant positivist/formalistic legal cultures, jealous of legal sovereignty and protective of conservative interests, and the entrenchment of a progressive juridical vision committed to the values of international human rights law. In addition to reshaping judicial actors' cognitive maps and awareness of certain enabling legal doctrines and instruments, this transformation modified their understanding of their professional mission as it relates to the ways they ought to conduct their duties and interpret the law in human rights cases.

Why did judges and prosecutors in some countries become committed to the cause of truth and justice? I argue that where human rights activists acknowledged the importance of traditional legal preferences as a clear blockage on the road to justice, and sought to tame the judiciary by turning themselves into agents of ideational change and capabilities diffusion, they managed to put criminals in jail. By taking seriously how judges and prosecutors think about these cases qua professionals of the law, litigants were able to design effective tactics of legal contention. Denouncing impunity in international forums, litigating abroad, or marching on the streets to put pressure on politicians would not suffice. They understood the importance of putting together professionalized teams of lawyers capable of introducing domestic judicial actors to new paradigms of rights-based jurisprudence, and teaching them how to pursue the goals of truth and justice legitimately within the conventions and parameters of the legal field.

Savvy litigants realized they faced three types of judicial actors – committed, indifferent, and recalcitrant – leading them to deploy two main strategies in order to bring about this necessary ideational transformation, and galvanize a critical mass of judicial actors in favor of their cause. First, committed and indifferent judges and prosecutors were targeted with pedagogical interventions. These included the organization of seminars for judicial personnel, establishment of informal contacts before and during critical stages of the litigation process, and the circulation of academic documents in court. Litigants thus taught members of the judicial community complex and often unknown international juridical doctrines and protocols. In the process, NGOs disrupted bureaucratic inertia and manufactured a plausible legal framework for judicial actors to justify the appropriateness of their actions. The ideas circulated in these venues had a technical component; i.e., they served as roadmaps for action. But they also had a normative one, because they legitimized unusual courses of action. Second, activists sought the replacement of recalcitrant judicial actors who staunchly resisted changes in patterns of legal interpretation, as a result of their unwavering commitment to positivism or their complicity with the previous regime. By deploying naming and shaming tactics in order to force resignations, and by promoting impeachments, human rights litigants deepened the shift in the legal and political allegiances of the judiciary.

Domestic judicial strategies operated primarily as a permissive cause. Litigants fundamentally altered the scope of conceivable outcomes, making possible certain legal solutions that in the absence of these interventions were literally "unthinkable." If doctrinal positions, technical skills, and professional commitments had remained unchanged, judicial actors would not have been able or willing to read constitutions or criminal codes in light of the greater protections afforded to victims by the international legal corpus. Moreover, these strategies marshalled a new logic of behavioral appropriateness within the legal field that catalyzed judicial collective action when the political and military establishments attacked pro–transitional justice outcomes. When litigants succeeded in institutionalizing a new set of standard practices, rekindling a shared vision of the role of the judiciary in processing rights claims, judicial actors incorporated a new professional mandate and set of values that they were willing to defend as a corporation. For example, presidents or soldiers who threatened judges or tried to contain transitional justice by invoking certain due process norms encountered resistance when judicial actors found it professionally unacceptable to ignore the demands of international law.

Given what is generally at stake in judicial dockets, the reproduction or transformation of legal preferences is an eminently political process that involves a variety of social forces that struggle to entrench within judicial bureaucracies legal ideas compatible with their normative commitments (DiMaggio and Powell 1991; Gillman 1993, 2002, 2008). The judicial battles at the core of transitional justice processes in Latin America, which pitted human rights NGOs against the military and its allies, exemplify these attempts to preserve and transform dominant legal visions in order to promote political causes. The ideas and legal arguments espoused by both groups either constrained or expanded the avenues to justice. Precisely because judiciaries were the epicenter of colonization strategies by both camps, the theory I propose indicates that litigants' chances of success increased when (a) they deployed strategies of institutional change before their rivals; (b) pedagogical interventions were framed in such a way that they were perceived by judicial actors as authoritative and elicited feelings of cognitive discomfort; (c) litigants' efforts were systematic, across both jurisdictions and legal issue areas; and (d) litigants were able to combine persuasion and replacement strategies to engineer widespread and enduring value changes in the judiciary.

In sum, ambitious programs of criminal prosecutions require deep institutional transformations within judicial branches, which involve both legal learning and changes in professional values. In turn, these changes depend on external inputs that actively expand the cognitive maps of judges and prosecutors, shake up their problem-solving predispositions, and contest control over their normative commitments. Human rights activists and their lawyers can manufacture this exogenous shock, crafting a new judicial culture through pedagogical and replacement strategies.

Deepening Our Understanding of Human Rights Prosecutions in Latin America

This book tells the story of how human rights litigants removed important blockages inside the judiciary to achieve their goals. The argument zooms in on how legal preferences and their remodeling by activists shape judicial responses to state repression, and in so doing deepens our understanding of transitional justice processes in three ways.

First, the following pages shed light on the relationship between the success of litigation battles and the strength of political/military veto players. It is often argued that these elites have the upper hand in deciding the fate of human rights prosecutions (Karl and Schmitter 1991; Zalaquett 1992; Pion-Berlin 1995, 1997). For example, according to Huntington (1991), the balance of power between the prodemocracy coalition and the authoritarian coalition at the time of transition determines whether or not there will be trials. In fact, the notion that "the victor tells the tale" squares well with several important cases of transitional justice across the globe (Nobles 2010).[5] Even when the phenomenon proves much more dynamic, and trials are not forever conditioned by the power of former dictators during transitions (Olsen et al. 2010; Kim 2012; Lessa 2013),[6] the general intuition about the role played by the stakeholders of power is still an important one (Lessa et al. 2014). Uninterested or ideologically opposed politicians can stall human rights prosecutions at any given point. By the same token, the rise to power of supportive presidents may revive the impetus for justice. In line with this view, some observers have attributed the recent wave of transitional justice in Latin America to the emergence of left-wing governments (Evans 2007; Karl 2007; Roehrig 2009).

However, by adding the legal preferences of judicial actors to the equation, it is possible to see that the goals and tactics of political and military actors need not overdetermine the outcome of these processes. In the same way as support from politicians or a weak military does not automatically translate into judicial victories, the presence of resourceful veto players does not necessarily lead to impunity. Judges and prosecutors can play an important role in blocking trials in otherwise favorable environments (due to technical incompetence, legal formalism, or recalcitrance). For

[5] The trials in Tokyo and Nuremberg are obvious examples. Similarly, when the Greek junta left power after a military defeat in 1974, human rights abusers were quickly taken to court and most cases were resolved within two years (Alivizatos and Diamandouros 1997). By contrast, after the negotiated Spanish transition (1975–1977), no attempts were made to prosecute those involved in the crimes of Franco's regime.

[6] For example, in Chile and Uruguay amnesties passed before or during the transition have not been an obstacle to protracted struggles for justice. In Chile a few years after Pinochet left power some courts issued condemnatory rulings (Collins 2010). Initially, the Supreme Court overturned the rulings, but since 1997 it has granted many exceptions to the amnesty (Hilbink 2007a). In Uruguay, there were popular referenda on the question of whether or not to uphold the amnesty law, and in all instances the pro–transitional justice camp lost. In the late 2000s, however, demands for justice were reactivated (Sikkink 2005; Lessa 2013). Important victories include a Supreme Court ruling in 2009 declaring the amnesty law unconstitutional, and a guilty verdict against former dictator Bordaberry in 2010. Finally, even in Brazil, where the issue of criminal accountability was absent from the political agenda in the aftermath of the 1985 transition, in the late 2000s prosecutors began to launch criminal investigations (see Chapter 6).

example, despite the projustice pressures exerted by the Kirchner administrations in Argentina (2003–2015), many courts actively tried to freeze the human rights docket, while others lacked the technical skills to deal with it successfully, severely hampering the progress of cases in several jurisdictions (Chapter 3). Similarly, in Brazil, the momentum gained by prosecutions in the later years of Dilma Rousseff's first term (2010–2015) was jeopardized by the courts, which continued to apply the amnesty law (Chapter 6).

By the same token, a judiciary that underwent a legal cultural transformation and has been infused with new professional values can effectively champion the cause in adverse situations. Removing judicial blockages can serve as a countervailing force on the effect of political opposition to transitional justice. In Peru, many civilian and military officers were sent to prison during Alan García's second term (2006–2011), a time when the president and members of his cabinet staunchly opposed the trials and tried to influence judicial decision making (Chapter 4). Likewise, during the 2010s some committed Guatemalan courts handed down condemnatory rulings in extremely high-profile cases of crimes perpetrated during the 1980s, despite fierce opposition from the political and military establishments.[7] In other words, despite lack of control over the purse or the sword, judges and prosecutors do not always strategically capitulate in the face of pressures from actors that have greater resources. This is in part because legal preferences turn them into less than perfect agents of politicians. Judicial bureaucracies reproduce their own legal cultures and ideologies, and when consistently spread throughout the organization, these values may lead judicial actors to resist in a corporate fashion outside imperatives to rule in any particular direction, actively champion risky causes, and defend professional standards.

With the allegiances of the judiciary in play, victims and their lawyers can eventually find in judges and prosecutors either allies or enemies, and this has implications for the success of trials regardless of the characteristics of the political environment. But even if macropolitical variables do

[7] Isolated victories include a ruling from August 2011 that found four military officers guilty of the Dos Erres massacre; a decision handed down in 2013 against former dictator Ríos Montt in which he was charged with genocide; and a sentence issued in 2015 against the former chief of the Guatemalan police for the perpetration of crimes against humanity during an attack on the Spanish embassy in 1980. It is important to note that the Constitutional Court invalidated the ruling against Ríos Montt, showing that there are still many fearful judges who refuse to participate in these cases, and many more who align themselves with the perpetrators, systematically stalling the proceedings.

not overdetermine the outcome, we must recognize that litigants' judicial strategies do not operate in a political vacuum (Lessa et al. 2014). The extent to which the political and military establishments are willing or able to oppose the human rights cause conditions victims' ability to turn a critical mass of judicial actors into allies, guaranteeing sustained prosecutorial waves. It is therefore important to build on existing studies, exploring the interaction between the strength of these veto players and the presence of adequate strategies of judicial transformation. As the case studies will show, the viability of persuasion campaigns increases where politicians have not purposefully stacked courts with recalcitrant, "unpersuadable" judges. The staying power of changes in legal preferences via pedagogical interventions also hinges on the absence of political backlashes, such as court packing initiatives. Similarly, in order to deepen shifts in the overall commitment of the judiciary by means of replacement tactics, activists often need their naming and shaming efforts to be reinforced by politicians, and almost invariably need their support to carry out impeachments and nominate friendly candidates. By putting the struggle over the judiciary at the forefront of the causal story, my analysis thus presents a more sober view of the impact of macropolitical factors, looking at how both these variables and litigation strategies affect the consolidation or removal of decisive judicial blockages on the road to transitional justice.

Second, the argument advanced in this book contributes to scholarship that looks at domestic human rights prosecutions as the product of global processes of norm socialization by specifying the mechanism that leads to the successful diffusion of these norms among domestic judicial actors. According to this literature, the driving force behind struggles for criminal accountability are transnational networks of activists and lawyers who seek to shape from abroad the conditions for the institutionalization of truth and justice at home (Brysk 1990, 1994, 2005; Sikkink 1993, 2005; Keck and Sikkink 1998; Risse-Kappen et al. 1999). The main goal of these networks is to socialize states into internalizing their international responsibility to investigate and punish severe human rights violations (Sikkink 2005, 2011). Activists use their specialized knowledge of international human rights law to exert pressure on governments that resist investigating the crimes (Lutz and Sikkink 2000). For example, during the 1990s Latin American NGOs often filed cases in foreign courts, invoking the principle of universal jurisdiction (Amnesty International 2001; Lutz and Sikkink 2001). The ensuing episodes of judicial activism, such as the trials in absentia of Argentine military leaders in Europe or the Pinochet saga of 1998 became important triggers of the current wave of criminal prosecutions (Hilbink 2007a; Huneeus 2010b; Roht-Arriaza 2005; Sikkink 2011). These tactics had an impact on state behavior by modifying the incentive structures faced by political leaders in the area of foreign policy as well as the values and principles of governmental actors (Risse-Kappen and Sikkink 1999; Cardenas 2007). In particular, the actions of European judges gave international visibility to the reigning impunity in the region, encouraging the opening of domestic avenues for resolving the issue according to accepted international legal standards.[8]

This influential approach offers insights into the empowering effect of well-crafted legal arguments and of the transnational epistemic communities formed in support of those doctrines. Moreover, the emphasis on the diffusion of ideas helps us make sense of radical shifts in general patterns of criminal accountability. But although it is undeniable that these international "norm-affirming" events are catalysts for bolder forms of accountability, the domestic mechanisms of suasion and normative change must be further unpacked. It is still unclear how norms become diffused among specific actors involved in the domestic judicialization process (Olsen et al. 2010). Mending this gap is important in order to understand better the conditions under which the development of global legal standards leads to the emergence of judicial norm entrepreneurs in some settings and not others.

This book is built on the assumption that for it to be effective, international diffusion must be coupled with differentiated processes of norm adoption, in which different domestic actors follow distinct routes to acceptance and compliance. In particular, whereas international political and diplomatic pressures can shame presidents into following human rights norms (Pion Berlin 2004), favorable judicial responses do not automatically follow suit. Judicial actors do not simply abide by the dictates of politicians. For one, they often face difficulties learning about, understanding, and absorbing the ideas promoted by foreign courts, and legally formulating the jurisprudential solutions demanded by transnational activists. Moreover, as suggested previously, judges and prosecutors can find the professional motivations and resources to put up a fight.

By theorizing about the organizational imperatives that lead judicial actors to think in very specific ways about human rights cases and their institutional responsibility in adjudicating them, I offer new insights into the diffusion strategies that can effectively turn them into champions of

[8] For example, Sikkink (2005) documents the diplomatic pressures exerted on President Menem by Scandinavian and French officials during state visits in the late 1990s.

the cause. The argument underscores the importance of uncovering the microfoundations of judicial behavior, investigating the interactions between litigants and judicial actors at the domestic level, and the effects of resocialization efforts attuned to judges' and prosecutors' professional concern with the legal legitimacy of their decisions. The analysis thus presents a more nuanced account of the judicial stream in the diffusion sequence, focusing on the way judicial actors become proficient in an alternative legal discourse and new investigative techniques, understand the jurisprudential innovations initiated in the international arena, and incorporate them into their daily decision making routines. There is a legal learning process relevant to explaining judicial behavior in cases of state repression, which is ignored if the analysis only considers, for example, presidents' foreign policy preferences. In other words, we must be able to explain how is it that litigants manage to shape the legal preferences of judicial actors in their favor, infusing them with new values relative to their professional obligations under international law.

Finally, this book adds a different perspective to work that looks specifically at the participation of judges and prosecutors in transitional justice processes. Whereas some suggest that projustice behavior is a symptom of judiciaries seeking atonement for their complicity with repressive regimes (Huneeus 2010b), others link changes in judicial involvement to reforms that enhance the formal independence of courts and their receptivity to rights claims, leading NGOs to step up litigation efforts (Hilbink 2007a; Collins 2010; Skaar 2011). By focusing on the impact of formal institutional changes, these approaches downplay the importance of the deep changes in informal legal cultures that were necessary for judges to deal successfully with the juridical complexities of human rights cases. Formal institutional reengineering does not guarantee the adequate training and normative commitment of a critical mass of judicial actors, both able and willing to sustain trials over time. Moreover, proimpunity politicians often use judicial reforms to stack courts with recalcitrant judges and create buffer zones against victims' efforts. Finally, reinforcing formal parchment barriers does not always deter members of the political and military establishments from intimidating committed judges and meddling with their affairs. For these reasons, instead of arguing that litigants simply respond to perceived changes in judicial receptivity, I argue that they manufacture it by activating informal mechanisms of institutional change, purposefully altering judges' and prosecutors' understanding of what is legally possible. They also cement their resolve to push investigations forward and withstand pressures. Prison sentences are therefore not the result of a formally insulated judicial branch, but of a deep politicization of the bench by human rights groups.

Why Focus on Criminal Prosecutions?

Scholars interested in regime transitions have pointed out that one of the most daunting challenges faced by new democracies is the question of how to deal with the violations of human rights and humanitarian law perpetrated by previous regimes (O'Donnell and Schmitter 1986; Linz and Stepan 1996; Huntington 1991; Hayner 2002; Elster 2004, 2006). The notion of transitional justice, or postconflict justice, encompasses a vast array of initiatives states can implement in order to address these wrongdoings, including prosecutions, reparations, memorials, truth commissions, lustration policies, and programs to retrain security forces (Cohen 1995; Bassiouni 2002; Teitel 2000, 2014; Roht-Arriaza 2006; Ambos et al. 2009; Nalepa 2010). This book adopts a narrower view of transitional justice. The focus is on criminal prosecutions aimed at establishing individual criminal responsibility for human rights violations. The political and legal challenges presented by criminal prosecutions make them an empirically and theoretically interesting subject.

From a political point of view, trials constitute one of the most demanding forms of transitional justice. When current or former members of the armed forces or leaders of politically representative groups run the risk of going to jail, the stakes in the process are much higher. Trials can lead to the destabilization of the democratic order and can accentuate the societal rifts opened up during the preceding armed conflict or authoritarian era (Zalaquett 1995; Osiel 2000). Criminal prosecutions also present a number of major legal challenges. Central to the evolution of the international legal regime throughout the twentieth century is the notion that states have a duty to prosecute international crimes (Méndez 1997; Simmons 2009).[9] In order to fulfill this duty, domestic judiciaries must incorporate

[9] This duty emerges from the Genocide Convention (1948), the Geneva Conventions (1949), and the Convention against Torture (1984). The Inter-American Court of Human Rights interprets the American Convention as imposing upon states the duty to investigate and punish serious human rights violations. Similarly, the European Court of Human Rights has declared that amnesties, pardons, and statutory limitations are inapplicable in cases of torture (ECHR, *Abdulsamet Yaman v. Turkey*, ruling of 2 November 2004). Whether criminal prosecutions are a mandatory part of this duty is controversial given the availability of other, nonretributive forms of justice (Ambos 2009). Orentlicher (1991) argues that although states have an international responsibility to investigate and punish these crimes, the scope of criminal accountability should depend on the regime's political and legal capacities to undergo such risky processes.

international jurisprudence and doctrines into their decisions, a task for which they are largely unprepared. Moreover, these sources of law often clash with standard understandings of the rule of law, triggering important debates about the extent to which trials can be held without undermining the legal order. According to Ruti Teitel, "The attempt to impose accountability through criminal law often raised rule-of-law dilemmas, including retroactivity in the law, tampering with existing laws, a high degree of prosecutorial selectivity, and a compromised judiciary" (2003: 76).

In other words, human rights trials are truly testing, not only because they are inherently complex, but also because they immerse judges in a sea of crisscrossing pressures, some of them exerted by extremely hostile and aggressive groups. Because of these challenges, they constitute defining moments in strengthening the ability of courts to protect the rights of citizens, and cement a constitutional culture that socializes political actors into respecting the legal boundaries of their institutional prerogatives (Larkins 1996). If judicial actors succeed in making the exercise of state violence accountable to republican procedures amid these difficulties and external influences, they can make a decisive contribution to securing the space of individual freedoms necessary for the flourishing of democratic politics (O'Donnell 2010). By contrast, their passivity, technical incompetence, or ineffectiveness may erode the ethical foundations of a regime based on equality before the law and respect for basic rights (Acuña and Smulovitz 1997).

By studying how judges and prosecutors respond to these demanding cases, it is possible to contribute to scholarly debates about the sources of assertive judicial action and judicial power. First, the radical jurisprudential changes required by criminal prosecutions of past torturers make this an excellent topic for analyzing the constraining and empowering effects of legal cultures on judicial behavior. By developing an argument explicitly grounded on a set of assumptions about the impact of legal preferences on judicial outcomes, this book strengthens the growing body of scholarship on the role of ideas in comparative judicial politics (Orren 1991; Hattam 1993; Hilbink 2007a, 2012; Woods 2008; Woods and Hilbink 2009; Couso 2010; Ingram 2012). I demonstrate the heuristic power of the framework, exploring the struggles that shape the reproduction and change of certain informal behavioral norms inside judicial branches, and their effect on the predisposition and ability of judiciaries to uphold certain rights at the expense of others. I thus show how ideas and professional values sometimes paralyze judiciaries, rendering them submissive and ineffective, whereas in other cases, they allow judiciaries to become forceful stewards of specific causes, defying external political constraints. The focus on legal preferences thus offers a fresh set of tools to explain shifts in patterns of judicial behavior, some of which are unexpected from the perspective of strategic theories popular in the field. Such theories emphasize judges' opportunistic, self-interested calculations in the face of uncertainty and threats from more powerful external players, as opposed to shared institutional visions and internalized standards of praxis.

Second, one of the driving forces behind the renewed interest in the role of ideas in judicial decision making is the spread of "neoconstitutionalist" doctrinal positions (Rodríguez Garavito 2009, 2011b; Couso 2010). Courts all over the world are beginning to loosen their formalist straitjackets, acknowledge the open nature of legal texts and rules, and assume a more activist role in the definition of the content and reach of constitutional rights (Gargarella, Domingo, and Roux 2006; Rodríguez Garavito 2011a). Unfortunately, we are still far from certain about the causes and mechanisms behind the spread of this rights-centered legal vision and its impact on assertive judicial decision making. The main challenge faced when exploring the causal impact of these new legal ideas is that as a set of norms and values, "neoconstitutionalism" is difficult to operationalize in order to carry out process tracing successfully. When an ideational variable is not adequately identified, it is hard to analyze who carries the ideas, where they take them, and how they implant them in others' minds. Because of the difficulties that result from vague operationalizations, existing studies tend to portray the causal link between the influx of new ideas and judicial outcomes as relatively straightforward, without delving into the conflictive processes of knowledge acquisition and normative evolution that characterize this phenomenon. By looking at a particular manifestation of "neoconstitutionalism," i.e., the doctrines derived from international human rights law vis-à-vis the treatment of mass atrocities, this book seeks to overcome some of these problems. A narrower focus on a clearly defined set of cases allows me to trace closely how specific ideas about the law held by judges and prosecutors change, zooming in on well-defined legal battles, identifying the actors involved, and determining how they clash as they try to entrench and dismantle certain standards of legal interpretation.

Because of the argument's focus on the role of legal preferences and their transformation when explaining shifts in jurisprudential patterns, the book also contributes to more general political science debates about norm diffusion (e.g., Beissinger 2002; Pevehouse 2002; Brinks and Coppedge 2006; Bunce and Wolchik 2011; Mainwaring and Pérez-Liñán

2013). The legal ideas that enabled successful criminal prosecutions at the domestic level were originally developed in the international arena, and in order to topple impunity regimes, judges and prosecutors in Latin America had to learn them anew. In addition to further unpacking the diffusion sequence as it pertains to the interactions between civil society and the domestic judiciary, my treatment of the mechanisms of ideational change involved in this process makes two contributions to our understanding of diffusion.

First, my analysis puts emphasis on the importance of technical knowledge as an enabler of shifts in normative commitments and patterns of political behavior. The diffusion of particular forms of expertise helps oppositions to run more effective electoral campaigns against authoritarian incumbents (Bunce and Wolchik 2011); shapes the design of environmental, economic, and health policies within and across states (Haas 1992; Peterson 1992); influences the content of treaties (Glasius 2005; Struett 2008; Deitelhoff 2009; García Iommi 2012); and affects the workings of international bureaucracies (Finnemore 1993, 1996; Barnett and Finnemore 2004). Like some of these studies, I emphasize the transmission of "know-how" as a crucial determinant of behavioral change and empowerment. Political action embedded in highly bureaucratic spheres has a technical dimension that cannot be overlooked. In this sense, the ability of judges and prosecutors to do and say things is as important as their motivations for championing certain jurisprudential outcomes. The account presented here shows that the inflow of knowledge about international law and special investigative protocols designed for cases of mass atrocities was decisive in order to explain why, regardless of their personal commitment to the cause, judges and prosecutors were capable of putting an end to impunity.

Finally, one of the central challenges of constructivist social science is to specify the conditions under which the diffusion of ideas has an impact on behavior. Showing that the consolidation of a new complex of ideas at the international level is concomitant with new ways of doing things among state actors is not the same as showing why and how the former are related to the latter. Scholars aware of this problem seek to explain success by exploiting cross-national variation in outcomes and looking at the moderating impact of contextual factors such as domestic institutions or national cultures (Checkel 1997, 2005; Legro 1997; Cortell and Davis 2000, Acharya 2004; Gheciu 2005; Shor 2008; Levitsky and Way 2010). The argument presented in this book builds on these theoretical developments by pointing to specific aspects of the diffusion process that facilitate the adoption of international norms relative to the prosecution of severe human rights violations. In addition to highlighting the importance of judicial strategies designed with a view on how judges and prosecutors *think* about their professional duties and *read* the legal corpus at their disposal, the theory and the evidence contribute to our understanding of the limits and possibilities of ideational change by studying how timing, the specific ways in which source and target interact, and the content of norms affect global socialization processes.

Tracing the Impact of Legal Preferences on Judicial Behavior

The Cases

This book seeks to refine our understanding of the causal process that leads to accountability for past human rights violations. The guiding premise is that explaining prosecutorial waves involves investigating the determinants of judicial behavior, and in order to do so it opens the "black box" of judicial institutions. I pay special attention to litigants' roles in these judicial battles, to the political context in which judges decide whether or not to open criminal prosecutions or rule against the perpetrators, and to the content of jurisprudence. The goal is to show that externally manufactured changes in legal preferences constitute a prerequisite for observing the explosion of pro–transitional justice rulings. In the absence of these changes, both political pressures in favor of prosecutions and efforts at international norm diffusion are futile.

The empirical chapters present intensive plausibility probes (George and Bennett 2004), focusing on two cases where we observe sustained waves of prosecutions against human rights violators (Argentina and Peru), and one in which we do not (Mexico). The choice of a small-N design responds to the fact that the central claims of the theory developed in Chapter 2 are claims about causal mechanisms, which specify the different steps in the story behind court outcomes. These kinds of explanations have the empirical burden of fully reconstructing all the nodes in the hypothesized causal chain in order to discard rival hypotheses and establish causation (Hall 2003). Consequently, an appropriate test consists of a careful diachronic documentation of ideational changes inside judicial branches. It also requires establishing whether these changes affect transitional justice in the hypothesized direction, and whether litigants are the main driving force. Tracing this process involves marshalling myriad data sources for each country, which is a highly demanding task that can only be done well by studying a few cases. Moreover, paying close attention to the content of a limited number of suits, the dynamics of judicial proceedings, and the context in which rulings are handed down reduces the risk of misinterpreting the decision making logic.

Argentina and Peru offer interesting "theoretical contexts" in which to explore the scope and plausibility of the argument. First, in both countries judiciaries evolved from being unresponsive bureaucracies into becoming suitable arenas for the advancement of the human rights cause. By analyzing these temporal changes within the same country, it is possible to control for a series of background conditions such as the brutality of state repression and the size and resources available to human rights organizations, while allowing variation in the strategies deployed by litigants. In the two case studies, I therefore explore shifts in the responsiveness of judges and prosecutors as the tactics of legal contention become more attuned to the importance of transforming legal preferences.

In the Argentine case, I identify two distinct stages in this evolution. The first stage covers the years from the mid-1980s until the early 2000s. During this period, litigants managed to build critical alliances with judicial actors in order to diffuse and entrench a new legal discourse favorable to their cause. Despite opposition from two successive administrations (Menem 1989–1999; De la Rúa 1999–2001), this led to a number of judicial victories – including truth trials and a landmark ruling declaring the unconstitutionality of amnesty laws. The second stage coincides with the beginning of an ambitious program of criminal prosecutions. Human rights groups forged bonds with the Kirchner administrations, prosecutors, and judges, redefining the priorities of the judiciary and its sense of mission vis-à-vis human rights. Most notably, they dismantled persistent islands of resistance to transitional justice by triggering a process of personnel turnover in the judicial branch.

In the Peruvian case, I document how starting in the early 2000s, the human rights movement deployed a massive pedagogical intervention in the judiciary, training judges and prosecutors in a new juridical discourse, thus opening up a world of previously unknown legal solutions for human rights cases and transforming a positivist and formalist legal culture. This strategic alliance forged between human rights activists and important groups within the judicial branch generated a number of ideological, technical, and political resources that facilitated collective responses on the side of judges and prosecutors against soldiers and politicians seeking to put an end to the trials by intimidating courts and refusing to cooperate with the judiciary.

Second, by unpacking the diffusion sequence that led to the success of calls for punishment, I am able to illustrate how the two strategies of legal contention identified by the theory (persuasion and replacement) operate in practice. In so doing, the positive cases help me build on existing explanations of transitional justice in Latin America. With regard to the impact of international norms, Argentina and Peru are two cases that during the 1990s were intensely scrutinized by the international community. Human rights movements in both countries successfully resorted to foreign courts seeking redress for state crimes. But as the case studies will show, litigants themselves were well aware that these international victories did not guarantee equivalent outcomes at home, and in line with the theory, they designed domestic strategies to transform the judiciary. In Argentina, for example, domestic pedagogical interventions began before the onset of aggressive international "norm affirming events." The international litigation efforts launched in the late 1990s resonated internally precisely because the transformation in judicial values was already under way. Moreover, even though by the 2000s the main legal obstacles for truth and justice had been removed in accordance with international norms, NGOs still had to further the local diffusion stream emphasized by the theory. Activists engineered personnel changes in order to cement the commitments of the judicial branch as a domestic norm entrepreneur. Similarly, in Peru, the numerous precedents handed down by the Inter-American Court of Human Rights against the state in the late 1990s and early 2000s had to be operationalized and explained to judges and prosecutors in order to modify their understandings of the law and of their professional duties. For example, litigants realized the importance of clarifying the terms under which international jurisprudence ought to be incorporated in domestic rulings.

In relation to the impact of the political environment, in both cases I am able to document assertive judicial behavior during periods in which the establishment opposed the trials (Peru 2006–2011 and Argentina 1990–2001), showing that a favorable political context is not always needed for observing positive transitional justice outcomes, and empirically establishing the decisive impact of legal diffusion strategies on judges' ability and willingness to defy soldiers and politicians. By looking at periods in which the military was weak and the political class was supportive of human rights (Peru 2000–2006 and Argentina 2003–2015), I further show that a favorable political environment does not suffice to turn judiciaries into responsive arenas. Within-case variation during these periods indicates that technical deficiencies and pockets of recalcitrance were instrumental in delaying the progress of prosecutions even under favorable conditions.

Finally, variation in the focus of litigants' strategies over time also provides empirical leverage to test the causal mechanisms at work intensively. First, NGOs' failure to engage with the judiciary in the terms identified by my theory during certain periods led to the absence of a strong or uniform commitment to the human rights cause among members of the judicial branch. Second, the substantive focus of pedagogical interventions on certain legal topics at the expense of others led to the forging of an uneven legal consensus. Those ideas that were extensively touched upon in the amicus briefs or during the academic activities organized by human rights activists evidence a deep penetration in the minds of judicial actors, whereas discrepancies remain around those questions not addressed by the diffusion efforts.

Although this variation in the implementation of adequate strategies of judicial change can be partially explained by litigants' own choices, the case studies illustrate how the political environment conditioned their ability to deploy these tactics. In Argentina, the anti–transitional justice camp led by President Menem manipulated judicial reforms to entrench conservative interests in the judiciary in the early 1990s, narrowing the scope of persuasion efforts by NGOs. The continuity of these judges in the bench limited the possibility of widespread judicial victories well into the 2000s, even though the proimpunity political coalition had by then lost power. But activists eventually took advantage of a shift in the political environment under the Kirchner administrations, denouncing judicial blockages and enlisting the new political allies to further the changes initiated via persuasion efforts with replacement strategies. In Peru, a favorable political climate in the aftermath of Fujimori's downfall facilitated widespread pedagogical interventions, which built judicial buffer zones that protected transitional justice victories. These proved crucial once proimpunity groups regained power in the mid-2000s. However, the lack of allies among politicians and the military during this second stage made it difficult to consolidate legal cultural shifts by means of replacement efforts, rendering judicial victories much more vulnerable to backlashes.

The Mexican case analyzed in Chapter 5 gives greater plausibility to the claim that when litigants do not deploy strategies aimed at transforming judges' legal preferences, courts never fully commit themselves to human rights cases, are unable to conduct effective investigations or imagine how to argue against impunity dispositions, and, of course, do not hand down condemnatory rulings. In this sense, contrasting positive and negative cases on the main independent variable clarifies the exact content of the litigation strategies that help engineer the outcome. For example, simply filing lawsuits or being vocal in the media or in the streets is not enough. Human rights movements in my three cases do this, but they only succeed when they activate pedagogical interventions and personnel turnover strategies with specific characteristics. The absence of these particular efforts leads to the persistence of formalist legal cultures, reflected in poor investigations and rulings that do not incorporate international law.

Mexico belongs to the universe of countries that experienced state sponsored violence in the form of systematic, widespread, and hierarchically organized attempts to eliminate left-wing groups. This is particularly important when considering its relevance as a negative case (Mahoney and Goertz 2004) because the nature of the crimes generated a number of legal and practical obstacles for criminal investigations and trials comparable to those in the positive cases. For example, when dealing with crimes committed by state actors in the distant past, the gathering of evidence proved difficult and domestic regulations such as statutes of limitations became an important juridical hurdle. Moreover, the international legal arguments that would have made it possible to overcome impunity were equally disconcerting for judicial actors trained in the Latin American legal tradition.

Additional case characteristics suggest that a positive outcome was indeed possible, enhancing its relevance for this study. First, Mexico has an active and vocal human rights movement that could have taken advantage of the unparalleled window of opportunity opened up in the early 2000s with the appointment of a special prosecutor by President Fox. In fact, the movement tried to litigate cases in court, courted the special prosecutor, and went to the Inter-American System, but never took legal preferences seriously or considered deploying the strategies of institutional transformation devised by their Argentine or Peruvian counterparts. Second, unlike Argentina and Peru, and less successful cases such as Uruguay, Mexico never passed an amnesty law benefiting state criminals. This a priori removed a key legal obstacle for the success of prosecutions. Finally, Mexico has a judicial branch with relatively high institutional capacity. For example, the judiciary underwent independence-enhancing reforms in the 1990s, especially at the level of the Supreme Court, which created the conditions for activism in the area of human rights.

Last but not least, the Mexican experience with transitional justice greatly facilitates rigorous process tracing, often difficult in negative cases, where, by definition, the mechanism identified by the theory is absent.

Unlike places where human rights trials were never attempted or occurred in a haphazard way, such as Brazil, Uruguay, Guatemala, or El Salvador, the creation of the Special Prosecutor's Office offers an arena in which we can observe sustained interactions among the relevant actors identified by the theory during a well-defined period. These interactions left myriad traces that enable me to document their ideas, strategies, and clashes, and look for evidence of disruptions in the diffusion process around the hypothesized nodes of the causal chain.

The Empirical Evidence

This book is based on more than twenty months of field research in the three countries, during which I conducted interviews with judicial personnel, activists, and politicians; fielded an anonymous survey of prosecutors; performed content and quantitative analysis of the rulings handed down by specific courts; conducted archival research in several venues; and attended trials. I use this evidence to investigate the dynamics behind attempts to colonize the judiciary, looking at efforts by pro– and anti–transitional justice groups to build coalitions with a critical mass of judges and prosecutors, or dismantle those forged by their adversaries.

The empirical chapters carefully reconstruct the informal spaces of interaction created by human rights activists in order to deploy their pedagogical interventions. Interviews with litigants, judges, and prosecutors, as well as information gathered in the archives of NGOs, allow me to document several key implications of the argument, including litigants' understanding of the importance of transforming legal preferences as the main motivation for engaging in these activities, the ideas that were circulated in these spaces, the ways in which they were explained, and the reach of the diffusion efforts. To explore the other strategy to craft a friendly judiciary, i.e., replacement, I use evidence of activists' naming and shaming of recalcitrant judges, and of their participation during nominations or impeachments, gathered from media sources and the records of judicial appointment bodies.

The analysis also characterizes the political environment surrounding prosecutions and trials in order to document the ability and willingness of politicians and the military to condition projustice outcomes. Relying on interviews with governmental and judicial actors, news archives, and the minutes of relevant congressional committees I trace the contours of the human rights policies pursued by presidents and legislatures, and look for evidence of informal intimidation tactics and court packing initiatives aimed at minimizing, deterring, or promoting judicial action in cases of state repression. This is important for two reasons. First, I am able to assess the levels of risk involved in handing down rulings for or against the defendants, and show that judicial actors often confronted powerful political and military players, following rekindled or traditional legal preferences. Second, by exploring efforts by anti–transitional justice administrations to secure reliable courts, and the timing of these efforts vis-à-vis activists' strategies of judicial change, I analyze the extent to which the former conditioned the success of the latter. The reactions of proimpunity actors to the inroads made by litigants into the legal imagination of judges and prosecutors are particularly revealing of how unsettling these changes in legal preferences can be from the point of view of those seeking to contain the judicialization process.

The most challenging aspect of the case studies is to show how legal preferences affect the thinking of judicial actors when deciding on human rights cases. Judges and prosecutors must recognize temporal shifts in their standards of adjudication as the impact of formal and informal litigation strategies accumulates, modifying their interpretative criteria, their technical capabilities, their approach to the investigations, and their professional commitment to push the cases forward. In other words, changes in legal ideas should be reflected upon and admitted, and prior formalist beliefs should be evaluated negatively, showing a high degree of normative suasion. This is the "smoking gun" evidence that would support the theory. It is not an easy test because judges and prosecutors, like any members of the elite, presumably want to present themselves in a positive light to the interviewer. Acknowledging the pedagogical impact of litigants' strategies amounts to (a) recognizing prior ignorance of these issues and (b) showing lack of originality in coming up with solutions for the legal problems presented by human rights cases.

Responses to survey questions as well as the numerous testimonies of judicial actors offered an invaluable window into these thought processes, especially the perceived legitimacy of different sources of law, the empowering effect of knowledge acquisition, and the importance of routines and standard practices in conditioning their professional undertakings. Moreover, the analysis of judges and prosecutors' subjective perceptions of their role in the battle for criminal accountability revealed the extent to which their actions were guided by a rekindled sense of a professional mission to adjudicate rights claims. To complement these data, the case studies rely on a close reading of indictments and decisions on interlocutory appeals and final rulings, to explore whether they effectively make use of international sources of law, refer to the political environment and the constraints it imposes on judicial behavior, and incorporate arguments expounded by litigants both in court and during pedagogical interventions. I also reviewed speeches and public statements delivered by judges in order to evaluate the relevance of the human rights cause in defining the institutional image the judiciary seeks to convey to the public.

Plan Ahead

In Chapter 2 I present a theory of the collapse of impunity in Latin America that begins with a series of assumptions about the nature of the judicial world and the behavior of its members. I conceptualize judicial decision making as a cognitive process based primarily on legal preferences, not strategic calculations. Armed with these theoretical tools, the chapter then unpacks the mechanisms of institutional change deployed by litigants in order to transform norms of legal praxis that are out of sync with antiimpunity arguments. I carefully identify the actors involved in these struggles, the ideas they seek to diffuse within the judicial branch, and the reasons why these tactics of legal contention are conducive to cementing the technical capacity and commitment of judges and prosecutors to the human rights cause. Chapters 3, 4, and 5 present the empirical findings obtained during field research in Argentina, Peru, and Mexico, respectively. Finally, Chapter 6 puts the three cases into sharper comparative perspective and shows how the argument might be useful to explain transitional justice outcomes in other Latin American countries, especially Brazil and Uruguay. The book concludes with a reflection about how legal preferences and the processes that lead to their reproduction and transformation offer new ways of thinking about the sources of judicial power and the nature of judicial independence.

2

Legal Preferences and Strategic Litigation

A Theory of Judicial Change

As the years since the end of dictatorships and internal armed conflicts in Latin America passed, prosecutions against those responsible for the perpetration of human rights violations became fraught with enormous challenges. In particular, the legal framework governing criminal procedures had to be reinterpreted keeping an eye on victims' rights to truth and justice, and investigating crimes that occurred several decades earlier proved increasingly difficult. From the perspective of judges and prosecutors, moving forward with these cases implied a radical transformation in the knowledge, practices, and values that underpinned their decision making routines, breaking with past interpretive standards. Prison sentences followed a reconfiguration of the locus of legal authority away from domestic legislation, in line with the imperatives of international human rights law. They also reflected the implementation of novel investigative approaches attuned to the historical and political specifics of the crimes. These approaches were imbued with a deep sense of obligation to exhaust all measures to build convincing accusations, amid official denial, fading memories, and scant "smoking gun" evidence. To understand the sustained wave of successful trials observed in several countries across the region we must therefore delve into the minds of judicial actors, exploring how they thought about the law and their duties as professionals in the legal field. Most importantly, we must uncover the processes whereby their legal visions shifted, embracing new paradigms of adjudication and a different sense of institutional mission. This chapter develops the theoretical apparatus to accomplish these tasks.

Judges and prosecutors operate in highly bureaucratized environments, characterized by formal and informal standards of praxis that often resist innovation. I introduce the notion of "legal preferences" to conceptualize this professional-cultural lens through which judicial actors approach the adjudication of rights claims. I argue that legal preferences shape the technical skills of judges and prosecutors, limiting creativity and favoring the reproduction of established problem solving templates. In addition, they nurture professional understandings of what constitutes appropriate legal praxis, crafting motives to resist outside pressures to rule in a different way. In so doing, legal preferences shape an active commitment to institutional goals. The entrenchment of these norms and practices thus affects judicial actors' ability and willingness to become influential political players in certain domains, defy politicians, redirect public policies, and, ultimately, distribute power to and from certain groups. Given the presence of this institutionalized interpretive prism, the emergence of new ways of seeing the law to favor formerly disadvantaged sectors of society rests on the development of the shared belief that alternative courses of action exist, and are legitimate within the rules and discursive parameters of the legal field. Moreover, judicial actors must become ready to defend unprecedented jurisprudential solutions from the criticisms and attacks launched by social forces with an interest in the preservation of the legal status quo.

My sociological institutionalist approach, anchored in the notion of legal preferences, offers an alternative to rationalist accounts with regard to the limits and possibilities in the exercise of judicial power. Rationalists tend to picture judges as strategic players who as members of the "least dangerous branch" lack access to the purse and the sword, and therefore adapt to the political environment in an effort to avoid conflict or political risks (Ferejohn and Weingast 1992; Epstein and Knight 1998; Epstein, Knight, and Martin 2001; Epstein, Knight, and Shvetsova 2001; Bergara et al. 2003). According to this literature, this is especially true in contexts of great institutional uncertainty such as the ones characteristic of Latin American democracies (Iaryczower et al. 2002; Helmke 2005; Pérez Liñán and Castagnola 2009; Scribner 2011). In other words, judicial behavior is conditioned by the degrees of freedom for action afforded by more resourceful political actors. By contrast, I propose a theoretical framework that looks at judges' and prosecutors' ability and willingness to wield autonomous influence on political outcomes as the product of an internal logic of appropriateness that trumps this external logic of consequences. Courts may be structurally well positioned to challenge a president or expand the rights of certain groups, but may lack the skills or the professional motivation to do so. Similarly, courts are often bound to lose if they embark on a collision course with powerful political actors. Sometimes, however, they choose to do so either because they follow what they believe is the right thing to do, or because they proceed to solve cases in the only way they know.

Understanding how legal preferences refract judges' and prosecutors' perceptions of the possibilities available in the cases they receive is of crucial strategic importance for those who want to promote political causes by means of judicialization. In particular, legal preferences condition the types of tactics of legal contention that are likely to lead to victories in court. Judiciaries have to be tamed, biasing their legal preferences, for them to turn into reliable stewards of specific interests. In the case of human rights trials activists faced unfavorable odds, as predominant positivist and formalist legal preferences were staked against them. Victories in the quest for truth and justice thus hinged upon their realization of the importance of igniting processes of ideational change within judicial branches. In the second part of this chapter I propose a theoretical mechanism activated by victims and their lawyers, to explain why in some places criminals were effectively prosecuted and punished. I argue that human rights activists implemented pedagogical interventions and personnel changing strategies, engaging in the political construction of a new legal vision that changed the norms guiding judicial action, reshaped courts' political will to become involved in struggles over transitional justice, and diffused the technical capabilities that made that involvement possible. The model relies on a careful characterization of the actors involved in the struggle, the legal ideas they intend to entrench in the judicial branch, and the conditions that make the activation of this crucial causal mechanism more or less likely. In particular, I theorize how anti–transitional justice interests in the political and military establishments may limit the possibilities of ideational change. As both camps seek to disseminate jurisprudential standards compatible with their political objectives, they turn the judiciary into a battleground of ideas about the law and conflicting institutional goals.

Human rights trials required a degree of judicial courage and defiance that challenges the traditional image of Latin American courts as ineffective, inconsequential, and obsequious to the political branches. Judges and prosecutors often put their careers at risk and defied domestic legislation, undermining the regulatory prerogatives of the executive and legislative branches. Throughout the process they acquired the technical skills to act in the judicial field in ways that they could not conceive of or imagine before, greatly expanding their sphere of influence to previously uncharted policy domains.[1] By looking at the behavioral effects of legal preferences

[1] This characterization of judicial behavior emphasizes three dimensions of the concept of judicial power often found in the literature: the ability of judges 1) to rule sincerely, 2) to command compliance with their rulings, and 3) to expand their spheres of influence and the reach of their prerogatives. For example, in his influential book Ginsburg states that judicial power "results from the interaction of three different components: the independent input

and their transformation, the pages to come identify new theoretical pathways leading to this kind of display of judicial power.

Legal Preferences and Judicial Behavior

What goes on in the minds of judicial actors when they must decide on a case? Influential rational choice scholarship pays special attention to how the institutional and political environment shapes judges' calculations (Epstein and Knight 1998). For example, several authors look at how formal barriers to the encroachment of politicians in the work of judiciaries (e.g. tenure, salary security, etc.) make bold, sincere behavior more likely (Domingo 1999; Domingo and Sieder 2001). Research done outside the United States, however, has identified informal mechanisms that often jeopardize the meaningfulness of these formal attributes of the bench (Iaryczower et al. 2002; Helmke 2005; Pérez Liñán and Castagnola 2009). As a result, in order to characterize the process whereby courts become autonomous actors, most rationalists now also take into account the political resources available to elected officials to circumvent court decisions or deactivate islands of independence within the judicial branch (Chávez 2003; Finkel 2008). The expectation is that courts are more likely to become involved in politically sensitive struggles when the power of their counterparts in the institutional game is circumscribed by formal institutions and/or their resolve is weakened by political fragmentation (Ríos Figueroa 2007; Helmke and Rosenbluth 2009; Chávez et al. 2011). The separation of powers, in particular, the judiciary's lack of both the sword and the purse, thus leads to strategic patterns of behavior. Under unfavorable conditions, judicial actors prioritize long-term goals such as job security over short-term assertions of judicial power that may lead to regrettable backlashes (Epstein, Knight, and Shvetsova 2001; Helmke 2005).

The strategic school revolutionized the field of comparative public law because it sensitized scholars to the importance of institutional constraints in the judicial decision making process, and to the fact that judges are deeply embedded in the political game. In spite of this crucial virtue, the

of the court in producing politically significant outcomes that are complied with by other actors" (2003: 252; see also Kapiszewski 2012). Most definitions, however, focus mainly on the first and second components (Larkins 1996; Cameron 2002; Staton 2010) and tangentially touch upon the third by introducing the notion of judicial authority or jurisdiction, referring to the formal prerogatives of courts to intervene in the cases brought before them (Stone 1992; Tate and Vallinder 1995; Finkel 2008).

approach has one central shortcoming: It sees processes of judicial decision making as fundamentally shaped by external factors. Courts' ability to wield power is at the mercy of the credibility and severity of the threats launched by politicians, legislators, or the military, and by the formal rules of judicial appointment and tenure designed by these actors. As a result, it leaves little room for identifying endogenous processes of empowerment and disempowerment borne out of the internal dynamics of judicial corporations, which may limit or encourage assertive action regardless of the preferences of elected officials or bureaucrats. Rationalists pay almost no attention to the resources and capabilities developed within judiciaries that nurture feelings of security to behave sincerely or a sense of mission to act in defense of certain positions.[2] It is this bias toward external factors that leaves strategic accounts ill equipped to explain, for example, why sometimes courts engage in severe interbranch conflicts, including battles they cannot win (Esptein et al. 2001; Helmke and Staton 2011; Kapiszewski 2012); or why courts privilege certain argumentative foundations to interpret their prerogatives and ground their decisions, with enormous consequences for their ability to define the contours of constitutional rights and the distribution of power in politics and society (Epp 1998, 2009; Hilbink 2012).

One way to take care of this problem is to look closely at the role of ideas about the law in judicial decision making processes. The entrenchment of certain beliefs about legal praxis among judges can have decisive effects on their ability to influence politics. Shared ideas can strengthen corporatist feelings and foster forms of internal associativism in defense of certain positions or prerogatives threatened by resourceful political majorities. Ideas and norms of behavior can also limit judges' ability to control the actions of elected officials even when the latter lack the resources to retaliate. For example, the hegemony of doctrines of legislative supremacy may lead judges to abdicate their powers of constitutional review (Hilbink 2007a; Couso 2010). From a theoretical point of view, it is therefore important to depict courts' motivations to wield power (or to refrain from it) as not dominated by a narrow form of self-interest. Judges and prosecutors may develop different types of conscious and unconscious goals, something that is increasingly recognized even by proponents of the strategic approach (Epstein and Knight 2013). For instance, by virtue of their

[2] The work of Staton (2004, 2010) and Vanberg (2001, 2005) constitutes an exception. For example, Staton argues that courts craft communication strategies in order to enhance their public legitimacy and increase their leverage in interbranch confrontations.

membership in the legal community, judicial actors may come to define their role in the political system in terms of producing legally sound jurisprudence; qua staffers of a bureaucratic body, they may be geared to abide by accepted standards of professional behavior.

Sociological institutionalism offers the tools to think about judicial behavior and judicial empowerment in these terms (Hall and Taylor 1996). The school was developed by organizational theorists under the influence of seminal contributions to the structure-agency debate in social theory (DiMaggio and Powell 1991). In particular, the cognitive turn in sociology led to the development of a notion of human action as embedded in taken-for-granted perceptual schemas used to make sense of the social world. Action grounded in the practicality of daily life runs contrary to the rationalist portrayal of actors as calculating creatures unconstrained by unconscious cognitive predispositions. Actors do not necessarily adhere to certain rules and practices because defecting would not be a best response given the actions of other players, but they stick to routines and existing templates because the latter become conventional aspects of political sociability. Conforming to conventions and routines reduces anxiety and reinforces a security system that endows social life with intelligibility (Giddens 1979, 1984), and nurtures feelings of social efficacy by yielding successful, scripted social encounters (Goffman 1974).

For sociological institutionalists, institutions take the form of cognitive frameworks that embody culturally constructed ways of judging and interpreting (Bourdieu 1977, 1984; Bourdieu and Wacquant 1992), as well as conceptions about appropriate patterns of action within organizations. These frameworks naturalize certain rituals and routines, provide meaning-ascribing tools to interpret the constraints and possibilities presented by the social environment, and lead to particular ways of conceptualizing problems and of perceiving the array of valid solutions (March and Olsen 1984). In the field of judicial politics, what distinguishes this brand of scholarship is the view that the goals judges seek when handing down rulings are both constituted and bounded by the characteristics of the organization they staff (Smith 1988, 2008; Gillman 1999). The possibilities offered by a case and the perception of existing jurisprudence and legal texts are mediated by legal visions or cultures/traditions of interpretation. These institutional lenses are political and historically constructed and constitute informal norms of behavior that indicate how things are done or ought to be done by judges as professionals of the legal field (Bourdieu 1986; Gillman 1999, 2002; Ingram 2012).

Judicial politics scholars working in the U.S. context tend to dismiss the idea that the law is an important determinant of judicial action. Segal and Spaeth famously argue that case facts or precedent do not limit judicial actors' drive to express their ideological positions (Segal and Spaeth 1993). In their view, legal discourse is a cloak used to disguise political choices. Others argue that judges use the law instrumentally in order to please certain constituencies, especially legal constituencies that value high quality juridical argumentation (Baum 2006; Graham 2009) or rely on precedent in order to prevent upsetting their superiors in the judicial hierarchy (Kastellec 2011; Lax 2011). Legal choices are thus seen as a fully conscious manipulation of the legal corpus that allows actors to rationalize reputational and ideological goals.

The argument put forward in this chapter is premised on different ontological assumptions. The quick dismissal of legal factors as relevant in judicial decision making is underpinned by a "positivistic understanding" of how legal interpretation works (Whittington 2000: 627). The implicit claim is that unless the law exerts an objective, material constraint on judges' individual orientations, it cannot be considered a relevant determinant of jurisprudential outcomes. Although I agree with Segal and Spaeth when they suggest that given the polysemic nature of the legal corpus, it cannot by itself act as a constraint, my position is that what matters is not what the law literally says, but the cognitive lens through which positive law, jurisprudence, and doctrine are interpreted. Most importantly, this lens is not the product of an asocial reading of the law by discrete judicial actors, but is in fact collectively constituted and reproduced by complex socialization processes that transcend individual behavioral predispositions.

As a result of these socialization processes in the legal academy and on the bench (Baum 1994; Kahn 1999), judicial actors' legal choices are decisively affected by a set of profession-specific values that I call legal preferences. Legal preferences are a defining feature of the cognitive lens through which judges and prosecutors conceptualize the disputes they are asked to adjudicate. They encompass views about what can be considered legitimate sources of law (domestic, international, customary); what are the legitimate sources of authority about the law (schools of thought); what are the acceptable forms of legal argumentation, templates of reasoned justification, and terms of art that may be used in courts' pronouncements; what amounts to a reasonable standard of proof when adjudicating criminal or civil responsibility; and conceptions about the reach of formal judicial prerogatives. These preferences stem from the judiciary's legal culture, "a structure of meaning ... passed on through socially transmitted norms of conduct and rules of decisions that influence ... cognitive processes and individual dispositions" (Bierbrauer 1994: 243). These internal norms or practices affect judicial action and the ability to wield judicial power.

In what follows, I propose three guiding assumptions about the role of these legal preferences in the workings of the judicial world. These are assumptions about how judges think and operate. First, technical capabilities and legal knowledge demarcate the world of conceivable and imaginable legal solutions for cases, thus influencing the array of policy domains in which courts can participate effectively. Second, ideas about the law and standardized adjudication practices constitute a reservoir of internal institutional resources that generate the political will to venture into sensitive debates over policy. Finally, judiciaries are politicized by alliances crafted by their own members and outside groups, entrenching norms and values relative to the exercise of judicial prerogatives. As a result, legal preferences reflect the institutionalization of interests in the judiciary, and produce organizational biases. This often implies the historical development of jurisprudential standards that are regularly applied, systematically favoring some type of plaintiff over others.

Legal Preferences and Technical Capabilities

Far from being epiphenomenal in decision making processes, legal preferences are constitutive of the game played by judicial actors. They are the means by which judges and prosecutors participate in social, economic, and political debates, reading and rewriting the law. These professional mores reproduce a habitus, which determines the predisposition of judges to act in certain ways (Bourdieu 1977, 1984). By promoting adherence to routine practices and standards of adjudication, legal preferences impose cognitive and technical limitations that bias judicial actors' regard for (or knowledge of) some types of legal instruments, doctrines, and precedents. They thus define the skills with which judicial actors are equipped to interpret the legal corpus, the practical tools necessary to conduct their duties, and the ensuing perceived possibilities for assertive behavior within the boundaries of the legal framework. This is hardly surprising because as Helmke and Levitsky suggest, "Actors operating within a particular formal institutional context develop norms and procedures that expedite their work or address problems not contemplated by the formal rules" (2006: 19). Anyone who rummages through judicial dockets discovers that judicial actors indeed operate on the basis of templates and repetition.

As members of the judicial field, they approach problems through the lens of that which is known, accepted, and previously tested.

The main effect of the skills, routines, and standards of legal praxis associated with certain legal preferences is that they reduce the number of ways in which judicial actors can legally respond to litigants' demands or to their own ideological or opportunistic considerations. Simply put, judges and prosecutors will never arrive at jurisprudential solutions they do not know about. This is not to say that judges never act strategically to advance their political, social, or economic goals better through legal interpretation, favoring causes or plaintiffs with whom they sympathize. In fact, legal arguments and doctrines are usually ambiguous enough to be subject to manipulations in order to fit the needs of a judge's preexisting ideological or policy agenda. What my approach indicates is that by virtue of their membership in a structured organizational environment, judges share technical knowledge associated with the practice of the law that conditions the number of ways in which nonlegal considerations can be reflected in rulings, rendering certain forms of behavior unthinkable. These deeply entrenched professional worldviews may therefore lead judicial actors to behave as *satisficers*, sometimes ruling out or simply ignoring available strategies to increase their power or pursue ideological agendas.

Using known legal instruments, lines of reasoning, and hermeneutic techniques is not simply a bureaucratic reflex; it also serves an important legitimating function. From a psychological point of view, the method that others and I routinely adopt to fulfill a task is endowed with an intuitive aura of reassurance. By contrast, solutions that must be justified on the basis of unusual arguments seem foreign and out of bounds. Like participants in other highly regulated spheres, judges and prosecutors are geared toward preserving the legal legitimacy of their decisions, and therefore avoid the unnecessary risks involved in using untested criteria. The latter may destroy the authority of the doctrines and routine practices to which they and their audiences are accustomed (Baum 2006). In addition, professional norms command a certain type of reasoned justification, one that falls within the limits of a specialized discourse to which clear parameters of argumentation apply (Friedman 2006; Bybee 2010).

This implies that those judges and prosecutors who as citizens could be allies of certain political causes need to be convinced that as legal operators they have acceptable weapons to become agents of those causes in the judicial field. More generally, radical deviations from established precedents or structural changes in the ways judicial actors understand their prerogatives necessarily follow the infusion of new technical skills that expand cognitive maps and multiply the array of legal solutions regarded as legitimate. As shown by Charles Epp, the meaning of constitutional provisions is not given by the letter of the law, but constructed during complex interactions between judges and outside forces (Epp 1998). As we will see later on in the case of transitional justice in Latin America, the lack of awareness among judges and prosecutors of international human rights doctrines and instruments, and of certain theories of criminal liability, posed a serious challenge for victims and their lawyers. Human rights NGOs could not expect to achieve justice if the arguments they expounded in court to overturn impunity dispositions were seen by judicial actors as incomprehensible, impractical, or lacking sound basis in positive law. Since these arguments contravened long-standing cultures of legal interpretation, received opinions had to be replaced, providing judges with an alternative discursive apparatus that resignified existing laws. At a more practical level, if, for example, in a case against military officers responsible for forced disappearances, judicial actors reproduced the techniques of criminal investigation used in regular homicide cases, it was very unlikely that they would be able to conclude that the evidence available was enough to incriminate the defendants. As a result, litigants had to retrain investigators, entrenching new evidence-gathering routines and criteria for evaluating and weighting clues.

Legal Preferences and Judicial Actors' Political Will

Common socialization processes, including standardized educational trajectories, nurture a specific way of thinking about the law among members of the bench. The ensuing patterns of behavior result less from strategic considerations than from a shared understanding of what is professionally acceptable. In this sense, following judicial routines and standard practices is often not a completely conscious undertaking, but rather a process whereby actors fulfill assigned roles and organizational expectations. These informal behavioral norms define judicial actors' perception of what is the appropriate scope of involvement in political affairs and shape the extent to which they can muster the will, courage, and resources to rule sincerely, fundamentally altering the cost-benefit analysis that determines whether or not to defy powerful political players. Legal preferences thus promote a logic of action with the potential of inducing judicial actors to engage in battles that would be ruled out from a purely rationalist perspective, or to shy away from fights they could conceivably win. Doing what a particular organizational role commands becomes more important than evaluating the costs of potential retaliations or of not pursuing a more activist agenda.

This is not to say, however, that these internalized norms always lead judicial actors to behave foolishly, fighting battles they cannot win. The point is simply that the institutionalization of ideas about appropriate legal praxis has an impact on the resources that courts can generate internally to improve their leverage in political struggles. In the first place, shared values enhance the collective determination of judicial players and their ability to stand up against powerful political actors. To put it differently, these ideas help overcome collective action problems. For example, the formation of formal and informal professional associations of judges or prosecutors driven by similar corporate identities can amplify their voices and enhance their individual sense of security (Hilbink 2007b, 2012). From the perspective of materially or politically more powerful groups, this can increase the costs of retaliation, making it more difficult for presidents or the military to subject judiciaries to their control.

Second, the development of corporate identities and institutional values is usually accompanied by the creation of complex symbolic infrastructures that cement the authority of the judiciary. In this respect, the imperative to fulfill behavioral expectations within judicial organizations responds to the interest in preserving the sources of courts' symbolic distinctiveness vis-à-vis other fields of action, which enhances judicial actors' authoritativeness when deciding over questions of great political importance. The internal construction of authority through the consolidation and external projection of legal symbolic systems can thus act as a shield in struggles with other organizations or political actors. This is no different from other professions, in which members are expected to express findings or opinions in a specialized language, or tailor explanations and narratives in the terms offered by accepted theoretical or conceptual paradigms. These discursive strategies are not only inevitable insofar as they are reproduced by internal socialization dynamics, but are also functional to the legitimation of an actor's position vis-à-vis its peers and external audiences that perceive in such practices an aura of authority, rigor, and knowledge (Shapiro 1981; Baum 2006). As a result, despite the obvious room for interpretative discretion, the professional duty of having to couch opinions in a specialized discourse is an "important legitimating ideal for courts" (Bybee 2010: 78; Clayton 1992). Legal reasoning, with its concomitant myth of legality (Scheb and Lyons 2000), constitutes the cornerstone of courts' "symbolic effectiveness" (Bourdieu 1984; Stinchcombe 1997). It is central to rendering the exercise of judicial power acceptable for the parties involved, including those who lose disputes. The symbols displayed in judicial rituals "tend to reinforce judicial legitimacy by teaching the lesson that courts are different from other institutions..., and are therefore worthy of respect" (Gibson and Caldeira 2009: 3).

By identifying legal preferences as a potential source of political will and authority to defend certain jurisprudential outcomes against external impositions, this second theoretical assumption indicates that the political environment does not necessarily determine the result of transitional justice efforts. Judicial corporate identities can turn judiciaries into resourceful opponents of elected officials and military actors pushing for rulings in either direction. For example, the widespread belief in the need to enforce international human rights treaties may lead judiciaries to ignore political pressures to perpetuate impunity. Similarly, a professional rejection of the legitimacy of nondomestic sources of law can limit the capacity of judiciaries to become suitable arenas for the defense of victims' rights. Human rights litigants' success is therefore a function of the extent to which they mold judges' and prosecutors' logic of behavioral appropriateness in their favor, enlisting them in their ranks.

Legal Preferences as Institutionalized Interests

Because legal preferences shape how judges and prosecutors respond to cases, and condition a professional sense of mission, their reproduction and transformation are not politically neutral (Hattam 1993; Pickerill and Clayton 2004; Gillman 2008; Novkov 2008). For example, if legal education and judicial practice promote a characterization of the bench as an institution that applies the literal meaning of written laws rather than one that has the prerogative to defy the legislator, the judicial battleground will be biased against change or against political minorities. Accordingly, the judiciary will operate as a conservative force (Hilbink 2007a). The complex of ideas, standards, and routines locked inside judicial organizations thus crystallizes power imbalances (Steinmo et al. 1992; Thelen 1999). As DiMaggio and Powell put it, "Institutional reproduction has been associated with the demands of powerful central actors, such as the state, the professions, or the dominant agents within organizational fields" (1991: 28).

Politically charged interpretive practices are manufactured and diffused by coalitions bridging actors within and outside judicial corporations, and are more or less pervasive depending on the strength of these alliances. In order to understand fully the position of the judiciary in any given political struggle and the ways in which it wields power distributing resources and entitlements, we must therefore explore how different groups manage to entrench their interests in the form of ideas about appropriate legal praxis, and thus promote particular types of judicial outcomes. In this sense, struggles to define what the law is, the limits of interpretive freedom, or the validity of certain doctrinal positions are at the heart of processes leading judicial corporations to become increasingly activist in particular policy domains. Winners transform these bodies into powerful and effective stewards of specific positions. As courts all over the world become the ultimate focal point of political confrontation, disputes over who the judges are and how they think intensify, leading politicians and civil society organizations to spend great amounts of political capital and resources in shaping legal preferences. Succeeding in the institutionalization of new interpretive standards can guarantee favorable jurisprudence over time, even after the demise of the coalitions that brought about the ideational changes (Gillman 1993, 2002).

Central to the construction of legitimizing legal discourses for innovative and transformative judicial involvement in political affairs is what some authors refer to as the "legal complex" (Halliday, Karpic, and Feeley 2007). This complex is made up of judges, prosecutors, private lawyers, public interest litigation groups, lawyers' professional associations, and academics. The web of relations established among them in pursuit of certain social and political causes constitutes the basis for effective policy transformation in the judicial field. Not only do these actors build on the discursive plane the technical fundamentals necessary for legal preference change, but they also give public visibility and mobilizational strength to these initiatives. The concerted actions of the legal complex can thus undermine the reproduction of practices and standards within judicial corporations, freshen up these institutions, redefine their mission, and open up a new world of legal solutions for social and political demands (Epp 2009: 24–25).

Large-scale changes in jurisprudential behavior – such as the cases of transitional justice studied in this book – follow ideational revolutions within judiciaries that result from such struggles. The quest for truth and justice presented to courts a set of legal arguments that departed radically from standard legal practice in Latin America, forcing pro- and antiimpunity groups to fight for control over the normative and professional commitments of judges and prosecutors. They likewise battled to diffuse awareness and impose acceptance of the legal discourses necessary to support those commitments. In particular, successfully promoting criminal prosecutions against human rights violators demanded from victims and their lawyers strenuous efforts in order to impose a new legal orthodoxy based on the values of international human rights law. Litigants had to put new ideas on the map, defying the institutional inertias that reproduce the cognitive frameworks underpinning judicial behavior. They also had to legitimize these new doctrines and convince judicial actors of the viability of that exercise of judicial power. In other words, in the struggle against impunity, litigants' success depended on igniting a process of institutional change that transformed formerly unreceptive and passive judiciaries into allied corporations. The result was that judges and prosecutors found themselves remarkably comfortable with jurisprudential innovations that were both intellectually challenging and politically risky.

After outlining my three central assumptions about how judges think and how judicial corporations become part and parcel of political struggles, the rest of the chapter deals with two remaining theoretical tasks. First, I specify the legal preferences underpinning judicial behavior in the region for most of the twentieth century. I also explain the arguments expounded by human rights litigants and their incompatibility with this long-standing tradition of legal interpretation. Second, I propose a theoretical mechanism that produces the necessary institutional changes for observing waves of prison sentences. I argue that successful litigants understand the empowering potential of nurturing an alternative sense of mission among judges, and identify the cognitive obstacles posed by a formalist and positivist tradition of legal interpretation. Inspired by this diagnosis, they design a series of strategies to transform technically deficient judiciaries, which by virtue of those deficiencies are biased against the transitional justice cause.

Identifying the Ideas, the Actors, and the Mechanisms of Change

The sentencing of human rights criminals is based on innovative interpretations of constitutional rights. Judges and prosecutors read into domestic legislation the values of international human rights law and seek to harmonize both legal bodies with the goal of expanding the sphere of victims' rights. This shift in legal visions is premised on the importance of undermining raison d'état considerations when evaluating how states treat their own citizens, a move that is in line with "neoconstitutionalist" currents of legal thought. Neoconstitutionalism promotes a greater predisposition to acknowledge the open nature of legal texts and expects judges to subject legislative acts to strong constitutionality and conventionality tests. The new doctrines thus release judicial actors from formalist straitjackets when they interpret the law, allowing them to become influential players in policy debates. In so doing, they put judiciaries at the center of debates over minority rights, the use of state violence, or the social effects of economic policy. In fact, the cultural transformation inherent in this rights-centered jurisprudence is often cited as the driving force behind the "judicialization of politics" in Latin America (García Villegas and Uprimny 2004; Sieder et al. 2005; Gargarella, Domingo, and Roux 2006; Kapiszewski and Taylor 2008; Rodríguez Garavito 2009, 2011a, 2011b).

Some explanations for this phenomenon focus on structural changes in legal regimes throughout the world, including the constitutionalization of judicial review, the creation of Constitutional Courts, and the drafting of bills of rights (Ginsburg 2003; Hirschl 2004).[3] By explicitly granting courts the prerogative to check legislation and by unequivocally recognizing myriad new rights, judges have been formally empowered (Gauri and Brinks 2008). In Latin America, the Spanish, French, and German constitutions had an impact on the new constitutions of Colombia (1991) and Peru (1979, 1993) that created Constitutional Courts independent of the judicial branch (Uprimny 2004; Dargent 2009; Rodríguez Raga 2011).[4] Similarly, recent reforms in countries including Costa Rica and Chile have led to the creation of special constitutional chambers within existing Supreme Courts (Wilson and Rodríguez Cordero 2006). Finally, the Mexican Supreme Court, although not formally a European-style Constitutional Court, has begun to behave like one as a result of a series of institutional changes promoted during the democratic transition (Magaloni 2003; Silva Meza and Silva García 2009). Other authors suggest that the new discourse of rights has penetrated judiciaries as a result of organizational changes that opened the door for new voices. The creation of Constitutional Courts, for example, led to the appointment of highly reputed legal scholars who were uncontaminated by the vices of positivist judiciaries (Nunes 2010). In addition, in countries such as Chile, judicial reforms led to the greater professionalization of the bench via the creation of judicial schools with competitive entry exams, and to the opening of numerous new positions in the judiciary. As a result in

[3] Ginsburg (2008) suggests that 158 out of 191 constitutions "include some formal provision for constitutional review" (81). These provisions range from the creation of separate Constitutional Courts in 79 cases to the granting of judicial review to ordinary courts or to a Supreme Court in 60 cases.

[4] For the development of neoconstitutionalism in Europe see Stone Sweet (2000).

part of the increasing presence of neoconstitutionalism in the Chilean legal academy, a new generation of jurists began to occupy posts within the judicial hierarchy (Couso 2007, 2010; Couso and Hilbink 2011).[5]

The story presented here deepens our understanding of the neoconstitutionalist revolution by further revealing the link between the influx of new legal preferences and judicial outcomes. It delves into the difficult processes of knowledge acquisition and normative evolution that underlie the adoption of neoconstitutionalist positions. To understand better the development of this jurisprudence, we must look beyond formal institutional changes and instead think about the conflicts involved in the emergence of alternative approaches to rights adjudication. For example, judges do not automatically embrace judicial review when the latter is constitutionalized, as this would imply too radical a change in their bureaucratic reflexes. Although the literature does mention changes in education and in the makeup of the academic world, qua causal mechanisms these accounts remain underspecified. They lack an adequate discussion of the actors involved in the spread of innovative paradigms, the resistance to the influx of new norms, and the processes whereby this resistance is overcome. In any ideational explanation, the ideas that support or challenge the status quo "must be able to be clearly identified and associated with specific political actors" (Berman 1998: 19) in order to trace connections between them and relevant outcomes. Documenting how diffusion opens up new possibilities for action and shuts down others requires a thick description of the actors carrying the ideas, their strategies to put them in play in decision making processes, and the pathways to acceptance and compliance by the target population. In other words, it is important to explore the processes whereby judges come to believe in the neoconstitutionalist paradigm and learn to apply these new tools when faced with actual cases.

I focus on a specific brand of neoconstitutionalism, namely, the (international) legal doctrines that regulate the investigation and juridical framing of mass atrocities, with an eye on victims' structural disadvantages in the proceedings. What is the content of the ideas in question and why do they affect the ability of judicial actors to become effective agents of truth and justice?

[5] Couso (2007) documents the rise in graduates from law degrees in the United States or Britain, who then returned to Chile with a new conception of the role of judges in the political system, and of the boundaries of legal hermeneutics.

States' Duty to Investigate, Prosecute, and Punish Human Rights Criminals

The international human rights regime,[6] developed in earnest as a response to the horror of the Holocaust,[7] was founded on the idea that governments can be held accountable at the international level for their behavior vis-à-vis their own citizens (Ratner and Abrams 1997). The United Nations Charter (1945), the Nuremberg Charter (1945), the Universal Declaration of Human Rights (1948), the Genocide Convention (1948), and the Geneva Conventions (1949) marked a momentous change in international relations.[8] The subject of these landmark multilateral treaties was not the preservation of state sovereignty or the regulation of interstate relations, but the protection of the human person from the arbitrary use of state power (Simmons 2009).

At the cornerstone of this transformation in international law is the development of the notion that certain forms of state repression constitute offenses against basic standards of civilization (Bassiouni 2011). These crimes violate norms of *jus cogens* and, according to a former chief justice of the Inter-American Court of Human Rights, damage the "juridical

[6] The international human rights regime consists of three main bodies of law. First, international human rights law protects individuals against their own governments in times of peace. Second, international humanitarian law regulates state behavior in times of internal and international armed conflicts. These first two bodies of law deal with states' international responsibilities. The distinction between international human rights law and humanitarian law has become less sharp in recent years. For example, crimes against humanity can be perpetrated both in times of peace and in times of conflict (see Aponte 2010; Meron 2000). Third, international criminal law emphasizes the existence of international crimes for which particular individuals can be held accountable. The international community may mandate that states investigate and prosecute certain crimes at the domestic level or may create international courts to deal with these cases. These are usually the crimes that constitute the greatest offenses against the human person and are therefore seen as crimes against humanity or in violation of basic standards of civilization. See Ratner and Abrams (1997: 8–15).

[7] On the effect of World War II on the development of the human rights regime, see Humphrey (1984). Before and after World War I, the Hague Treaties and the first three Geneva Conventions began to regulate explicitly the customs of war with the goal of protecting individuals from state abuses during times of international armed confrontation. See Bassiouni (1986, 2003).

[8] Other important multilateral agreements on the protection of the human person include the 1968 Convention on the Non-Applicability of Statutory Limitations to War Crimes and Crimes against Humanity, the 1984 Convention against Torture, and the 1998 Rome Statute that created the International Criminal Court.

conscience of humanity."[9] Genocide was the first international crime to be codified in a multilateral treaty in 1948 (Ratner and Abrams 1997). Other criminal definitions emerged with the evolution of international customary law (Bassiouni 1996).[10] Crimes against humanity, for example, involve a series of common crimes such as murder, enslavement, deportation, imprisonment, torture, rape, forced disappearances, and persecutions on political, racial, and religious grounds, perpetrated in a systematic fashion against specific groups of civilians.[11]

The idea that crimes against humanity and other grave international crimes must be investigated, and their perpetrators punished, is an increasingly valued norm in the international human rights regime.[12] Domestic legal barriers to the progress of criminal prosecutions are considered unacceptable (Orentlicher 1991; Kok 2007; Van der Voort and Zwanenburg 2001). The most consistent jurisprudence on the matter is perhaps the one developed by the Inter-American Court of Human Rights.[13] In the celebrated *Barrios Altos* decision against Peru, the court argued:

[9] I/A Court HR, *Barrios Altos v. Peru*, ruling of 14 March 2001, concurrent opinion of Judge Cançado Trindade, paragraphs 24 to 26. The "norms of jus cogens reflect core constitutive values and commitments of the international community" (Ratner and Abrams 1997: 18).

[10] There are different approaches "to determine whether a norm has achieved the status of customary international law. The most common formulation ... stipulates two basic requirements: 1) that the norm be reflected in consistent state practice, and 2) that the practice be adhered to out of a sense of legal obligation (opinio juris)" (Ratner and Abrams 1997: 16–17).

[11] The Hague Convention of 1907 was one of the first times that the idea of "crimes against humanity" appeared in international law. The notion of "elementary laws of humanity" was also acknowledged in the 1919 report presented to the Preliminary Peace Conference after World War I (Ratner and Abrams 1997). After World War II, the Nuremberg Charter defined crimes against humanity as the "murder, extermination, enslavement, deportation, and other inhumane acts committed against any civilian population, before or during the war, or persecutions on political, racial or religious grounds in execution of or in connection with any crime within the jurisdiction of the Tribunal whether or not in violation of the domestic law of the country where perpetrated" (text can be found at http://avalon.law.yale.edu/imt/imtconst.asp [last accessed 16 November 2015]). In the 1990s, Article 3 of the statute of the International Criminal Tribunal for Rwanda defined them as crimes "committed as part of a widespread or systematic attack against any civilian population on national, political, ethnic, racial or religious grounds" (text can be found at www.unictr.org/sites/unictr.org/files/legal-library/941108_res955_en.pdf [last accessed 16 November 2015]).

[12] The Geneva Conventions, the Genocide Convention, and the Convention against Torture demand that states take action against impunity. The Convention on the Non-Applicability of Statutory Limitations to War Crimes and Crimes against Humanity also dictates the removal of domestic obstacles to the progress of prosecutorial efforts.

[13] Latin America was a pioneer in the development of the international human rights regime. In the aftermath of World War II the American nations issued the American Declaration of

> This Court considers that amnesty dispositions, statutes of limitations and the establishment of exculpatory dispositions that seek to impede the investigation and punishment of those responsible for serious human rights violations such as torture, summary, extralegal or arbitrary executions and forced disappearances, all of which are banned because they contravene non-derogable rights recognized by International Human Rights Law, are inadmissible.[14]

The court has also emphasized states' duty to develop judicial structures that ensure the prevention and timely punishment of these crimes.[15] In addition, it has argued that states have an international responsibility to fulfill these obligations,[16] and has justified the inapplicability of the *non bis in idem* (double jeopardy) principle when a previous prosecution has not been conducted impartially.[17] This Inter-American jurisprudence is also illustrative of the use of customary international law to show that the existence of a long-standing norm against impunity trumps any domestic legislation valid at the time of the crimes. For example, the court has referred to the Nuremberg Charter and various United Nations resolutions to document the decades-old international understanding that prohibits torture, forced disappearances, and other inhumane acts (Dondé 2010).

Human rights litigants in Latin America strategically use the legal norms developed as part of the international human rights regime. International human rights law puts into sharper focus victims' right to truth and justice, often at the expense of procedural rules that benefit defendants. First, international customary law and the norms of *jus cogens* are used to define organized and systematic attacks against civilian populations as crimes against humanity. This applies irrespective of whether or not these criminal definitions were present in local criminal codes at the time of perpetration (in most cases they were not). The international community has

the Rights and Duties of Man in Colombia and thus exerted great influence at the United Nations' San Francisco conference that led to the 1948 Universal Declaration of Human Rights (Glendon 2008). Countries in the region would later agree on the establishment of the Inter-American Human Rights System (Goldman 2009; Huneeus 2010a).

14 I/A Court of HR, *Barrios Altos v. Peru*, ruling of 14 March 2001, paragraph 41, my translation. The court arrived at the same conclusion in the case of "crimes against humanity," which are different from "serious human rights violations." See I/A Court of HR, *Almonacid v. Chile*, ruling of 26 September 2006, paragraphs 96 to 113.

15 See, for example, I/A Court HR, Case of Radilla-Pacheco v. Mexico, ruling of 23 November 2009.

16 See for example I/A Court HR, *Case of Velásquez-Rodríguez v. Honduras*, ruling of 29 July 1988.

17 For the court's doctrine of fraudulent double jeopardy, see, for example, I/A Court HR, *Case of La Cantuta v. Peru*, ruling of 29 November 2006.

long recognized the gravity of these crimes, indicating that these definitions were already part of the legal repertoire. Even if at the time of perpetration states had not endorsed this tacit international consensus against mass atrocities by ratifying treaties or conventions, perpetrators should have been aware of the prohibitions on state action imposed by accepted standards of civilized behavior. This argumentative move allows litigants to question the validity of amnesties passed by congresses and approved by presidents, as well as other impunity dispositions such as statutes of limitations or pardons. The perpetration of crimes against humanity imposes the duty to investigate and punish those involved upon states, regardless of when and where the crimes were carried out. This duty extends beyond the removal of formal barriers for prosecution to include "due diligence" in the pretrial phase. In practice, this means that judges should exhaust all measures to establish criminal responsibility, especially in the face of official denial and the absence of direct incriminating evidence.

Second, criminal definitions derived from international human rights law expand the scope of victims' rights in other ways.[18] In the Latin American context, the notion of forced disappearances is particularly illustrative. The concept, which was developed in earnest in the 1980s and therefore was not present in most local penal codes when the crimes were perpetrated,[19] is defined as follows by the Inter-American Court of Human Rights:

> The multiple and continuous violation of various rights consecrated in the [American] Convention, since it not only produces an arbitrary deprivation of freedom, but also violates the personal integrity and security of the detainee and puts his/her life at risk, placing him/her in a state of complete defenselessness and leading to other related crimes.[20]

The "pluriofensive" nature of the crime is extremely important for victims' claims to truth and justice. First, forced disappearances are continuous

[18] In order to make use of use of the notions of "crime against humanity" and "forced disappearance" in domestic lawsuits, defendants are first charged using criminal definitions included in local penal codes valid at the time of perpetration. The context and the systematic nature of the crimes are then invoked to justify redefining the charges as serious international crimes that were part of unwritten customary standards of state behavior at the time when they were perpetrated. This redefinition leads to a reinterpretation of the rights of the victims and their relatives with regard to the validity of statutory limitations, double jeopardy, and amnesties (Yacobucci 2005; Filippini 2006; Parenti 2010; Quinteros 2010).

[19] The Organization of American States, for example, declared forced disappearances to be crimes against humanity in 1982.

[20] I/A Court HR, *Gómez Palomino v. Perú*, ruling of 22 November 2005, paragraph 92, my translation. See also I/A Court HR, *Velásquez Rodríguez v. Honduras*, ruling of 29 July 1988.

crimes.[21] The crime continues to be perpetrated for as long as the whereabouts of the victim remain unknown. This means that statutory limitations begin to run out only when the body is found. Second, the refusal to provide information about the fate of the victim is an essential part of the criminal definition. Consequently, criminal responsibility can also be assigned to those who participate in the organization that plans, executes, and covers up the disappearances without directly kidnapping, hiding, or murdering the victims. This was usually the role of military dictators and other high-ranking officials. Finally, the denial of information not only affects the victim's fundamental rights to life, liberty, and so forth, but also those of his/her relatives, who must endure uncertainty. This expands the universe of legally recognized victims and opens the way for claims based on the right to truth as well as the right to justice.[22]

Third, in addition to overcoming formal juridical obstacles, the language of crimes against humanity allows litigants to invite judges and prosecutors to pay attention to the context in which the crimes were perpetrated. Awareness of context is crucial in order to make up for the lack of direct incriminating evidence when trying to establish individual criminal responsibility. Crimes against humanity are usually perpetrated by clandestine groups that do not leave traces of their operations in official records.[23] When they do, commanding the state apparatus allows them to guard or destroy the evidence effectively. Moreover, the oral testimonies of the victims' relatives, survivors, or eyewitnesses normally lack precision or are contradictory as a result of trauma and the passage of time. Because of these inherent evidentiary limitations, systematic human rights violations cannot be treated using the same standards applied, for example, in regular homicide cases (Espinoza 2010; Vargas 2010). In addition to the profuse use of indirect and circumstantial evidence, the oral testimonies of individual witnesses who escaped or were released from concentration camps should acquire special value. For example, in cases of sexual

[21] For an extended analysis of the crime of forced disappearance see Modolell González (2010).

[22] On how forced disappearances affect the right to truth, see I/A Court HR, *Caso Castillo Páez v. Perú*, ruling of 3 November 1997, paragraph 90. The jurisprudence of the Inter-American Court of Human Rights also indicates that "impunity propitiates the chronic repetition of human rights violations and the total defenselessness of victims and their relatives" (I/A Court HR, *Paniagua Morales and others v. Guatemala*, ruling of 8 March 1998, paragraph 173).

[23] For example, during the Peruvian internal armed conflict, military officers in charge of forced disappearances used pseudonyms. This makes it particularly hard to establish who was deployed where, and reconstruct the chain of command.

violence perpetrated decades ago, these witnesses become what in human rights criminal doctrine is known as "necessary witnesses."[24] Despite their imprecisions, their testimonies constitute the only data source available to reconstruct the crimes and identify the culprits. In regular criminal cases they would never constitute the main basis for conviction, but their use in human rights prosecutions reflects sensitivity to context and to the international responsibility to seek justice.

Finally, in order to ascribe individual criminal responsibility to all members of the criminal enterprise, litigants promote the use of innovative theories of criminal liability. These doctrines were developed in conjunction with international criminal law and humanitarian law (Mettraux 2009) and are particularly useful when arguing cases against military or political leaders who did not directly perpetrate the crimes, but whose input was necessary for their design and implementation. In the Latin American context, the theory of "command responsibility," or in Spanish *autoría mediata*, has been extremely influential.[25] *Autoría mediata* implies the existence of an illegal, hierarchically structured organization, in which the interchangeability of immediate perpetrators guarantees the man behind the scene, i.e., the leader, his dominion over the execution of the plan (Roxin 2006). Given the lack of written orders, the use of contextual and historical evidence such as military manuals or newspaper archives is crucial to determine command responsibility.[26] In order to use this doctrine,

[24] The first time this concept was used in Latin America was in the 1985 ruling against members of the Argentine military juntas.

[25] This translation should be read with caution. Some jurisprudence understands "command responsibility" as arising from an act of omission, i.e., when leaders fail to control their subordinates (Mettraux 2009). The Spanish term *autoría mediata* does not refer to a crime of omission because it assumes that the leader or high-ranking official participates in the design of the repressive strategies. It is also important to note that other theories of criminal liability have been developed to address this type of crime. Here I only refer to *autoría mediata* because it has been the most influential in Latin America. Other doctrinal shifts in the area of criminal liability are the product of international jurisprudence on human rights violations. For example, the International Criminal Tribunals for the Former Yugoslavia and Rwanda and the International Criminal Court of Justice have made important contributions to the development of a theory of criminal liability for "joint criminal enterprises." For an excellent analysis of these doctrines see Olásolo Alonso (2010).

[26] Mettraux uses as an example the way the International Criminal Tribunal for the Former Yugoslavia evaluated evidence to impute command responsibility: "In an oral ruling of 2 July 2007, a Trial Chamber of the ICTY held that 'evidence of a general publication which is directed to a department [in this case, the police as an institutional branch of the Ministry of Interior] is information which, on its face, can be expected to be within the knowledge of the Minister of that department and the Minister's immediate successor.' Despite the absence of any evidence that this information had in fact become available to the accused,

which is often the only way to send former presidents or junta leaders to jail, judicial actors must adapt it to national contexts in the absence of explicit legislation (Prusak 2010).

To summarize, the use of international criminal and human rights law allows litigants to invoke states' international responsibilities to investigate the crimes and punish the perpetrators irrespective of domestic legal barriers, adequately characterize the crimes, and adapt standards for evaluating evidence. As a result, victims and their lawyers are able to claim a series of rights, and remove legal obstacles to the launching of criminal prosecutions.

The Positivist Conundrum

Critics of the human rights legal discourse contend that the recognition of victims' rights compromises the rule of law. According to these lawyers, provictim groups construe their demands on the basis of vaguely defined terms such as "crimes against humanity." These terms are derived from subjective interpretations of the norms arising from customary practices, supposedly accepted and binding when the crimes were committed. In addition to resorting to unwritten sources of law, litigants ask judicial actors to impute individual criminal responsibility on the basis of criminal definitions codified in international legal instruments after the date when the crimes were perpetrated. Finally, litigants are accused of demanding sui generis exceptions to rules of criminal procedure that were present in penal codes at the time of the crimes, such as statutory limitations. In line with this critique, Ratner and Abrams (1997) warn that since much of international criminal law is not codified, there is a greater reliance on interpretations of customary law. This interpretation is "fraught with dangers for defendants in criminal cases, who may face judges with different methodologies and approaches to the derivation of custom or other law. Moreover, over-reliance on scholarly writings, where progressive views often seek to move the law forward, could instead lead to prosecutions that run afoul of defendants' rights" (Ratner and Abrams 1997: 20).

The interpretation of domestic law in light of international law is also controversial because numerous human rights treaties explicitly outline

who was a Minister of the Interior of Macedonia at the relevant time, this information was regarded prima facie as relevant to establishing his mens rea for the purpose of the doctrine of superior responsibility" (Mettraux 2009: 10; footnotes omitted, italics in original).

the rights of individuals facing criminal charges. In fact, imposing limitations on the arbitrary exercise of state power as it pertains to criminal prosecutions has been one of the main motivations driving the development of international human rights law.[27] For example, in a critique of the jurisprudence of the Inter-American Court of Human Rights, Ezequiel Malarino accuses the court of expounding a *punitivist* conception of human rights: "Hand in hand with victims' super-right [*sic*] to justice, the Inter-American Court is creating a true 'statute of the victim' opposed to the 'statute of the defendant', consecrated in the [American] Convention; that is, a non-written Bill of Rights of the victim that neutralizes the written Bill of Rights of the defendant" (Malarino 2010: 46). In so doing, the Inter-American Court demands that state actors modify their penal systems in order to accommodate the court's interpretation of victims' rights, retroactively adapting due process rules.

At the core of the antiprosecution case is the argument that by invoking this type of international criterion, litigants encourage judges and prosecutors to water down the legality principle. The notion of *nullum crimen sine lege, nulla poena sine lege paevia, scripta, stricta et certa* (no crime and no punishment without a prior, written, unambiguous and easily understandable law) is a fundamental axiom of modern criminal law (Guzmán Dálbora 2010). Respect for this axiom constitutes a guarantee of legal certainty for the defendant. The legality principle limits the punitive powers of states as it forbids the retroactive application of the law, censures the conviction for crimes not unequivocally defined in written statutes at the time when the crime is committed, limits the possibility of interpreting the law by analogy (individual conduct should be clearly defined to be considered criminal), and commands the enforcement of statutes of limitations.[28]

The incompatibility of the case put forward by human rights litigants with these principles of modern criminal law naturally elicits qualms

[27] The international recognition of due process is enshrined in Articles 8–12 of the Universal Declaration of Human Rights (Donnelly 1986) and in Articles 8 and 9 of the American Convention on Human Rights (Malarino 2010).

[28] With regard to statutes of limitations see Kok (2007). This debate was already occurring during the 1969 Convention on the Non-Applicability of Statutory Limitations to War Crimes and Crimes against Humanity. Many states refused to sign or ratify the document arguing that it provided ambiguous and legally imprecise definitions, thus violating the principle of legality. There was also a heated discussion about whether the application of the instrument should be retroactive. For a summary of these debates see Corte Suprema de Justicia de la Nación Argentina, Arancibia Clavel, Enrique Lautaro s/homicidio calificado y asociación ilícita y otros, ruling of 24 August 2004, concurrent vote of Justice Carmen Argibay.

among Latin American judicial actors. It clashes with judges' and prosecutors' legal preferences, their bureaucratic instincts, and dominant views about appropriate professional conduct. Although arguments derived from international human rights law represent the only normative source that enables judges to challenge the validity of amnesties and to ignore statutes of limitations, using them can be extremely controversial because it involves applying the law retroactively and defying the positivization of the law. Toppling impunity regimes via unconstitutionality rulings, or by granting exceptions that are not explicitly legislated, also implies redefining the traditional deferential position of Latin American courts vis-à-vis written laws and the political branches entitled to enact them (Couso 2010; Pásara 2010). Finally, the difficulties involved in processing these arguments are enhanced by the fact that only recently has international human rights law become part of universities' curricula in Latin America. Adding to the lack of familiarity with this legal corpus, judges and prosecutors do not normally use it to solve the vast majority of the criminal prosecutions they deal with on a daily basis (López Medina 2004; Pásara 2010). From their point of view these ideas are highly experimental and, in some cases, do not make a lot of sense.

To become causally powerful, human rights ideas must overcome a series of crucial cognitive and behavioral obstacles inside judicial branches. Relaxing or simply ignoring the legality principle in cases of gross human rights violations requires a paradigm shift in the way those in charge of administering justice perceive the normative system that regulates their professional activities. In Latin America, this normative system is part of a long tradition that affirms the supremacy of domestic written law and promotes a vision of the law as a series of rules to be applied and not as a set of constitutionally enshrined principles to be interpreted, reconciled, or ranked as demanded by the case under consideration.[29] After reviewing the legal literature produced in the region during most of the twentieth century, Javier Couso concludes that up to the 1980s "the dominance of legal positivism and a deferential understanding of the role of the courts vis-à-vis the political system was absolute" (2010: 152). Judges, who are a product of this culture, come to see the bench as an instance in which only the formal legality of norms, and of private actions as literally described by those norms, is checked. In this context, the notion that laws are clear and that their application requires no interpretation is widespread (Cuneo 1980; Pérez Perdomo 2006; Schauer 2008).

[29] Stone Sweet (2000) refers to this latter vision as "higher-law constitutionalism."

At the turn of the century, Andres Bello, one of Latin America's most prominent and influential legal thinkers, crystallized the spirit behind positivist legal preferences:

> Even if the law exhibits a notorious injustice, the judge ought to apply it as it is: "Dura lex, sed lex" (tough law is nonetheless law). If we allow judges to correct the injustice of legislation, these would be replaced according to the conscience of judge, and individuals would not know what to do, since each person has his own ways to understand fairness, and fairness would then inspire the most anomalous and contradictory decisions. (Quoted in Couso 2010: 150)

More recently, in the 1970s the president of the Superior Court of Lima, Peru, stated:

> We suffer from mistaken and pungent criticisms for our decisions.... A judge cannot erect himself into a legislator by interpreting the law due to the obsolescence of legal instruments ... because so doing would mean erecting the will of the judge into a source of law, something which is doctrinally inadmissible and very dangerous. (Quoted in Pásara 2010: 37)

During the same period, the chief justice of the Chilean Supreme Court explained:

> The mission of the Court is to defend the current legal order. We lack – as is evident – the power to alter the latter through interpretation.... The renovation of the legal order can only be pursed through new legislation. Therefore the violation – directly or indirectly – of legality is unacceptable, because without law there is no justice.... Judges ought to act strictly within the framework of existing legality. (Quoted in Couso 2010: 151)

A Colombian legal academic opposed to these formalist tendencies recalls their impact on his education:

> The dominant way of teaching law, against which we rebelled, promoted at a basic level learning by heart the rules contained in laws and codes as a necessary step to remember and remain loyal to them.... "Legality," as a tool of social control began there, in our memory, in order to pave the way for a journey in which the formalist techniques of legal interpretation prevailed. (López Medina 2004: 2; my translation)

In a similar critical vein, a current Mexican Supreme Court Justice proclaims the obsolescence of these still very popular ideas among his colleagues:

> [The duty of a judge] is not simply to subject himself to the law, but to engage in a critical analysis of its meaning in order to control its

> constitutional legitimacy. And the legal science has ceased to be … mere description to become critical. (Silva Meza and Silva García 2009: xxi, ft.13; my translation)

In sum, there are two main reasons why the hegemony of positivist/formalistic legal preferences constitutes an important impediment to the pursuit of truth and justice. First, these legal preferences narrow the scope of judges' and prosecutors' technical skills. The international legal arguments that make prosecutions possible must be learned from scratch. As indicated by the sociological institutionalist framework outlined previously, radical departures from standard legal praxis involving awareness of new bodies of law require the expansion of cognitive maps, allowing the judicial imagination to contemplate alternative ways of doing things. Making these alternatives known to the relevant actors is the first logical step toward breaking institutional inertia biased in favor of certain types of legal solutions. Second, the case for transitional justice takes judges and prosecutors outside their comfort zone. They must therefore find the motivation to adapt their bureaucratic routines. For one, the jurisprudential innovations sought by human rights litigants entail a high degree of experimentation. Even those most favorable to the cause require reassurance that the symbolic effectiveness of their actions will not be jeopardized. As argued earlier in the chapter, in order to take professional risks by increasing their profile in any given policy area, judges and prosecutors must be able to justify their interventionism legally in a language that conforms to certain professional standards. Moreover, since investigating human rights crimes is particularly demanding and dangerous, judicial actors must be given good reasons to go above and beyond their terms of reference, often by reconfiguring what they perceive these terms of reference to be.

These two obstacles are particularly consequential in the presence of powerful political actors opposed to the opening or reopening of prosecutions. Here the professional motivation needed to push the cases forward is, of course, greater. In the absence of an alternative legal vision, the positivist/formalist orthodoxy can engender a submissive reflex among judges and prosecutors faced with cases filed by human rights lawyers. Judicial actors lack the reasons, and hence the ideational resources to oppose these political players. In addition, under these circumstances the old orthodoxy provides a legitimizing discourse for the decision to perpetuate impunity and to avoid entering into a collision course with powerful majorities or elected officials. In order to alter the status quo in a politically adverse scenario, judges must therefore be able to marshal the symbolic effectiveness of a new set of norms, appealing to potential allies in the social, political, and legal worlds. The new orthodoxy has to penetrate deeply into their identities for it to trigger risky, assertive behavior in the midst of outside pressures to the contrary. As these new professional standards evolve and become ingrained in the functioning of judicial bureaucracies, it becomes more difficult for judges to accept political directives or threats to ignore them. At the same time, they become armed with ideational resources to resist attacks.

Transforming Legal Preferences

Reflecting on the drivers of judicial change, a Mexican Supreme Court judge stated, "Litigants are the unknown soldiers of jurisprudence."[30] Organized litigation groups can disrupt judiciaries' bureaucratic inertia, filing cases that raise new questions and forcing courts to turn their gaze to different argumentative strategies. As Charles Epp famously put it, "Combining rights consciousness with a bill of rights and a willing and able judiciary improves the outlook for a rights revolution, but material support for sustained pursuit of rights cases is still crucial. A support structure for legal mobilization provides this missing ingredient" (1998: 17). In fact, public interest litigation has led to important breakthroughs in the protection of individual rights, the creation of new entitlements, and the launching of progressive policy reform.[31] Following these findings, the main intuition behind the causal story told in this book is that victim NGOs play a central role in unlocking the path to successful human rights trials.

Human rights groups that equip themselves with professional teams of public interest lawyers and engage in sustained litigation are more likely to achieve victories. Sustained litigation generates positive information

[30] Interview, Mexico City, 27 July 2010.

[31] On the impact of the American civil rights movement see, for example, McAdam (1982), Wasby (1983), Tushnet (1994, 2004), and Patterson (2001). For a skeptical view of the real impact of civil rights litigation in the United States see Rosenberg (1991). On the legal strategies to secure equal employment opportunities and labor rights in the United States see Burstein (1991) and McCann (1994). Baird (2007) adds an interesting twist to the literature on public interest litigation in the United States arguing that litigants do not set the agenda of the U.S. Supreme Court, but that they largely respond to judges' signals indicating their interest to rule on a particular issue area. On the role of transnational litigation see Keck and Sikkink (1998), Sikkink (2005), Cichowski (2007), CELS (2008b), and Simmons (2009). On the achievements of public interest litigation groups in the areas of gay rights and access to health care in Latin America see Wilson and Rodríguez Cordero (2006) and Bimbi (2010). On the achievements and failures of human rights lawyers under authoritarian regimes see Moustafa (2007).

feedback. Through trial and error, litigants use test cases to find where in the system judges are more responsive or what arguments are viable given the existence of impunity regimes. Litigants can thus incrementally exploit loopholes in the law in order to develop jurisprudential benchmarks from which to launch bolder challenges. But even though sustained litigation is a crucial precondition for successful transitional justice efforts, it is not enough. This is where my argument departs from traditional analyses of legal mobilization. In addition to their formal moves in particular lawsuits, litigants must adopt a much more active approach and influence judges and prosecutors' receptivity to human rights cases.

Formal litigation and conventional pressure politics cannot on their own elicit positive responses from judicial actors. There is a need to compensate for cognitive deficits, making the "unthinkable" possible by shedding new light on juridical problems and turning unusual legal moves into routine components of decision making protocols. Litigants need to be able to put themselves in the shoes of judicial actors, imagine how these professionals of the law might react when confronted with antiimpunity arguments, and consider the knowledge and skills at the disposal of judges and prosecutors to deal with the complexities of cases of state repression. In view of the unusual nature of their demands and the doctrines used to support them, litigants should seriously evaluate how traditional legal preferences mediate jurisprudential outcomes, and in line with my sociological institutionalist approach, conclude that they constitute an important obstruction on the road to prison sentences.

In order to remove this blockage, civil society organizations must deploy surreptitious, behind the scenes efforts to transform the ideas that circulate inside judicial institutions. These are important in order to secure consistent macrolevel jurisprudential shifts over time, as opposed to isolated victories. The mechanisms of legal contention must aim at producing widespread changes in both the technical capacity and the political will of the judicial corporation, investing its members in the fight against impunity. At the heart of this process are informal attempts to deinstitutionalize constraining legal preferences via the diffusion of international human rights norms.

In order to come up with a correct diagnosis of the problem and decide to invest resources in ideational change, human rights activists have to be able to understand the problem in legal, as opposed to purely political terms. Recruiting teams of well-trained lawyers is therefore of paramount importance. Lawyers are more likely to see the chasm that separates standard practices and precedents from antiimpunity arguments grounded in international human rights law, and conclude that regardless of political momentum in favor of their cause, success ultimately hinges upon the extent to which judicial actors can understand and process those arguments. In this sense, lawyers are in a better position to see the biases in traditional legal education that lead Latin American judicial actors to be either skeptical of the viability of paths to justice or confused about how to proceed. This is in part because human rights lawyers are themselves the product of similar socialization processes and often went through an arduous intellectual journey to visualize alternatives to the legal status quo.

In their efforts to conquer the allegiances of the judiciary, human rights NGOs face three types of judicial actors – committed, indifferent, and recalcitrant. Each group in turn differs with regard to their personal views about state repression and the need for truth and justice. The label "committed" is used here to refer to those judges and prosecutors who favor the human rights cause. This predisposition could be a function of ideology or personal experiences with repression. Indifferent judges and prosecutors are those with no prior personal commitment to human rights. This could be the result of weak ideological positions or lack of knowledge of the extent and nature of state repression. Finally, among recalcitrant judges one finds those who exhibit a deeply ingrained positivist legal worldview. They are individuals who have written about criminal law in the terms prescribed by the traditional legal orthodoxy or who unequivocally support the defendants, because of either personal connections with former military officers or collaboration with the previous regime. This diversified pool of judicial actors must be matched with differentiated strategies of institutional transformation.

The informal mechanisms that trigger the aforementioned change in legal preferences include persuasion via pedagogical interventions and replacement via "naming and shaming." Whereas the first two groups of judicial actors may be the targets of pedagogical interventions, recalcitrant judges essentially are not susceptible to ideational change. This third category is the focus of replacement strategies. Crafting courts that are viable outlets for advancing human rights is as much about disseminating the tools for judges and prosecutors to act in this direction in a highly technical environment as it is about creating an institutional commitment to new forms of legal praxis. On the one hand, through pedagogical interventions litigants raise awareness of judicial actors' obligations under international law, plant the seeds of a renewed professional imperative to defend the cause, and enable members of the judicial community to enact those values without breaking with the parameters of action that govern the legal field. On the other, replacement strategies remove judicial blockages that survive the passage of time, accelerate the pace of institutional change, and protect the inroads made through persuasion.

Persuading the Persuadables with Pedagogical Interventions

Litigant groups that informally diffuse throughout the judiciary arguments derived from international law and jurisprudence will be more successful in toppling impunity regimes. As suggested, the arguments that enable the overcoming of amnesties or the restrictions imposed by statutes of limitations need to be learned anew by judges and prosecutors. In this regard, litigants face an uphill battle because judicial actors are not novices when it comes to the law. Likewise, they hold more or less stable positions about what is right and wrong in their professional milieu. Further still, these positions are not easily reconciled with the new legal vision promoted by human rights NGOs. Several important assumptions about criminal and constitutional law must be revised for these new norms to resonate with judicial actors. As some constructivist scholars have argued, we should not expect socialization to be easily achieved in this type of environment (Checkel 2005; Gheciu 2005).

As a result of this normative incongruence, the socialization of judges and prosecutors into new traditions of legal interpretation must be crafted with great care. Diffusion requires more than simply quoting the new normative baggage in formal documents filed in court. Crucially, it relies on the creation of informal pedagogical spaces outside the courtroom where litigants can interact with judicial actors face to face, explain alternative ways of adjudicating and investigating human rights cases, and diffuse specialized legal knowledge.[32] By organizing academic events for judicial personnel, activists become, quite literally, teachers of new norms of professional conduct. In addition to making up for the deficits of formal legal education, victims and their lawyers use pedagogical interventions as a way to immerse judicial actors in human rights circles and build strong personal connections. These linkages and alliances are instrumental in expanding the reach of pedagogical efforts because they facilitate future flows of information and ideas in the form of highly targeted persuasion

[32] The literature on American courts shows that the information transmitted by litigants in this form is relevant when judges make their decisions, especially in areas that are controversial. See Johnson, Wahlbeck and Spriggs (2006).

strategies during crucial moments in the judicialization process. This is especially important if judges and prosecutors face unexpected difficulties or need additional reassurances about the appropriateness of specific legal moves. Ultimately, incorporating judges and prosecutors into human rights networks is key to changing legal preferences, because socialization is by definition a process whereby actors are drawn into "the norms and rules of a given community" (Checkel 2005: 804).

The extent to which judicial actors are more or less predisposed to participate in these out of court pedagogical activities is, of course, a function of whether or not they are personally committed to the cause of truth and justice. Even though committed judicial actors may at first find the new legal orthodoxy foreign and implausible, it is still likely to resonate with their personal values, making persuasion easier. Their predisposition to rule in favor of the victims notwithstanding, pedagogical interventions are, on the one hand, deeply empowering for this group of judges and prosecutors and, on the other, essential to making sure their rulings effectively undermine impunity.

Regarding the empowerment of committed judicial actors, pedagogical interventions construct road maps for action couched in a discourse that fits the parameters of argumentation in the legal field. Far from offering political reasons for punishing the perpetrators, successful litigants disseminate a highly technical and sophisticated legal infrastructure. For example, giving judges the tools to explain the implications of international legal obligations in domestic judicial proceedings allows them to legitimize deeply controversial decisions and provides a sense of professional security by assuring them that they are not jumping off a jurisprudential cliff. One of the key empirical implications of the argument is therefore that committed judicial actors should welcome and praise pedagogical efforts in these terms, underscoring their role in allowing them to act upon their convictions while following the behavioral expectations of their professional environment. In addition, this active supply of information via pedagogical interventions and the informal channels created afterward is important because it signals to committed judicial actors the existence of groups within the legal complex among whom the new legal discourse is highly popular, providing extra reassurance that they are not acting alone.

In terms of guaranteeing the effectiveness of jurisprudential moves, it is important to note that although it is entirely possible for a handful of entrepreneurially committed judges to decide on their own to make moves against impunity, litigants should not expect this goodwill to translate automatically into adequate rulings. They must still actively supply information and ideas to their natural allies in the bench. Human rights lawyers are the true specialists and have the time and resources to invest in finding the best possible legal pathways. Despite their commitment, these judges and prosecutors are almost always inexperienced in this kind of case. Litigants must exploit their own expertise in order to make sure that their allies know exactly how to proceed and, most importantly, that each juridical step against impunity modifies the argumentative landscape in a way that expands the sphere of victims' rights. For example, a judge may on her own initiative grant a habeas corpus petition to the relatives of victims of forced disappearances on strictly procedural grounds. However, if she has been trained by litigants to invoke international sources of law, the judge might in addition develop the notion of a "right to truth" to support her decision. Reading this right into existing law can greatly empower the plaintiffs.

In order to secure favorable judicial outcomes across jurisdictions, at different stages of the litigation process, and over time, litigants have to reach beyond a handful of committed judges and prosecutors. Human rights movements must use pedagogical interventions to induce a wider politicization of the judiciary, turning the institution into a conflict-ridden arena in which the possibilities of legal hermeneutics are redefined in support of certain objectives and forging strategic alliances with a large critical mass of judicial actors. This has the potential to modify the judiciary's corporate identity. For example, pedagogical interventions are a way for committed and converted judges to get to know each other and forge professional bonds, fostering the formation of extensive judicial networks or associations bound by their members' adherence to a new legal orthodoxy and its values. These forms of ideational-cum-social capital can be effectively leveraged against the opponents of transitional justice, catalyzing collective reactions to outside threats or putting pressure on potential defectors within the institution.

For this to happen, pedagogical interventions must also target indifferent judicial actors. This is much harder, as the norms litigants intend to diffuse are highly dissonant with respect to established legal preferences. Litigants' ideas are also unlikely to resonate with these judges' personal values. Indifferent judges lack the motivation to take professional risks and think outside the box in order to push complex investigations forward. For example, it was not uncommon for Latin American military authorities to deny the existence of the infamous flights of death planned during the 1970s, in which political prisoners were drugged and thrown into the ocean. It took a lot of creativity and motivation for judges to find alternative ways to gather evidence of these crimes. Some savvy judicial actors looked in the local newspapers of coastline cities and in the records of cemeteries in the area to see whether, around the dates of the alleged flights, unidentified corpses had been found on the beach. These kinds of initiatives are harder to expect from indifferent judges. Not only is solving human rights cases less of a priority for them, but they also often perceive these cases as a nuisance that disrupts routines and makes them vulnerable to external pressures. In this sense, it is important to bear in mind that judges and prosecutors confront an environment of crisscrossing pressures, in which defendants and their allies also engage in lobbying tactics, deploying resources both to intimidate and to court members of the bench. Because of this, human rights activists and their lawyers cannot simply rely on the ideal of judicial impartiality. They must win the hearts and minds of judicial actors, and personally invest them in the cause by convincing them of the legitimacy and superiority of the new legal vision.

Pedagogical interventions create a common discursive space in which indifferent judicial actors and human rights lawyers can begin to understand each other. They provide nontrivial information about the magnitude and historical significance of the crimes in an effort to instill a sense of urgency. As some social psychologists have pointed out, making new information available can lead individuals to "engage in a high intensity process of cognition, reflection, and argument" (Johnson 2003, quoted in Goodman and Jinks 2013: 25). Most importantly, however, in order to succeed, litigants must carefully design pedagogical interventions to trigger two psychological processes that increase the chances of luring indifferent judges into their camp.

First, litigants need to make pedagogical initiatives attractive and endow them with a sense of legitimacy in order to persuade indifferent judges to attend and listen. Although the very nature of these informal academic venues makes them an ideal site to achieve this, I contend that litigants are more likely to be successful if they carefully choose the agents who will speak on their behalf in front of judges and prosecutors. The literature on diffusion indicates that the internalization of norms and practices is sometimes a function of emulation (Beissinger 2002; Pevehouse 2002; Bunce and Wolchick 2011) and the authority of the source (Kopstein and Reilly 2000; Levitsky and Way 2010). With regard to emulation effects, Bunce and Wolchik indicate that innovations are "less original than they seem. While 'newness' is central to the idea of innovation, innovation nonetheless owes at least some of its originality to past developments" (2011: 280). In this sense, litigants must raise awareness of rulings handed down by similar courts in other countries, and, most importantly, they ought to recruit speakers among respected judges or prosecutors who have successfully resolved similar juridical dilemmas. Facilitating these contacts between the target population and their accomplished peers at home and abroad gives the former reassurance that toppling impunity regimes is legally viable and politically possible. For example, in Chapter 4 I show that the contacts fostered by NGOs between Peruvian judges and their Argentine counterparts who conducted the famous 1985 trial against the military juntas were important in guaranteeing a positive outcome in the 2009 Fujimori case.

With regard to authority, pedagogical interventions must have the appearance of being neutral settings (Gheciu 2005). As parties in the legal dispute, human rights litigants cannot appear to be exerting undue influence on the arbiters. NGOs are more likely to be successful if those who speak on their behalf are respected law professors, international experts, or members of prestigious international institutions dedicated to the promotion of human rights on a global scale. An amicus brief signed by a well-known constitutional lawyer or a lecture delivered by the legal scholar who developed the innovative theories of criminal liability used by human rights activists in their suits will look more authoritative and worthy of consideration. Similarly, forming partnerships with universities in the organization of pedagogical initiatives can be a crucial component of campaigns to spread a new legal orthodoxy. These academic linkages can make pedagogical interventions a particularly effective strategy in hostile political environments. In unfriendly contexts, judges feel safer attending events organized in universities than those held in NGO headquarters because the former inoculate them from accusations of partiality.

Second, pedagogical interventions should become moments of intense reflection that pause bureaucratic inertia and lead indifferent judges and prosecutors to think carefully about the implications of impunity. In other words, informal contacts forged during academic events and thereafter must be used to interrupt the reproduction of routines incompatible with prosecutions, such as the automatic invocation of statutes of limitations or amnesty laws. This is achieved by triggering feelings of discomfort associated with cognitive dissonance, that is, the holding of two or more contradictory beliefs:

> This phenomenon is part of a family of cognitive processes related to the basic human need to justify one's actions to oneself and others. Substantial empirical evidence demonstrates that individuals experience

> discomfort – including anxiety, regret, guilt – whenever they confront cognitions about some aspect of their behavior inconsistent with their self-conception (including any social roles central to their identity). Individuals are highly motivated to minimize this dissonance by either changing their behavior or finding ways to justify their past behavior. (Goodman and Jinks 2013: 27)

I argue that in human rights cases, this can happen by moving to the fore three crucial contradictions. First, cognitive dissonance may arise out of the contradictions often found in the legal status quo regarding the possibility of punishing the perpetrators. For example, in some cases amnesties allow for the prosecution of certain crimes and not others. As we shall see in Chapter 3, Argentine litigants' success in framing their case around this type of contradiction led indifferent judges to consider the need to rethink the legal status quo.

Second, exposing judicial actors to information about repression and suggestive evidence about individual criminal responsibility may produce a disjuncture between, on the one hand, the belief that victims were indeed wronged by the state and, on the other, the assumption that the legal system does not easily correct these wrongs. This has the potential of becoming a powerful *legal* motivation for indifferent judicial actors to modify their allegiances, narrowing the chasm that separates antiimpunity arguments from existing legal preferences. As we shall see in the case studies, some indifferent judges and prosecutors were persuaded of the need for justice after being sensitized by such evidence, and eventually explained their reasons for action by making reference to their professional duty to punish serious crimes. This evidence combined with greater awareness of the extent of repression legitimizes victims' claims and makes it harder for judges to rationalize and morally justify the automatic dismissal of cases. By playing positivist legal preferences against this sense of duty, litigants can thus open up a space for the acceptance of alternative standards of legal praxis that allow judges to iron out the inconsistencies.

Third, exposing judges and prosecutors to the normative foundations of international human rights law is also likely to disrupt bureaucratic inertia and generate discomfort with a mechanical reproduction of the legal status quo. At the heart of this body of law is the notion that states, and judges, have an international duty to prosecute international crimes. Using pedagogical interventions to manufacture a deep awareness of this alternative source of legal authority and professional duties forces indifferent judicial actors to question their exclusive, thoughtless, instinctive allegiance to domestic law. At the same time it empowers them by giving them the legal reasons to erode the primacy of the latter and reconcile the contradictory imperatives emanating from both bodies of law. Moreover, turning their gaze toward their external obligations can enhance judges' and prosecutors' sense of duty to modify the status quo in the face of blatant contradictions in the impunity regime or between the evidence and impunity. By encapsulating the debate in strictly juridical terms regarding the correct integration of competing sources of law, litigants draw attention to substantive legal questions about what is professionally correct, or what the law demands, rather than what is opportune, and to what the facts say as opposed to what the powerful would like to hear. In this sense, it is important that the facts of the cases resonate with international criminal definitions such as crimes against humanity, which activate the jurisdiction of international human rights law in domestic prosecutions. For example, bombarding judicial actors with several cases that illustrate the systematic nature of state terrorism or holding training sessions about the dynamics of violence can increase the perceived juridical viability of extemporaneous international definitions that require individual crimes to be part of broader repressive efforts.

Under What Conditions Is Lasting Judicial Change More Likely?

Engineering a far-reaching resocialization of judges and prosecutors, and giving them the tools and the motives to fight against impunity, is a complicated task that requires a well-designed and executed plan. Activists must take legal preferences seriously and target both committed and indifferent judicial actors with pedagogical interventions that exhibit the characteristics outlined in the previous section. I now identify an additional set of factors that make their chances of success more or less likely, generating additional observable implications against which to evaluate the argument. These are related to both the features of the political environment and the choices of litigants themselves.

Litigants' success depends first and foremost on the extent to which pedagogical interventions are either systematic or isolated initiatives. When it comes to effective teaching, sociologists have long recognized the importance of sustained interactions between the parties involved (Bourdieu and Passeron 1977). As argued previously, because of its incongruence with positivist/formalistic legal preferences, the legal infrastructure designed to fight against impunity is difficult to understand and internalize. If litigants consistently organize academic events before and throughout the judicialization process, it is more likely that judicial actors will learn how to use the new investigative techniques and juridical doctrines, and that they will be persuaded about their legitimacy. In addition, more or less regular exposure has the potential of sparking real interest among the target population, which may in turn lead some judges and prosecutors to further their studies, apply to postgraduate degree programs in human rights law, and take other actions.

The intensity of persuasion efforts can vary along two dimensions. First, efforts can be focused on a handful of courts. This is not an issue when judiciaries grant exclusive jurisdiction over human rights cases to some judges, but it can be highly problematic when this is not the case, especially in federal systems. If there is a court or geographic bias in diffusion strategies, we should observe corresponding patterns of intercourt or subnational variation in transitional justice outcomes. Second, pedagogical interventions can be biased in favor of certain topics. There are two distinct moments during human rights trials in which the use of different sets of innovative legal arguments is required. In the first stage, what matters is whether or not amnesties and statutes of limitations are valid. Here litigants try to modify patterns of constitutional interpretation via the diffusion of international human rights norms. In the second stage, judicial actors must confront a series of issues related to how to organize court proceedings. Litigants must therefore diffuse techniques that allow judges to deal with the lack of direct evidence, foster the accumulation of cases to uncover patterns and establish the scale of the repression, and promote the adoption of protocols to treat traumatized witnesses in ways that guarantee reliable testimonies. Depending on the intensity with which human rights litigants diffuse these two distinct sets of skills, we should observe variation in the levels of consensus among judges and prosecutors across legal issue areas. For instance, amnesties could be circumvented and cases reopened, but indictment and conviction rates may not be uniform across jurisdictions because the criteria used to evaluate the evidence remain formalistic in some of them.[33]

[33] Variation in the content of pedagogical interventions can result from various factors. Litigants may poorly diagnose the importance of diffusing both sets of ideas, and spend more time on the most pressing legal questions, which often involve removing obstacles to launching the investigations, namely, amnesties and statutes of limitations. It is also possible that once these obstacles are removed and proceedings unravel quickly, litigants have little time to switch the emphasis of their diffusion strategy to the practical aspects of investigating state crimes. Finally, it is important to note that legal norms tying international human rights law to the inapplicability of amnesties or statutes of limitations are supported by a rich international legal corpus, in particular, the influential jurisprudence of the Inter-American Court of Human Rights. Litigants lack equally authoritative statements

So far I have assumed that the content, reach, and ultimately the success of pedagogical interventions are a function of litigants' diagnosis of the problem, and their technical expertise to address it effectively. However, the characteristics of the political environment play an important role in conditioning litigants' ability to remove judicial blockages. To put it simply, under certain conditions it is hard to engage and persuade judicial actors. As indicated in previous sections, my explanation sees judiciaries as the target of attempts by myriad actors to entrench ideas about the law in the routine practices of judges and prosecutors. The goal of these groups is to guarantee stable jurisprudential outcomes in favor of their long-term normative or distributive interests. In this sense, the potential for autonomous judicial behavior in human rights cases should lead proimpunity groups, including presidents and members of the military establishment, to try to preserve the hegemony of positivist/formalistic legal preferences, and contain the judicialization process using legal and illegal forms of pressure and institutional cooptation. When these actors are strong and resolved, litigants will have a more difficult time trying to change how judges understand the law and their institutional mission, which could eventually lead to the forging of a weaker, uneven, and unstable consensus around their alternative vision.

Given these crisscrossing pressures, the timing of litigants' pedagogical interventions vis-à-vis similar or more coercive strategies deployed by their opponents matters to explain the level of success of their resocialization initiatives. Pedagogical interventions can be deployed in hostile political environments, as when carefully planned they can be quite inconspicuous, protecting the attendees from accusations of partiality or even more dangerous retaliatory measures. All they require is a critical mass of judicial actors who are willing to participate and, crucially, who are open to persuasion.[34] But if in any given country there is a powerful anti–transitional justice coalition that successfully colonizes courts with recalcitrant judicial actors *before* litigants organize their own campaign, the potential target population for pedagogical interventions is reduced quite dramatically. Similarly, in the absence of widespread changes in state personnel after democratic transitions, authoritarian enclaves in

about the ways judges and prosecutors should plan and conduct investigations. For example, because the Inter-American Court does not look into questions of individual criminal responsibility, it has remained silent on this second set of issues.

34 My theoretical framework obviously assumes that there are no structural impediments (e.g., repression) that prevent civil society actors to organize and create these pedagogical spaces.

the judiciary can make some courts impenetrable for litigants. In these contexts, there are fewer persuadable judicial actors. As a result, litigants will have to plan more targeted interventions and adopt a more piecemeal approach to judicial change, leading to more gradual victories. As I will show in Chapter 3, Argentina is an example of this. Despite the nonnegotiated nature of the democratic transition, there was a high degree of personnel continuity in the judiciary after 1983, which, coupled with the recovery of the proimpunity coalition in the 1990s, conspired against the efforts of NGOs to trigger a fast process of institutional change.

By contrast, in those contexts in which litigants enjoy a first-mover advantage to approach judicial actors, for example, because immediately after the democratic transition proimpunity forces are in utter disarray, or because the transition is accompanied by the removal of a dictator's closest cronies from the bench, NGOs will be able to engage in more ambitious and systematic efforts to craft a friendly judiciary. In particular, this may allow activists to erect buffers against future backlashes against truth and justice should the balance of power shift again. When facing this kind of resocialized judiciary, soldiers and politicians seeking to put an end to the judicialization process are likely to encounter resistance from judicial actors. Guided by a rekindled logic of appropriateness, judges and prosecutors will defend the new institutional goals from outside encroachments. As a result, personal or professional intimidation efforts may not prove as effective. In addition, attempts to stop trials in this way may require more widespread use of coercive tactics – a move that can bring about high reputational costs for politicians and that is generally difficult to carry out on a large scale. The case of Peru (analyzed in Chapter 4) is an example of this alternative scenario.

Although successful resocialization efforts certainly increase the costs of these backlashes, attempts to counter processes of judicial transformation cannot be ruled out completely. If an anti–transitional justice coalition comes to power and is ready to adopt aggressive measures, its efforts can severely water down the institutional consensus against impunity crafted by activists and their lawyers. This of course can have a negative impact on the staying power of ideational change. By promoting a counternarrative about the nature of state repression and the behavior of security forces, these backlashes can erode emerging commitments among indifferent judicial actors and stabilize the hegemony of traditional legal preferences. More worrisome for the victims, however, is the possibility that the newly empowered coalition engages in court packing or manipulates administrative procedures to remove unreliable and rebellious judges from sensitive courts. Where judicial terms are fixed and committed judicial actors begin to leave the bench as the proimpunity coalition comes to power, this is much easier to achieve, as these actors can now take advantage of an unparalleled opportunity to appoint recalcitrant replacements. In other words, even after robust socialization efforts by victims and their lawyers, we are likely to observe intertemporal variation in the progress of human rights cases when shifts in the political environment are accompanied by a changing balance of power among the social, partisan, and military forces seeking to influence who the judges are and how they think. As will become clear later on, the contrast between the gradual but steady progress of trials in Argentina and the less robust outcomes in Peru following a backlash in the late 2000s illustrates that the political context can moderate success in this way.

Finally, the effect of pedagogical interventions is likely to be more powerful when reinforced by a second mechanism of institutional change: replacement strategies. If in addition to persuading a critical mass of judicial actors, human rights groups successfully remove recalcitrant, "unpersuadable" judges or prosecutors, they are more likely to accelerate the pace of institutional change and significantly increase the costs of backlashes. By decisively expunging a legal philosophy that constrains judicial action and biases outcomes, replacement further consolidates the entrenchment of a new institutional vision in the area of human rights. The replacement mechanism involves promoting impeachments to replace the old guard with new, friendlier or more approachable judicial actors. Litigants may also force resignations by naming and shaming judges or prosecutors who, for example, collaborated with the repressive apparatus, have unequivocal links to the defendants, or purposefully stall the proceedings. In order to be effective, human rights litigants need not be successful in all of their removal efforts. In fact, a few disciplining actions may be enough to deter similar judges from stalling interlocutory appeals indefinitely, closing down investigations, or systematically handing down acquittals.

In the same way as committed judges and prosecutors may defy proimpunity politicians pressuring for acquittals, recalcitrant judges can rebel against generalized calls for truth and justice. Consequently, even under favorable political conditions, combining both strategies of institutional change is more likely to lead to sustained and uniform waves of trials. As the case studies will show, a few recalcitrant judges can severely jeopardize the course of prosecutions. In Latin America, several members of the judiciary who remained in their jobs after democratic transitions were active accomplices of state terrorism. At the onset of the judicialization process, many of them had already climbed through the ranks of the institution, and occupied positions in key courts with the power to block appeals, appropriate dockets, and stall trials. These conservative judicial actors were close to the defendants on a professional and ideological level, and on a personal one. Defending the hegemony of the old legal orthodoxy was crucial in order to advance their interest in perpetuating impunity.

Replacement strategies rely on taking the battle to transform the judiciary into the light of day, building a broad base of alliances. Particularly important are allies in the press who can expose recalcitrant judges, and members of the bodies in charge of appointing and removing judicial actors. These bodies often include legislatures and judicial councils staffed with politicians, members of lawyers' professional associations, and judges.[35] As a result, this mechanism of institutional change can be most effectively activated in a partisan and public opinion environment that supports transitional justice. In unfavorable political environments it is unlikely that litigants will have the necessary clout to activate and influence removal and appointment processes. This contrasts with pedagogical interventions, which, as we saw, can operate with a lower level of public visibility. Litigants can surreptitiously draw judicial actors to their academic events without the help of politicians. If properly designed, pedagogical interventions can be safely carried out even in hostile environments, protecting judicial actors from external pressures. Argentina exemplifies how the presence of a decisively favorable political environment in the 2000s allowed litigants to further judicial change initiated via pedagogical interventions with replacement strategies. I argue that the high levels of institutional transformation achieved in this context largely explain why it became the country with the greatest number of human rights trials in the world.

Conclusion

This chapter presented a framework for understanding judicial behavior that emphasizes the production and reproduction of informal behavioral norms within judicial corporations. I argued that judicial behavior cannot be reduced to strategic responses to the surrounding political

[35] During the 1990s a wave of judicial reform throughout Latin America led to the creation of these bodies in countries including Peru, Argentina, Chile, and Mexico (see Hammergren 2007; Finkel 2008).

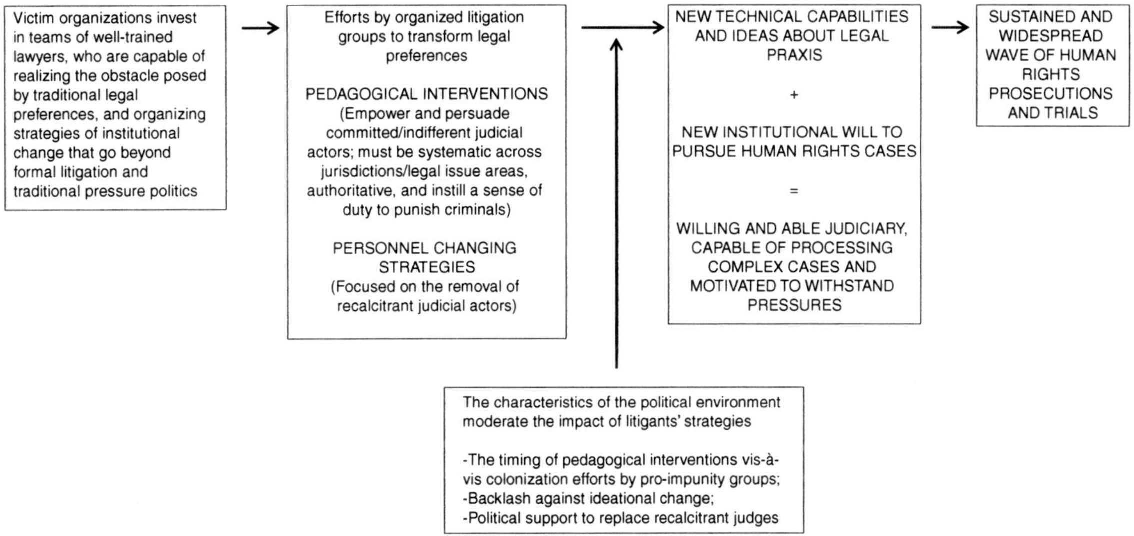

Figure 2.1. Explaining the Success of Human Rights Prosecutions in Latin America.

environment. Deeply internalized legal preferences offer the motivation and resources for judges and prosecutors to disregard those calculations and act in accordance with professional standards and institutional goals. These preferences are not politically neutral, but are the product of struggles in which outside political groups, in alliance with judicial actors, seek to secure favorable jurisprudence and safeguard their interests. As a result of the cognitive limitations and normative commitments derived from legal preferences, radical changes in patterns of judicial behavior, such as those associated with successful human rights trials in Latin America, require profound shifts in dominant juridical visions. Influencing judges and prosecutors via transformations in norms of interpretive praxis and judicial personnel is crucial in order to observe durable and stable macro-jurisprudential shifts in favor of formerly disadvantaged groups.

The second part of the chapter identified the complex of conflicting legal preferences at the heart of the struggle for human rights, associating different ideas with specific groups of actors. I argued that human rights litigants seek to replace an old legal orthodoxy biased in favor of impunity with a neoconstitutionalist conception of criminal justice that favors prosecutions. I explained the contention mechanisms that lead to positive outcomes in the area of transitional justice, as well as the conditions that increase the likelihood that they will be effective in bringing about prison sentences. In this regard, the model emphasizes both litigants' choices when designing their tactics of legal contention, as well as the moderating impact of the political environment. Figure 2.1 shows a diagram summarizing the main theoretical argument. In the chapters that follow I put these insights to work using the case studies of Argentina, Peru, and Mexico.

3

Argentina

Pedagogical Interventions and Replacement Strategies in the Struggle for Human Rights

This chapter analyzes the Argentine experience with the judicialization of human rights violations perpetrated during the military dictatorship that ruled the country between 1976 and 1983.[1] In the three decades following the democratic transition, Argentina gradually became the country with the largest number of criminal cases against human rights violators in the world. In line with the model presented in Chapter 2, throughout this period, different factions with stakes in transitional justice tried to colonize the judiciary, manipulate the legal preferences of judges and prosecutors, and redefine their institutional goals. Ultimately, however, organized victim groups and their lawyers prevailed, guaranteeing stable and consistent jurisprudential outcomes that favored their interests.

The uniqueness of the Argentine case can be explained by NGOs' early realization of the importance of manufacturing alternative legal preferences to give judicial actors the technical capabilities and professional motives to defy impunity laws and pursue complex investigations. Activists' cohesiveness and high levels of legal professionalization led them consistently to deploy both pedagogical interventions and replacement strategies, thus triggering deep ideational changes in the judicial branch. As we shall see in subsequent chapters, this dual approach differentiated the Argentine movement from its counterparts in Peru and Mexico. NGOs' efforts removed decisive judicial blockages on the road to truth and justice, generated productive synergies with processes of international norm diffusion, pushed judges and prosecutors to defy the limits imposed by a hostile political environment during key moments in the 1990s, and exploited the possibilities afforded by the rise to power of a supportive political coalition in the 2000s.

[1] For an explanation of the origins of the military dictatorship in Argentina see O'Donnell (1988). For an account of the violations perpetrated during this period, see CONADEP (1984).

Argentina offers within-case variation in terms of the macropolitical context in which litigants implement strategies of judicial transformation. As a result, this case study serves two important analytical goals. First, it aims to show that, regardless of political support for the cause, activists must take seriously how judicial actors think about human rights cases and their associated professional duties. Otherwise, trials may well be stalled by incompetence, bureaucratic inertia, or sheer recalcitrance. Second, variation in the characteristics of the political environment sheds light on the conditions under which efforts at legal preference change are more or less likely to bring about widespread institutional changes in the judicial branch.

From the passage of amnesty laws and pardons in the late 1980s and early 1990s, to the first judicial ruling declaring the unconstitutionality of the amnesties in 2001, human rights activists focused their efforts on opening up a legal space for assertive judicial behavior. Their strategies included organizing pedagogical activities for committed and indifferent judges and prosecutors, filing lawsuits for cases not covered by the amnesties, promoting truth-seeking trials, and sustaining the flow of information to key judicial actors. Activists used these tactics both to make judges and prosecutors aware of the imperatives of international human rights law and to diffuse acceptance of these doctrines. On the one hand, I demonstrate that these pedagogical interventions indeed shifted legal visions and motivated judges to erode the impunity regime, defying the constraints imposed by the Supreme Court and two different national administrations (Menem 1989–1999 and De la Rúa 1999–2001), which adamantly refused to reopen the trials. In this sense, it is important to highlight that litigants' astute realization of the need to find allies in the judiciary and nurture rebellious values among them was crucial because despite the fact that the military had little control over the terms of the Argentine democratic transition, proimpunity interests were back in power rather soon after 1983. On the other hand, the narrative also suggests that these domestic strategies of judicial change began before the international litigation efforts that put impunity in the global agenda in the late 1990s. Argentine litigants thus paved the way to amplify the judicial effect of external normative pressures, equipping judges with the necessary tools to confront nontrivial legal issues not addressed by the pronouncements of international courts. This bolsters the point advanced earlier regarding the need to trace diffusion streams at the domestic level.

Although during the 1990s litigants galvanized a critical mass of judges and prosecutors willing and able to rule in favor of the victims, their pedagogical interventions had a limited reach. As a result, jurisprudential success was also limited. This was in part due to the efforts by the anti–transitional justice camp to colonize the bench with recalcitrant judges early on in the process, which limited the pool of persuadable judges once litigants launched pedagogical interventions. In addition to allowing for the survival of these recalcitrant positions in several jurisdictions, the unevenness of activists' strategies of judicial transformation in the 1990s left many committed and indifferent judicial actors ill-equipped to deal with complex human rights cases. When Néstor Kirchner came to power in 2003 and launched a decisive push in favor of criminal accountability, these same judges were still not ready to respond effectively to the new call for truth and justice. The political environment had now changed dramatically in favor of the victims, but the resilience of islands of bureaucratic incompetence and recalcitrance continued to condition the success of criminal prosecutions in some provinces and courts.

Focusing on this internal variation over time and across space, this chapter challenges the conventional wisdom that credits presidential support for the explosion of trials and prison sentences during the Kirchner years. In so doing I reinforce my argument about the centrality of shifts in legal visions to the story behind criminal accountability for human rights violations. Despite unprecedented levels of success at the aggregate level in the 2000s, there were important differences in outcomes across legal issue areas and subnational jurisdictions, which are better explained by the absence of legal preference change among key judges. A highly favorable political environment at the national level was not enough to break the esprit de corps of certain sectors of the judiciary that opposed the trials, or indeed to overcome blockages due to technical incompetence. Changes in the political environment, however, allowed activists to ignite a second mechanism of institutional transformation in order to make up for these shortcomings. I show how NGOs garnered the support of their new political allies and activated replacement strategies that ultimately catalyzed the unprecedented wave of prison sentences observed to this day, and decisively cemented the positive direction of the judicialization process. In other words, the Argentine case illustrates both the highly interactive effect of litigant's strategies and the changing political environment on transitional justice outcomes, and the importance of combining both persuasion and replacement in order to trigger the deep institutional changes necessary to remove judicial blockages.

In the following pages, I reconstruct the microlevel interactions between judicial actors and litigants. I explore how legal preferences conditioned the way the former perceived human rights cases and how the latter were instrumental in transforming legal visions so as to make justice possible. The analysis begins with a brief history of the origins of the judicialization process in the 1980s in order to show that during those years, the judiciary displayed an uneven commitment to the human rights cause. As we shall see, this led both pro– and anti–transitional justice coalitions to realize the need for intervention in the judicial branch in order to secure ties with reliable allies. In other words, I first describe the strategic environment that both camps confronted at the dawn of the democratic era.

Judicial Behavior and Amnesty Laws: Lessons from the 1980s

During the 1980s, some judges and prosecutors promoted investigations and trials beyond what the transitional government deemed prudent. Despite these isolated instances of judicial rebellion, most judges had an ambivalent attitude toward truth and justice. This indifference, coupled with growing concerns about the precariousness of the new democracy, led most courts to endorse the amnesty laws signed by the administration in 1986 and 1987. Exploring the erratic participation of the judicial branch during this period allows us to understand the battle over the hearts and minds of judges and prosecutors that characterized the following decades.

Upon his inauguration in 1983, President Alfonsín of the Radical Party (UCR) issued an order to launch investigations against the members of the military juntas. The administration argued that the juntas

> conceived and instrumented a plan of operations against subversive and terrorist activity, based on clearly illegal methods and procedures.... Approximately between the years 1976 and 1979, thousands of people were illegally deprived of their liberty, tortured and killed as the result of the application of these procedures, inspired by a totalitarian doctrine of national security. (Quoted in Sancinetti 1987: 173, my translation)

The government's initiative led to a historic ruling handed down in 1985 by the Federal Appeals Court of the City of Buenos Aires.[2] The judgment, however, did not put the human rights question to rest. In the famous *punto 30* of the ruling, the judges instructed military courts to begin new judicial proceedings against lower level policemen and soldiers who had

[2] Videla and Massera were sentenced to life imprisonment; Viola, Lambruschini, and Agosti to 17, 8, and 3 years and 9 months in jail, respectively; Galtieri, Anaya, Lami Dozo, and Graffigna were acquitted.

been in charge of the military's governing apparatus.[3] The executive had always planned to expedite the judicialization process by circumscribing it to those with the highest levels of responsibility, so the court's decision to extend the trials beyond the junta leaders constituted a bold act of defiance (Pion-Berlin 1997: 84–88).[4]

In order to appease a still-powerful military, Alfonsín devised a strategy to limit the reach of the new wave of investigations. Early in 1986, the Ministry of Defense issued instructions to military prosecutors to exclude from the prosecutions those who had followed superiors' commands from higher level officers, thus mandating a generous interpretation of the principle of due obedience (Smulovitz 1995; Norden 1996: 103). Contemporary sources also indicate that the government struck a deal with the chief of the armed forces, promising to issue pardons at the end of the presidential term (Morales Solá 1990; Norden 1996: 127–128). Finally, in December 1986 Alfonsín sent to congress the Punto Final Law, which enforced a strict 60 day limit for filing new cases (Sancinetti 1987). The law was passed days after the Buenos Aires Province Federal Appeals Court handed down a second condemnatory ruling against high-ranking members of the police and was a response to the news of growing discontent among the military rank and file, delivered to the president by the leadership of the armed forces (Verbitsky 2003; Novaro 2009).

Several judicial actors rebelled against the government's containment strategy. First, the members of the now very prestigious City of Buenos Aires Federal Appeals Court threatened to resign if the administration insisted on issuing instructions to military prosecutors (Pion-Berlin 1997: 96). These threats were accompanied by massive demonstrations organized by the human rights movement and attended by members of all political parties, including the UCR (Acuña and Smulovitz 1995; Novaro 2009). As a result of this widespread opposition, the minister of defense resigned and the president ordered the rewriting of the instructions to

[3] According to a law passed by congress immediately after the 1983 elections, the Supreme Council of the Armed Forces had original jurisdiction over human rights cases.

[4] For example, in 1983 Alfonsín sent to congress a bill to nullify the self-amnesty law approved by the military before the transition. The government sought to include in the law a clause that would exempt those who had followed superior commands from any criminal responsibility. In congress, several groups pushed back and sponsored amendments that expanded the universe of cases susceptible to prosecution. When the law was finally passed, it stated that officers who had followed orders would be exempt from any criminal responsibility except when they had perpetrated "atrocious and abhorrent" crimes. Ample room was thus left for judicial discretion when deciding whom to prosecute (Manzetti 1993).

avoid, at least until the passage of the Punto Final law, arbitrary restrictions on prosecutions (Norden 1996; McGuire 1997).

Second, during 1986 some federal appeals courts began to usurp jurisdiction over cases of state repression involving junior officers. They accused the Supreme Council of the Armed Forces of delaying judicial proceedings in order to favor their military colleagues. Following the decision of the Buenos Aires court to intervene in cases of crimes perpetrated in the largest clandestine detention centers (the cases *ESMA* and *1er Cuerpo del Ejército*), appeals courts in cities including Rosario and Bahía Blanca took control of their respective human rights dockets (Novaro 2009). Civilian federal judges justified this move by invoking Law 23049, which established that although military courts had original jurisdiction, civilian courts had the right to intervene if cases suffered delays of six months or longer.

Finally, toward the end of 1986, federal appeals court judges in such cities as Buenos Aires, Bahía Blanca, Rosario, and Comodoro Rivadavia decided to suspend their summer holidays in order to process as many indictments as possible before the end of the 60 day window established by the Punto Final law (Acuña and Smulovitz 1995). By the end of February 1987, more than 300 officers were facing judicial proceedings, a move that decisively undermined the effectiveness of the de facto amnesty. The Bahía Blanca federal prosecutor at the time explained in an interview the motivations behind this reaction:

> When in December 1986 I requested the Federal Appeals Court of Bahía Blanca to swiftly process the incoming lawsuits, the government fiercely attacked me. I publicly stated that I would not cave in to those pressures because despite being a federal prosecutor I was not subject to the executive's instructions. I was part of an independent entity and would abide by existing legal principles. What we were investigating were not isolated patterns of behavior during the fight against subversive groups, but specific crimes defined in the Argentine Criminal Code. From my point of view, it was unacceptable that through the *Punto Final* Law the government sought to establish a series of privileges for some members of the population. In the end, I did not question the constitutionality of the law because by February we had been able to issue all of the indictments.[5]

The corrosive effects that the actions of this and other judicial actors had on the Punto Final law also implied a bold defiance of the executive's insistence that prosecutors make use of the principle of due obedience.

[5] Interview, Buenos Aires, 9 November 2010.

In January 1987 the aforementioned prosecutor publicly declared that he would act in accordance "with the principles of legality and impartiality, without receiving commands from the executive."[6] A federal judge also recalls the combative spirit prevalent among some of his colleagues during the months immediately following the approval of the Punto Final law: "I found a court that was willing to pursue the path demarcated by the 'punto 30,' bringing the territorial bosses in charge of executing the anti-subversive repressive plan to justice. The time frame for filing cases expired between February 19 and 22, 1987. I basically didn't sleep."[7]

This high-profile involvement of judicial players in salient political struggles was unprecedented. Their actions radically departed from the preferences of the executive branch and the military, the two actors that throughout the twentieth century had reduced the judiciary to a submissive and politically irrelevant organization (Oyahnarte 1972; Smulovitz 1995; Iaryczower et al. 2002; Chávez 2004; Helmke 2005; Spiller and Tomassi 2009; Chávez et al. 2011). According to some scholars, rising levels of formal judicial independence explain judicial feistiness during this period (Skaar 2011). The problem with this explanation is that the formal structure of the judiciary, including appointment procedures, was not reformed during the 1980s (Smulovitz 1995). Others have focused on informal political dynamics that eased prior constraints on judicial autonomy (Filippini 2007; Novaro 2009). For example, Novaro (2009: 36–37, 44) suggests that Alfonsín's ambivalent and erratic human rights policies, the perceived disorientation of his administration, and the divisions within the UCR encouraged courts to defy him.[8] This account is more plausible because it is clear that since 1983 Alfonsín had been notoriously unable to control the judicialization process.

Despite their merits, explanations that emphasize changes in formal rules or broad political dynamics obscure the fact that very few judicial actors actually became involved in thorny political territory. The aforementioned bursts of judicial assertiveness are less puzzling if one takes into account that they were not representative of the attitude of the judiciary qua institution. To be sure, in the aftermath of the transition Argentines "discovered the law" and the possibilities afforded by the judicialization of social and political conflicts. Members of the judiciary became media

[6] *Clarín*, 25 January 1987.

[7] Interview, Buenos Aires, 20 May 2011.

[8] Novaro also highlights President Alfonsín's principled commitment to the separation of powers as one of the reasons why he was not more decisive in his attempts to control the judiciary (2009: 66).

stars as never before, revealing the "potentially subversive and mobilizing character of legal rhetoric" (Smulovitz 1995: 88; 2002). The high profile acquired by some juridical battles, especially the human rights trials, allowed certain judicial actors to stage concrete displays of a new commitment to the rule of law. But this commitment was not generalized. As a former prosecutor stated in an interview, "Judicial activity was circumscribed to a few protagonists. It wasn't massive. What explains certain types of behavior is the personal commitment of the actors and the will of the judges. It was similar to what happened during the dictatorship with the granting of habeas corpus petitions: granting those petitions was a personal choice."[9]

The reason for this patchy commitment to the human rights cause is that in many ways the Argentine judiciary remained unchanged. For example, Alfonsín confirmed 70 percent of the judges that were active during the dictatorship.[10] This continuity meant that the outgoing dictators had appointed the majority of the sitting judges in the new democracy.[11] According to Verbitsky (1993), the juntas fired 32 percent of the judges in the city of Buenos Aires and 42.4 percent of those in the interior of the country, and replaced them with loyalists. It was highly unlikely that many of these individuals would feel compelled by the values and goals of the new political era. According to a former federal judge: "The judiciary had a strong authoritarian component ... pro-military in many respects" (quoted in Novaro 2009: 44 ft. 28, my translation).[12]

The government made very few important new appointments. In addition to the notable exception of the Supreme Court, Alfonsín nominated the members of the City of Buenos Aires Federal Appeals Court. Some of them belonged to the small group of judges who during the dictatorship had granted habeas corpus petitions to the relatives of the disappeared and who had declared the unconstitutionality of the amnesty approved by the military government in 1982. Others were young lawyers with little experience in the judiciary. It is therefore not surprising that they were among the few who at first behaved according to the new logic of judicial autonomy and respect for the rule of law. This was precisely the mission for which they had been enlisted. They not only weighed in during public

[9] Interview, 9 November 2010.

[10] *La Nación*, 3 August 1984.

[11] Conservative provincial elites with strong influence in the senate successfully sponsored the confirmation of federal judges with jurisdiction in their districts. Many of these judges had begun their judicial careers during the dictatorship (Novaro 2009: 44).

[12] For a similar description of the posttransition judiciary also see Sancinetti (1987: 14–15).

debates about the judicialization process, sometimes threatening to resign in order to put pressure on political actors, but also jealously guarded the court's autonomy and professional integrity. For example, when some of these judges left the bench disgusted with Alfonsín's retrenchment in the area of human rights, the president of the court, Andrés D'Alessio, made sure that the vacancies were filled with individuals who were also committed to the cause. Horacio Cattani, who replaced one of the outgoing judges, explained his appointment in the following terms:

> When D'Alessio asked me to join the court I told him I was skeptical that the Senate would confirm my appointment. I was neither a Peronist nor a Radical, and I would not be subject to partisan control. D'Alessio told me: "Let me take care of that. In a few months you will be sworn in." The court was fully committed to maintain its standing and prestige. It was fantastic.[13]

The integrity of this court was perhaps unique. According to one of Alfonsín's closest advisers, "Judges lacked a group or institutional identity" (quoted in Novaro 2009: 217, my translation), which in turn impeded the consolidation of uniform jurisprudential criteria vis-á-vis human rights prosecutions. Similarly, a then federal judge describes the attitude of other members of the judiciary in the weeks prior to the 1985 trial:

> It was a period of great solitude. People in Tribunales [the headquarters of the federal judiciary in Buenos Aires] did not support us. They were scared, afraid. When we met with them in the corridors, they asked us: "Is it true that you will hold this trial? Are you nuts?" … Many thought it was impossible to bring the leaders of the military regime to justice. (Ricardo Gil Lavedra quoted in Eliaschev [2011], my translation)

In fact, judges in several federal courts were reticent or simply unwilling to follow the leadership of their counterparts in the City of Buenos Aires. For example, after the historic 1985 ruling, the La Plata Federal Appeals Court, which had jurisdiction over important cases such as *2do Cuerpo del Ejército*, refused to take the human rights docket from the hands of military courts. According to a federal judge, "La Plata did not want to have anything to do with the case. They wanted the court in the City of Buenos Aires to do it."[14] The Córdoba Federal Appeals Court also refrained from exerting pressures on military tribunals to speed up the proceedings. At the same time as the judges in Buenos Aires were taking decisive steps to

[13] Interview, Buenos Aires, 20 May 2011.

[14] Interview, Buenos Aires, 20 May 2011. In the end it was the Buenos Aires Federal Appeals Court that demanded that the Supreme Council of the Armed Forces hand over the case.

regain civilian jurisdiction over human rights cases, judges in Córdoba granted the Supreme Council of the Armed Forces further extensions (Novaro 2009).

The Supreme Court was also highly erratic in its behavior vis-à-vis human rights cases. On the one hand, Alfonsín's prestigious appointees upheld the constitutionality of Law 23049, which granted civilian courts the right to take human rights cases from military courts (Garro and Dahl 1987a; Novaro 2009: 38 ft. 17); confirmed the City of Buenos Aires Federal Appeals Court's ruling against the military juntas; and in *Videla* (1986), expanded the conditions under which subordinate officers could be subject to criminal prosecutions, thus limiting the applicability of the principle of due obedience (Garro and Dahl 1987b).[15] Less than a year later, however, the court reversed its position on this question. In *Camps* (1987), it validated the constitutionality of the second amnesty law, the Due Obedience Law, which barred criminal prosecutions against all subordinate officers.[16] Justice Petracchi explained the court's exercise in judicial restraint in the following terms:

> It is relevant to point out that the law cannot be interpreted turning a blind eye on the particular political context that motivates it, or with indifference towards the effects that this Court's decision to declare it void could produce. Notwithstanding the serious deficiencies in the norm, this Court cannot ignore that irrespective of the letter of the law, there is a clear political decision on the side of the legislator, which the judicial branch should not evaluate. (CSJN, Decreto 280/84 PEN, 1987, my translation)

The political context Justice Petracchi references in his opinion was one dominated by growing fears of a military insurrection. After federal courts undermined the effects of the Punto Final Law, the military rank and file became increasingly worried about new trials (Romero 2002: 263).[17] Early in 1987, some junior officers began to receive court orders mandating them to testify in the various ongoing cases. Several officers decided to ignore these orders, openly defying civilian authorities. During the Holy Week of 1987, tensions exploded as a group of Malvinas veterans organized a mutiny in a military barrack outside the capital. It was in the wake

[15] During most of 1985 and 1986, the administration lobbied the Supreme Court in order to persuade the judges to force upon lower courts an expansive interpretation of the principle of due obedience. The Supreme Court resisted these pressures (Manzetti 1993: 192).

[16] For a legal analysis of the law see Sancinetti (1987).

[17] Severe cuts to the military budget also added to the growing discontent among generals. In 1989 salaries were only half of what they had been in 1983 (Manzetti 1993: 189–190).

of this uprising that Alfonsín decided to send the Due Obedience Law to congress (Manzetti 1993: 193; Norden 1996). Because of the uncertainty generated by the uprisings (Manzetti 1993: 201), the Supreme Court felt it was unwise to worsen the precariousness of the political situation by striking it down.

As I have suggested thus far, a lack of professional interest in human rights cases, the absence of significant institutional and personnel changes, fear of the military, and persisting loyalties with the previous regime, all contributed to the uneven commitment and erratic responses of judges and prosecutors to transitional justice. The 1980s thus left one central lesson for pro– and anti–transitional justice groups: If the judiciary were left to act autonomously, there was no guarantee that it would deliver consistent jurisprudential outcomes in one direction or the other. As a result, dominating the judicial branch by modifying legal preferences became a central component of the strategies deployed by both camps in the following years.

For anti–transitional justice groups, the instances of judicial autonomy observed during the 1980s were a source of concern given their proven ability to jeopardize attempts to put trials indefinitely on hold. It took two military uprisings and the passage of a second amnesty law to contain these "rebellious" judicial actors. In this sense, Alfonsín's reluctance to exert decisive pressures on judicial actors to impose the government's moderate prosecution policy (Pion-Berlin 1997; Novaro 2009) was now regarded as incompatible with the need to put an end to the military question. According to one of Alfonsín's closest advisers, not controlling the judiciary "can be very dangerous, especially when you have in your hands something like the prosecution of military officers, because there is a need to unify jurisprudential criteria" (quoted in Novaro 2009: 217, my translation).

On the other side were pro–transitional justice groups who began the democratic era with a militant skepticism about the transformative capacity of the judiciary (Acuña and Smulovitz 1995; Filippini 2007; Novaro 2009). Created in the 1970s, organizations such as the Asamblea Permanente por los Derechos Humanos (APDH), Madres de Plaza de Mayo, Abuelas de Plaza de Mayo, and Centro de Estudios Legales y Sociales (CELS) drew together politicians from all political parties, lawyers, intellectuals, and victims of state repression (Brysk 1990; Mignone 1991). Most of these groups initially opposed the judicial path drawn by the administration to deal with the human rights question (Jelin 1994). Antigovernment protests began as early as 1983 when congress debated Alfonsín's plan to reform the Code of Military Justice in order to establish a legal framework for the trials. Their opposition to the government also included criticisms of the plan to create an independent truth commission.[18] In addition, their lack of trust in the judiciary's ability to carry out the trials led them to propose a "political trial" instead of a conventional one (Mignone 1991: 158). Consistent with this position, most human rights groups rejected the ruling handed down by the City of Buenos Aires Federal Appeals court in 1985 (Novaro 2009: 201).[19]

As sectors of the judicial branch began to respond favorably to the human rights cause, some NGOs – in particular CELS and other organizations staffed primarily by human rights lawyers – departed from the movement's position and became more cooperative with the judicial process (Mignone 1991: 160).[20] Vecchioli (2010, 2011) explains that while in exile during the dictatorship, high-profile human rights and labor lawyers established links with international organizations such as the International Commission of Jurists and the International League for the Rights of Man. These connections were instrumental in providing the funding and know-how to professionalize the staff of these local NGOs further and gave them the resources to assist effectively in the judicialization process (see also Dezalay and Garth 1998). The impact of CELS's professionalism and legal orientation, for example, is evidenced by the fact that it alone filed six hundred of the two thousand charges against military officers received by federal courts between February and August 1984 (Osiel 1986; Norden 1996; Pion-Berlin 1997: 91).

These cooperative human rights lawyers limited their interactions with judicial actors to the formal stages of the judicial process (e.g. filing charges, facilitating witness testimonies, providing evidence). They did not engage in the type of transformative strategies described in Chapter 2 as the most effective or conducive to achieving stable and enduring jurisprudential outcomes. In many respects, human rights organizations allowed the judiciary to act alone. The personal commitment of some

[18] Many activists declined the government's invitation to be members of the CONADEP (Fernández Meijide 2009). Most human rights organizations instead favored the creation of a bicameral commission in congress.

[19] They objected to both the prosecutor's strategy to base the accusation on a limited number of cases (approximately seven hundred), and the court's decision to acquit some of the junta leaders (Sancinetti 1987).

[20] Victim NGOs did of course participate in judicial proceedings, but always remained more skeptical. There were two main forms of participation: testifying as witnesses and transferring information about the crimes from NGO archives to the courts.

members of the judiciary led to the construction of ad hoc alliances, but no systematic efforts were made to diffuse uniform criteria across different jurisdictions. For example, according to the chief prosecutor in the 1985 trial against the juntas, "I had no informal meetings or conversations with human rights lawyers about the legal strategy chosen by the prosecution. I did approach prestigious academics, but that wasn't helpful because most of them expressed profound disagreements with our approach."[21] A former federal prosecutor also recalls that the focus of these organizations was on formal litigation strategies: "When I decided to question the Due Obedience Law, Horacio Verbistky [member of CELS] helped me a lot by publishing the decision in the newspaper he directed. But I did not have a direct legal collaboration with CELS."[22]

As human rights groups became less skeptical of the "judicial path," they realized the need to intervene forcefully in the judiciary. The isolated victories and subsequent backlashes of the 1980s indicated that the number of committed judicial actors did not constitute a large enough critical mass to launch a decisive and effective corporate reaction in favor of victims' rights. This became even more apparent when the City of Buenos Aires Federal Appeals Court, whose members had been at the forefront of transitional justice efforts, handed down a unanimous ruling accepting the Supreme Court's position with regard to the Due Obedience Law. Five of the judges, Gil Lavedra, Valerga Araoz, Arslanian, Peres, and Cattani, did so reluctantly, invoking their duty to follow Supreme Court precedents. By contrast, D'Alessio emphatically defended the Supreme Court's criteria dismissing counterarguments based on Argentina's obligations under the Convention against Torture as inapplicable because of the retroactivity principle, and arguments based on customary international law as mere rhetoric (Sancinetti 1987). This foreshadowed the presence of traditional legal preferences incompatible with the possibility of circumventing the impunity laws. Not even committed judges could be counted among reliable allies when it came to legal interpretation. They simply saw no legal alternatives to the status quo. Building strong bridges with the judiciary in order to entrench new professional visions and equip friendly judges with powerful juridical reasons to innovate and defy their superiors was therefore a pending task, one to which they would dedicate time and resources in the years to come.

[21] Interview, Buenos Aires, 20 December 2010.
[22] Interview, Buenos Aires, 9 November 2010.

The Anti-Transitional Justice Coalition Takes over the Judiciary

Alfonsín left the presidency in 1989. Soon after his inauguration, President Menem of the Peronist Party granted pardons to the junior officers who had organized the two military uprisings that haunted the final years of the Radical administration (Manzetti 1993: 195; Norden 1996: 140; McGuire 1997). Despite this concession, there was another uprising in December 1990, which made it clear that the military question was far from being resolved. Menem violently crushed the rebels, and took additional steps to appease the military further. On 29 December, he issued a second set of pardons, this time benefiting eleven members of the dictatorship who were serving time in jail as a result of the 1985 ruling. Together with the amnesty laws, these presidential pardons became the pillars of the Argentine legal impunity regime.

When CELS lawyers filed suits before the Supreme Court denouncing the unconstitutionality of the pardons, the government realized that the judiciary would once again be the epicenter of the debate on how to handle the legacies of the dictatorship. Judges could still be an obstacle to closing down the military front once and for all. For some of Menem's closest advisers, "homogenizing the [Supreme] Court vis-à-vis the executive"[23] became a priority in order to prevent the administration's policies from suffering the same fate as Alfonsín's (Ferreira Rubio and Gorretti 1998).[24] Government officials therefore became staunch supporters of the doctrine of judicial restraint and sought to shape a court with legal preferences conducive to noninterference in political questions. In fact one of Menem's cabinet ministers had been one of the main proponents of this doctrine when he was a member of the Supreme Court in the 1960s (Oyhanarte 1972).

Peronists could not trust the judiciary's willingness to stop the few human rights cases still in progress, especially those not covered by the amnesty laws (i.e. the illegal kidnapping of the children of the disappeared). For example, since 1988, first Alfonsín and then Menem had

[23] These were the terms used by Eduardo Bauzá, the president's general secretary. *La Nación*, 26 September 1989.

[24] The reasons for doing this exceeded the military question. Menem and his advisers also anticipated that adverse judicial rulings could jeopardize the full implementation of their market reform agenda (Murillo 2001; Levitsky 2003, 2005). In the 1980s, the judiciary had not only undermined Alfonsín's transitional justice strategy but was also inimical to key economic decisions such as the declaration of the state of emergency of the pension system (Kapiszewski 2012).

implored the Supreme Court to usurp jurisdiction over these cases, move them to a quick close, and stop further indictments and subpoenas. These pressures were not effective (Verbitsky 1993: 33–34). Similarly, Menem's judicial lobbyists could not prevent other acts of judicial defiance. After the government issued the first set of pardons, two federal prosecutors asked their respective appeals courts to nullify them. This confirmed politicians' worst fears about the dangers of allowing the persistence of islands of judicial commitment to the human rights cause and they tried to minimize the damage. One of these prosecutors recalls the tense days that followed his decision:

> The toughest days of my judicial career were those before and after I asked the Federal Appeals Court of Bahía Blanca to declare the unconstitutionality of the pardons. The Menemist avalanche to destroy me was terrible. Before I filed my petition the Solicitor General sent me a letter stating that I could not question an unobjectionable presidential decree. I told him that between a decree and the Constitution, I would choose the latter. He replied saying that he agreed with me, but that as prosecutors we could not question a political decision made by the President. They also tried to bribe me and later, to suspend me.... At some point in your life you have to act according to what you think is right, both juridically and ethically. Even my father warned me that I could lose my job, but if I had capitulated I would have gone home defeated.[25]

If the military question was to be put to rest, Peronists had to prevent these rebellious attitudes. The strategy devised by the Menem administration to cement the reliability of the judiciary involved decisively infiltrating the bench and engaging in court packing. The government intended to send a credible threat to judicial actors: Not acting as requested by the government could have severe professional and personal consequences. The plan was launched on 15 September 1989 when the president sent to congress a bill to increase the number of Supreme Court justices from five to nine.[26] Justices Belluscio, Bacqué, Petracchi, and Fayt reacted by issuing a statement (the famous 44th Accord) in which they denounced the executive's plan as contrary to judicial autonomy and the judiciary's democratic

[25] Interview, Buenos Aires, 9 November 2010.

[26] Among contemporary observers, it came as no surprise that the president announced his plan only a few days before an army general had to attend a hearing at the San Martín Federal Appeals Court (Verbitsky 1993). His subpoena had been delayed for a month, after the government with the aid of a military doctor managed to produce a medical certificate temporarily exempting the general from his day in court. Since the hearings could not be postponed indefinitely, the government needed the judiciary to shelve the case to prevent the general's absence in court from being interpreted as a new act of military defiance.

mission to uphold the constitution (Ferreira Rubio and Gorretti 1998; Helmke 2005). When it became clear that the president would get away with the initiative, two justices resigned. Menem was thus able to name six new judges and build a friendly majority in the Supreme Court. The newly appointed judges, Barra, Cavagna Martínez, Levene, Nazareno, Moliné O'Connor, and Boggiano, were very conservative and had strong personal and political ties to President Menem (Baglini and Orlandi 1993: 80–82).

The fact that the administration was anxious to receive jurisprudential support for its signature initiative in the area of transitional justice is illustrated by a public statement made by one of Menem's closest legal advisers: "If any claimant or prosecutor questions the possibility of pardoning indicted officers, and if this Court declares the unconstitutionality [of the pardons], that day the Chief of the Army will come to us and we will have an infernal mess" (quoted in Verbitsky 1993: 142). The new court responded to the government's wishes and endorsed the constitutionality of the presidential pardons on two occasions: December 1990, days after the last military uprising and before the second set of pardons was signed by the president, and October 1992, when the military threat was no longer present. In the former case, the majority explained that under the Military Code of Justice the family of the victim lacked standing, thus invalidating the interlocutory appeal demanding the rejection of the pardons. In the latter, they invoked U.S. jurisprudence on judicial restraint.

Attempts to mold the legal preferences of the judiciary did not stop at the level of the Supreme Court. By the end of the 1980s, there was a growing consensus in the legal community in relation to the need to introduce structural changes in the judiciary.[27] Menem took advantage of this impetus for reform and proposed a new Code of Criminal Procedures. Some of the changes passed by congress in 1991 included the creation of Federal Oral Tribunals and a Court of Cassation (Finkel 2004, 2008). This gave the executive an unparalleled opportunity to staff the new courts with allies, and to get rid of inconvenient judges.

The creation of Federal Oral Tribunals doubled the number of seats in the federal judiciary. As a result, during his first term (1989–1995) Menem set a record by making more than seven hundred nominations (Llanos and Figueroa 2008). He strategically filled some of the new seats with Federal

[27] Several important changes were proposed during Alfonsín's presidency, but congress rejected them all. Initiatives included the creation of family and youth courts and the modification of the Code of Criminal Procedures to introduce, among other things, the possibility of trial by jury (Smulovitz 1995: 102).

Investigative Court judges who had caused trouble to the administration in several high-profile corruption and human rights cases. Among their many duties, Federal Investigative Courts are the ones that conduct the initial investigations in cases involving federal officials and decide whether or not to submit cases to trial courts. The promotion of his judicial enemies was not a magnanimous gesture; it allowed the government to "expel judges upwards" (Baglini and Orlandi 1993: 87) from seats in the courts in charge of deciding on the activation of sensitive cases, to positions with less room for discretion. To replace them, Menem appointed loyalists.

The most blatant attempt to colonize the judiciary was the saga behind the creation of the Court of Cassation, a court of last appeal in criminal cases. The administration nominated personal and political allies of the president. Most importantly, the nominees had direct links to the dictatorship and were unsympathetic to the transitional justice cause. Of the thirteen judges, some had worked at the infamous Camarón, a criminal court created to deal with political crimes during the 1970s; others had worked in the judiciary during the dictatorship in courts that systematically denied habeas corpus petitions filed by the victims of state repression; one of them had filed a libel case against a prominent Peronist leader who publicly denounced the dictatorship in the late 1970s; another had filed a criminal case against a Grandmother of Plaza de Mayo who shouted at him during a hearing in a case about the illegal abduction of her grandchild by the armed forces; yet another had been fired by the chief prosecutor in the 1985 trial against the junta leaders on the grounds that his personal defense of state terrorism made him ill-suited to investigate the generals; and four had voted to uphold the constitutionality of Menem's pardons as members of the City of Buenos Aires Federal Appeals Court (Verbitsky 1993).[28]

By appointing these judges, Menem created a buffer zone that would systematically stop or delay the progress of human rights cases. In fact, the entrenchment of judges with anti–transitional justice legal preferences in the upper echelons of the federal judiciary was effective in guaranteeing stable and reliable jurisprudential outcomes for the next decade and a half. As we will see later on, removing these judges from the bench was one of the main goals of the human rights movement when it activated aggressive replacement strategies in the 2000s.

[28] In fact, the only two members of the City of Buenos Aires Federal Appeals Court who were not promoted to the Court of Cassation were those who had signed the minority position in that ruling. For a profile of the judges appointed by Menem see *Página 12*, 1 April 2007.

Identifying the Challenge Ahead: The Problem of Legal Preferences

When Menem's takeover of the judiciary was consummated, human rights organizations faced an important challenge: They had to reenlist judicial actors behind their cause. But the nomination to the federal bench of stewards of the impunity regime put pro–transitional justice groups at a clear disadvantage. Since they were not the first movers in the struggle to colonize the bench, they faced a growing number of recalcitrant judges. As a result, victims and their lawyers had to plan highly targeted strategies of institutional transformation. In this context, the main priority became to identify indifferent or committed judges, modify their legal preferences by first giving them the technical tools to activate dormant cases, and then persuade them to make risky legal moves.

The impunity regime and the Supreme Court rulings endorsing it had effectively killed all judicial activity in the area of human rights. A former federal judge explained in an interview that committed judicial actors needed fresh ideas to overcome those legal and jurisprudential obstacles:

> The slow progress of the human rights question during the 1990s was a direct consequence of the passage of the laws and the pardons. They were laws approved by Congress! When some actors questioned them in court, judges upheld their constitutionality.... An overwhelming majority of courts validated the laws and the pardons. Certain aspects of the judiciary had to be restructured in order to make it possible to observe courts declaring the unconstitutionality of those legal instruments. That took a very long time.[29]

In the interview, the judge also made reference to the fact that toppling the impunity regime via unconstitutionality rulings implied a departure from the Argentine judiciary's doctrine of "self-restraint in political questions" (Oyhanarte 1972: 96, my translation), which had been one of the "constants in Argentine judicial politics" (ibid: 116, my translation) since the late nineteenth century.[30] To make matters worse, Menem's Supreme Court appointments had cemented the hegemony of this approach to legal interpretation. Although during the 1980s some courts had departed from this principle in human rights cases, at the end of the day, the highest courts in the land accepted the amnesties and the pardons. On what legal

[29] Interview, Buenos Aires, 17 December 2010.

[30] The most radical expression of this doctrine was the Supreme Court's famous accord in the wake of the 1930 military coup, which recognized the legitimacy of the new authorities. After the ousting of President Frondizi in 1962, the Supreme Court reinforced this doctrine, accepting the irreversibility of the coup.

grounds would lower courts now accept the demands of human rights groups, defying in the process both politicians and their superiors in the judiciary? How could the cases be reignited without violating, for example, the principle of double jeopardy, which protects an individual from being prosecuted twice for the same crime?

The human rights community identified international human rights law as the only legal corpus that could be used to back challenges to the status quo. The strategy looked promising, especially after the Inter-American Commission of Human Rights published a country report in 1992 denouncing the amnesties and the pardons as illegal under the American Convention on Human Rights (Fillipini 2007). Unfortunately, however, the implementation of these novel arguments required of judicial actors understanding, endorsing, and implementing legal instruments and principles rarely used in Argentine jurisprudence. In other words, NGOs' legal strategy was at odds with existing legal preferences, which were in turn biased in favor of impunity.

During the trials of the 1980s, courts did not have to resort to international human rights law. For example, since there were no amnesties or pardons in place and statutes of limitations were for the most part still running, there was no need to use categories such as crimes against humanity to define the crimes in a way that made them subject to procedural exceptions. Moreover, there is evidence that at the time not even the most committed members of the federal judiciary were either aware of or sympathetic to the international legal case against impunity. In an interview, the leading prosecutor in the 1985 trial stated:

> At the time Argentina was the only country in which civilian courts created in the nineteenth century tried former military leaders. We applied the criminal code of 1922, valid at the time of the crimes. By contrast, in Nuremberg a military court, a "victors' court," applied criminal law retroactively and violated the legality principle. Nothing of the sort happened in Argentina. The juntas were found guilty of perpetrating common crimes unequivocally described in existing, written law.... Moreover, we were well within the limits specified by statutes of limitations.

He then went on to criticize the criteria promoted by human rights organizations in the 1990s and 2000s to reopen the investigations:

> Argentina was one of the last countries to ratify the Convention on the Non-Applicability of Statutory Limitations for War Crimes and Crimes against Humanity. It's the least ratified convention! ... It is wrong to declare statutes of limitations void on the basis of that convention when it wasn't part of domestic law at the time of the crimes. I am against the idea of

> invoking the principles of international law. I do not think the legality principle, which took centuries to be accepted by nations worldwide, should be thrown out of the window.[31]

Similarly, his then colleagues in the City of Buenos Aires Federal Appeals Court also publicly expressed their opposition to the use of international law. As we saw earlier, in his opinion in the 1987 decision accepting the constitutionality of the Due Obedience Law, Judge D'Alessio dismissed customary international law as "mere rhetoric" (Sancinetti 1987: 147, my translation). In a recent interview two former members of that court made a similar argument. Judge Torlasco, for example, argued that current human rights cases "would have normally been subject to statutes of limitations according to Article 18 of the Constitution." In a disapproving tone he pointed out that judges are "applying the Convention on the Non-Applicability of Statutory Limitations retroactively."[32]

Certain passages of the 1985 historic ruling against the juntas also point to the lack of penetration of international human rights principles in judges' understanding of criminal law. For example, in cases in which the air force had transferred detainees to either the army or the navy early on during the dictatorship, the court acquitted the representative of the air force in the junta invoking the exhaustion of statutory limitations. Since the notion of crimes against humanity was not used, this made perfect legal sense. The lack of juridical innovation is also exemplified by the treatment of disappearances. For example, on several occasions the court concluded that the lack of evidence about the final whereabouts of the victims inhibited the court from assuming their death and proceeded to acquit the defendants (Sancinetti 1987: 41–44). This was in part because the judges did not see these crimes through the lens of international criminal definitions. As argued in Chapter 2, these legal categories raise awareness of the contextual specificities of this type of crime and lead judicial actors to ignore the decision making routines they follow in regular homicide cases, in which finding the body is usually the starting point for any investigation.

Finally, the arguments used by the prosecutors who questioned the pardons in the late 1980s and early 1990s provide further evidence of the fact that the international legal case against impunity was not part of judicial actors' cognitive maps. For instance, Prosecutor Cañón did not use those criteria when he asked the Bahía Blanca Federal Appeals Court to declare the unconstitutionality of the pardons. Instead, his argument was

[31] Interview, Buenos Aires, 20 December 2010.
[32] *La Nación*, 15 August 2010, my translation.

cast exclusively on domestic legal grounds as a separation of powers issue, characterizing the pardons as an illegal encroachment of the executive in the affairs of the judiciary (Verbitsky 1993: 147–148). As he stated in an interview, "In those days we followed the principles of domestic law. The only non-domestic source of law I made reference to during the 1980s and early 1990s was Roxin's theory of command responsibility."[33]

When these domestic legal arguments against the pardons and the amnesty laws failed, it was clear that the pro–transitional justice coalition had to find new ones. By the early 1990s they were already persuaded that the only way forward was to invoke international human rights law and customary law. However, the rejection or lack of awareness of these principles by their allies within the judiciary necessitated wide diffusion of the acceptance of human rights doctrines. If the discourse of human rights law was alien to these committed judges and prosecutors, matters could only be worse among indifferent ones. The judicial blockage against transitional justice was therefore not only made up of recalcitrant judges, but also of their ill-equipped committed and indifferent colleagues. As we shall see, litigants had in mind a model of judicial decision making remarkably similar to the sociological institutionalist framework advanced in Chapter 2. Their diagnosis of the problem highlighted the role of traditional legal preferences in engineering judicial acquiescence. Leading NGOs were thus able to see that in order to become agents of truth and justice within the parameters of action that govern the legal field, judges and prosecutors had to be given acceptable juridical tools and taught how to use them. Legal visions had to shift so that committed and indifferent judicial actors could see viable alternatives, marshal legitimate reasons to challenge the president and their superiors in the judicial hierarchy, and, in the process, feel safe to follow their convictions as professionals of the law.

Transforming Legal Preferences with Pedagogical Interventions

In the early 1990s, changes in the country's legal structure opened a window of opportunity for pro–transitional justice groups to make their case successfully before federal courts. On the one hand, in the case *Ekmekdjian v. Sofovich* (1992), the Supreme Court ruled that international law had primacy over domestic law. Although the case was unrelated to the issue of transitional justice, it set an important precedent in Argentine jurisprudence. Second, Article 72 of the constitution, reformed in 1994, granted

[33] Interview, Buenos Aires, 9 November 2010.

constitutional status to a series of international treaties including the American Declaration of the Rights of Man, the American Convention on Human Rights, the Convention on the Prevention and Punishment of the Crime of Genocide, the Convention against Torture, and the Convention on the Rights of the Child. The incorporation of international human rights instruments thus reinforced the viability of an antiimpunity legal strategy based on nondomestic legal arguments.

Contrary to the view expressed by some scholars, however, the mere existence of a new legal window of opportunity did not automatically translate into changes in patterns of judicial behavior. This new window would have been causally inert in the absence of a more complex process whereby judges (a) were made aware of the international instruments now added to the constitution, (b) were persuaded that abiding by those treaties was mandatory, and (c) were taught how to incorporate them into their daily jurisprudential routines. In fact, CELS lawyers were very much aware of the need to accompany these formal changes with changes in informal legal preferences. In its 1994 annual report the NGO's executive directors made it clear that "recognizing the constitutional status [of international treaties] means the [opening] of a real possibility to work with new tools to improve the protection of human rights, *at the same time as it opens numerous alternatives that will depend on our imagination and ingenuity to turn them into results*" (CELS 1995a: 5, my emphasis and translation). In addition to disrupting entrenched bureaucratic inertias, the diffusion effort had to engineer a strong commitment to the cause in order to motivate judicial actors to defy the ruling party. Not only was Menem at the peak of his power (he secured reelection in 1995), but the administration had also strengthened its alliance with the military by, for example, appointing individuals with a dictatorial past to manage the government's security policies (Novaro 2009). As part of this move, Menem publicly vindicated the role of the military during the dirty war and accused human rights organizations of seeking the resumption of "la subversión" (CELS 1995a: 63).

The strategy to diffuse international legal principles within the federal judiciary was primarily designed by CELS and the Abuelas de Plaza de Mayo (hereafter, Abuelas). It had three main components. First, in the early 1990s, CELS' lawyers designed a series of pedagogical initiatives to teach judges about the requirements of the new constitution in the area of human rights and international law. Second, activists activated the so-called truth trials. Finally, since the amnesty laws were designed so that they did not apply to the cases of children abducted during the dictatorship, litigants filed numerous criminal lawsuits in federal courts concerning these crimes. These three strategies had varying degrees of immediate success in entrenching ideas about international law among judicial actors. However, in the medium run, they led to a major victory, namely, a landmark ruling by a federal criminal court in 2001 declaring the amnesty laws to be unconstitutional.

Designing Pedagogical Interventions

Between 1992 and 1996, CELS organized a series of academic activities in order to train judges and prosecutors informally in the domestic use of international human rights law. To reconstruct the motivations and reach of these initiatives I conducted archival research at the NGO's headquarters. The documents I found are incredibly rich: letters between CELS's president, Emilio Mignone, and the speakers he invited to the seminars; grant proposals outlining the pedagogical goals of the organization; transcripts of the discussions; attendance records; and reports submitted to the international agencies that funded the pedagogical initiative.

The following is a passage from a funding request sent in 1992 to the International Commission of Jurists, which reveals CELS's diagnosis of the problem posed by traditional legal preferences. The excerpt makes it clear that even before the constitutional reform, CELS was planning a long-term diffusion effort, hoping that by making judges one of their main targets, international law would eventually trickle down into local jurisprudence:

> The course's goal is to analyze the use of international and regional human rights conventions in Argentina's domestic law.... This analysis will include a study of the relevance [of international human rights law] and the objections and obstacles that oppose it.... In countries like Argentina ... both judges and lawyers, and even universities, scholars and legal journals frequently ignore [the obligation to abide by those norms], depriving citizens of the rights and protections they safeguard. For this reason, CELS deems it convenient to organize a regional seminar that brings together legal scholars, judges, lawyers, university professors and advanced law students ... with the goal of analyzing this problem and diffusing the conclusions among the aforementioned groups.... [The meeting] will constitute the first step of a movement that will translate into workshops, seminars, research, publications and judicial rulings conducive to a comprehensive domestic use of the norms of international human rights law.[34]

[34] Letter from CELS to ICJ, 6 July 1992. On file with the author. My translation.

Records also show that the seminars put special emphasis on the technical aspects of the use of treaties and conventions in court briefings and rulings. Most importantly, they highlight that CELS thought about how to maximize the persuasive power of the pedagogical interventions. In line with my argument about the importance of carefully choosing the agents of diffusion to enhance the legitimacy and authoritativeness of the message, the organizers invited national and foreign experts in constitutional law and international human rights law to deliver the lectures. Among the speakers, one finds Carlos Nino, German Bidart Campos, and Eugenio Zaffaroni, three of Argentina's most influential legal minds. Well-known international experts such as Augusto Cançado Trinidade, who would later become president of the Inter-American Court of Human Rights, were also invited. During an interview a member of CELS recognized that inviting others to speak on behalf of the NGO was indeed instrumental in raising the appeal of the events among judicial actors. It was not the victims putting forward a self-interested legal argument, but disinterested parties explaining what was right or wrong in contemporary legal praxis:

> One of the really successful strategies was to try to find very prestigious individuals within the judiciary and in the legal profession who would come and endorse our initiatives. We invited them, we explained to them our objectives and they were given a prominent role in the program. Their presence made it easier to overcome certain prejudices among judges and prosecutors, who perhaps would have refused to come if the speakers had been CELS's lawyers.[35]

By organizing these academic workshops CELS "added an educational component to its institutional objectives."[36] These pedagogical interventions became progressively more ambitious, especially after the 1994 reform. Whereas the first seminar organized in 1992 convened a very select group of lawyers and judicial actors (35 in total), in 1996 the institution reports an attendance rate of more than 150 individuals per day during three days of intense academic discussions. Since the speakers also submitted essays that were published in edited volumes, it is likely that the ideas and legal solutions proposed in the seminars traveled beyond the immediate participants.[37] Additional evidence of CELS's emphasis on the importance of diffusing these new ideas even further is the publication

[35] Former CELS executive director, interview, Buenos Aires, 3 November 2010.

[36] Ibid.

[37] The most influential is Abregú and Courtis (1997).

in 1995 of an annotated constitution, which carefully analyzed the 1994 reform from a human rights perspective.

These pedagogical interventions constituted the first attempt to diffuse the ideas that would later allow some judicial actors to open cracks in the impunity regime. The seminars provided the building blocks of a common discursive space in which the advocates of international law and the judges could understand each other, and begin to share similar legal preferences. Moreover, the immersion of certain judges and prosecutors into the networks of human rights activists and lawyers facilitated informal contacts between the two camps during the judicial proceedings initiated later in the decade. Given the narrow political space for transitional justice initiatives during the Menem years, these informal connections were crucial in order to plan risky legal moves carefully. For example, in the archival data I found the names of fifty-one judicial employees who attended the 1996 seminar. Among them, I was able to identify four individuals (Horacio Cattani, Pablo Parenti, Manuel Garrido, and Felix Crous) who would later play a tremendously influential role in championing the human rights cause in the Buenos Aires judiciary as judges, clerks, and prosecutors. I also interviewed judges and prosecutors from Buenos Aires, Mar del Plata, and Bahía Blanca who were at the forefront of the institutionalization of truth trials in the second half of the 1990s, and they all reported their attendance at these seminars.[38] Finally, by engaging judicial actors in strictly juridical terms, the seminars allowed CELS's lawyers to begin to isolate legal questions from political ones. As we shall see later, this initiated the conversion of indifferent judges in key courts. A growing sense of professional duty to punish the perpetrators of undeniably severe crimes minimized the impact of political calculations in judicial decision making.

Despite these important contributions, the pedagogical interventions had one central shortcoming: Their geographical scope was rather narrow. My sources explained that very few judges and prosecutors outside the City and Province of Buenos Aires participated. For example, a human rights lawyer stated in an interview:

> We had difficulties moving outside the capital city. I always say that Argentina is like a dwarf with the head of a giant. Everything is concentrated.... You have no idea of the lack of knowledge and awareness of international law that we found in the interior of the country. I once gave a talk in Córdoba and a member of a provincial Supreme Court came to tell

[38] Interviews Mar del Plata, 16 November 2010; Buenos Aires, 9 November 2010; Buenos Aires, 5 February 2011; Buenos Aires, 20 May 2011.

> me that after listening to my lecture she concluded that she had to go back to university. She did not know anything about international law.[39]

As the discussion of the truth and child abduction trials will also demonstrate, most of the other legal and extralegal initiatives launched by leading human rights organizations in Argentina during the 1990s suffered from the same shortcoming. By focusing their interventions on a few judges, human rights groups obtained jurisprudential victories in only a handful of courts. Nevertheless, given the dire circumstances they faced after Menem's colonization of the judiciary, it is not surprising that activists had to concentrate on building few but strong alliances with committed judicial actors.

Institutionalizing the Duty to Investigate the Fate of the Disappeared

After preparing the ground for legal preference change via the seminars described above, human rights organizations were ready to engage in formal litigation efforts that would eventually strike fatal blows to the impunity regime. These moves allowed them to maintain sustained interactions with important judicial actors, further diffusing technical knowledge and motivating them to push the limits of possibility afforded by the political environment.

Litigants began by asking the City of Buenos Aires Federal Appeals Court to recognize victims' right to truth on the basis of the jurisprudence of the Inter-American Court of Human Rights in *Velázquez Rodríguez v. Honduras* (1988) and an interpretation of Argentina's obligations under the American Convention on Human Rights. They argued that despite the limits on criminal prosecutions imposed by the amnesty laws, the judiciary could still request information from the executive and the armed forces in order to establish the fate of the disappeared. The initial diffusion of this idea among the relevant judicial actors can be understood by closely looking at the jurisprudence of the court between March and July of 1995. Judge Horacio Cattani, who attended the seminars earlier in the decade, was the nexus with human rights organizations.

In 1995 a newspaper published an interview with a former navy officer who candidly described the methods used to disappear political prisoners during the dictatorship (CELS 1995b; Payne 2008). Three weeks later a lawyer without direct links to the main human rights NGOs filed a petition asking the judges to inquire about two French nuns who had

[39] Interview, Buenos Aires, 2 December 2010.

been detained and then disappeared. In a unanimous decision, the court accepted the petition, but made it clear that this was not an attempt to open a formal investigation to determine criminal responsibilities.[40] The ruling did not make reference to international law. Instead, the judges described their decision as guided by a "humanitarian" spirit.

The situation changed when the same court accepted two requests for information filed by Emilio Mignone and Carmen Lapacó. In contrast to the lawyer who filed the first case, Mignone and Lapacó, who were founders of CELS, made a much more sophisticated argument based on international law. Their briefs introduced to the debate the idea of a right to truth and to mourning, rights that CELS explicitly recognized as not being part of Argentine domestic law (CELS 1999). In so doing, they built the foundations for juridical innovation, asking the court to make an expansive, nonformalistic reading of victims' rights. In Mignone's case, all five of the judges ruled in his favor, and three did so by fully endorsing the new doctrine. Cattani, Luraschi, and Cortelezza concluded their joint opinion by stating that they were acting "in observance of the fundamental principles of international human rights law," among which they included victims' and society's rights to know the truth about what happened during the dirty war.[41]

International law made further inroads into the discussion when, invited by CELS, two global NGOs – Human Rights Watch (HRW) and the Center for Justice and International Law (CEJIL) – and the prestigious jurist Eugenio Zaffaroni filed an amicus curiae brief "to subject to the court's consideration some arguments derived from international human rights law related to the state's responsibility with regards to the victims of forced disappearances."[42] The court's decision to accept the brief constituted a landmark in the truth-seeking process for a number of reasons. First, for the first time in Argentine jurisprudence, a federal court was

[40] Cámara de Apelaciones en lo Criminal y Correccional de la Ciudad de Buenos Aires, *Méndez Carreras, Horacio s. presentación en c. Nro. 761 E.S.M.A. Hechos que se denunciaron como ocurridos en el ámbito de la Escuela de Mecánica de la Armada*, ruling of 20 March 1995. On file with the author.

[41] Cámara de Apelaciones en lo Criminal y Correccional de la Ciudad de Buenos Aires, *Mignone, Emilio s/presentación en causa Nro. 761 E.SM.A. Hechos que se denunciaron como ocurridos en el ámbito de la Escuela de Mecánica de la Armada*, ruling of 20 April 1995. See also *Lapacó, Carmen s/presentación en causa nro. 450*, ruling of 18 May 1995. On file with the author.

[42] Cámara de Apelaciones en lo Criminal y Correccional de la Ciudad de Buenos Aires, *C. 761 Hechos ocurridos en el ámbito de la Escuela de Mecánica de la Armada*, ruling of 18 May 1995. On file with the author. My translation.

open to considering arguments beyond those expounded by the parties in a case. Second, the brief incorporated a wealth of information about international law, treaties, doctrine, and jurisprudence that had been absent from the proceedings. Finally, the ruling made it clear that amicus briefs would only be accepted when filed by "non-governmental organizations with a valid and genuine interest in the subject, and proven specialization in it," in "exceptional cases of the magnitude of the present one."[43] This was important because from now on, NGOs' international connections would be allowed to take a prominent role in the domestic judicialization process, endowing international legal arguments with an aura of authority and legitimacy.

The inflow of new legal ideas clearly strengthened the position of the allies of NGOs in the court, providing them with a better case to pursue their commitment to truth and justice. This is how Judge Cattani describes the truth seeking process before and after the inflow of these new legal arguments:

> After the issuing of the pardons some of us decided to reactivate human rights cases very slowly and very cautiously. We didn't want to call the attention of politicians or the media. We were fearful that at some point the Ministry of the Interior would step in and complicate things. The other problem was that some members of the court were staunch Menem supporters.... But we began working on the basis of a bad legal argument. Why did we continue with the investigations? One of the answers was that there were still some unidentified human remains. Other things were also still pending. For example, when victims needed official documents to process their petitions for monetary reparations under Menem's reparations law, they came to the court to request formal proof that their relatives had been victims of state repression.... The entire legal approach changed when CELS intervened in Mignone's case. The whole question of the right to truth was something introduced to us by them. Now we had a much better argument to justify our judicial proceedings, despite the existence of the impunity laws. The "humanitarian" argument was useful, especially at the beginning of the process and in particular when trying to persuade some of my Menemist colleagues, but it did not affirm new rights or establish the basis for future triumphs as the right to truth argument did.[44]

This extract reveals important features of the initial stages of the process of legal preference change. First, the "humanitarian argument" was initially helpful because it highlighted inconsistencies in the legal status quo. The impossibility of launching judicial proceedings meant that families lacked

[43] Ibid.

[44] Interview, Buenos Aires, 20 May 2011.

information about the whereabouts of their relatives, information that they needed, for example, to apply for the reparations scheme. Moreover, there were unidentified human remains, which had to be dealt with at some point. By merely filing requests for information litigants were thus able to play judges' professional duty to identify human remains or assist in administrative processes against their inclination to abide by the formal ban on further investigations. The ensuing thought process preempted behavioral inertia, i.e., the reflex reaction of invoking the amnesties to dismiss any case associated with the dictatorship automatically. Holding contradictory beliefs about how to proceed is likely to have generated the feelings of discomfort identified in Chapter 2 as conducive to persuasion. Indifferent judges reflected on their actions, drawing some of them closer to the victims' perspective on these issues. Second, the testimony suggests that despite the presence of committed judges, litigants still had to exploit the informal contacts afforded by the links forged during pedagogical interventions to supply these actors with adequate technical skills. This was important so that when acting upon their convictions, judges altered the juridical landscape in productive ways. In this case the "humanitarian" argument could only take the victims' case so far, and litigants could not wait for allies such as Cattani to make further innovations ex nihilo and on their own initiative. After all, the legal and political margin for action was too narrow, and the argumentative terrain of the right to truth was doubtless uncharted.

At the end of the day, however, the court decided there were no grounds to insist on obtaining the relevant information. Some recalcitrant judges such as Riva Aramayo continued to offer a formalistic reading of the law: The court could not declare the existence of new rights such as the right to truth. Moreover, she argued that her colleagues could not make exceptions to the judiciary's routine practices invoking the special nature of dictatorship era cases.[45] Others concluded in a second ruling on *Lapacó* that since the authorities had responded to the court's formal request for information by denying the existence of documents about the whereabouts of the disappeared, there was nothing else the judiciary could do. Taking further actions on the basis of the state's international responsibility to investigate, a responsibility that had been partially fulfilled, would amount to a flagrant violation of the rules against

[45] See Riva Aramayo's opinion in Cámara de Apelaciones en lo Criminal y Correccional de la Ciudad de Buenos Aires, *Causa 761 Hechos ocurridos en el ámbito de la Escuela de Mecánica de la Armada*, ruling of 18 July 1995. On file with the author.

double jeopardy. This would also inevitably require judges to inquire about the individual criminal responsibility of members of the armed forces, a course that was barred by the amnesties and Supreme Court jurisprudence.[46]

This made it clear that the acceptance of the new legal ideas was still precarious. Given the general hostility of the political environment to the human rights cause, activists' strategies could not fully convert most judges. Their actions did, however, have the nontrivial effect of empowering committed judges, providing them with technical tools to start carving out alternatives to the legal status quo. When CELS lawyers appealed to the Supreme Court in an effort to expose more judges to their case, they also found support further up in the judiciary. As expected, the Menemist Supreme Court ruled against them, but two judges (Petracchi and Bossert), as well as the solicitor general, embraced the international legal arguments in support of the right to truth. For example, according to the solicitor general, pursuing further investigations did not violate the rules against double jeopardy (CELS 1999). As we shall see, these timid and inconclusive affirmations of the existence of a right to truth would be exploited later on in the process.

Truth seeking gathered momentum in the second half of the decade. As described in the previous section, during this time pedagogical interventions became more ambitious and several federal judges touched by these initiatives started to show a true commitment to the human rights cause. They knew that the armed forces would continue to deny any knowledge about the whereabouts of the disappeared, so they decided to derive more ambitious prerogatives from the notion of a "right to truth" and went beyond submitting formal requests for information. In a rather unorthodox and radical move, criminal courts in various jurisdictions subpoenaed members of the military to question them and started to hold regular hearings to obtain information.

For many scholars, this phenomenon was a direct result of growing international pressures circa 1998, in particular the growing interest in cases of state repression by European judges (e.g. Lutz and Sikkink 2001; Roht Arriaza 2005). According to this view, as these pressures mounted, domestic courts found greater space to inquire about the fate of the disappeared. Although of undeniable importance in putting the question of

[46] See Cortelezzas's opinon in Cámara de Apelaciones en lo Criminal y Correccional de la Ciudad de Buenos Aires, *Causa 761 Hechos ocurridos en el ámbito de la Escuela de Mecánica de la Armada*, ruling of 18 July 1995. On file with the author.

impunity on the global agenda, the Pinochet case in London or the trials in absentia of Argentine generals in Italy and France cannot on their own explain the impressive progress of the truth-seeking effort. Judicial receptivity to these and other international signals is better understood if we take into account the gradual process of legal preference change ignited earlier in the decade. The diffusion of new legal ideas and technical skills from within facilitated productive synergies with subsequent external pressures and demonstration effects.

First, the alliances built with judicial actors in previous years triggered a positive feedback effect on some international legal moves. In fact, committed prosecutors partnered with their European counterparts to facilitate international information flows:

> I went to all the courts that had cases stalled in their dockets and introduced the judges to the Italian prosecutor. I asked for copies of everything the prosecutor needed. With the information the prosecutor obtained via these non-official channels, he now knew exactly what to request via official diplomatic channels. As you can see, putting the judiciary to work, and allowing foreign courts to successfully put pressure on Argentina was a craft![47]

In addition, although ultimately unsuccessful, early domestic victories made possible highly relevant international norm-affirming events. For example, after the Supreme Court had the final say in *Mignone* and *Lapacó*, CELS was in a much better position to look for answers abroad. The NGO filed a complaint with the Inter-American Commission of Human Rights, which led the Menem administration to sign a friendly accord in 1999 committing to finding ways to remedy victims' condition. The solicitor general followed up by instructing prosecutors to "analyze all procedural options within their reach to collaborate with the relatives of the disappeared ... and avoid raising jurisdictional questions ... that could put obstacles to the investigations" (quoted in CELS 1999, my translation). This suggests that international tactics did not trigger, but deepened an ongoing erosion of the impunity regime.

Second, apart from noting this complex domestic and international interactive process, it is also important to bear in mind that the progress of truth seeking beyond those first timid decisions handed down by the City of Buenos Aires Federal Appeals Court required more than just pressures from abroad. Although courts had now recognized the existence of a right to truth, a series of procedural and legal issues had to be resolved before

[47] Federal prosecutor, interview, Buenos Aires, 9 November 2010.

judges were able to gather information actively. In this sense, international pressures would have been inert in the absence of further technical development at home that was able to translate those abstract normative imperatives into actionable causes within the legal field. After all, these criminal courts were being asked to carry out investigations that would not have any criminal consequences. Seen from this angle, truth seeking demanded the disruption of some very basic bureaucratic routines, and judges had to learn how to do it.

From the early 1990s, NGOs worked intensely on developing the doctrinal basis for these unusual legal moves. In 1995, the aforementioned amicus brief filed by CEJIL and HRW on behalf of CELS planted the seed for more assertive behavior, including the issuing of subpoenas to military officers. The brief introduced the idea that courts' responsibility in the search for truth was not limited to promoting administrative acts such as formal requests for information, but also included obtaining testimonies from victims and alleged perpetrators. CEJIL and HRW indicated that courts should identify via these testimonies those individuals who participated in the illegal detentions, as well as those who gave logistical support to the military. This was the doctrine that judges followed in the second half of the decade as NGOs deepened their contacts with key federal courts.

Third, the domestic diffusion of technical capabilities was crucial in order to empower committed judges to withstand internal political pressures contrary to those originating abroad. Litigants' guidance allowed them to justify the appropriateness of their actions in an increasingly hostile context. As judges in several provinces began to subpoena former members of the military, defense attorneys invoked the amnesty laws and argued that these cases should be put under the jurisdiction of military courts (CELS 2000). In one instance, the recalcitrant Court of Cassation agreed. Toward the end of 1999, it ordered the Bahía Blanca Federal Appeals Court to surrender all court documents, and refused to accept duplicates with the intention of fully removing the case from the hands of pro–transitional justice judges. The Supreme Court was quick to support this decision, and effectively stalled the progress of truth trials in Bahía Blanca for more than a year (CELS 2000). Menem's appointees thus continued to work on behalf of the military, evidencing the long-lasting impact of his colonization efforts (CELS 2001). To make matters worse, in addition to these stalling tactics, committed judges had to deal with open acts of defiance, as a growing number of military officers began to ignore the subpoenas. Finally, when some federal judges took even bolder steps and ordered the arrest of army and navy officers who did not want to testify, they were fiercely attacked:

> The conservative media and the political establishment came after us. For example, the federal police in charge of the security of the court stole drugs that had been seized in another case, and when this became public the media accused us of supporting drug-traffickers, of not taking seriously cases involving current as opposed to past criminals. Why were we investigating crimes that took place 30 years ago if we could not be effective in the investigation of contemporary cases? Politicians even filed charges in the Judicial Council, and lots of individuals who were incriminated by witnesses during the hearings, filed libel cases against us.[48]

In this context, affirming their commitment to the truth-seeking crusade in open defiance of the government and their superiors in the judicial hierarchy required more than just courage or international support. Committed judges needed clarification regarding the procedural grounds on which to require the presence of alleged perpetrators in court as part of a noncriminal investigation, let alone arrest them. As one of them explained:

> It was doubtful that we had the power to do this kind of moves. We had constructed a legal space based on the right to truth that allowed us to say, "we want to know certain things," but that wasn't enough. For example in the early stages of the process Massera [N.B. former member of the military junta] agreed to testify in court. Lots of activists and human rights lawyers attended the hearing and they began to ask Massera for documents they thought he had hidden in his house. He agreed to let us look for those documents. When we arrived several journalists asked us if we were conducting an official search. Of course we weren't! We were not allowed to issue that kind of warrant in these cases. We were there because the guy let us in! We had been able to ask questions because he had agreed to it! Formally, we had no power.[49]

Several judicial actors also revealed that human rights organizations, and CELS in particular, used informal contacts to supply the legal basis that judges later used to justify and legitimize unorthodox moves. The following excerpt from an interview with a federal judge illustrates the extent to which this leading organization grounded its strategies of legal contention in a profound understanding of legal preferences as the foundation of judicial behavior. They knew they had to give judges good reasons to act

[48] Interview, Mar del Plata, 16 November 2010.
[49] Interview, Buenos Aires, 20 May 2011.

within the parameters of the law. Qua professionals of the legal field, their allies in the bench could not act out of sheer personal convictions:

> We would not have been able to do many of these things without the intervention of CELS. It was the most active organization, and the most committed to democracy. They never suggested crazy moves and always offered the best juridical backing.... If someone tells you, you should do this or that, and that person has the prestige of Eugenio Zaffaroni, then as a judge you are put in a very different position. It's a way of empowering you to do things.... For example, it was not clear which Code of Criminal Procedures we had to use [during the truth trials]. The new code approved in 1991 or the one valid before that date? Well, our decision was based on the advice given to us by CELS.[50]

What this evidence shows is that the international diffusion process was in some cases preceded and in others accompanied by a crucial domestic one. Human rights lawyers made available a series of innovative legal arguments and persuaded judges to use them in order to expand the sphere of victims' rights. By asking prestigious international organizations and jurists to act on their behalf, they enhanced the legitimacy of their position. As the last extract makes clear, however, these informal pedagogical interventions also answered nontrivial questions about how to conduct the daily court proceedings in this kind of case. Although international human rights law and international norm-affirming events can be very helpful in raising the visibility of the problem of impunity, and in solving the macrojuridical questions at the heart of these processes, they are not designed to address the minutiae of judicial decision making at the domestic level. Exerting public pressure on relevant actors through the media or public demonstrations, or passively expecting international norm-affirming events to win over judges' hearts and minds, clearly would have fallen short of the objective of activating and sustaining these trials. For these strategies do not offer guidance on how to navigate uncharted juridical territories.

The victories obtained in the search for information about the whereabouts of the disappeared demonstrate that encapsulating the human rights issue within the logic of courts and legal proceedings can offset the limitations imposed by a hostile political environment. Litigants used pedagogical interventions to immerse an important group of judicial actors in human rights circles, and to teach them how to defend their acts of defiance legally. They thus unleashed a truth-seeking process that engendered

[50] Interview, Buenos Aires, 7 February 2011.

its own momentum. The truth trials exposed judges to a wealth of evidence of horrendous crimes that further invested them in these cases by making ever more apparent the blatant contradiction behind these uncovered facts and the legal status quo. Judges and prosecutors were thus persuaded that it was their duty as judicial professionals to iron out these inconsistencies, and cemented their belief in the moral imperatives behind victims' demands. This turned them into reliable allies of the pro–transitional justice coalition. As one of them stated in an interview:

> During the days of the truth trials I was accused of malicious prosecution for ordering the arrest of a navy officer who had allegedly raped one of the victims disappeared in a clandestine detention center. He was obviously in jail for only a few hours because the impunity laws were still in place.... Of course I anticipated the political consequences that my decision would have, but I didn't care! If there is one thing I learnt during this process is that I care about what victims think of me. I care that victims think "at last I found a judge that I can trust."[51]

In fact, this rekindled sense of professional mission could not be stopped by either Menem or his successor, UCR's Fernando de la Rúa. The trials became so institutionalized that hearings continued well into the 2000s when there were no longer legal barriers to pursue more orthodox criminal strategies.

Persuading Judges to Exercise Their Duty to Punish the Perpetrators

In addition to the explosion of truth trials, there was intense judicial activity in another set of cases related to state repression: the abduction of babies born in clandestine detention centers. According to Abuelas, an organization created to find the missing children, detainees gave birth to approximately five hundred babies, who were then illegally adopted (Abuelas de Plaza de Mayo 2007, 2009). The progress made in these cases in the late 1990s led to a historic ruling declaring the unconstitutionality of the amnesty laws in 2001.

Despite not being formally barred by the amnesties, the abductions involved a series of challenging legal issues.[52] Litigants had to build a case

[51] Interview, La Plata, 13 November 2010.

[52] The moral outrage caused by these crimes made it harder for politicians to include them in the amnesty laws. In addition, on several occasions both the Alfonsín and Menem administrations supported Abuelas's cause. For example, Menem's secretary for human rights invited one of Abuelas's lawyers to a United Nations preparatory meeting for the Convention of the Rights of the Child and helped them to lobby successfully for the inclusion of articles that recognized the human right to an identity, and the international responsibility of states

that proved the existence of a systematic plan that permitted the illegal adoption of babies. This was important in order to charge junta leaders on the basis of their command responsibility, and to show that although six of these crimes were included in the 1985 ruling against them, new prosecutions would not constitute an instance of double jeopardy. Once again, litigants galvanized indifferent judicial actors by planning diffusion efforts aimed at transforming judges' legal preferences and sense of professional duty. Most of the cases filed by Abuelas's lawyers fell into the hands of two investigative federal courts in the Buenos Aires area led by Judges Servini and Marquevich, who thus became the locus of activists' persuasion efforts.

Judge Marquevich was the first to issue a favorable ruling. In 1997, he indicted a military doctor responsible for delivering babies in clandestine maternity wards. A year later, he shocked the public when he put former president Videla in preventive imprisonment accusing him of designing a systematic plan to abduct children. The head of Abuelas's legal team explained the impact of the ruling in the following terms: "That day many victims felt that they no longer had reasons to be afraid. We began to receive tons of phone calls and letters from people who were now ready to talk, and tell things about their experiences in the clandestine detention centers."[53] Following Marquevich's lead, a few weeks later Judge Servini issued a similar arrest warrant against Videla's colleague in the military junta, Emilio Massera. In January 1999, another federal judge did the same with seven other high-ranking former military officers (CELS 1998; Skaar 2011).

Marquevich's decision had important legal consequences. Echoing the doctrines that human rights organizations had been trying to diffuse among judicial actors since the early 1990s, Marquevich affirmed the supremacy of international law. He also set an important precedent by being one of the first judges in the country to use the notion of crimes against humanity. He reasoned that since this criminal definition is derived from customary law, it was not subject to statutory limitations. He also explained that the nature of the crimes allowed rules about statutory limitations to be set by treaties and international conventions signed after their perpetration, thus granting an exception to the legality principle (CELS 1999: 98–99). The terms of the indictment allowed the victims later to question an interlocutory appeal filed by the defendant, which claimed that the decision

to protect that right. According to the head of Abuelas's legal team during the 1990s, this strengthened their case before domestic courts. Interview, Buenos Aires, 2 December 2010.

53 Interview, Buenos Aires, 2 December 2010.

violated rules regarding double jeopardy.[54] Human rights lawyers argued that not only was the criminal definition invoked in the ruling different from the one used in 1985, but also since Videla was the one who planned the illegal operation, he was in fact still perpetrating the crimes by not telling the truth about the whereabouts of those children.

As we saw in previous sections, some of the judges and prosecutors who were at the forefront of the truth trials were connected to human rights circles, especially after participating in various pedagogical activities organized by the NGOs. Understanding the spread of the new legal orthodoxy among them is easy: Their proximity to the community of victims and their lawyers made these judges more receptive to legal arguments that allowed them to back radical departures from existing jurisprudence. By contrast, the federal judges who indicted former junta leaders between 1997 and 1999 in abduction cases were not natural allies of the movement. In fact, the level of informal contacts between litigants and these judges was low. For example, some of the arrest warrants took activists by surprise. As a result, for the most part litigants diffused international legal arguments via formal briefs, but used information obtained during the few informal encounters with the judges to adjust their strategy in ways that enhanced the credibility of their experimental ideas. From judges' professional point of view, impunity began to look incompatible with strong evidence of horrendous crimes.

Since 1996, litigants had bombarded Marquevich with very similar and related cases. This led him to identify criminal patterns indicative of a broad and systematic criminal plan, a realization that was compatible with the legal reasoning expounded in the formal briefs written by Abuelas's lawyers to justify the indictment. The systematic nature of the repression indeed resonated with international criminal definitions, activating the jurisdiction of international law in domestic juridical proceedings. This is how the head of the NGO's legal team explained the judge's decision making process:

> [We] explained our arguments in our written communications with the court. However, in conversations I had with him as part of the natural relationship between a lawyer and a judge, I noticed that the numerous cases we filed had persuaded him that these were not isolated events. That is exactly what we

[54] The defendants filed several interlocutory appeals in the Buenos Aires Federal Appeals Court invoking statutes of limitations, the absence of direct criminal responsibility, and double jeopardy. Although some of these former military officers were granted the privilege of house arrest or even released from preventive imprisonment, the court did not accept the interlocutory appeals, leaving the cases open. In these abduction cases, the supremacy of international legal principles was thus affirmed at two different levels of the judiciary (CELS 2000, 2001).

> needed to bring Videla to court, so we clearly had something to work with. After I realized this change in the judge's perception of the cases I immediately requested that the court summon a former military doctor who had witnessed the crimes. Fortunately, he decided to tell everything. He even answered the questions about the chain of command that I had requested the court to ask. He explained the location of the clandestine maternity wards, the individuals who gave him the orders, the officers present when the orders were given, etc. This is how the chain of command finally came to light, as did the criminal responsibility of superior officers. A week later Marquevich arrested Videla.[55]

In Servini's case, these strong indications of a carefully designed plan orchestrated from above also inspired an alternative sense of professional duty. Reflecting on the absence of adequate institutional responses to victims' legitimate demands, she explained her decision in the following terms: "As a mother and a grandmother I understood these women. I would have gone mad if that had happened to me. I felt that something had to be done."[56]

As argued in Chapter 2, the dynamics of court proceedings can insulate juridical issues from political ones by directing the attention of judicial actors to evidentiary and legal questions that highlight their responsibility not to turn a blind eye to blatant wrongdoing. Suggestive evidence of state repression and exposure to victims' ordeals narrowed the space to invoke technical excuses to dismiss these inconvenient cases. Judges were thus compelled at least to consider available ways to find a legal remedy, pushing their legal preferences closer to international law. In these particular cases, enlisting indifferent judges in the ranks of the pro–transitional justice coalition was no small feat, as the president's position was explicitly opposed to the arrests. For example, Menem led the case in favor of the idea that the pardons prohibited a second prosecution for the same crimes (Skaar 2011). But concerns about potential political retaliation lost centrality when judicial actors were confronted with reliable testimonies indicating the responsibility of certain individuals in the perpetration of abhorrent crimes.[57] As one of the human rights lawyers told me, "Once we managed to separate discussions about the facts and the law from the ideological and political debate, judges began to respond."[58]

[55] Interview, Buenos Aires, 2 December 2010.

[56] Interview, Buenos Aires, 5 November 2010.

[57] Marquevich's decision clearly upset certain sectors of the establishment. Years later, these animosities took a toll on his judicial career when he was accused of misconduct in these and other cases, and impeached.

[58] Interview, Buenos Aires, 6 December 2010.

Apart from providing another arena for activating this legal logic and defying the limits of political possibility, child abduction cases also gave human rights organizations the chance to strike their first blow against the impunity laws. In the judicial cases analyzed thus far, neither litigants nor judges questioned the constitutionality of the amnesties. As a result, when the judiciary accepted arguments about the legal viability of truth-seeking trials, or in favor of the indictment of military officers for having planned the abduction of hundreds of babies, this revealed a series of contradictions at the heart of the Argentine judicialization process. Victims could discover what happened to their loved ones and identify those responsible, but could not ask the judiciary to prosecute the wrongdoers. Similarly, police and military officers could go to jail for abducting children, but no one could ask a court to punish them for the torture and murder of the parents of those children. In 2000, human rights NGOs found a case in which these contradictions became crystal clear, enabling them to convince a judge to declare the unconstitutionality of the impunity laws. As in previous instances of the judicialization process, framing the case around these inconsistencies was an important foundation of the persuasion process, as it disrupted bureaucratic inertia.

Victoria Poblete was kidnapped with her parents in the 1970s and was later given to a family with close connections to the military. After Victoria recovered her identity, Abuelas's legal team filed a criminal lawsuit against her adopted parents in Judge Cavallo's federal investigative court. The available evidence in this case was exceptionally conclusive, to the point that Abuelas knew who had been responsible for transporting the baby from the clandestine detention center to her new home. Knowing the identity of those who had stolen the baby also meant knowing the identity of those who had been involved in the disappearance of the biological parents. CELS lawyers took note of this, asked their colleagues at Abuelas for permission to intervene in their case, and filed an interlocutory appeal in the same court demanding that the judge also prosecute the defendants for the crime of forced disappearance.[59] They invoked myriad international legal instruments to persuade Judge Cavallo that the impunity laws were invalid and could not stand in the way of justice. On 6 March 2001, the judge responded favorably, striking down the laws.[60]

[59] The internal deliberations within CELS and between CELS and Abuelas's lawyers were confirmed during interviews with members of both organizations.

[60] Juzgado Nacional en lo Criminal y Correccional Federal Nro. 4 de la Capital Federal, *Causa Nro. 8686/2000 caratulada Simón, Julio, Del Cerro, Juan Antonio s/sustracción de menores de*

The ruling was a remarkable achievement because at this point not even the Inter-American Court of Human Rights had declared the amnesties illegal under international law. Cavallo explained that the recognition of *jus cogens* as a source of law in Article 118 of the constitution, as well as the constitutional status of several treaties, allowed him to conclude that customary international regulations against crimes against humanity were operative in the 1970s. He was therefore entitled to use this category to define the forced disappearance of Victoria's parents. Not prosecuting these crimes would also amount to a violation of the state's international responsibilities, which in turn justified the nullification of the amnesties.[61]

It is important to reconstruct at a microlevel the dynamics that made this radical breakthrough in the judicialization process possible and assess whether they support my theoretical assumptions about judicial behavior and the process that leads to transitional justice victories. What impact did the political environment have on the court's decision? Did the judge feel constrained by the traditional legal orthodoxy? Did his legal preferences change in the process? Did human rights litigants trigger those changes by activating informal diffusion strategies?

As mentioned, in 2000, CELS lawyers began to articulate their strategy with Abuelas. Before formally filing the brief, the first step was to contact the judge informally.[62] This was not difficult for two reasons. First, the judge had a personal relationship with the president of CELS. Second, his clerks were immersed in human rights networks. For example, they appear in the attendance records of the seminars organized in the early 1990s. During these meetings CELS lawyers confirmed that the judge shared their discomfort relative to the contradictions crystallized in the case: The defendants were being indicted for stealing a baby but could not be indicted for causing the disappearance of her parents. The next move involved assuring the judge that it was legally possible to remove the legal obstacles posed by the amnesty laws. In an interview, Cavallo explained the problem as follows:

> It was a very new topic. It raised all sorts of intractable philosophical and legal questions.... At some point we realized that we had to violate some

10 años, en particular, sobre el contenido de la presentación del Centro de Estudios Legales y Sociales, ruling of 6 March 2001. On file with the author.

61 Examples of the extensive academic commentary triggered by the ruling can be found in CELS (2008b).

62 Human rights lawyers, interviews, Buenos Aires, 2 December 2010 and 20 December 2010.

crucial principles of criminal law, in particular the legality principle. We needed to make sure we got that right.[63]

The judge felt that he needed the appropriate legal tools in order to depart from standard legal praxis. This was particularly important in Cavallo's case, because as he also stated in the interview, these were questions he had never considered before. In other words, he did not belong to a group of scholars or practitioners who had long been trying to find a legal solution to the problem of the amnesties. Legal preferences mattered: He was not willing to destroy "all that we know and hold dear about modern criminal law." In his words, "I seriously evaluated whether I could reach that decision or if it was nonsense. It was an experiment, and it could fail."[64]

Having solid legal foundations was not only important for professional reasons, but also for political ones. Cavallo knew that if he did not uphold the laws, his career could be in trouble. After President de la Rúa took office in 1999, his administration systematically tried to avoid adding a conflict with the military to its already long list of political and economic problems. For example, the president denied all requests by European governments to extradite members of the military who were being investigated by foreign courts (Skaar 2011). Consistent with this policy, when the administration found out that Cavallo was considering striking down the laws, the minister of justice personally lobbied him. In this context, the judge needed a good case in order to defy the government.

When Cavallo was finally persuaded, he sealed a deal with CELS by asking them to file a request formally to nullify the Punto Final and Due Obedience Laws. Litigants had to make sure to cite as many international precedents as possible.[65] A brief drafted by a prestigious institution such as CELS would not only provide him with a large amount of additional information, but also send the government the signal that he was not acting alone. The first ruling declaring the unconstitutionality of the impunity laws was therefore a "collaborative"[66] effort, in which human rights lawyers and activists put to work their contacts within the judiciary informally to persuade a judge to act in their favor.

Consistent with my theoretical expectations, litigants succeeded because they took legal preferences seriously as an important dimension

[63] Interview, Buenos Aires, 21 October 2010.
[64] Ibid.
[65] This was confirmed during interviews with both the judge and two human rights lawyers involved in the case.
[66] Interview, Buenos Aires, 21 October 2010.

of judicial decision making. By shifting the judge's legal vision toward international law, CELS activated a professional space for innovative judicial behavior. This idea was nicely condensed in an interview with one of the members of the City of Buenos Aires Federal Appeals Court that nine months later upheld Cavallo's ruling:

> During these informal exchanges with CELS's lawyers we often told them: "give us more of this and less of that." We could negotiate with them. They understood our needs. CELS knew perfectly well that they needed to put their best legal talent to draft those briefs, and that they couldn't just bring the victims to move us. They had to design and offer us clever juridical solutions. That is exactly what they did.[67]

Another judge made a similar point about the importance of CELS's pedagogical interventions and their focus on the technical aspect of judicial decision making:

> CELS provided us with the intellectual resources we needed. They organized conferences, published books, and even built strong personal ties with some members of the judiciary. I remember once telling them "what do you want me to do, I have my hands tied by the amnesty laws." They then intervened and told me "That is not true, here are all these alternative solutions to put an end to impunity."[68]

Summary

Judiciaries are coveted by myriad groups who seek to entrench legal preferences compatible with their interests. The institutionalization of legal visions engenders bureaucratic inertias that lead to long-term biases in judicial decision making, favoring solutions that have important implications for the distribution of power in politics and society. The struggle over the allegiances of Argentine judicial actors in the 1990s is a clear example of these dynamics. The anti–transitional justice coalition moved first, successfully colonizing the bench with judges who agreed, both legally and politically, with the perpetuation of impunity. This significantly narrowed the pool of judicial actors who could be successfully approached by victim groups. NGOs nevertheless focused their persuasion efforts on key courts, and achieved important victories. Their highly skilled legal teams allowed them to understand the crucial role played by legal preferences in courts' behavior. They intelligently crafted

[67] Interview, Buenos Aires, 20 May 2011.
[68] Interview, Buenos Aires, 26 October 2010.

formal and informal legal moves that equipped their allies on the bench, who were at a loss as to how to justify challenges to the status quo legally, with appropriate tools. Their pedagogical interventions also led international legal ideas to make inroads into the minds of indifferent judges. By encapsulating the human rights question within the logic of the law, NGOs eased the constraints imposed by a hostile political environment, and gained the favor of judges such as Marquevich and Cavallo as well as of those who pushed and sustained the truth trials between 1995 and the mid-2000s. As we shall see, however, the limited reach of these pedagogical interventions and the resilience of recalcitrant judges erected serious obstacles to the progress of cases, even after the political climate shifted decisively in their favor.

The Explosion of Transitional Justice in the 2000s and the Limits of Persuasion

Until the early 2000s judicial activity in the area of transitional justice focused for the most part on the truth and child abduction trials analyzed previously. The 2001 ruling paved the way for the filing of new criminal lawsuits against former military and police officers for the disappearance, torture, and murder of political prisoners. In response to petitions to reopen the cases stalled by the amnesties, several federal courts concluded that even though Cavallo's decision lacked confirmation by the Court of Cassation or the Supreme Court, they could still initiate proceedings. Instead of automatically invoking the amnesty laws, some judges argued that their validity had to be explored on a case-by-case basis after conducting a thorough investigation.

The course of the judicialization process changed dramatically between 2004 and 2010 when the Argentine Supreme Court handed down a series of rulings declaring the inapplicability of statutory limitations in cases of crimes against humanity, the retroactive unconstitutionality of the amnesty laws, and the unconstitutionality of the pardons (ADC 2008: 435–458).[69] The highest court in the land thus endorsed the international legal case for transitional justice, triggering an explosion of trials in Federal Oral Tribunals (FOTs). FOT No. 5 of the City of Buenos Aires

[69] Landmark rulings include Corte Suprema de Justicia de la Nación, *Arancibia Clavel, Enrique Lautaro y otros s/ homicidio calificado y asociación ilícita*, ruling of 24 August 2004; Corte Suprema de Justicia de la Nación, *Simón, Julio Hector y otros s/privación ilegítima de la libertad*, ruling of 14 June 2005. Corte Suprema de Justicia de la Nación, *Videla, Jorge Rafael s/ recurso extraordinario*, ruling of 26 April 2010. On file with the author.

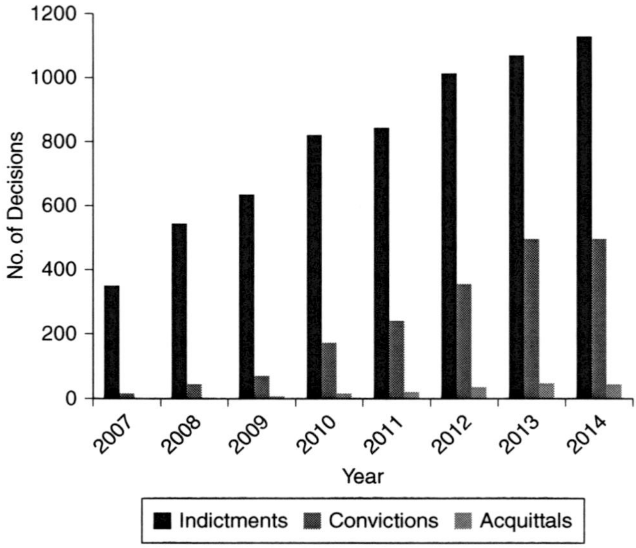

Figure 3.1. Trial Statistics (2007–2014).
Note: Some individuals have been indicted and convicted more than once. The indictment figure for 2014 only includes data up to July.
Source: Indictments: Solicitor General's Office; Convictions and Acquittals: CELS.

issued the first condemnatory ruling in 2006, sentencing a former military officer to twenty-five years in prison.[70]

The evolution of criminal trials after 2006 was dramatic. As Figure 3.1 shows, the annual number of indictments nearly quadrupled between 2007 and 2014, rising from 349 to 1,128. During these years, the number of convictions also increased exponentially, especially after 2010. Whereas in 2009 there were 130 convictions, by 2014 courts had handed down 1,883. The overall conviction rate for this period is an impressive 91.7 percent. These rulings were handed down in 135 trials (Figure 3.2). After carefully reading these decisions, it is clear that, in general, judges rejected the enforcement of statutes of limitations, defined the crimes using international legal categories, and gave a prominent role to indirect evidence, contextual factors, and witness testimonies to establish individual criminal responsibility, especially in those cases in which the accused were not the immediate perpetrators.[71]

[70] Tribunal Oral Federal No. 5 de la Capital Federal, *Causas N° 1.056 y1.207*, ruling of 4 August 2006. On file with the author.

[71] All rulings are on file with the author.

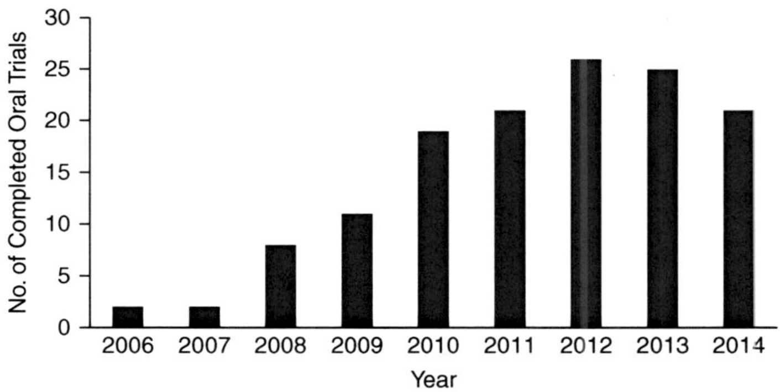

Figure 3.2. Number of Completed Oral Trials by Year (2006–2014).
Source: CELS.

This dramatic turnaround in the fate of human rights cases is explained by a variety of factors. The first is the diffusion of a new legal orthodoxy by human rights organizations initiated during the 1990s, made authoritative by Supreme Court rulings issued between 2004 and 2010. The interview data presented in the previous section suggested that in the 1990s the judicial actors who were pioneers in adopting international human rights norms were at first doubtful and insecure about taking those jurisprudential steps. The following testimonies illustrate how different the attitude of judges and prosecutors involved in the new wave of trials is:

> The Supreme Court rulings in *Simón* and other cases shook the minds of many people. They were the outcome of the consolidation of a new current of ideas within the judiciary. Today, for example, nobody questions the validity of customary international law as a source of law. What we do discuss among colleagues is the question of how to make sure that these trials finish as quickly as possible in order to close a chapter in Argentine history.[72]

> There is no problem with investigating these cases even after the exhaustion of statutes of limitations. Statutes of limitations are not a fundamental principle of criminal law. They have to do with process, and procedural rules can be changed without affecting the rights of the defendants. It's not an issue.[73]

> Many people outside the judiciary, especially legal practitioners, don't understand what we are talking about when we say that prior to the 1970s

[72] FOT judge, interview, Buenos Aires, 9 February 2011.
[73] Investigative Federal Court judge, interview, Buenos Aires, 19 November 2010.

> there was an international consensus crystallized in principles of international human rights law that makes it possible to establish, for instance, the inapplicability of statutory limitations for crimes against humanity, or that any law that contradicts these principles is invalid. At least in this court this is no longer a debate.[74]

> We are not violating the principle of legality. These are simply cases that we are not used to investigating on a daily basis, and they require us to use international legal norms that we don't normally invoke.... I grew up intellectually in the 1990s, when the truth trials were under way. I was a student and then a young practitioner during those years, so as the judicialization process moved forward I organically incorporated those new ideas. The ones who did have to be persuaded and transformed in their legal visions were those who took the first steps towards truth and justice. They belong to a different generation.[75]

As these quotes indicate, the new legal discourse became internalized among some members of the judiciary, thus replacing the bureaucratic routines that in the past led to formalistic patterns of judicial decision making. For example, the problem of statutory limitations became a non-issue. By adhering to new juridical standards, many judges see investigating and punishing grave human rights violations as their mission to fulfill and as part of the international responsibilities of the Argentine state. Some of the testimonies also highlight the impact of generational change. A new cohort of future judges, prosecutors, and clerks grew up intellectually in an academic and professional environment in which novel issues were being debated. NGOs' diffusion efforts altered the terms of the debate. In addition to this doctrinal transformation, the litigation efforts of the 1990s led courts to amass a wealth of evidence. This greatly facilitated the task of issuing indictments and handing down prison sentences in the following decade. Without the emerging legal consensus and this readily available evidence, which human rights NGOs helped to create, it is unlikely that the judiciary qua institution would have been able to process the avalanche of cases that flooded their dockets in the 2000s effectively and efficiently.

Changes in the political environment also improved the chances of success of the judicialization process. The arrival of Néstor Kirchner (Peronist Party) in 2003 put an ally of the human rights movement in the presidential palace. In his first two years in office, he promoted a series of signature policies in the area of transitional justice. For example, he systematically

[74] FOT judge, interview, Buenos Aires, 11 February 2011.

[75] Federal prosecutor, interview, Buenos Aires, 26 November 2010.

retired army generals who publicly expressed support for the dictatorship, pushed for the repeal of the amnesty laws by parliament in 2003,[76] changed the composition of the Supreme Court by appointing pro–transitional justice justices between 2003 and 2005, created a special team in the Solicitor General's Office charged with monitoring the investigations conducted all over the country and providing technical support to prosecutors,[77] and instructed his human rights secretary to act as a claimant on behalf of the state in cases filed in federal courts (Skaar 2011; CELS 2011).[78]

For some, Kirchner's leadership is enough to explain the phenomenon (e.g. Roehrig 2009). The chief prosecutor in the 1985 trial echoed this conventional wisdom when he compared current trials with his own experience: "It's like hunting lions in the zoo."[79] In other words, the combination of a nonexistent military threat and a supportive administration meant that victims no longer faced obstacles in the quest for justice. But was the achievement of hundreds of prison sentences as easy as hunting lions in the zoo? It is certainly plausible to argue that the diffusion of international legal ideas among federal judicial actors was a trivial background condition and that later changes in the political environment are what ultimately explain why we observe a new wave of criminal trials. In this part of the chapter, however, I will present evidence that challenges this account and reinforces the explanatory centrality of legal preferences and judicial change. Geographical and temporal patterns of judicial decision making during the 2000s suggest that a sizable portion of the judiciary did not automatically give in to the president's demands. Legal preferences mediated the response of judicial actors to these external stimuli. In fact, further changes inside the judicial branch were still necessary to bring about this remarkable outcome. Although the new political climate certainly catalyzed more effective strategies of judicial transformation on the side of litigants, these still had to be designed and implemented in order to remove judicial blockages made up of resilient pockets of recalcitrance and bureaucratic inertia.

[76] In 1998 congress had already repealed the laws with no retroactive effects. Both repeals were symbolic gestures. Notwithstanding, the law approved by congress in 2003 led the Buenos Aires Federal Appeals Court to send the files it had accumulated during the truth trials to investigative federal courts. This precipitated the start of new investigations before the Supreme Court nullified the amnesties.

[77] On the creation of this special unit see Resolución PGN 14/07, Procuración General de la Nación, 7 March 2007. On file with the author.

[78] These policies were continued by Kirchner's successor, Cristina Fernández (2007–2015).

[79] Interview, Buenos Aires, 20 December 2010.

Bureaucratic Inertia and Recalcitrance

I begin by showing that in the jurisdictions or legal issue areas in which the diffusion of the new legal orthodoxy by NGOs was limited, changes in the political environment did not lead judges to abide by a powerful president's intense policy preferences. This demonstrates the importance of changes in legal preferences. In some cases, particularly that of the Court of Cassation created and packed by Menem in the early 1990s, judges continued to be loyal to their anti–transitional justice patrons. In others, judicial actors held onto their preexisting legal preferences in debates about the rules that govern judicial proceedings in cases of crimes against humanity, in ways that put them at odds with the goals of victims and the administration. And yet another group of judges found it difficult to deal effectively with proceedings that exceeded their technical knowledge and fundamentally defied their routines of legal praxis.

The Court of Cassation showed a notorious lack of commitment to the progress of human rights cases in the initial stages of the new wave of the judicialization process. This is hardly surprising given that until 2008, seven of Menem's thirteen original appointees were still occupying seats in the court. For example, by December 2010 the court had only reviewed nine of the rulings handed down by FOTs. Between 2006 and 2010, it took the judges an average of 15.6 months to decide whether or not they would uphold lower court decisions. Data from 2012 also show that the cases that were still pending confirmation had been in the court's docket for up to a maximum of 28 months. As with the truth trials of the 1990s, moreover, these judges paralyzed important cases.[80] The court, for instance, shelved the case involving the crimes perpetrated in the largest clandestine detention center (ESMA) for more than a year because the second and fourth chambers could not agree on which one had jurisdiction over the interlocutory appeals filed prior to the trial stage.[81]

The Court of Cassation's handling of preventive imprisonments was also a matter of intense controversy. Before cases reach the trial stage, defendants are often put under arrest. According to Argentine law, preventive imprisonments can only last for a maximum of three years. If at the end of that period the accused has not received a condemnatory ruling, s/he should be released until the trial. Human rights lawyers claim

[80] These figures are based on my own calculations on the basis of data found at www.cels.org.ar (last accessed 16 September 2014).

[81] The Court of Cassation is divided into four chambers with three members each.

that these rules should not apply to cases of crimes against humanity because, among other reasons, the defendants can use their political connections to flee the country if set free before the trial. In a clear act of defiance, between 2006 and 2011, the Court of Cassation ordered the release of numerous military officers. Interestingly, not even the strongest and most direct political pressures led the judges to change their position on the subject (or to accelerate the confirmation rate of FOTs' rulings, for that matter).

The events that followed the 2008 release of Alfredo Astíz, who was an emblem of the dictatorship's repressive plan, offer an opportunity to assess the behavior of the court vis-à-vis these external stimuli systematically.[82] The day after the court's decision, Kirchner's wife and successor, President Cristina Fernández, appeared at an event organized by human rights NGOs and publicly shamed the judges, accusing them of trying to perpetuate impunity.[83] To step up the pressure, three months later human rights groups filed an impeachment request against the judges who signed the release. These attacks were launched in a context characterized by a unified government, and a powerful president with clear and strong preferences regarding this issue. Moreover many of the judges in the court had no tenure security.[84] If the strategic model of judicial behavior is correct, under these conditions, judges should have responded favorably to the threats, lowering the rate of releases. By contrast, if orthodox routines of legal interpretation or recalcitrance were at play, we should not observe such differences across time.

In order to test this proposition, I analyzed decision making patterns in 232 rulings handed down by the Second Chamber of the Court of Cassation on preventive imprisonments between 2007 and 2010.[85] I coded the rulings 1 if they upheld the arrest and 0 if they released the prisoner. I then ran two separate bivariate regressions to explore whether the rate of releases decreased after politics intervened by putting the judges in the spotlight, thus moving strategic considerations to the fore. Figure 3.3 presents the model exploring the impact of the president's menacing speech, and Figure 3.4 shows the results of the model exploring the impact of the

[82] Astíz was responsible for the disappearance of the founder of Mothers of Plaza de Mayo.

[83] *Página 12*, 19 December 2008.

[84] Some of the judges in the Second Chamber were provisional judges, temporarily sitting in for retired judges. Evidence suggests they coveted a permanent position. In fact, they applied for one when the Judicial Council launched the official appointment process.

[85] The Second Chamber is the one that concentrates most of the cases of human rights violations. Moreover its members were the ones attacked by the president.

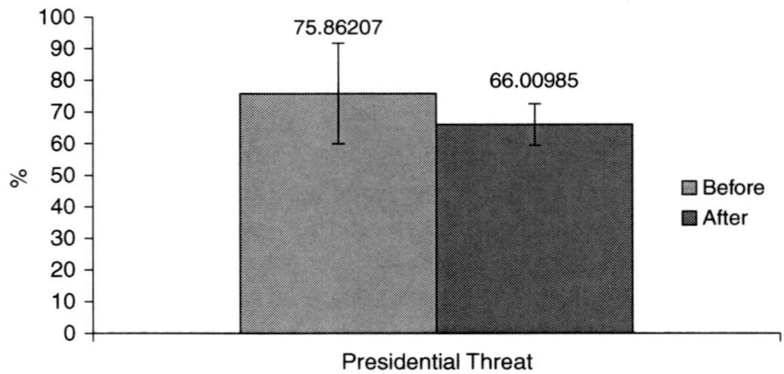

Figure 3.3. Decisions on Preventive Imprisonments by the Court of Cassation before and after the President's Threat (2007–2010).
Note: Bivariate regression. Whiskers represent 95 percent confidence intervals.
Source: Court of Cassation.

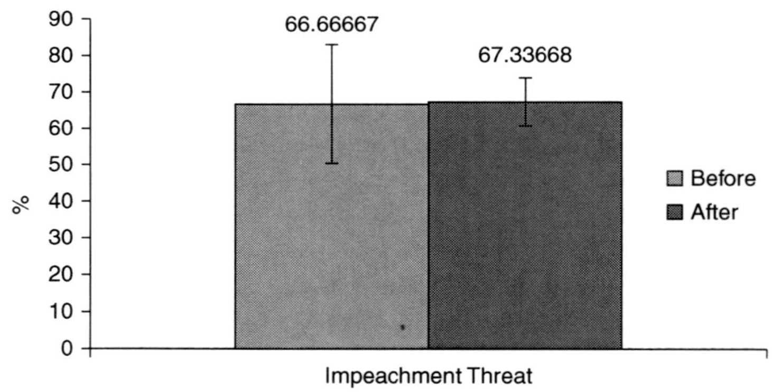

Figure 3.4. Decisions on Preventive Imprisonments by the Court of Cassation before and after the Impeachment Threat (2007–2010).
Note: Bivariate regression. Whiskers represent 95 percent confidence intervals.
Source: Court of Cassation.

aforementioned impeachment request. In neither model is the effect significant, suggesting that judges did not behave opportunistically. One of the judges confirmed this in an interview: "After the threats we continued to rule as we saw fit."[86]

[86] Interview, Buenos Aires, 16 December 2010.

Human rights activists were certainly correct in pointing out that among Menem's appointees, the decision to overturn preventive imprisonments was motivated by their recalcitrance. Long-standing membership in the anti–transitional justice coalition led these judges to obstruct human rights cases and score points for the defendants. But among the newest members of the court, i.e., those who were not the product of court packing efforts in the early 1990s, the question seems to have been one of strict legality. In other words, upholding the imprisonments ran contrary to established legal preferences. When asked about the harsh critiques he received from NGOs and the government, one judge explained that by releasing the prisoners he did not intend to undermine the judicialization process:

> We had to rule on preventive imprisonments that had expired 6 years ago. In non–human rights cases we always apply the same criteria, the criteria we teach our university students. Why would we change it?... Questions such as the applicability of statutory limitations have all been answered, and I personally endorse the solutions offered by the Supreme Court. Torturers should know that they cannot rely on the absence of a written law defining crimes against humanity in order to avoid trial. Disappearing people is against any basic moral standard, even though the crime was not included in the country's criminal code. But questions about process are still unresolved. There is a debate, and my views do not coincide with those of human rights organizations.[87]

It is indeed possible that in addition to recalcitrance, the court's opposition was the product of principled rejection by some judges of part of the new juridical orthodoxy promoted by the human rights movement.[88] The issue of preventive imprisonments, for instance, was never included in the discussions during the pedagogical interventions or the truth trials conducted in the 1990s. It surfaced with the progress of criminal prosecutions in the following decade. The uneven penetration of new ideas and values may thus help us understand the absence of a more robust consensus among nonrecalcitrant judges in certain areas of the broader legal debate.

The Court of Cassation delays in processing appeals as well as its decisions regarding preventive imprisonments are illustrative of how

[87] Interview, Buenos Aires, 26 October 2010.

[88] His positions on other legal issues in the transitional justice debate give credibility to this statement. For example, he voted with the majority in a decision striking down Menem's presidential pardons even before the Supreme Court's 2010 ruling. Cámara Nacional de Casación Penal, *Videla, Jorge Rafael y Massera, Emilio Eduardo s/ recurso de casación*, ruling of 3 July 2009. On file with the author.

Table 3.1. *Indictments Filed in FOTs (December 2010)*

Jurisdiction (province)	Indictments	Filed in FOTs	Indictments Filed in FOTs, %	Intensity of Truth Trials During the 1990s
Chaco	63	36	57.14	Low
Misiones	19	10	52.63	Low
Córdoba	319	150	47.02	High
City of Buenos Aires	380	138	36.32	High
Tucumán	129	42	32.56	Low
Province of Buenos Aires	314	93	29.62	High
Santa Fe	102	30	29.41	High
Rio Negro	160	35	21.88	Low
Chubut	29	5	17.24	Low
Salta/Jujuy	88	14	15.91	Low
Mendoza	466	61	13.10	Low
Entre Ríos	28	1	3.57	Low

Source: Solicitor General's Office. The total number of indictments is higher than the one reported in Figure 3.1 because here I count each indictment, not each indicted individual.

unreformed legal preferences and recalcitrance added tensions to the judicialization process, despite the presence of a strong executive with salient preferences vis-à-vis the outcome of the trials. Another example of judicial resistance is found when one compares courts in the City of Buenos Aires, the Province of Buenos Aires, Córdoba, and Santa Fe, with courts in the rest of the country, where the diffusion strategies designed by litigants in the 1990s were not deployed. In order to take a look at this geographical variation, Table 3.1 uses as an indicator of performance the rate at which indictments issued by investigative federal courts were filed in FOTs to initiate oral trials (column 4). The chosen indicator is useful for three reasons.[89] First, it controls for the size of the docket. The indicator shows the extent to which cases advance to the trial stage, irrespective of the number of individuals under investigation or those who receive

[89] Ideally the analysis would also incorporate the rate at which the alleged perpetrators mentioned in the dockets were indicted by investigative judges. Unfortunately I could not get that information.

indictments. Second, the indicator reflects the impact of the stalling tactics or the inefficiency of appeals courts in each jurisdiction. The reason why indictments cannot be automatically sent to the trial courts is that federal appeals courts must usually decide on a series of legal issues raised by defendants in interlocutory appeals. Appellate judges can therefore delay the progress of the case by not resolving those appeals in due time. Finally, I focus on 2010 because among the years that make up the initial stage of the new wave of transitional justice, it is the one with the highest number of oral trials. This suggests that enough time had passed since the onset of the process for cases to have cleared procedural hurdles and reached the trial stage.

Although the relationship between the rate reported in column 4 and the holding of truth trials in the 1990s is far from perfect ($r = 0.26$), there is an identifiable pattern. The average rate among those jurisdictions that had truth trials in the 1990s is 35.6, whereas that of the provinces in the interior of the country is 26.8. These differences suggest that those federal appeals courts in which human rights organizations did not litigate cases in the 1990s were less willing and able to process the cases that landed on their dockets in the following decade. As a result of the absence of truth trials and diffusion efforts, activists had no opportunities to build alliances with judges, expose them to new arguments and a wealth of evidence about the abhorrent crimes perpetrated by the military, and, ultimately, change their legal preferences. When the judicialization process resumed in the 2000s, these judicial actors were less well versed in the new legal orthodoxy and poorly trained in the investigative and juridical techniques needed to work these cases efficiently and effectively. In addition, appellate judges who were not targeted by human rights organizations were more likely to be unsympathetic to their cause, appropriate dockets, and intentionally delay the progress of the cases. Let us analyze how bureaucratic inertia and recalcitrance also played a role among these judges.

With regard to the impact of bureaucratic inertia, interview evidence gathered during fieldwork is illustrative. The judicial actors I interviewed made it abundantly clear that human rights cases were disruptive of the routines and standard practices to which judges and prosecutors in the interior of the country are accustomed. Those with no experience in the truth trials had an especially hard time understanding the requirements of these cases, which posed unique technical and practical challenges. This slowed the judicialization process in those jurisdictions, as suggested by the figures in Table 3.1. For example, a member of the

Solicitor General's Office in charge of providing legal support to provincial prosecutors explained the sources of indifference:

> These individuals do not have an open mind. In Salta, for instance, they have no experience in dealing with these cases.... They operate with an extremely formalistic understanding of the law and of the way the judiciary should work. As a result we have a hard time getting them to respond favorably to our requests. It is hard to make them understand the historic importance of the trials. But beyond these political issues, it is also hard for them to understand that according to Supreme Court jurisprudence it is their responsibility to make an effort to speed up the proceedings. The Court has clearly stated that fulfilling the international responsibilities of the Argentine state also involves getting rid of formalistic interpretations of the law that slow down the progress of the cases. Either they do not feel the pressure of these instructions, or they are not aware of them.[90]

Another member of the special team in the Solicitor General's Office reinforced the point made by his colleague:

> It was difficult to persuade judges and prosecutors in the interior of the country that it was their job to apply international criminal law to these cases. In response they would tell us: "Don't come to me with strange ideas. During our entire career we were perfectly fine by focusing on domestic law." These cases go against the inertias characteristic of any bureaucracy, interrupting the routines of their members.[91]

Yet another gave me a specific example of how these dynamics play out in practice, delaying the progress of the cases from the investigative stage to the trial stage:

> Where technical deficits are more apparent is in the resistance to accumulate individual cases in larger mega-cases involving a multiplicity of victims. This resistance reflects a lack of understanding of the fact that these were not isolated homicides or kidnappings but were all instances of a systematic plan to disappear political opponents. Because they were all a consequence of the same criminal enterprise, they should be investigated together. Thinking of these cases as isolated events responds to a cultural reflex of members of the judiciary. That is how they are used to proceed. They were never trained to act differently.... For example, during the truth trials the Córdoba Federal Appeals Court produced a mega-case including crimes perpetrated by the 2nd division of the army based in Córdoba but with jurisdiction in other provinces of the northwest such as La Rioja. When the prosecutors outside Córdoba began investigating the crimes perpetrated in

[90] Interview, Buenos Aires, 26 November 2010.
[91] Interview, Buenos Aires, 2 November 2010.

Table 3.2. *Defendants under Arrest by Prison Type (2008)*

Jurisdiction	In Military Barracks, %	In Regular Prisons, %
City of Buenos Aires	9	51
Province of Buenos Aires	13	26
Rest of the country	78	23

Source: CELS (2008a).

> their provinces, they essentially dismembered the mega-case! This slowed down the proceedings.[92]

Finally an appellate judge who regularly reviews the decisions made by courts in the interior spoke about the technical deficiencies he finds in many of the cases:

> We read decisions sent by lower courts in the interior over and over again, because many of them are disastrous. Who are the ones who issue those rulings? Are they expert jurists? No! They have no expertise in these questions. It is very nice to talk about crimes against humanity, but at the end of the day you have to know how to evaluate and analyze the evidence. A standard legal education is clearly not enough to successfully do this in cases of human rights violations that took place decades ago, in part because of the nature of the evidence that we must use.... I understand it is very hard to study while one is working in a court. If one hasn't been studying these issues for a long time, it is hard to do a good job from a technical point of view. Roxin's theory of command responsibility is not as simple to apply as some people think.[93]

With regard to the second factor, recalcitrance, my interviewees mentioned the preexisting political loyalties of some judicial actors in the interior of the country as one of the causes behind the slow progress of human rights cases in those jurisdictions. Figures presented in Table 3.2 reinforce the suspicion that these judges were biased toward the defendants. According to official statistics, judges outside the City and Province of Buenos Aires were more likely to offer much more favorable arrest conditions to the defendants, placing them in military barracks under the supervision of their former subordinates. Defendants who are under the watch of their own colleagues in the military enjoy more privileges, especially the possibility of making illegal escapes. Among the former military

92 Interview, Buenos Aires, 27 October 2010.
93 Interview, Buenos Aires, 26 October 2010.

officers arrested in military barracks, 78 percent were sent there by judges in the interior of the country. The geographical pattern is reversed when one looks at those arrested in regular prisons.

To illustrate further the patterns of complicity between judges and military officers, and their impact on the trials, I collected additional data on two jurisdictions that rank poorly in terms of the indicators used in Table 3.1: Mendoza and Salta/Jujuy. In the early 2010s, Jujuy courts had around 115 cases of human rights violations involving 158 victims in their dockets. Yet, no trials were held in this province until 2013. Similarly, in Salta only one trial took place between 2004 and 2012. Since the case involved a single victim of forced disappearance, it was not even representative of the broader patterns of state repression in the region. These two northwestern provinces are under the jurisdiction of the Salta Federal Appeals Court, whose cozy relationship with the military goes a long way in explaining the dire situation of human rights cases at this stage in the process. Judicial actors were so determined to halt the trials that not even the most decisive pressures exerted by the national government via the Solicitor General's Office were able to induce strategic behavior among them.

Judge Rabbi Baldi, president of the Salta Federal Appeals Court, was appointed after his predecessor resigned in 2009, accused of collaborating with the military in the perpetration of crimes against humanity during the 1970s. Unfortunately for the victims, the new judge also had connections with the armed forces: His brother-in-law was investigated for crimes committed by the Fifth Division of the Army. In fact, in 2008 the judge used his contacts in the police to delay a search in his sister's house. As a federal prosecutor explained in an interview:

> In Salta the judge who had original jurisdiction in many of these cases was removed due to his participation in the crimes!... Like in many other jurisdictions of the interior of the country, it is not uncommon that the accused have all sorts of personal relations with judicial actors. Everyone knows each other. These are very small provinces, which have the characteristics of feudal societies. Federal judges have great connections, and an enormous amount of influence and authority.[94]

Rabbi Baldi's commitment to stall human rights cases is also clearly shown by the fact that he systematically rejected interlocutory appeals filed by litigants and prosecutors questioning decisions made by his protégé in the neighboring province of Jujuy, the federal investigative judge Olivera

[94] Interview, Buenos Aires, 26 November 2010.

Pastor. The latter was appointed in 2004 after Rabbi Baldi heavily lobbied the Judicial Council. Olivera Pastor had under his jurisdiction all the cases of victims disappeared in his province. To begin with, the judge was reluctant to accumulate cases. This would have greatly facilitated the proceedings, in addition to allowing defense lawyers to show the systematic nature of the dictatorships' repressive plan. As a result of the refusal to create "megacases," there was an average of 1.3 victims per case. The pressures exerted by the Solicitor General's Office failed to convince the judge to change his criteria. For example, data from the six accumulation requests filed by this office illustrate not only Olivera's recalcitrant position against accumulation, but also his contempt for the political signals sent by the government, as it took him an average of seven months to decide whether or not to group the cases of 76 victims. More importantly, by April 2011, only 15 of the 170 alleged perpetrators who were still alive in the province had been indicted. This was partly because between 2007 and 2011 the judge rejected 88 percent of the prosecution's requests to call in the military for questioning, a compulsory step before a judge can issue an indictment.[95]

In the province of Mendoza, where the dictatorship caused the disappearance of almost two hundred people, the situation during the second half of the 2000s was not very different from the one described in Salta and Jujuy. In 2008, for example, there were only 15 indictments and not a single former military officer was serving time in jail. The Federal Appeals Court was responsible for nullifying all arrest warrants issued by investigative federal court judges in Mendoza and neighboring provinces over which the court had jurisdiction. In a rather scandalous decision the judges even defended the good faith of a former fugitive, who now promised to abide by future court orders if he was set free for the duration of the investigations. As a result of these actions, in 2010 there were 466 pending indictments, and only 13 percent awaited trial; by late 2011 only one oral trial had been held and the percentage of indictments at the trial stage was a meager 14.94 percent. Contributing to this hostile environment, during the 2000s the press reported several attacks on human rights activists, including the electrification of the fence surrounding the house of a prominent lawyer.[96]

The situation is hardly surprising if one considers that as in the case of Salta/Jujuy, the members of the Federal Appeals Court and the federal

[95] These figures were obtained from the Solicitor General's Office. On file with the author.

[96] *Página 12*, 28 November 2008.

prosecutor had strong connections with the military. One of the prosecutors working in Mendoza as part of the special team in the Solicitor General's Office explained the situation:

> These were judges who supported the theory of the two demons. There was an enormous resistance to investigate the past. But it wasn't a resistance based on a disagreement with the norms of international law. It was ideological, and also personal, given their connections with the defendants. They thought that by stalling the cases they could buy time for the human rights fervor to wither away.[97]

His colleague reinforced the idea that judges had clear motivations to stop the cases:

> Judges usually face a dilemma. If they reject all of the appeals filed by the defendants they can be accused of not guaranteeing due process; if by contrast they are permissive with those requests, they can be accused of protecting torturers. But in the case of Mendoza, the members of the judicial branch had an extremely permissive attitude with the stalling tactics of the defendants. They delayed decisions on interlocutory appeals and released the detainees. They applied the worst legal doctrines. They rejected the accumulation of the cases, they did not accept as a crime the crime of forced disappearances, etc.[98]

Most of the judges involved in these cases were judges or prosecutors during the dictatorship, and at one point or another publicly declared their friendship with the military officer who was appointed by the juntas to govern Mendoza in the 1970s. According to the president of CELS, the judges "do not want a parade of witnesses telling the people of Mendoza what they did during the military dictatorship."[99] In 2009, a special team sent by the Supreme Court to organize evidence regarding state repression in the province confirmed this suspicion. They found that two of the aforementioned judicial actors, Judge Romano and Prosecutor Miret, had participated in torture sessions. The evidence was so clear that Romano was later accused by human rights organizations of the perpetration of 103 crimes against humanity.

The behavior of the Court of Cassation and of some judges in the interior of the country therefore suggests that despite the presence of an extremely supportive political environment after Kirchner won the presidency in 2003, the judicialization process faced serious obstacles. In this sense, it

[97] Interview, Buenos Aires, 16 December 2010.

[98] Interview, Buenos Aires, 16 December 2010.

[99] *Página 12*, 21 April 2010.

illustrates the long-lasting impact of the court packing initiatives led by the anti–transitional justice political coalition in the 1990s. The institutionalization of proimpunity values in the judiciary motivated resistance to the new wave of prosecutions. As argued, Menem's early colonization of the bench also limited the possibility of widespread legal preference change via pedagogical interventions. This too had far-reaching implications. The unevenness of the diffusion process explains the technical deficiencies found in the interior of the country. Judges' legal preferences clearly mediated the impact of external stimuli, as many judicial actors could not respond effectively to the pressures of the administration and human rights organizations. In sum, corporate and ideological commitments, as well as ignorance of certain investigative techniques or jurisprudential solutions, made judges and prosecutors imperfect agents of elected politicians. Within-case variation in Argentina thus reinforces the theoretical claim that positive transitional justice outcomes require deep institutional changes inside judicial branches. It does so by highlighting the importance of legal preference change in the 1990s, which enabled the swift processing of suits in some courts when the political conditions shifted. Moreover, it underscores how limited ideational transformations in other courts rendered insufficient the sudden empowerment of a pro–transitional justice electoral coalition.

Cementing Judicial Change via Replacement Strategies

The opportunities afforded by a favorable political environment led human rights NGOs to reinforce the process of judicial change ignited via pedagogical interventions with replacement strategies. In order to dismantle islands of resistance to their cause and remove resilient judicial blockages, in the second half of the 2000s, activists filed impeachment requests, named and shamed recalcitrant judges, and sponsored the nomination of friendly lawyers to seats in key federal courts. As the trial statistics presented earlier indicate, the effects of these efforts were felt most decisively in the 2010s, when the scope of the judicialization process expanded dramatically.

The first major attempt to have a say in who occupies seats in the federal bench was launched in 2002, when civil society organizations drafted a document entitled "A Court for Democracy." In it they promoted changes in the composition of the Supreme Court (CELS et al. 2002). NGOs proposed changes in the nomination process to increase its transparency. In particular, they demanded the opening up of an institutional space for civil society to scrutinize the nominees. In addition, they argued that the president and the senate should strive to ensure gender, regional, and expertise diversity among candidates for the court. Finally, the document insisted that the nominees should meet certain ethical and professional standards (ADC 2008). After he was sworn in, Kirchner instructed his party to begin impeachment proceedings against some of the members of the Supreme Court. The decision was immensely popular because of the public's discontent with Menem's appointees (Ruibal 2009). These political pressures led to the resignation of three justices. In 2004 and 2005, congress removed two more, thus putting an end to Menem's so-called automatic majority. Facing the prospect of having to fill vacancies in the Supreme Court, Kirchner's minister of justice approached CELS's lawyers indicating that the government was ready to endorse their ideas.[100] Between October 2003 and February 2005, Kirchner made four nominations following the protocol designed by the NGOs.[101] According to one of the civil society organizations behind the initiative, the new system forced the executive branch to use greater care in choosing the candidates, allowing the citizenry "to evaluate and debate about them" (ADC 2008: 32, my translation).

When the senate confirmed the nominees, human rights organizations' strategy to promote personnel changes in the federal judiciary achieved its first major victory. Among those who were eventually appointed to the court were a historic ally of the human rights movement and one of Latin America's most prestigious legal scholars (Eugenio Zaffaroni), a judge from the International Criminal Court and former political prisoner (Carmen Argibay), and two respected civil law experts (Ricardo Lorenzetti and Elena Highton). My sources indicate that when the president met with the potential candidates before publicly announcing the nominations, he asked them about their position on the constitutionality of the amnesty laws. In fact, when interviewed by the media during the nomination process, the future president of the Supreme Court, Ricardo Lorenzetti, made his pro–transitional justice position crystal clear.[102]

As we saw in previous sections, under its new composition, the Supreme Court handed down a series of key rulings that enabled the relaunching of the judicialization process. Most importantly, the institutional mission of the court changed dramatically. There is evidence to suggest that the

[100] CELS lawyer, interview, Buenos Aires, 20 December 2010.

[101] Kirchner was entitled to make six nominations. In 2005, however, the president accepted a proposal from civil society organizations to reduce the court's size from nine to seven. As a result, he could not pack the court.

[102] *Página 12*, 3 September 2004.

renewed court thought of transitional justice as its signature issue and built a brand around it. According to one of its members:

> The emphasis on human rights cases has had a tremendously positive impact on the court's legitimacy. The court consciously gave this issue a prominent position in its institutional agenda.[103]

Consistent with this institutional mission, the Supreme Court created an interbranch commission to monitor the progress of human rights cases across the country.[104] Moreover, throughout this period, the court was at pains to inform the public about judicial activity in human rights cases. A newly created in-house news agency constantly issued press releases about important rulings, the progress of trials around the country, and the issuing of indictments in high-profile cases. An analysis of the agency's tweets between January 2009 and December 2011 indicates that 23.5 percent of the time the Supreme Court sought to inform the public about judicial activity it highlighted the achievements of federal courts in human rights cases. Similarly, 32 percent of the speeches delivered by the president of the Supreme Court between 2002 and 2011 were about the state of these cases, emphasizing their priority status in the court's agenda. Analyzing statements to the media made by the president of the court during the same period indicates that 28 percent made reference to human rights cases.[105]

The second major battle launched by human rights organizations to promote personnel changes in the federal judiciary was the one involving the composition of the infamous Court of Cassation. The objective was to remove the recalcitrant judges appointed by Menem in 1991. The saga began in 2003 when defense attorneys filed an interlocutory appeal to question the constitutionality of the law passed by congress to repeal the amnesties. A year later the court had still not handed down a decision, blocking further proceedings by lower courts. Contributing to this delay, the appeal was caught in a jurisdictional battle between the Second and Fourth Chambers of the Court of Cassation. When the plenary finally decided to hand it over to the latter, it caused a general outcry

103 Interview, Buenos Aires, 17 December 2010.

104 The commission gained notoriety when it summoned in the president of Salta's Federal Appeals Court to question him publicly about the sorry state of the judicialization process in his jurisdiction.

105 Issues such as judicial independence, domestic violence, and budgetary constraints received prominent but less central treatment. These data were obtained by conducting an online search of articles published in *Página 12* between 2002 and 2012. The keyword used was "Ricardo Lorenzetti."

among victim organizations because it was well known that the judges of the Fourth Chamber had clear anti–transitional justice positions. The Asociación de ex Detenidos Desaparecidos and the Liga Argentina por los Derechos del Hombre filed a lawsuit against the entire court for taking this decision. They later recused the Fourth Chamber arguing that it was the "military chamber." Tensions escalated when, in a ruling rejecting the recusals, Judge Bisordi referred to one of the human rights lawyers as a "delinquent terrorist."[106] Joined by other human rights organizations, the lawyers alluded to by the judge filed an impeachment request in the Judicial Council. In November 2005 the Judicial Council ruled to fine Bisordi. Although a majority in the council agreed with the claimants that Bisordi's ideological positions made him unfit to rule in human rights cases, they failed to impeach him and the other two members of the Fourth Chamber.[107]

By 2007, the court had still not ruled on the appeal despite the famous 2005 Supreme Court decision that nullified the impunity laws and had more than two hundred similar appeals pending decision. As a result of their reluctance to hand down a ruling, the judges were slowing progress, especially in an emblematic case involving crimes against humanity perpetrated in the largest clandestine detention center (*ESMA*). This made it easier to call attention to the stalling tactics. In March of that year, human rights organizations tried once again to get rid of the recalcitrant judges. In contrast to the previous attempt at removing the judges, this time they managed to garner the support of President Kirchner. Sixty-one former political prisoners who were plaintiffs in four cases stalled by the court (*1er Cuerpo del Ejército*, *Campo de Mayo*, *ESMA*, and *Plan Cóndor*) filed a suit in the Judicial Council against Judges Hornos, Capolupo, Riggi, and Bisordi. Five days later, Kirchner made a speech fully endorsing the efforts of human rights organizations. He stated: "I tell the judiciary, and I know that in the Judicial Council they will also hear: please, enough! Trials and punishment! This is what we need. I swear that I push and push, but there are judges and prosecutors who turn a blind eye."[108] Two days after that, Judge Bisordi took a leave of absence but insisted that he would not resign, and a week later another judge, who was not formally questioned in the

[106] *Página 12*, 23 September 2004.

[107] *Página 12*, 2 November 2005. When the Court of Cassation finally accepted the recusal, it appointed two judges to rule on the interlocutory appeals concerning *ESMA*, both of whom had strong links to the dictatorship and the defendants. NGO lawyers also successfully recused them. See *Página 12*, 7 April 2005.

[108] *Página 12*, 25 March 2007.

suit but who was sympathetic to the defendants, resigned after securing her retirement package. Finally, in November both Bisordi and Cupolupo stepped down, leaving only two of the judges in question still standing.[109] Following these resignations, the court began to hand down decisions on the interlocutory appeals in line with Supreme Court precedents. Moreover, it confirmed the prison sentences issued by FOTs in two oral trials (CELS 2011).

The attempts to purify the court did not end here. As I mentioned in the previous section, in December 2008 the judges of the Second Chamber decided to end the preventive imprisonment of high-profile torturers. When these judges were sworn in seven months earlier to fill some of the vacancies in the court temporarily, they had expressed their commitment to human rights cases. Judge Yacobucci, for example, told the press: "We have all the well-known human rights cases and we will pay special attention to make sure that everything is done without delays."[110] In fact, in the following two years they confirmed eight condemnatory rulings handed down by FOTs. Despite this improvement in the court's performance, the criteria used to rule on preventive imprisonments did not satisfy human rights organizations. In response to these unpopular decisions, they filed an impeachment suit against them. One of the judges reflected on the effects of these tactics:

> Bonafini [the president of Mothers of Plaza de Mayo] said she would come after our families. We were accused of protecting the perpetrators. They accuse everyone who does not rule like they want. Some because they grant house arrests, others because instead of sentencing all of the accused they acquit a few.... Some judges in lower courts resigned, fearing they could suffer a similar fate.[111]

As I showed in the previous section, these pressures did not change the chamber's decision making patterns, but they were effective in forcing the resignation of five more judges, both old and new, between 2010 and 2011. One of them did so after human rights activists filed two suits against him, accusing him of collaborating with the dictatorship's plan to abduct babies.[112]

What had taken Menem less than a month in the early 1990s took human rights organizations nearly six years in the 2000s. But the constant

[109] *Página 12*, 6 November 2007.
[110] *Página 12*, 18 April 2008.
[111] Interview, Buenos Aires, 26 October 2010.
[112] *Página 12*, 8 November 2011.

pressure exerted on the court in the form of criminal lawsuits and impeachment requests paid off because it put the situation in the spotlight, calling the attention of politicians supportive of their cause. In 2011, President Fernández announced her nominees, finally changing the composition of the Court of Cassation. Among the candidates confirmed by the senate and applauded by the NGOs was a human rights lawyer from the Province of Santa Fe. There is evidence that the attitude of the court toward human rights cases changed as a result of the new composition. In addition to a significant increase in the rate of confirmation of FOT rulings,[113] the new judges issued a new set of rules designed to speed the appeals process[114] and created a registry of victims/witnesses to spare them the emotional ordeal of having to testify about the same crimes in different oral trials.[115]

At the same time, as they tried to reform the Court of Cassation, human rights organizations also activated personnel turnover strategies targeted at lower federal courts. First, they promoted investigations of those judges who had collaborated with the dictatorship. According to the Solicitor General's Office, in 2011 there were between forty-five and sixty former judges and prosecutors formally accused of perpetrating crimes against humanity.[116] Second, and perhaps most consequential for the progress of cases in the interior of the country, activists also sought to remove recalcitrant lower court judges and prosecutors. A careful reading of the Judicial Council's rulings in cases debated between 2003 and 2012 indicates that 29 percent of lower federal court judges who went through impeachment proceedings faced accusations filed by NGOs concerning their behavior in human rights cases. Table 3.3 complements this figure by listing different types of actions taken against members of the judiciary. The data were obtained by conducting research in the archives of national and provincial newspapers, the Judicial Council, NGOs, and the Solicitor General's Office. In total I was able to identify twenty-four different replacement initiatives undertaken between 2003 and 2011 in eight different provinces. In seventeen of them, human rights cases were removed from the orbit of recalcitrant judges and prosecutors.

In absolute terms, these figures are not all that impressive. However, a detailed look at the judges and prosecutors involved reveals that in some jurisdictions such as Chaco and Mendoza, activists were able to overhaul

[113] By August 2014, 35 percent of these rulings had been reviewed and confirmed.

[114] For example, judges no longer evaluate evidence that has already been accepted as valid in related cases.

[115] *La Nación*, 14 January 2012.

[116] *Página 12*, 28 August 2011. In 2010 one of these former judges received a prison sentence.

Table 3.3. *Judicial Actors Denounced by Human Rights Organizations*

Jurisdiction	Year	Judicial Actor*	Action Taken by NGOs**	Outcome
Buenos Aires	2010	1 Investigative Court judge	Suit filed in the Judicial Council (Abuelas de Plaza de Mayo)	In progress
Chaco	2003	3 Federal Appeals Court judges	Suit filed in the Judicial Council (CELS, HIJOS)	Suspended; not impeached; removed from case
	2004	1 federal prosecutor (Federal Appeals Court)	Criminal lawsuit for collaboration with the dictatorship; complaint filed in the Solicitor General's Office (CELS, HIJOS)	Removed from the case
	2004	1 federal prosecutor (Investigative Federal Court)	Criminal lawsuit for collaboration with the dictatorship; complaint filed in the Solicitor General's Office (CELS, HIJOS)	Removed from the case
	2004	1 federal prosecutor (Investigative Court)	Complaint filed in the Solicitor General's Office (CELS, HIJOS)	Removed
	2004	1 federal prosecutor (Federal Appeals Court)	Complaint filed in the Solicitor General's Office (CELS, HIJOS)	Removed
City of Buenos Aires	2005	1 Federal Oral Tribunal judge	Suit filed in Judicial Council (CELS)	Resigned
	2005	1 federal prosecutor (Federal Oral Tribunal, Federal Appeals Court)	Complaint filed in the Solicitor General's Office (CELS)	Resigned
	2005	1 Investigative Court judge	Suit filed in Judicial Council	No action taken
	2009	1 Federal Oral Tribunal judge	Suit filed in Judicial Council (Secretariat of Human Rights)	The judge asked to be transferred to a different court with no human rights cases in the docket

(continued)

Table 3.3 (*cont.*)

Jurisdiction	Year	Judicial Actor*	Action Taken by NGOs**	Outcome
Córdoba	2011	1 Federal Investigative Court judge	Suit filed in Judicial Council (Abuelas de Plaza de Mayo)	In progress
	2011	1 Federal Appeals Court judge	Suit filed in Judicial Council (no information)	In progress; the judge was successfully recused
Jujuy	2011	1 Federal Investigative Court judge	Suit filed in the Judicial Council (human rights organizations)	Resigned
Mendoza	2008	4 Federal Appeals Court judges	Suit filed in Judicial Council (Movimiento Ecuménico por los Derechos Humanos and Fundación Liga Argentina por los Derechos Humanos)	3 resigned; 1 impeached
	2010	1 federal prosecutor (Federal Appeals Court)	Suit filed in Judicial Council (Asociación de Ex Detenidos Desaparecidos)	Removed; impeached
Salta	2007	1 Federal Appeals Court judge	Suit filed in Judicial Council (human rights organization)	Resigned
Santa Fe	2009	3 Federal Oral Tribunal judges	Suit filed in Judicial Council (Human rights NGOs and Ministry of Justice)	No Information

Notes: *In parenthesis is the type of court in which the prosecutor litigates cases.
**In parenthesis is the name of the NGO and/or government agency that filed the lawsuit or complaint. The category "human rights organization" is used when the available information does not specify which NGO was behind the initiative.

the federal judiciary totally, changing the fate of human rights trials in those places. For example, Table 3.1 showed that in 2010, the Chaco federal judiciary was the top performer in terms of the percentage of indictments that were filed in FOTs. This performance is puzzling because Chaco was not significantly affected by the diffusion efforts launched by human rights organizations in the 1990s. The answer to this puzzle is that the shortcomings of the pedagogical interventions were compensated by the activation of intense replacement strategies in the 2000s. Chaco was the site of a well-known massacre perpetrated by the military in the 1970s. When the case was reopened after 2003, human rights organizations realized that the two federal prosecutors in charge of the investigations had collaborated with the military in the perpetration of crimes against humanity. They immediately filed criminal lawsuits against them and managed to remove them from the case. They also filed complaints in the Solicitor General's Office to remove their replacements because they systematically stalled the cases. Moreover, in 2004 CELS and the local chapter of HIJOS, an organization that gathers the sons and daughters of the disappeared, also launched serious accusations in the Judicial Council against the members of the Chaco Federal Appeals Court who nullified all the arrest warrants issued by a federal investigative judge. Although the impeachment failed, the judges were suspended. Following the removal of recalcitrant judges, the head of the solicitor general's special team of prosecutors charged with assisting in human rights cases was sent to Chaco to monitor the proceedings closely. In 2010 the local FOT finally sentenced eight former military officers to life imprisonment for their criminal responsibility in the Margarita Belén massacre. Chaco thus became a "leading case" of the effectiveness of naming, shaming, and suing judges and prosecutors who put up obstacles to human rights investigations.

The Mendoza federal judiciary, whose stalling tactics I have discussed, suffered a similar fate between 2008 and 2012. When it became clear that the province was an outlier in the national judicialization process, human rights organizations trained their eye on the federal judges. Activists soon discovered evidence of the judges' past connections with the defendants, which explained the absence of condemnatory rulings in the province. After the NGOs publicly accused several members of the Federal Appeals Court of promilitary bias, the Supreme Court intervened, assigning reliable judges to human rights cases. Impeachment proceedings were subsequently initiated against six of Mendoza's federal judges. Two of them, the ones also accused of perpetrating crimes against humanity, were impeached while the remaining four resigned. The turnaround in the situation of human rights cases was impressive. For example, a year after the judges were removed, the province passed from having four cases in the trial stage to having twenty (CELS 2010). In 2013, the percentage of indictments at the trial stage rose to an impressive 49.91 percent. According to a federal prosecutor:

> The decisive factor was the partnership between the new prosecutors and the victims. For the first time there were judicial players in Mendoza willing to push the cases from within the judiciary. Before we got there the defendants put obstacles, the judges supported them and the prosecutors turned a blind eye.... Once the victims managed to remove the judges, our job was much easier.[117]

In sum, after 2003 human rights organizations sought the removal from the bench of judges and prosecutors who proved unfriendly to their cause. In so doing, they deepened the process of judicial transformation and cemented the ability and willingness of the judiciary to process human rights cases. Argentina thus illustrates the positive synergies that result when litigants' strategies of judicial change occur in favorable political environments. Activists deployed replacement efforts at all levels of the judiciary, altering the composition of key courts. In the cases of the Court of Cassation and lower federal courts, NGOs acted as whistle-blowers, eventually catching the attention of politicians, from Presidents Kirchner and Fernández to government and opposition representatives in the Judicial Council. Members of the political class proved willing to reinforce shaming tactics, initiate impeachment proceedings, and nominate friendly judges.

Conclusion

After their experience in the 1980s, Argentine pro– and anti–transitional justice coalitions sought to galvanize a critical mass of judicial actors in order to guarantee stable jurisprudential outcomes that favored their interests. This chapter documented a decades-long struggle over who occupied seats in the federal bench, and how judges and prosecutors understood their duties as professionals of the law. I thus traced the political origins of legal preferences as they relate to human rights cases. The narrative showed that these professional worldviews engendered bureaucratic routines, standards of praxis, and institutional commitments that at different points in time were instrumental in either perpetuating or disrupting the impunity regime.

[117] Interview, Buenos Aires, 16 December 2010.

After the passage of the amnesty laws in the late 1980s, litigants faced an uphill battle when it came to unleashing the potential of the judiciary as a vehicle for truth and justice. Although the military had left power in rather unfavorable conditions, proimpunity forces soon regained political clout. Moreover, as a result of this reempowerment and the personnel continuities that accompanied the 1983 transition, the judiciary became packed with recalcitrant judges. In the end, however, human rights activists prevailed because they focused their efforts on changing the ideational makeup of the judiciary. In the 1990s, they emboldened committed judges and won over a few influential indifferent ones. From early on in the process several NGOs understood that legal preferences severely condition judicial decision making. Given the experimental nature of the case in favor of prosecutions, judges and prosecutors had to be infused with a new logic of behavioral appropriateness. Innovation needed to be seen as compatible with the parameters of reasoning and argumentation that govern action in the legal field. Aware of this challenge, litigants deployed a campaign that shifted legal visions. They led key judicial actors to contemplate a new horizon of jurisprudential solutions, embrace the values that underpin international human rights law, and acquire the skills to act upon those preferences. The professional values diffused via pedagogical interventions motivated judicial actors to defy the impunity regime at a time when the political environment strongly preferred to maintain the status quo. In other words, changing legal preferences empowered some members of the bench to push the limits of political possibility at critical moments in the judicialization process, in ways not anticipated by strategic understandings of judicial decision making.

In line with the theoretical argument developed in Chapter 2, persuasion worked for a number of reasons. First, NGOs endowed pedagogical interventions with an aura of legitimacy. They enlisted domestic and international experts to speak on their behalf, raising the appeal and authority of the message. Second, expanding their networks in the judiciary allowed them to plan more targeted efforts, establishing informal contacts with judicial actors in a position to shatter the legal infrastructure that protected the perpetrators. Third, these informal encounters were characterized by juridical talk, not by traditional pressure politics. Litigants thus framed the question of impunity in strictly legal terms, pointing at inconsistencies in the law and presenting evidence that resonated strongly with international criminal definitions. This was important because they paused bureaucratic inertias and encouraged indifferent judges to think about the legal and professional implications of impunity. For some judges, it became clear that something had to be done to iron out those inconsistencies and remedy victims' situations. Finally, domestic diffusion efforts began before international litigation strategies, and were therefore instrumental in amplifying their effect. Litigants turned certain Argentine courts into fertile ground for the cascading of international norms. On their own, external signals would not have been enough to equip and motivate judicial actors to become agents of truth and justice.

There were of course limits to persuasion. In the 1990s, human rights NGOs implemented a highly targeted effort to modify legal preferences, in part because of the timing of their intervention vis-à-vis similar efforts by the anti–transitional justice camp. Menem's court packing initiatives entrenched enemies of transitional justice and reduced the pool of persuadable judges. In this sense, Argentina illustrates how macropolitical conditions can moderate the effect of litigants' correct diagnosis of the problem and ambitious campaigns of legal preference change. Where pedagogical interventions were weak, judges and prosecutors showed reluctance to process these suits, or had a hard time dealing with their idiosyncratic features. This was true even in the 2000s, when the political environment had shifted decisively in favor of the victims. The presence of powerful political allies, however, allowed NGOs to address these shortcomings via replacement strategies. They unearthed evidence of judicial collaboration with the military regime, denounced inexplicable delays in the proceedings, and mobilized resources to remove judges or shame them into resignation. These efforts furthered the institutional transformation ignited in the 1990s, leading to a widespread shift in the values that underpin judicial decision making across the country and levels of the judiciary. As we shall see in the following chapter, although Peruvian activists were equally conscious of the obstacles posed by traditional legal preferences, and successfully implemented pedagogical interventions to modify them, their inability to reinforce these victories with personnel changes put them in a more precarious situation than their Argentine counterparts.

4

Peru

Pedagogical Interventions and Human Rights Trials in Unfriendly Territory

This chapter tells the story of transitional justice in Peru after the internal armed conflict and Fujimori's authoritarian regime. The focus is on the surge of human rights trials between the 2000 democratic transition and the present. During this period, judges and prosecutors catalyzed a comprehensive program of criminal prosecutions by handing down exemplary condemnatory rulings and managed to fend off attacks against these jurisprudential achievements. Human rights NGOs played a central role in this process, removing important judicial blockages. The Peruvian case offers within-case variation in the contexts in which litigants deploy strategies of legal preference change, shedding light on the limits and possibilities of an externally induced judicial transformation. Although pedagogical interventions initially galvanized a critical mass of judges and prosecutors willing to champion the victims' cause, the growing hostility of the political environment after the mid-2000s caused problems at critical stages during the judicialization process, leading to less robust results than in the Argentine case.

NGOs' high level of legal professionalization – borne out of their experience with domestic and international litigation before the transition – allowed them to diagnose correctly the problems posed by formalistic legal preferences early on in the process, and thereafter design a campaign to diffuse new capabilities. These strategies transformed a formerly passive and ineffective judiciary, whose lack of legal imagination had for decades stunted its ability to protect individual rights and the standing of the Peruvian state vis-à-vis the international responsibilities. Litigants understood that despite the numerous cases decided against the country by the Inter-American Court of Human Rights, the incorporation of international legal standards into local jurisprudence would not happen by default. In other words, they knew they had to become conveyor belts of these innovative doctrines and teach judicial actors how to operationalize them in the domestic judicialization process. In order to do so effectively,

NGOs increased the appeal of their interventions by carefully selecting the agents of diffusion and partnering with prestigious academic institutions. Pedagogical efforts were also highly systematic, manufacturing deep awareness of international legal imperatives. There was, however, some variation in the topics discussed in these venues, which led to concomitant variation in jurisprudential achievements. This strengthens the claim that pedagogical interventions mattered. Rulings and investigations evidence a strong consensus in those issue areas that were systematically touched upon during pedagogical interventions (e.g. the use of international criminal definitions), whereas they reflect a lack of expertise in others (e.g. evidence treatment, leading, for example, to several controversial acquittals). The Peruvian case thus shows that international norm diffusion requires a carefully planned domestic resocialization of judicial actors if it is to have a corrosive effect on impunity regimes.

Peruvian NGOs decided to transform the legal cultural underpinnings of judicial decision making immediately after the democratic transition, when the political environment was favorable to their cause. They did so because in their view, the success of criminal investigations required more than support from politicians; it depended on the presence of highly skilled judicial actors. The early manufacturing of judicial commitment to the cause, which was made possible both by NGOs' correct diagnosis of the problem and by the space afforded by the posttransition political climate, proved even more important when the balance of power shifted against them in the mid-2000s. Prior changes in ideas and standards of legal praxis motivated courts to pursue now dangerous investigations, defying the dictates of the newly empowered proimpunity establishment. In this regard, Peru offers an example of what in Chapter 2 I referred to as "backlash." The strengthening of these actors led to repeated attempts to stop the judicialization process by denying access to official documents and evidence, intimidating judges and prosecutors, and manipulating the legal framework. But this backlash was effectively resisted by key members of the judicial corporation, suggesting that provided certain changes occur in judicial values, a favorable political environment is not necessary to obtain prison sentences for human rights criminals. As we saw in the Argentine case, the pages ahead will document instances in which rekindled legal preferences led judges and prosecutors to refuse to act as agents of politicians.

By putting into sharper focus the empowering effect of legal preference change, the aforementioned backlash also shows that it was informal institutional change, not the strengthening of formal parchment barriers after democratization that allowed judges and prosecutors to prevail in interbranch confrontations. Heightened formal judicial independence after Fujimori's departure in 2000 certainly did not deter the proimpunity coalition that came to power in 2006 from engaging in all sorts of shenanigans to undermine the protective character of formal rules and, in so doing, exhaust judicial commitment to truth and justice. Its limited success notwithstanding, what the experience with backlash does underscore is that the staying power of legal preference change can be jeopardized by shifts in the balance of power. The change in the political environment cemented the resilience of remaining pockets of judicial resistance to the cause by empowering recalcitrant judges, and made it impossible for litigants to activate replacement strategies. As a result, trials did not ultimately have the same intensity as in the Argentine case. In fact, at several points during this period, committed judges had to fight hard against some of their recalcitrant colleagues to prevent the overturning of important jurisprudential milestones.

This chapter has a different structure from Chapter 3, which reflects the shorter duration of the Peruvian judicialization process. I first provide an overview of the dependent variable, i.e., the outcome of criminal investigations. The narrative then contextualizes these rulings, characterizing the growing hostility of the political environment. I then explain prosecutorial success by exploring the effect of pedagogical interventions on legal preferences. The analysis pays special attention to the extent to which the rise to power of a proimpunity coalition conditioned the effectiveness of litigants' strategies.

From Judicial Acquiescence to Action

In May 1980, Peru celebrated its first democratic presidential election after twelve years of military rule. On Election Day, in a small village in the province of Ayacucho, an armed organization known as the Shining Path burned the ballot boxes, making its entrance into the national political scene. This episode was the prelude of a bloody internal conflict in which the armed forces and national police confronted the terror tactics of the ruthless Maoist group (Stern 1998). Over the next decade and a half, the violent military campaign against the Shining Path would leave an estimated toll of 67,756 deaths: 31,331 attributed to the Shining Path, 20,458 to national security forces, and the remaining 15,967 to other actors involved in the conflict.[1] Victims were subject to sexual violence,

[1] These figures are estimates that appear in the Final Report of the Truth and Reconciliation Commission. See Comisión de la Verdad y Reconciliación (2003), appendix no. 2.

torture, extrajudicial killings, massacres, and forced disappearances. State agents perpetrated 122 massacres (i.e. collective executions of five or more victims) and the Shining Path was involved in 215. When it came to forced disappearances, the main culprit was the government.[2] The Truth and Reconciliation Commission's Final Report, released in August 2003, characterized these crimes as serious human rights violations, which in some cases constituted breaches of the standards set by international humanitarian law.[3]

The conflict spanned several presidential terms – Fernando Belaúnde (1980–1985), Alan García (1985–1900), and Alberto Fujimori (1990–2000). All three were democratically elected governments, but during the third period there was a regime change after Fujimori staged a self-coup in 1992.[4] Although most of the deaths occurred during the 1980s, Fujimori's strategy vis-à-vis the Shining Path was particularly ruthless. His tight alliance with the armed forces and the intelligence services led to the creation of a clandestine paramilitary group known as Grupo Colina, which was responsible for two of the most emblematic massacres of the period, Barrios Altos in 1991 and La Cantuta in 1992.[5] Moreover, during his presidency, amnesty laws were passed in 1995 in order to exonerate military and police officers from their responsibility in human rights violations perpetrated between 1980 and 1995.[6]

The 1990s were also characterized by judicial complicity and acquiescence (Carrión 2006). With the exception of the *La Cantuta* case, military courts usurped jurisdiction over all cases involving state agents in order either to close the investigations or to hand down acquittals.[7] No thorough investigations were conducted to establish the truth about the

[2] Comisión de la Verdad y Reconciliación (2003), volume VI, chapter I. For a description of forced disappearances during this period also see Report No. 55 of the Office of the Ombudsman, available online at www.defensoria.gov.pe.

[3] Comisión de la Verdad y Reconciliación (2003), volume I, chapter IV.

[4] Although Fujimori held elections after a new constitution was drafted in 1993, Peru did not become a full democracy until he left power in 2000. For a history of this period see Conaghan (1998, 2002), Conaghan and Basombrío (1996), Tanaka (1998, 2005, 2006), Cotler and Grompone (2000), Carrión (2006).

[5] See APRODEH (2008) and Burt (2007) for a full account of these massacres.

[6] For a full account of the context in which the amnesty laws were passed see Defensoría del Pueblo (2001).

[7] In *La Cantuta* case military officers were sentenced by military courts as part of a deal with the government that included the passage of amnesty laws within a year. As shown previously, the government kept its promise. See Villarán (2007).

whereabouts of the conflict's victims or to punish those responsible.[8] The attitude toward those suspected of terrorism was markedly different. The government passed a series of antiterrorism laws, which established a draconian legal framework to deal with these cases. The new regulations greatly undermined the rule of law and violated due process: They gave defense lawyers no time to prepare the cases, allowed judges to conduct interrogations without appearing in front of the accused, gave military courts jurisdiction over civilians, enabled detentions without official warrants, and promoted indictments on the basis of ambiguous criminal definitions such as "treason." Not surprisingly, these laws led to the incarceration of hundreds of innocent civilians.[9]

In a context characterized by the state's abdication of its duty to protect citizens from violence, human rights organizations became crucial actors. They amplified victims' voices, documented rights violations, and engaged in strategic litigation both in the Inter-American system of human rights and in domestic courts, especially after the country transitioned back to democracy. In 1985, more that forty regional and national NGOs created an umbrella organization known as the Coordinadora Nacional de Derechos Humanos (CNDH).[10] During its first five years of existence, the CNDH intensely denounced and documented human rights violations. During the 1990s, it began to forge alliances with international organizations such as Human Rights Watch, Amnesty International, and the International Center for Justice and International Law. This strategy facilitated contacts with the Inter-American Commission of Human Rights, which intensified its concern with the Peruvian situation by giving it a prominent treatment in its annual reports, and by regularly paying visits to the country.[11] The lack of an adequate response by the local judiciary also led Peruvian NGOs to take cases to the Inter-American Court of Human Rights. These efforts resulted in a series of rulings that highlighted the state's international responsibility to investigate and punish the crimes.[12]

[8] During the 1980s, congress did launch a few investigations but proved very ineffective. One of the cases investigated at the time was a massacre later known as the *Cayara* case that took place during García's administration. See Villarán (2007).

[9] See De la Jara (2001).

[10] For a comprehensive history of the CNDH, and for a list of its members, see Youngers (2003). The main organizations that make up the CNDH are Instituto de Defensa Legal (IDL) and Asociación Pro Derechos Humanos (APRODEH).

[11] See Villarán (2007).

[12] Landmark rulings include I/A Court HR, *Case of Neira Alegría v. Peru*, ruling of 19 January 1995, and I/A Court HR, *Case of Durand y Ugarte v. Peru*, ruling of 16 August 2000, both

Finally, during the 1990s, the CNDH mounted an ambitious media and litigation campaign in defense of innocent civilians imprisoned under the aforementioned draconian antiterrorism legal framework. Because of its defense of alleged terrorists, the human rights community was fiercely accused of defending the interests of the Shining Path.

The active presence of human rights organizations in the international scene largely contributed to Fujimori's rapid loss of prestige and support. After a series of corruption scandals shook the political arena in late 2000, Fujimori resigned and fled to Japan (Tanaka 2005). His resignation initiated a political transition to democracy, which one of my interviewees defined as the "NGO transition."[13] Human rights NGOs actively participated in the broad coalition that backed President Valentin Paniagua's transitional government (2000–2001). Activists and their allies staffed crucial cabinet positions in the Ministries of Foreign Relations, Justice, and Women's Affairs, and in state agencies such as the Office of the Ombudsman and the Solicitor General's Office. This instantly improved Peru's relations with the Inter-American system,[14] facilitated the design of an ambitious reparations program for the victims of the conflict, and shaped the political conditions suitable for the creation of a Truth and Reconciliation Commission.

The Truth and Reconciliation Commission played a pivotal role in the transitional justice process initiated by domestic courts in 2004.[15] Apart from extensively documenting the atrocities and the political context in which they were perpetrated, the commissioners filed forty-seven emblematic cases. Human rights organizations not only staffed the commission with their own members; they were also responsible for shaping its mandate and agenda. As a former CNDH's executive director who was a minister in Paniagua's cabinet stated in an interview, "When the cabinet debated the proposal to create a truth commission, I did not participate in those discussions as a minister but as a human rights activist infiltrating the government."[16]

regarding forced disappearances during the massacre at El Frontón prison in 1986; I/A Court HR, *Case of Castillo Páez v. Peru*, ruling of 3 November 1997 on the forced disappearance of Ernesto Castillo Páez; and I/A Court HR, *Case of Barrios Altos v. Peru*, ruling of 14 March 2001 on the Barrios Altos massacre that took place in 1991. This last ruling nullified the amnesty laws.

13 Interview with a member of the right-wing party Unidad Nacional, Lima, 28 May 2010.

14 In 1999, Fujimori removed Peru from the contentious jurisdiction of the Inter-American Court of Human Rights, claiming that it defended terrorists.

15 Some investigations were reopened in 2001 after the Inter-American Court handed down the famous *Barrios Altos* ruling.

16 Interview, Lima, 30 April 2010.

The first posttransitional government ended in 2006 when Alejandro Toledo transferred the presidency to Alan García. The climate favorable to the NGO agenda came to an abrupt end. García was a former president accused of being responsible for hundreds of human rights violations in the late 1980s. Not surprisingly his government was extremely hostile to transitional justice efforts. His presidency also coincided with the regaining of electoral strength by Fujimori's party. As the figures that follow will show, however, the vast majority of Peru's transitional justice achievements took place in this hostile political environment. These achievements included both judicial rulings handed down by domestic courts rejecting formalistic arguments invoking statutes of limitations and amnesty laws, and prison sentences against a former president and dozens of military and police officers.

The poor record of the judiciary in protecting individual rights and sanctioning state abuses changed dramatically during the 2000s. Apart from the aforementioned cases filed by the Truth and Reconciliation Commission, the Office of the Ombudsman submitted another 14 and, following a friendly accord with the Inter-American Commission of Human Rights, the government presented an additional 159.[17] These initiatives marked the beginning of a judicialization process that involved hundreds of victims and more than 750 military and civilian officers responsible for torture, extrajudicial executions, forced disappearances, and other major crimes.[18] Figure 4.1 shows the progress of the sixty-one cases filed by the Truth Commission and the ombudsman during the early years of the process.[19] Initially, the number of preliminary investigations decreased, and the number of shelved cases increased. As the years passed, however, new investigations were launched. In 2013, for example, there were ongoing formal investigations of 194 former army officers, 37 former navy officers, 31 former policemen, and 11 civilians, while 681 active and retired members of the military were still under preliminary investigation.[20] These figures suggest that cases moved slowly up the judicial ladder, with only a few of them reaching the trial stage.

17 See Report No. 139, Office of the Ombudsman, available online at www.defensoria.gov.pe.

18 *El Comercio*, 6 June 2010.

19 The last year for which disaggregated data are available is 2008. The Office of the Ombudsman is the only agency that has access to the docket. The data reported can be also found in Report No. 139, Office of the Ombudsman, available online at www.defensoria.gov.pe.

20 See Report No. 162, Office of the Ombudsman, available online at www.defensoria.gov.pe.

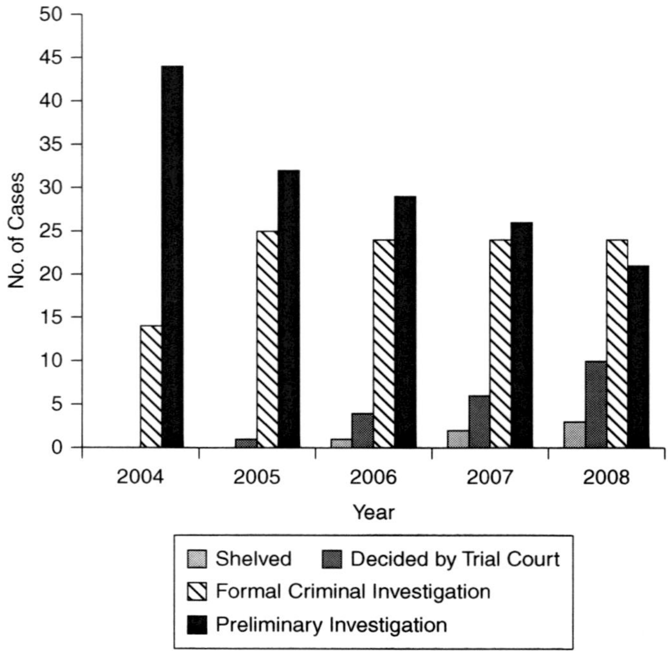

Figure 4.1. Progress of Cases Filed by the Truth and Reconciliation Commission and the Office of the Ombudsman (2004–2008).
Source: The Office of the Ombudsman.

There are several reasons why the progress of human rights cases was slow during this period. One factor is the convoluted route they had to follow within the judiciary. Most suits were processed in courts semispecialized in conflict-related crimes.[21] Provincial prosecutors had to conduct preliminary investigations and decide whether to indict the accused or close down the case. If they filed an indictment, a provincial judge also gathered evidence and decided whether there was probable cause to move to the trial stage. Subsequently, a higher-level prosecutor would investigate the case again and send another indictment to the National Criminal Court, where trials were held. At this point, it was not uncommon for victims to have to wait months for trials to begin because courts easily became overloaded, creating a bottleneck. Finally, after the National Criminal Court handed down a decision, parties usually appealed to the

[21] These specialized courts also dealt with other forms of organized crime such as money laundering, human trafficking, and drug trafficking.

Supreme Court, where yet another prosecutor presented the charges.[22] Defendants often used this convoluted system to their advantage, flooding courts with interlocutory appeals demanding the enforcement of statutes of limitations or the amnesty laws passed by Fujimori, and insisting that the criminal definitions used to indict the defendants were not part of the Peruvian legal framework when the crimes were perpetrated.[23] As a result of these appeals, cases were immersed in a stop-go dynamic up and down the judicial ladder.

However, the main reason for the slow progress of cases was the inherent difficulty involved in the investigation of these crimes. Smoking gun evidence was hard to come by because the rights violations had taken place a long time before the investigations, and the forced disappearance machinery left very few traces. In this sense, witness testimonies were usually all that was left to reconstruct who took the victims or what happened to them later on. The problem was that these individuals often contradicted themselves or offered vague recollections. Moreover, the armed forces were quite reticent to provide information about which officers were deployed in each region. This information was crucial to identify the perpetrators because in Peru officers used pseudonyms during the conflict. As a result, survivors or witnesses never heard the actual names of those in charge of the abductions or the clandestine detention centers. In fact, the inability to identify the perpetrators by name is the reason behind 80 percent of the decisions to shelve cases. Finally, many investigations involved trips to remote and inaccessible regions to gather the testimony of people who only speak indigenous languages. This not only was time consuming, but also required very specific resources, which were often lacking. As the Office of the Ombudsman described it in its 2013 report on the state of the judicialization process:

> In a visit to the city of Ayacucho in March 2013, we established that Supra-Provincial criminal prosecutors do not have a direct landline, fax machine, copier, scanner, film camera, photo camera or laptop for when prosecutors must travel to other provinces to gather testimonies. Moreover, we were informed that in order to conduct exhumations they must themselves purchase tents, special boots and other required materials. (Report No. 162, Office of the Ombudsman, p. 104, my translation)

22 The crimes perpetrated by the paramilitary group known as Grupo Colina followed a similar path but not in these specialized courts. Instead, these cases were investigated in special anticorruption courts of the Lima circuit. Finally, former president Fujimori was tried by a special panel of Supreme Court justices.

23 The Spanish term used in Peru is *pedidos de excepción*.

Despite these procedural and practical obstacles, by international standards the activity of courts between 2004 and 2014 was intense. In addition to a landmark trial against the leadership of the Shining Path, the National Criminal Court held thirty-seven oral trials, twenty-one of which took place during Alan García's term (2006–2011). Overall, forty military and police officers were sentenced to between ten and fifteen years in prison, and ninety-six were acquitted (Table 4.1).[24] The court's overall conviction rate was 29.4 percent. With regard to the nature of the crimes, twenty-four of these trials dealt with forced disappearances, homicides, torture, and massacres perpetrated in the 1990s during the final months of Alan García's first administration and Fujimori's first term in office. Although some trials involved massacres perpetrated in the 1980s, at the time of writing the most emblematic cases of that period were either in the final investigative stages or undergoing trial.[25] Finally, all of the rulings handed down by the National Criminal Court were appealed. The Supreme Court fully upheld nine rulings and invalidated twelve, requesting a new trial for all or some of the defendants usually because it disagreed with how the National Criminal Court had evaluated the evidence. It is worth noting that the Supreme Court only once ordered a retrial following a conviction (Chilliutira case).

Parallel to the activity of the National Criminal Court, the first chamber of the anticorruption circuit in Lima handed down a series of exemplary rulings against the members of the paramilitary group created during the Fujimori administration. In 2008, the three judges ruled against four members of the Grupo Colina and acquitted five others for the forced disappearance and murder of students at La Cantuta University in 1992. Later that year, when the police captured two other members of the Grupo Colina involved in these crimes, the court also issued prison sentences. In November 2005, the judges had already sentenced two other members of the paramilitary group after they confessed the crimes. In *La Cantuta* case, the Supreme Court confirmed the acquittals and seven of the prison sentences and requested a new trial for one of the officers found guilty. In 2010, the same anticorruption court put an end to an oral trial that lasted five years, sentencing nineteen members of the paramilitary group to between four and twenty-five years in prison for perpetrating crimes

[24] The second *Pucara* trial (October 2014) constitutes an exception. In that case, the National Criminal Court sentenced three former members of the military to 20 years in prison, the highest punishment allowed for the crimes in question.

[25] The most notable example is the Accomarca massacre of 1985. The trial began in 2010 and has suffered innumerable delays. It was still ongoing at the time of writing.

Table 4.1. *Rulings in Oral Trials Held at the National Criminal Court (2006–2014)*

Case	Decade of Perpetration	Date of Ruling	Convictions	Acquittals	Upheld by Supreme Court	President at the Time of the Ruling
Castillo Páez	1990s	March 2006	4	12	Yes	Toledo
Céspedes Montalvo I	1990s	November 2006	0	1	Yes	García
Chuschi	1990s	February 2007	2	4	Yes	García
Céspedes Montalvo II	1990s	February 2007	0	1	Yes	García
Barrantes I	1990s	February 2007	0	5	Partially*	García
Bustíos	1990s	October 2007	2	0	Yes	García
Mancilla	1990s	October 2007	0	3	Yes	García
Aponte Ortiz I	1990s	November 2007	2	0	Yes	García
Santa Bárbara I	1990s	March 2008	1	1	No**	García
Haro/Mautino	1980s	July 2008	0	5	Partially*	García
Matero	1990s	August 2008	0	5	No***	García
Osorio I	1980s	December 2008	0	1	No***	García
Tarazona	1990s	2008	1	0	Yes	García
Pomatanta I	1990s	February 2009	1	2	No***	García
Los Cabitos	1980s	October 2009	0	4	No***	García
Los Laureles	1980s	October 2009	0	7	Partially*	García
Acocro	1990s	2009	1	3	Yes	García
Barrantes II	1990s	March 2010	1	0	No***	García

(*continued*)

Table 4.1 (*cont.*)

Case	Decade of Perpetration	Date of Ruling	Convictions	Acquittals	Upheld by Supreme Court	President at the Time of the Ruling
Pucara	1980s	June 2010	2	8	No***	García
Universidad Nacional del Centro I	1980s	June 2010***	0	2	No***	García
Pomatambo y Pracco Alto	1980s	October 2010	0	4	Yes	García
Chilliutira	1990s	June 2011	2	0	No***	García
Pucayacy II	1980s	October 2011	2	0	No decision	Humala
Pomatanta II	1990s	October 2011	1	3	No decision	Humala
Gutierrez Quintero	1990s	2011	1	1	No decision	Humala
Osorio II	1990s	2011	0	1	No decision	Humala
Castillo Cisneros	1980s	2011	0	1	No decision	Humala
Baldeon	1990s	January 2012	1	0	No decision	Humala
Chipana Wayra	N/A	2012	0	1	No decision	Humala
Aponte Ortiz II	1990s	2012	1	1	No decision	Humala
Santa Barbara II	1990s	2012	1	2	No decision	Humala
Constantino Saavedra II	1990s	2012	0	4	No decision	Humala
Los Laureles II	1980s	November 2013	0	6	No decision	Humala
Villanueva	1990s	September 2013	2	0	No decision	Humala

Universidad Nacional del Centro II	1980s	May 2014	2	0	No decision	Humala
Morales Ortega y otros	1990s	May 2014	0	7	No decision	Humala
Pucara II	1980s	October 2014	10	1	No decision	Humala
TOTAL			40	96	CONVICTION RATE: 29.4%	

Sources: The National Criminal Court does not make its rulings available to the public. I found some of the rulings by doing research in the court's archives and used this material as the main primary source for reconstructing the history of the court's performance. These rulings are on file with the author. Whenever I could not locate the text of any given decision I consulted the NGO that represented the victims in a particular case and conducted online searches in the daily newspaper *La República*.

Notes: *Indicates that the Supreme Court requested a new oral trial for some of the defendants. **Indicates that the Supreme Court requested a new oral trial. The most common reasons for requesting a second trial were irregularities found in the proceedings and insufficient evidence. Some of these rulings are on file with the author; others have not been made public. ***Indicates a split decision.

against humanity in the *Barrios Altos*, *El Santa*, and *Yauri* cases. Among them was Valdimiro Montesinos, former chief of the intelligence services and symbol of Fujimori's repressive apparatus. Eleven officials were acquitted.[26] The conviction rate of this Lima based court was an impressive 62.8 percent.

In addition to high-ranking military, police, and intelligence officers, the judicialization process included suits against a former president. After the Chilean judiciary extradited Fujimori in 2007,[27] the Peruvian Supreme Court decided he would face three trials. The first trial concerned severe human rights violations that took place during his presidency, including the massacres and forced disappearances known as *Barrios Altos* and *La Cantuta*. The trial began in early 2008 and lasted until April 2009 when the court sentenced Fujimori to twenty-five years in prison for the crimes of aggravated homicide, assault, and kidnapping.[28] The judges concluded that the status of Fujimori as a former head of state justified the maximum punishment allowed by Peruvian law (Burt 2009). Fujimori's trial constitutes an exceptional achievement in transitional justice worldwide: For the first time in history a democratically elected head of state was convicted by courts in his own country of human rights violations.

The trial received international acclaim for its fairness and impartiality[29] and attracted the daily attention of the Peruvian public. In January 2006, almost three years before the oral hearings started, only 26 percent believed that if Fujimori were to face a trial he would be treated impartially, and 41 percent thought that courts would be biased against him. The Supreme Court was aware of the mistrust it generated among the public and saw the trial as an opportunity to legitimize itself.[30] According to Prusak, given "the high profile and politically sensitive nature of the trial,

[26] All rulings handed down by the first criminal chamber of the anticorruption circuit are on file with the author.

[27] After spending time in Japan, in 2006 Fujimori traveled to Chile with the expectation that being in a neighboring country would facilitate a political comeback. Instead he was imprisoned and eventually extradited. Peruvian human rights organizations joined efforts with their counterparts in Chile to lobby for the extradition (e.g. they traveled to Chile with the victims on multiple occasions) and supplied the legal arguments that made this victory possible (Human Rights Watch 2009).

[28] Suprema Corte de Justicia de la Nación (Peru), *Exp. Nº 10–2001/ Acumulado Nº 45–2003–A.V,* ruling of 7 April 2009. On file with the author.

[29] See Amnesty International (2009) and Human Rights Watch (2009).

[30] The average approval rating of the judiciary between 1991 and 2009 was 26.8 percent. The figure does not include the ratings received in 2003, 2004, and 2006 because of missing data. Source: APOYO. The data are on file with the author.

the Peruvian justices were hyper-vigilant in ensuring that the defendant was afforded all due process and procedural protections necessary to make the trial fair and legitimate" (2010: 889).[31] For example, the judges made sure that the trial was broadcast live to the Peruvian public and that the press had full access to the proceedings. To this end, they authorized myriad domestic and international observers to attend the hearings. As one of the three judges told me in an interview:

> For us it was an opportunity to show what a trial looks like. The support of the media was important in order to broadcast the trial to the whole country. It was a pedagogical opportunity. The trial was like a civics class taught on a massive scale.[32]

These efforts paid off, and by the time the court was ready to hand down its decision the public held the judges in very high esteem. For example, in a survey conducted in January 2009, individuals were asked whether they "approved or disapproved of the performance in the trial of César San Martín," the judge presiding over the hearings. He received a 37 percent job approval and only 34 percent offered no answer, suggesting that the vast majority of the population could now identify a Supreme Court judge by name.[33]

The figures presented thus far indicate that judges regularly and consistently issued punishments and acquittals from the inception of the judicialization process. The condemnatory rulings handed down by these three courts used international law and jurisprudence to characterize the crimes in question as "forced disappearances" and/or "crimes against humanity."[34] In the rulings of the National Criminal Court for which the full text is available, I found an average of 15.2 references to international human rights treaties or the jurisprudence of international courts per decision.[35] These

[31] For example, after the defense attorneys argued that Fujimori had severe health problems, the judges decided to shorten the duration of the hearings.

[32] Interview, Lima, 28 May 2010.

[33] The survey was conducted by IPSOS APOYO. The data are on file with the author.

[34] For example, "crimes against humanity" are not codified in Peruvian law. For a discussion of the problems raised by these issues see Quinteros (2010).

[35] I could only obtain 13 rulings: *Castillo Páez, Chuschi, Bustios, Universidad Nacional del Centro I, Constantino Saavedra, Santa Bárbara I, Matero, Efrain Aponte I and II, Los Laureles I, Mancilla Calle, Haro y Mautino,* and *Pomatanta I.* These rulings make reference to the Inter-American Commission of Human Rights, the Inter-American Court of Human Rights, the UN, the Inter-American Convention on Forced Disappearances, the International Criminal Court, the American Convention on Human Rights, the International Covenant on Civil and Political Rights, the OAS, the Universal Declaration of Human Rights, the American Declaration of the Rights and Duties of Man, the Convention

doctrinal innovations made it possible to overcome formalistic readings of the legality principle, and thus disregard the exhaustion of statutes of limitations or prior rulings by military courts and aggravate the punishment of those found guilty. For example in *Chuschi*, the National Criminal Court justified its characterization of the crimes as "forced disappearances," a criminal definition not operative at the time of perpetration, but one that affords greater protection to the victims:

> One of the consequences of considering the crime of forced disappearance as a permanent crime is that although it is true that according to the legality principle prohibitive legislation must precede the crime, in the case of permanent crimes the applicable criminal legislation is not necessarily that which was valid when the crime was perpetrated. The criminal behavior continues until the whereabouts of the victim are established. As a result if during this period a new, more serious criminal type becomes part of the legislative framework it can be applied. (*Chuschi*, National Criminal Court, pp. 101–102)

Similarly in *Bustios*, a case tried in the early 1990s by military courts, the National Criminal Court used Inter-American jurisprudence to grant an exception to the *non bis in idem* principle:

> Exceptions to the enforcement of the *non bis in idem* principle are grounded on states' responsibility to investigate, prosecute and punish. The right to be protected against multiple judicial proceedings initiated by the state should be considered alongside the requirement that those who violate international human rights law must be brought to justice. (*Bustios*, National Criminal Court, pp. 4–5)

In cases such as *Castillo Páez*, *Fujimori*, *La Cantuta*, and *Barrios Altos*, judges also explicitly applied a nonformalistic human rights vision to evaluate the evidence. In these cases, judges recognized that given the nature of the crimes in question, it was unfair to demand that prosecutors and human rights litigants produce direct incriminating evidence in order to establish individual criminal responsibility, such as official documents ordering the disappearance of a prisoner. Evidence about the historical context in which the crimes were committed, as well as oral testimonies and journalistic investigations, thus became crucial. For example, in Fujimori's trial the Supreme Court argued that common knowledge about how state-sponsored criminal organizations work "indicates that the usual

on the Prevention and Punishment of the Crime of Genocide, the Convention on the Rights of the Child, and the Convention on the Non-Applicability of Statutory Limitations to War Crimes and Crimes against Humanity.

practice is not to register the issuing of illegal commands in a [formal] request or document, because what is crucial is the concrete, effective and real power that is exercised by the heads of the organization, and that those below recognize".[36] Moreover, "it is precisely the clandestine nature and the illicit practices of an organization what leads to rule out, for obvious reasons, the possibility of proving its existence and the acts it perpetrated using [written] normative instruments."[37]

The preceding rulings show that judges adapted the standards of normal criminal prosecutions to the nature of the cases in question by applying human rights criteria. More importantly, in all cases, acquittals were decided on the basis of interpreting available evidence, and not by invoking legal formalisms such as amnesties or statutes of limitations to stop criminal prosecutions. In this sense, during the course of the investigations and trials, lower courts had to decide on numerous interlocutory appeals filed by the defendants invoking these formalisms or other written rules of criminal procedure with the intention of stopping the trials. The data on these appeals suggest the development of a culture of legal interpretation that transcends plain-meaning interpretation and delves into questions about fundamental rights and state responsibilities, which may or may not be part of positive law.

Between 2004 and 2008, for example, eight interlocutory appeals were filed invoking the validity of amnesties, and thirteen invoking statutes of limitations. An additional thirty-five argued that criminal definitions used in the indictments were not included in Peruvian law at the time of the events, and seventeen claimed that the trials could not proceed because they concerned matters already adjudicated (Table 4.2).[38] In total, twenty-four of these appeals were granted, while the remaining forty-nine were rejected.[39] Of the twenty-four interlocutory appeals accepted by lower courts, nineteen correspond to objections raised against the definition of the crimes. Unlike the exhaustion of statutes of limitations or the enforcement of amnesties, accepting this type of request does not stop criminal prosecutions, but simply implies that prosecutors must reframe their accusations.

[36] Suprema Corte de Justicia de la Nación, *Exp. Nº 10-2001/ Acumulado Nº 45-2003-A.V*, ruling of 7 April 2009. On file with the author.

[37] Ibid.

[38] This is because some of the cases in question were investigated and closed by military courts in the 1980s and 1990s.

[39] All of these figures correspond to decisions made by the National Criminal Court and, when appeals did not reach that level, by lower courts.

Table 4.2. *Interlocutory Appeals Filed by Defendants (2004–2008)*

Type of interlocutory appeal	Accepted	Rejected
Amnesties	0	8
Statutes of limitations	2	11
Definition of the crime	19	16
Double jeopardy	3	14

Source: Report No. 139. Office of the Ombudsman.

These jurisprudential innovations ignited by lower courts were consolidated and deepened by a series of decisions handed down by the Constitutional Court throughout the 2000s.[40] This court made a series of criteria concerning the interpretation of the obligations of the Peruvian state in investigating and punishing gross human rights violations authoritative. In order to do so it consistently read the 1993 constitution in light of international treaties and the rulings of the Inter-American Court of Human Rights. The impact of this court's activism in the area of human rights is widely recognized within the judiciary. For example, in one of the questions included in an original survey of human rights prosecutors, respondents were asked to rate on a scale of 1 to 10 the importance of Constitutional Court rulings in tracing the jurisprudential path to truth and justice.[41] The average response was 8.5, indicating the existence of a general consensus about the role of constitutional judges in the judicialization process.

On several occasions the Constitutional Court recognized the right to truth and the need for the state to commit itself to fight against impunity in cases that involve serious offenses against humanity. In a 2004 ruling, the judges defined the right to truth as an implicit right recognized by the constitution, since "the Nation has the right to know the truth about unjust and painful facts or events produced by multiple forms of state and non-state violence.... In this sense the right to truth is an inalienable

[40] Landmark rulings include STC 2488-2002-HC/TC, ruling of 18 March 2004; STC-2798-2004-HC/TC, ruling of 9 December 2004; STC 4677-2005-HC/TC, ruling of 8 December 2005; STC 4587-2004-PA/TC, ruling of 11 November 2005; STC 679-2005-PA/TC, ruling of 2 March 2007; STC 3938-2007-PA/TC, ruling of 5 November 2007; and STC 01271-2008-PA/TC, ruling of 8 August 2007. I cite the rulings using the nomenclature employed by the Constitutional Court, which will facilitate readers' search for these documents on the court's Website: www.tc.gob.pe.

[41] See later discussion for details about the survey.

collective juridical good."[42] The magnitude of these atrocities, which the court has repeatedly referred to as "crimes against humanity," mandates that the state cannot establish limits to its prerogative to conduct a criminal investigation, prosecute, and punish those responsible, even if "a long time has passed since the date when the illicit act was committed."[43]

The Constitutional Court was also a central actor in setting limits on the jurisdiction of military courts.[44] In the early to mid-2000s, disputes between civilian and military courts over which system had the right to intervene in the judicialization process threatened to jeopardize transitional justice in Peru. Defense lawyers claimed that their clients should be put within the orbit of military tribunals because the crimes they were accused of were committed while serving as military officers. They did so anticipating the lack of impartiality of military judges when investigating their peers. When deciding on this issue, the Constitutional Court consistently ruled in favor of excluding gross human rights violations from the jurisdiction of military courts. It rejected the formalistic definition of military misconduct as "crimes committed on active duty"[45] and defined them as regular crimes subject to civilian jurisdiction. Moreover, the court ruled that even in those cases in which military judges can intervene, they are not exempt from applying normal due process clauses and the human rights criteria established by the American Convention.

The Constitutional Court's expansive reading of rights embedded in the constitution cemented the criteria developed by lower courts to reject the interlocutory appeals filed by defense lawyers. In doing so, courts at different levels of the judiciary established that there could not be positive or formal legal barriers to redress conflict-era human rights violations. As shown previously, this allowed victims and their lawyers to achieve crucial victories in the judicialization process. The decisions issued by civilian courts led to the incarceration of perpetrators of all ranks for crimes committed under different political regimes. Those found guilty include members of the powerful Peruvian armed forces and the leaders of a political

42 STC 2488-2002-HC/TC, ruling of 18 March 2004, Consideration No. 8, my translation.

43 Ibid.

44 Landmark rulings include STC 0017-2003-AI/TC, ruling of 16 March 2004; STC 0023-2003-AI/TC, ruling of 9 June 2004; STC 0004-2006-AI/TC, ruling of 17 April 17 2006; STC 0006-2006-PI/TC, ruling of 13 June 2006; STC 0012-2006-PHC/TC, ruling of 15 December 2006; STC 8353-2006-PHC/TC, ruling of 9 April 2007; STC 01605-2006-PHC/TC, ruling of 30 June 2008; 00005/2007-PI/TC, ruling of 26 August 2008; 01524-2007-PHC/TC, ruling of 9 December 2008; 05567-2007-PHC/TC, ruling of 3 February 2009, and 00002-2008-PI/TC ruling of 9 September 2009.

45 The Spanish term is *delitos en función*.

group that governed the country for a decade and continued being a relevant actor after the democratic transition.

Human Rights Trials in Unfriendly Territory

What explains this intense judicial activity around the investigation and punishment of gross human rights violations in Peru? This question is more intriguing if one considers that during the period in which most judicial victories were achieved, courts were subject to all sorts of intimidation tactics deployed by sitting presidents and the military, with the goal of undermining their commitment to the progress of the cases. As mentioned before, some of my interviewees referred to the 2000 political transition as "the NGO transition." During those years, human rights activists were a powerful voice in the political arena and staffed the state with their members. The issue of coming to terms with the past was a high priority and activists managed to implement their agenda. Congress investigated corruption scandals that had Fujimori and his cronies as the main protagonists; two consecutive presidents (Paniagua 2000–2001 and Toledo 2001–2006) offered support for the creation and operations of the Truth and Reconciliation Commission, heavily influenced by the human rights movement; and the judiciary created a semispecialized court system to deal with criminals belonging to both state and nonstate organizations. But when I conducted fieldwork in 2010, the good days had been over for quite some time. In the words of an activist lawyer, "The political discourse against the judicialization process has become the dominant voice."[46] Another one acknowledged that "our enemies have become more powerful; the armed forces have regained their political influence and the government has forged an alliance with them in order to anchor its power."[47] Yet a third concluded: "We are weaker now and our adversaries take advantage of that in order to strengthen their influence over important arenas where our legal battle takes place."[48]

The political space for action in the area of transitional justice indeed narrowed after 2006. The rise to power of APRA's Alan García, together with the electoral recovery of Fujimori's party,[49] completely changed the

[46] Interview, Lima, 14 April 14 2010.
[47] Interview, Lima, 21 April 2010.
[48] Interview, Ayacucho, 5 May 2010.
[49] In the 2006 legislative elections Fujimori's daughter, Keiko, was the candidate who received the largest number of votes. In 2011, she almost won the runoff presidential election against Ollanta Humala, garnering 48.6 percent of the vote.

environment. Between 1985 and 1990, Alan García presided over some of the bloodiest years of the armed conflict.[50] As a result of his status as commander in chief of the police and the armed forces during those years, he was later accused of being responsible for several massacres, including the murder of hundreds of convicts at El Frontón and Castro Castro prisons.[51] It therefore comes as no surprise that his second presidency was characterized by a hostile attitude toward the judicialization process. The vice president, a former general also accused of being involved in human rights violations, and the minister of defense were both extremely vocal in their support for the army officers affected by the trials. On several occasions, the president himself demanded an end to what he saw as a political persecution against those who "defended the interests of the fatherland."[52]

Changes in the presidential palace were accompanied by a recovery of the military's political leverage. After the collapse of Fujimori's regime, the armed forces were in disarray.[53] As Figure 4.2 suggests, in 2002 they received the lowest approval rating since 1997, but they subsequently regained political prestige, achieving levels of support similar to those registered during the early 1990s, immediately after the capture of the leader of the Shining Path, Abimael Guzmán. This improvement in their public standing is correlated with higher levels of political leverage due to their strategic role in the government's antinarcotics policy[54] and in dealing with the rise in violent social conflicts in the interior of the country.[55] In 2009, for example, the Constitutional Court justified a decision that expanded the independence of military courts vis-à-vis judicial oversight institutions in a case unrelated to the judicialization of human rights violations. It stated that the country witnessed "the reinvigoration of terrorism in alliance with drug trafficking" and hence the armed forces needed greater autonomy.[56]

50 Although the greatest number of deaths in any given year took place in 1984 (approximately 4,000), during García's presidency the violence spread to more districts and reached the second highest peak of deaths in 1989 (more than 2,500 approximately). See Comisión de la Verdad y Reconciliación (2003), volume I, chapter III, p. 117.

51 Investigations in *El Frontón* and *Castro Castro* cases are still ongoing.

52 *El Comercio*, 6 June 2010.

53 For an analysis of the politicization of the armed forces during the 1990s and the internal conflicts that emerged as a result, see Comisión de la Verdad y Reconciliación (2003), volume II, chapter III.

54 According to the United Nations, Peru is now the largest cocaine producer in the world. See United Nations (2010). For a journalistic account of the rise in military antinarcotics activities see *La República*, 5 May 2010.

55 For an analysis of the exponential increase in violent protests see Meléndez and León (2009).

56 STC 00001-2009-PI/TC, ruling of 4 December 2009.

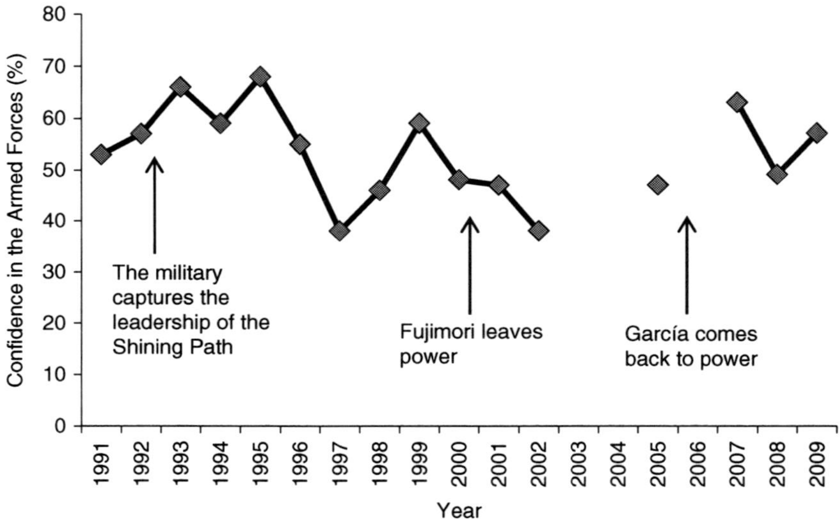

Figure 4.2. Confidence in the Armed Forces (1991–2009).
Source: APOYO, based on nationally representative surveys. Figures represent responses to the question "In general, would you say you feel confidence in the Armed Forces or not?" No data are available for the years 2003, 2004, and 2006.

The greater reliance of the government on the armed forces to confront security and governability challenges naturally improved the standing of the institution in relation to human rights investigations. In the aforementioned survey of prosecutors, 100 percent of respondents strongly agreed with the statement that the Ministry of Defense and the armed forces generated obstacles to the progress of the investigations (Table 4.3). The results also indicate that the lack of cooperation from these actors was perceived as more problematic for the success of the judicialization process than the excessive workload, or the lack of adequate material resources to carry out their duties.

Given the questions asked, the preceding data cannot fully gauge judges' and prosecutors' perceptions of the extent to which García's support for the armed forces increased their leverage vis-à-vis human rights investigations. In order to document temporal variation in the tolerance of elites, I rely on qualitative evidence gathered during interviews. In all of my interviews with judges and prosecutors the lack of collaboration of the armed forces and the Ministry of Defense was the first thing mentioned when asked about the main obstacles they faced. My sources unanimously pointed out that the reticence to release

Table 4.3. *Prosecutors' Perceptions of the Obstacles Faced during Investigations*

Question	Average response
Please indicate how much you agree with the following statements... Strongly agree = 4; Somewhat agree = 3; Somewhat disagree = 2; Strongly disagree = 1	
The Ministry of Defense creates obstacles that make the progress of the investigations for human rights violations slow	4
Large dockets make the progress of human rights investigations slow	2.6
The lack of material resources makes the progress of human rights investigations slow	3.3

Source: Original survey. Target universe: All prosecutors involved in human rights cases. Anonymous survey administered online. Link to survey sent via email by chief prosecutor on behalf of the author. Response rate: 43.5 percent.

documentation about the activities of the military and the police during the armed conflict worsened after 2006. For example, the head of the anticorruption team in the Attorney General's Office who presented charges against Fujimori and his allies for human rights violations, indicated:

> At first, gathering information was difficult because the military was still controlled by Montesinos's allies.... Paniagua [the transition president between 2000 and 2001] removed many of these high commanders, and made our job much easier. In contrast to the current situation, during those years we did not face problems when asking the Ministry of Defense to send us information. In fact, with the aid of a very courageous judge, we even broke into military intelligence headquarters and found documents, human remains and the ovens in which they were cremated.[57]

In the words of a prosecutor working in Ayacucho:

> The lack of collaboration by the Ministry of Defense is the biggest problem we face. The lack of information is key to explain the slow progress of many cases. If we cannot identify the military personnel active in this area in the 1980s and 1990s, we cannot individualize those responsible for the crimes we investigate, and therefore cannot file indictments. The military has those records. All that we have are the aliases of the alleged perpetrators that the victims heard while in prison or when their relatives were kidnapped.[58]

[57] Interview, Lima, 19 March 2010.
[58] Interview, Ayacucho, 1 May 2010.

A judge offered a similar perspective on this issue:

> During Toledo's presidency [2001–2006], while I was an anticorruption judge I took part in the investigations against the Grupo Colina. . . . In those years there was a lot of room for us to act, and we achieved many things. In fact we captured a lot of fugitive military and police officers. This shows that there was political will; otherwise the police would not have responded to our requests to find these individuals. Nowadays the situation is different. We have submitted a number of arrest warrants but those in charge show no interest in following through. . . . Also, on many occasions the armed forces and the Ministry of Defense refuse to submit the documentation we ask for. I now feel that they are in a more powerful position to overlook our requests.[59]

In addition to concealing information, the García administration strived to create resource imbalances between the parties involved in the trials, thus strengthening the position of military and police officers. For example, in 2006 the government sent to congress a proposal to grant the Peruvian Agency for International Cooperation the authority to punish civil society organizations that were considered to have violated regulations on the reception of international aid effectively. The bill was intended to enhance government control over NGO funding, which originates disproportionately in foreign countries and foundations. The law was passed and resulted in sanctions against human rights NGOs. Similarly, the Ministry of Defense was also active in ensuring that those accused of human rights violations had access to the services of prominent Lima attorneys.[60] For instance, the state approached the same private law firm hired by Fujimori's family, seeking advice for the defense of military officers. This possibility was never offered to the victims of state repression. Many of them still lack access to lawyers because NGOs do not have the resources to take on thousands of cases.[61]

García also forged a parliamentary alliance with Fujimori's party. The president could never count on a legislative majority and was forced to build coalitions to pass his agenda through congress. After the 2006 elections, Fujimori's followers consolidated a cohesive legislative caucus, which became the second largest in parliament after other more numerous

[59] Interview, 6 May 2010.

[60] See Presidential Decrees N° 061-2006 and N° 022-2008-DE/SG. On file with the author.

[61] Estimates indicate that only 39.1 percent of the victims involved in the judicialization process have access to lawyers. See Report No. 139, Office of the Ombudsman, available online at www.defensoria.gov.pe.

blocs disintegrated (Valladares 2010).[62] When Fujimori's extradition was imminent, and during his trial, these legislators threatened to break the tacit alliance they had with APRA in order to gain leverage in their negotiations with the government. Despite Fujimori's conviction, the alliance did not break and both parties consistently voted together in favor of the president's policies (Panfichi 2009).

The inroads that Fujimori's followers made into the parliamentary arena after 2006 turned congress into another institution hostile to human rights NGOs, whose capacity to lobby congress to pass their legislative proposals was very limited. One indicator of this is the low participation of human rights NGOs in the debates of the Justice and Human Rights Committee in charge of analyzing bills related to the human rights agenda. Between 2000 and 2009 the Justice and Human Rights Committee met 167 times, and only on 5 of these occasions were members of human rights organizations invited to present their point of view or participate in debates. In contrast, other civil society organizations had easy access to legislators. For example, the Energy and Mining Committee met 75 times between 2005 and 2009. Civil society and business representatives were invited to 23 of those meetings.[63] The high presence of civil society actors in debates at the Energy and Mining Committee is due to the fact that the committee dealt with a policy area in which there was greater consensus among political elites, and between them and powerful business organizations.[64] This comparison suggests that congress was not necessarily an inhospitable arena for lobbying tactics, but that human rights organizations were not welcome. This was confirmed by numerous sources including the highest-ranked clerk in the Justice and Human Rights Committee[65] and by human rights activists themselves. According to one of them:

> Congress is a lost cause for us. If in the previous congress [2001–2006] we were invited on a handful of occasions, in the current one the situation is even worse. Congress has adopted a confrontational attitude towards us that has worsened with time. The Justice and Human Rights Committee is mainly concerned with passing laws to control the activities of NGOs. Fujimori's lawyer is the committee's president, so there's no room for us there.[66]

62 García's APRA and the Fujimoristas are the only legislative caucuses that were not decimated by the lack of party discipline. See Meléndez and León (2010).

63 This information was gathered by analyzing the minutes of these meetings.

64 The mining industry is one of the pillars of Peru's economy.

65 Interview, Lima, 22 March 2010.

66 Interview, Lima, 14 April 2010.

The hostility toward the human rights cause peaked in 2010, when García issued Presidential Decree No. 1097. Human rights activists and sectors of the media characterized the move as an amnesty in disguise. In contrast to other more subtle tactics deployed to minimize the impact of the investigations and trials, this decree intended to strike a fatal blow against the entire judicialization process. In August, congress interpreted a recent Constitutional Court ruling as demanding a series of amendments to the Criminal Code of Military Justice.[67] In order to comply with the ruling, legislators passed a law granting the executive the power to introduce those modifications by decree. In September, the changes were announced and unexpectedly included a series of guidelines related to the treatment of human rights cases by civilian courts.[68] One of them mandated the immediate closing of all criminal prosecutions that had been open for more than fourteen months. Another instruction forced upon courts an interpretation of the Convention on the Non-Applicability of Statutory Limitations to War Crimes and Crimes against Humanity. The decree stated that since Peru ratified the convention in 2003, the criteria used by courts to ignore statutes of limitations in cases of human rights violations could not be applied to crimes committed before that year – i.e., to all of the cases still under investigation. The initiative also questioned the legitimacy of the rulings handed down until that day because courts had applied the convention retroactively in all of those decisions.

The decree triggered the immediate reaction of human rights organizations. They took center stage and denounced the government for trying to stop the judicialization process with unconstitutional guidelines.[69] Constitutional law professors allied to the human rights movement explained in the media the arguments judges should use in order to apply judicial review to overturn the decree.[70] They emphasized the possibility of using international jurisprudence to do so, in particular the rulings of the Inter-American Court. Experts argued that if judges implemented the decree, they would be violating the state's international responsibility to investigate and punish gross human rights violations.

[67] STC 00001-2009-PI/TC, ruling of 4 December 2009. Congress's interpretation of the ruling was questionable because the court did not explicitly mandate this.

[68] It was later revealed that the minister of defense received advice from Fujimori's lawyers when drafting the decree. See *IDL-Reporteros*, 24 September 2010.

[69] Examples of public statements by human rights NGOs can be found in *La República*, 2 September 2010 and 8 September 2010, and *Caretas*, 9 September 2010.

[70] *La República*, 3 September 2010.

Several days after the decree was published, one of the accused in the *Barrios Altos* case asked the first criminal chamber of the anticorruption circuit court in Lima to terminate the trial and close the case.[71] Judges were quick to respond and handed down a unanimous ruling declaring the decree unconstitutional.[72] The fact that the ruling was unanimous is quite telling of the outrage the decree triggered among judges, because one of the three members of this chamber had consistently voted to acquit defendants in other cases. In addition to this court's decisive response, the prosecutors in charge of human rights cases released a document carefully explaining why they refused to apply the decree. In what amounted to a manifesto of what they perceived to be their new institutional mission, they emphasized that if the new regulations were accepted, and cases were closed either because statutes of limitations were invoked or there were delays in the investigations, the country would be sanctioning impunity, thus aggravating victims' situation.[73] This corporate reaction by members of the judicial branch allowed them to prevail in their confrontation with the executive. As my sociological institutionalist approach indicates, sharing certain values regarding the correct exercise of judicial prerogatives increased their ability to overcome collective action problems and enhanced the decisiveness of their efforts to defend their position actively. In the process, the president incurred great political costs. After he failed to explain why the decree was not aimed at obstructing transitional justice, the president derogated the norm. In addition, he was forced to restructure the cabinet by firing the prime minister and the ministers of justice, defense, and finance.

This episode is interesting because it clearly reveals two aspects of the Peruvian judicialization process. First, the tolerance of political actors for the investigations and trials was extremely low. Second, human rights organizations could count on a series of crucial allies in the judiciary who, in spite of adverse political conditions, expressed their commitment to the progress of the cases in no uncertain terms. But beyond all this posturing, was it in fact professionally or personally risky to defy politicians? Did judges and prosecutors enjoy the protection of formal institutional safeguards that minimized the costs of defiance? In other words, can formal judicial independence explain the outcome of the judicialization process amid political hostility? Or was it in fact necessary to reconfigure judges and prosecutors'

[71] *La República*, 6 September 2010. The trial had lasted for more than 14 months.

[72] Expediente 28–2001, ruling of 15 September 2010. On file with the author.

[73] *La República*, 9 September 2010.

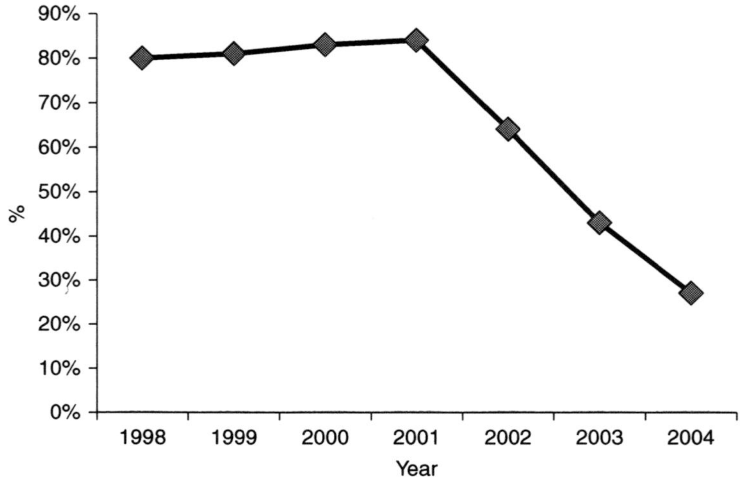

Figure 4.3. Untenured Judges in the Peruvian Judiciary by Year (%).
Source: Justicia Viva (2006).

legal preferences and their understanding of their institutional mission externally, providing them with normative and professional incentives to discount very real risks? The next two sections answer these questions.

Formal Judicial Independence and Informal Intimidation Tactics

After the political transition in 2000, some of the institutional conditions highlighted in the judicial politics literature as guarantors of formal judicial independence were restored (Ferejohn 1998; Domingo 1999; Ríos Figueroa and Taylor 2006; Ríos Figueroa and Staton 2014; Ríos Figueroa 2011). During Fujimori's authoritarian regime several judges and prosecutors were sacked in order to fill those positions with government allies. Moreover, the proportion of untenured judicial actors increased, exposing judges and prosecutors to the fear of losing their jobs if they opposed the regime's wishes (Finkel 2008; Dargent 2009). When Fujimori resigned as president, the transitional government reinstated a number of those judges. Among them were three former members of the Constitutional Court, who in 1997 had ruled against Fujimori's intention to run for a third term and were subsequently impeached. Figure 4.3 shows that the levels of untenured judges also declined, enhancing the formal political insulation of the judiciary.

As Dargent's (2009) analysis of the Constitutional Court suggests, the higher levels of political pluralism and fragmentation that accompanied the transition also opened up spaces for bolder patterns of judicial behavior with greater impact in sensitive policy areas – often against the government's wishes. In this context, it was harder for parties to galvanize enough votes in congress to appoint extremely partisan nominees.[74] Moreover, once seated, judges knew that high levels of interparty consensus had to be reached in order to impeach them. Furthermore, my interviews with several Supreme Court and Constitutional Court justices indicate that after the democratic transition, they felt more secure in their positions. Fujimori's takeover of the judiciary was still a very traumatic and vivid memory. As a result, "any politician who seeks to imitate the previous regime would pay an incredibly high political cost because he or she would be reproached both locally and abroad."[75]

Formally independent judges, however, were not a guarantee that transitional justice efforts would succeed. As in Argentina during the Menem years, the Peruvian anti–transitional justice coalition engaged in systematic attempts to prevent the judiciary from further pushing human rights cases forward. These players came to the realization that judicial autonomy would put their interests in jeopardy and decided to act in order to undermine that autonomy and the incipient commitment of certain judges and prosecutors to the human rights cause. Their tactics aimed at inducing strategic behavior among judicial actors involved in the investigation and trials by highlighting the risks entailed in defying powerful political and military groups. There were three types of interventions: personal threats, the manipulation of the rules governing the internal workings of the judiciary, and "judicial clientelism." All of them undermined the protective character of formal institutional safeguards.

After the mid-2000s, judges and prosecutors were constantly exposed to intimidation tactics and anonymous threats. Their investigations and rulings affected extremely powerful actors, which could count upon the necessary information and means of violence to do harm. When I interviewed them, several judges and prosecutors mentioned they were victims

[74] Any lawyer can apply for a position in the Constitutional Court. Applicants are ranked according to a number of meritocratic criteria including past experience, academic qualifications, publications, and performance in candidacy exams. A special congressional committee interviews those at the top of the ranking. A congressional supermajority is needed in order to approve the nominations.

[75] Supreme Court judge, interview, Lima, 28 May 2010.

of these tactics. For example, a judge recounted her traumatic experience in the following terms:

> I constantly receive threats, especially by military officers during the hearings. Once one of these individuals tried to intimidate us saying that he knew where my colleague in the court and I spent time when we weren't at work. It was clear that he knew exactly at what time we left the office, etc. My colleague's son has also been shot.[76]

The government also enforced disciplinary sanctions against judicial actors. These initiatives were intended to set standards of acceptable behavior, especially among judges and prosecutors who sought to be promoted or ratified in their posts. The anti–transitional justice coalition used to its advantage a formal rule that stipulates that judges and prosecutors must be evaluated every seven years, and can be removed on the basis of those evaluations. In this context, disciplinary sanctions or formal accusations of malicious prosecution[77] can harm an individual's chance of keeping his or her job. The most notable example is that of Cristina Olazábal, a prosecutor in charge of investigating the *Cayara* and *Accomarca* massacres perpetrated during García's first presidency. In 2006, she indicted García and a number of former military officers, a decision that put her job security at risk. After García was sworn in as president, the nation's chief prosecutor initiated an internal investigation and presented charges against Olazábal arguing that she had engaged in malicious prosecution. She was subsequently untenured and demoted.

This episode became emblematic of the executive's determination to undermine the commitment of judicial actors vis-à-vis human rights cases. As one of Olazábal's colleagues admitted:

> What happened to Cristina Olazábal is frightening. We need to be very careful when confronting with these individuals. After that unfortunate episode many prosecutors have seriously considered whether to move on with the investigations or to put them on hold.[78]

A high-ranking prosecutor also described how this episode affected his subordinates:

> The accusation presented against Olazábal is something that I think should not have happened. It has spread a lot of fear among prosecutors. I can

[76] Interview, Lima, 23 March 2010.

[77] In Spanish the word *prevaricato* refers to a charge brought against a judge or prosecutor who wrongfully applies the law.

[78] Interview, Ayacucho, 1 May 2010.

> make a mistake, but it's my opinion and cannot lead to formal charges for malicious prosecution! Instead of backing prosecutors and giving them the tools they need to face extremely complicated and dangerous investigations, the chief prosecutor attacks them. These shenanigans are aimed at discouraging prosecutors, at dilapidating their commitment to truth and justice.[79]

Finally, a provincial judge also acknowledged that judges were not exempt from these fears. He explained that since the aforementioned episode, many of his colleagues have been "afraid to launch bold accusations using innovative definitions that characterize the crimes with the appropriate legal language, like Cristina did.... They do not want to suffer the consequences."[80]

Prosecutors and judges interpreted the Olazábal case as a warning sign and a reminder that their professional futures did not necessarily depend on their merits as public servants. In this sense, arbitrary disciplinary sanctions were combined with the activation of well-known patterns of judicial clientelism in order to produce the desired effects. García's political party, APRA, was mentioned in many of my interviews with judges and prosecutors as having expanded its influence over the judiciary between 2006 and 2011. With the aid of some judicial authorities, García manipulated appointments and arbitrarily transferred judges from some courts in order to keep them away from sensitive human rights cases. The message was clear: Being out of sync with powerful political actors, or not having the right political connections could lead to a stagnant judicial career or to its abrupt termination. The testimony of one of the judges interviewed for this study crystallized the consensus about APRA's relationship with the judiciary:

> The judiciary is full of staunch APRA supporters, especially here in Lima. I was part of the anticorruption courts and could have been promoted to a criminal chamber. Instead I was sent back to a regular criminal court. My problem was that in the 1980s I was a high-ranking clerk in a special Supreme Court panel that tried four of García's ministers. As a result, for APRA I am a persona non grata. These are the informal mechanisms that do not kick you out of the game, but make your life really difficult. They are the ones who decide on your professional future. When I was about to begin investigating the *El Frontón* case, they sent me to another court. They obviously know about my position with regard to, for example, statutes of limitations, so they got rid of me.[81]

[79] Interview, Lima, 26 May 2010.
[80] Interview, Ayacucho, 3 May 2010.
[81] Interview, Lima, 26 March 2010.

The party's past record in office enhances the credibility of my sources: APRA's colonization of the bench in the late 1980s was one of the central arguments used by Fujimori in the early 1990s when he launched the restructuring of an institution that was at the time seen as corrupt and inefficient (Lovatón 2003; Finkel 2008). Ironically, Fujimori used the discourse of accountability and transparency to bias the judiciary in his favor as well as to undermine its autonomy.

Changes in the balance of power thus diminished the effectiveness of gains in formal judicial independence achieved after the democratic transition. In a move intended to institutionalize its interests in the judicial branch and halt the judicialization process, a highly determined proimpunity coalition informally circumvented parchment barriers seeking to deter committed judges and assign human rights cases to the orbit of friendly ones. The extant literature on judicial behavior and common sense both indicate that in this type of political environment, one should observe high levels of judicial caution and timid rulings. In transitional justice processes, this pattern should be enhanced, not only because the liberty of powerful individuals is at stake, but also because the legal arguments that judges and prosecutors must endorse to make those politically risky moves defy some of the most basic rules of professional behavior in criminal prosecutions. When ruling against the defendants, judges challenge not only the political and military establishments, but also the legal establishment. Why put their careers on the line if received legal understandings indicate that statutes of limitations constrain the punitive power of the state? Why jeopardize their physical integrity if the criminal definitions invoked by litigants were not part of positive law at the time when the crimes were committed? Why take such risky moves if they could easily argue against the retroactive application of international treaties and conventions? These questions point to the need to inquire about the sources of a widespread commitment to justice and the penetration of an alternative legal discourse that made it possible.

Transforming Legal Preferences with Pedagogical Interventions

So far I have shown that the political environment was not one that favored the human rights cause. But despite the use of aggressive intimidation tactics by proimpunity actors, judges and prosecutors did not act strategically: They did not bury their heads in the ground, halt cases, systematically hand down acquittals, or passively accept instructions from the executive branch. One could argue that progress after 2006 is a result of the momentum generated by a previous political climate supportive of the judicialization process. We continued to observe positive outcomes only because during the initial posttransition period judicial actors could collect evidence and file indictments. Judges and prosecutors were simply finishing what they had started in the early 2000s. This perspective is, however, unsatisfactory. The existence of extremely bold condemnatory rulings after 2006 and the reaction of judges and prosecutors to initiatives such as Decree 1097 indicate there was something else going on. Moreover, the Peruvian judiciary had a bad record when it came to the protection of individual rights and virtually no experience in processing complex legal arguments based on international human rights law, so even prosecutorial progress before 2006 requires an explanation. In this sense, it is important to identify what changed in the judiciary after the democratic transition, the driving force behind this change, and the reasons why the transformation was resilient despite García's backlash.

In line with the theory presented in Chapter 2, the outcome in the Peruvian case is better accounted for by an explanation that looks at changes in the legal preferences harbored by judicial actors and in their institutional commitments. Even when political elites supported their cause, NGOs were aware that a favorable political environment was not enough to guarantee effective and committed judicial behavior. An incompetent judiciary still represented a considerable blockage on the road to justice. Human rights lawyers also astutely anticipated that if in the future political tolerance for transitional justice decreased, judges who did not have articulate pro–transitional justice legal arguments would be more likely to capitulate in the face of fierce pressures. They proceeded to take advantage of the opportunities afforded by the favorable posttransition climate to deploy an ambitious diffusion effort within the judiciary. This signaled the presence of a vocal and organized support structure willing to back courageous judges and prosecutors publicly. Most importantly, however, NGOs designed pedagogical interventions in order to craft a constituency of judicial actors for whom ending the judicialization process contravened a series of norms and legal understandings internalized as guiding premises of their professional undertakings. In so doing, activists empowered judges with the legal tools necessary to defeat impunity and sustain an ambitious program of criminal prosecutions over time.

The Purpose of Pedagogical Interventions: Identifying the Problem of Legal Preferences

In the immediate aftermath of the 2000 democratic transition, human rights litigants were aware of the poor record of the Peruvian judiciary in the defense of fundamental rights during the internal armed conflict.

Their own experience with domestic litigation in the 1990s indicated that triggering important changes within the institution was a precondition for achieving victories in a future judicialization process. In order to deal with human rights cases successfully, judicial actors had to modify their standards of legal praxis radically, engaging in unprecedented interpretations of the law and changing their passive approach to these criminal investigations. In other words, as their Argentine counterparts did, litigants correctly diagnosed that extant legal preferences would constitute a primary obstacle in their struggle.

According to the Final Report of the Truth and Reconciliation Commission, during the 1980s, judges and prosecutors abdicated their prerogative to investigate the crimes perpetrated by both parties involved in the conflict (the military and the Shining Path), and in the 1990s, they passively endorsed and applied draconian antiterrorism legislation. In other words, the victims could not count on the support of a critical mass of committed judicial actors:

> The judiciary lacked a real capacity to act, or what is even worse, did not have the will to act in defense of the constitutional order.... [It became] an agent of violence against persons, either because – structurally – judicial operators were constrained by the organization of the judiciary and by ineffective norms, or because those same operators acted in such a way that they left the citizens whose rights they must defend, in a state of destitution. (Comisión de la Verdad y Reconciliación 2003: volume III, chapter VI, pp. 249–250, my translation)

For example, the Final Report describes how prosecutors delegated their investigative duties to the police, systematically failing to check those proceedings in order to guarantee respect for civil rights and due process, as well as satisfactory outcomes – particularly when the subjects of those investigations were security officers. Similarly, judges recurrently allowed military tribunals to usurp jurisdiction in cases of state repression, indirectly facilitating acquittals.[82]

The judiciary's inability to perform its constitutional duties during that period has been attributed to two factors: the lack of adequate material resources and deficient technical capabilities. Figure 4.4 shows the evolution in the percentage of the state's budget allocated to the judiciary between 1980 and 2000. During the course of two decades, the judicial branch was never assigned more than 1.5 percent of the state's total expenditures. This obviously had an impact on the capacity of the judiciary to

[82] See Comisión de la Verdad y Reconciliación (2003), volume III, chapter II, Section 6.

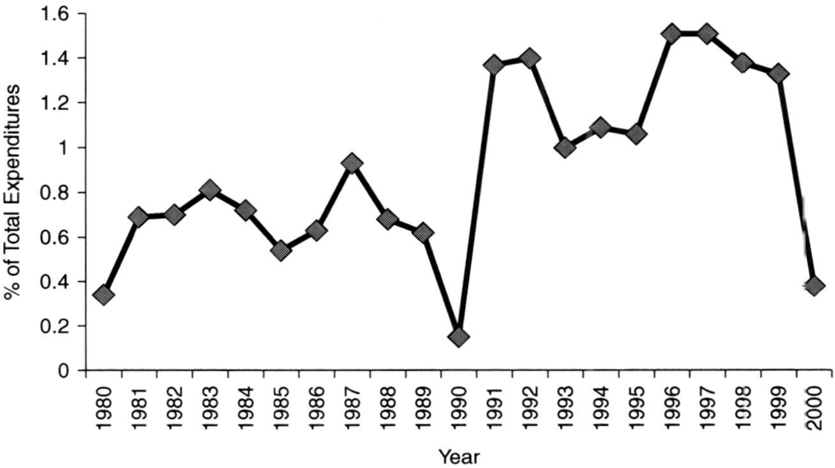

Figure 4.4. Resources Allocated to the Judicial Branch (1980–2000).
Source: Comisión de la Verdad y Reconciliación (2003).

conduct investigations that required, among other things, trips to remote areas in the Peruvian highlands where the crimes were perpetrated, expensive forensic tests, and translators for the non-Spanish-speaking victims called in to testify as witnesses.[83]

With regard to technical capabilities, the consensus in the literature and among legal practitioners interviewed during fieldwork is that Peruvian judicial actors suffered from enormous knowledge deficits. In the words of Peru's most prestigious legal sociologist, "Doctrinal training has separated ... the law from its social consequences.... The inoculation of a professional ideology within universities weakens the student's critical spirit.... We have concrete evidence about the prevalent presence of mediocre professionals in the judiciary, with an inadequate or barely acceptable technical expertise" (Pásara 2010: 133–135, my translation). The Final Report of the Truth and Reconciliation Commission similarly points to traditional legal preferences as a conditioning factor. Until the 2000s, Peruvian judicial actors ignored their duty to enforce checks and balances because of their lack of adequate training in "constitutional law and the lack of awareness of international human rights instruments"

[83] Of the victims 75 percent spoke Quechua as a first language. According to Jo Marie Burt this "is an astonishing figure given that only 16% of Peruvians are not primary Spanish speakers" (2009: 393).

(Comisión de la Verdad y Reconciliación 2003, vol. 3, chapter 2, 255, my translation). Judges limited themselves to a "strict and mechanical enforcement of norms, without considering principles, values and fundamental rights" (ibid: 256, my translation). The influence of positivism and formalism indeed led them to operate with a restricted interpretation of the reach of their formal prerogatives, failing to take a more active role in controlling the legality and due diligence of proceedings in conflict related cases. An indicator of the presence of a constraining legal vision is that although the Peruvian Constitution grants judges the power of judicial review,[84] until the 2000s, it was rarely used. In fact, in the 1980s and 1990s, the Constitutional Court, created in 1979 and reformed in 1993, checked the constitutionality of laws only on a handful of occasions (Dargent 2009).

In the eyes of Peruvian human rights activists, limited technical capabilities and deeply ingrained routines of praxis constituted an important foundation of judicial decision making, one that they had to reshape actively. The diffusion of legal and jurisprudential tools derived from international human rights law was necessary for prosecutors to file indictments, and for judges to circumvent the legal formalisms invoked by the defendants. Moreover, they sought to instill in judicial bureaucrats the motivation to conduct highly demanding investigations effectively. Litigants were able to make a correct evaluation of the challenge ahead not only because they had experienced prior frustrations with the domestic judiciary, but also because they had experimented with these enabling doctrines when they litigated in the Inter-American human rights system in the late 1990s. Although effective in triggering international rulings repudiating impunity and with the potential of unlocking the path to justice at home, they knew firsthand the chasm that separated these ideas from those harbored by domestic judicial actors. This experience had also allowed them to nurture the human resources to embark upon a pedagogical effort of unprecedented proportions, and the international contacts to increase its appeal and effectiveness.

Armed with this diagnosis, and with the resources that made it possible in the first place, human rights NGOs devised myriad strategies to equip judges and prosecutors with the technical capabilities and the values they lacked in order to process cases of state repression successfully. Their pedagogical initiatives were varied. Activists organized academic seminars, facilitated informal contacts between Peruvian judicial actors and prominent national and foreign legal experts, and produced authoritative

[84] Article 234 of the 1979 constitution, and Article 138 of the 1993 constitution.

documents and briefs explaining to judicial actors how to incorporate international legal instruments and jurisprudence in their rulings in order to fulfill the responsibilities of the state regarding the punishment of mass atrocities.

To begin with, the human rights movement staffed the legal team of the Truth and Reconciliation Commission with this educational goal in mind. As the lawyer in charge of the team stated in an interview:

> We knew that apart from gathering evidence about the violations documented in the Commission's Final Report, we had to expand its original mandate to provide a clear, almost pedagogical interpretation of the Peruvian legal framework in light of international law. We had to make it clear that it was unacceptable and illegal to use legal formalisms and a parochial reading of the law to stop the judicialization process.[85]

Echoing this concern, the Final Report strategically made reference to these interpretive routines as one of the factors limiting the ability of the judiciary to deliver justice to the victims:

> The lack of audacity to overcome the existing narrow legal framework with creative interpretations of the law, the lack of civic courage to defy the threats of powerful actors ... were and still are the defining features of the culture of our judicial operators, that must be overcome because otherwise we run the risk of perpetuating a dangerous Achilles' heel of democracy. (Comisión de la Verdad y Reconciliación 2003: volume II, chapter VI, 249–250, my translation)

Human rights activists in the commission sought to appeal directly to the judicial community, offering a scathing critique of its record during the conflict while providing a legal framework that could guide judicial proceedings in order to avoid repetition of past experiences. A document backed by the Peruvian state was thus made available so that judges and prosecutors could consult it and invoke it in their decisions. This first pedagogical strategy is a clear example of how, in the first few years after the democratic transition, NGOs used high levels of institutional access to begin to remove judicial blockages by modifying the streams of ideas that flowed inside the judiciary.

In addition to the inclusion of this legal brief in the Final Report, the influence exerted by activists led the Truth and Reconciliation Commission to recommend the creation of specialized courts to deal

[85] Interview, Lima, 10 March 2010. See Comisión de la Verdad y Reconciliación (2003), volume I, chapter IV.

with human rights cases. The new system was to be put under the aegis of the National Criminal Court. The issuing of this recommendation was a major victory because it offered human rights litigants the opportunity to lobby for the creation of an institutional setting in which to activate mechanisms of norm diffusion. After the Final Report was published, they approached the judges at the National Criminal Court to encourage them to demand the creation of this special jurisdiction. As several human rights lawyers explained in my interviews with them, the presence of specialized courts would give them the opportunity to build a strong relationship with a small group of judges and prosecutors, and facilitate the design of a plan to teach their judicial counterparts the aforementioned doctrines and legal ideas:

> Our relationship with the judges of the National Criminal Court began in the early years of the transition when we litigated cases of terrorism before that court. Besides those formal interactions, we approached them informally to persuade them to demand jurisdiction over cases involving human rights violations. Once this special subsystem was created, we knew that it was an unprecedented opportunity to make sure that they shared our same legal criteria when assessing the difficulties presented by these cases. We now had a demarcated group of judges and prosecutors that we could approach by inviting them to seminars and discussions and by circulating academic materials among them. We thus began to share with judges and prosecutors the same educational initiatives we designed for our own legal teams.[86]

A prominent human rights lawyer further explained the need for these targeted pedagogical interventions:

> We had to cover what we anticipated would be the main legal hurdles in the judicialization process. The inapplicability of amnesties, the previous adjudication of these cases by military courts, the inapplicability of statutory limitations, the limits to military jurisdiction, the definition of forced disappearances as continuous crimes and the techniques to apply international human rights law in criminal procedures, were juridical issues that had never been confronted by courts before. There were no precedents in Peru. We had a couple of international rulings and a ruling that refused to apply the amnesties in 1995, but nothing else. We knew these would be the main arenas of confrontation during investigations and trials, and it was therefore crucial to ensure a minimum level of expertise in these matters among judges and prosecutors.[87]

[86] Interview, Lima, 14 April 2010.
[87] Interview, Lima, 10 April 2010.

The jurisprudential criteria identified by this lawyer as constituting the main argumentative battleground in the judicialization process were the ones developed by the Inter-American Court of Human Rights in the various cases decided before the 2000s. As we saw before, some of those cases were litigated by these same NGOs against the Peruvian state. In this sense, the excerpt is revealing of the fact that Peruvian activists were aware of the continuing need to make norm diffusion a top priority by extending the diffusion stream beyond the international arena and into domestic courts. Like their Argentine colleagues in the 1990s, they understood that the juridical standards consolidated abroad would not automatically trickle down. Judges and prosecutors had to be exposed to these ideas and taught how to use them effectively.

Litigants did not want judicial actors to excuse themselves from applying these innovative criteria because of lack of knowledge or awareness. This could be the perfect pretext for those not willing to become involved in thorny territory. But unfortunately the problem was more acute: Even those judges willing to expose themselves to political pressures found it difficult to understand the legal options available to them. In an interview, a human rights lawyer gave me examples of the extensive technical deficits he found among lower court judges and prosecutors at the onset of the judicialization process, which further motivated the pedagogical interventions:

> At the beginning of the process, between 2001 and 2004 some of the indictments issued by prosecutors and the first arrest warrants issued by provincial judges were written by us. They would come and tell us "I would like to issue these warrants but I have no idea how to do it." This was a warning sign about the obstacles we could face if we did not act inside the judiciary, as opposed to simply being vocal in the media or staffing government agencies. At first we began by distributing documents and briefs, but then we decided to invite them to seminars and lectures given by experts in the field.[88]

One of his colleagues in the province of Ayacucho, the epicenter of the internal armed conflict and the site of many investigations, highlighted the problem of traditional legal preferences in the following way:

> In our universities these topics are not part of law programs. Even though I studied law relatively recently, in the 1990s, I never took a human rights course. In addition, especially here in Ayacucho, human rights are considered subversive. The situation was even worse in the 1980s, when most of

[88] Interview, Lima, 21 April 2010.

> the judges and prosecutors active today studied law. As a result, judicial actors have a narrow focus on internal law and are not used to invoking international norms and precedents. This was a huge problem for us at the beginning of our litigation efforts because central to those efforts was the use of the arguments and instruments of international law. Without expanding judges' and prosecutors' legal knowledge and without encouraging them to transform their legal praxis, it would have been impossible to punish human rights violators. Creating a new legal current within the judiciary was the key to our success.[89]

In other words, the pedagogical efforts were intended to struggle against a jurisprudential inertia reproduced by the educational system and enhanced by the taboo built around the human rights legal discourse, often seen as supportive of the interests of terrorist organizations. Securing the domestic diffusion of international legal standards was important in order to raise awareness of the availability of alternative courses of action compatible with transitional justice. Neither institutions of higher education nor the lingering prejudices regarding the actors involved in the conflict guaranteed that these ideas would be adopted in the absence of more aggressive and targeted interventions.

The Effect of Pedagogical Interventions: New Legal Horizons and Professional Duties

As we have seen, Peruvian judicial actors eventually broke with this inertia and embraced the new legal orthodoxy in their rulings on conflict related crimes. Although the sequencing is suggestive of some level of impact, it is necessary to evaluate the claim that this was a product of the pedagogical efforts. In a survey of prosecutors conducted in 2010, almost seven years after the launching of the pedagogical initiatives, the average respondent reported attendance in more than 3 of these courses,[90] and only three respondents said they had studied international human rights

[89] Interview, Ayacucho, 5 May 2010.

[90] There are no public records of the number of seminars organized by NGOs or of the mechanisms whereby academic materials were distributed among judges and prosecutors. The process was truly informal. In fact, I accidentally became an agent of norm diffusion. Academics at the Catholic University knew of my upcoming trip to Ayacucho and asked me to distribute among the judges and prosecutors I was set to interview a recently published book with the proceedings from one of their workshops (see Quinteros 2010). In that seminar, a series of experts gave lectures on how to deal with a number of legal hurdles such as statutes of limitations, how to justify charges against military commanders not directly responsible for the crimes, and how to interpret national law in light of international jurisprudence.

Table 4.4. *Prosecutors' Assessment of Litigants' Pedagogical Interventions*

Question	Average Response
Please indicate the number of seminars on human rights organized by civil society that you attended since 2004. One = 1; Two= 2; Three = 3; More than three = 4	3.4
Did you take International Human Rights Law Courses in law school?	YES = 15% (3 respondents)
Please indicate how much you agree with the following statements... Strongly agree = 4; Somewhat agree = 3; Somewhat disagree = 2; Strongly disagree =1	
The lack of training makes the investigation of human rights crimes more difficult	2.01
After attending these seminars I am more likely to use international legal instruments in my decisions	3.75
In the seminars I became familiar with legal instruments I previously did not know about	3.45
After attending these seminars I am more likely to accept indirect evidence to ascribe individual criminal responsibility	2.55

Source: Original survey. Targeted universe: all prosecutors involved in human rights cases. Anonymous survey administered online. Link to survey sent via email by chief prosecutor on behalf of the author. Response rate: 43.5 percent.

law in law school, confirming the deficits in traditional legal education. When asked about their agreement with the statement "After attending these seminars I am more likely to use international legal instruments in my decisions," the average response was 3.75 out of a maximum of 4 on the agreement scale. Similarly, the prosecutors who participated in the survey showed high levels of agreement with the statement that in the seminars they became familiar with legal instruments they previously did not know about. Finally, the average respondent somewhat disagreed with the idea that the lack of training makes the progress of the judicialization process difficult, indicating that at the time of the survey human rights groups had made a good job at improving prosecutors' technical skills and broadening their knowledge horizons (Table 4.4).

The judges and prosecutors I interviewed for this study were surprisingly candid in accepting their prior ignorance of these legal tools and the positive impact of activists' strategies in their ability to prosecute and punish criminals who violated human rights. In the words of a provincial prosecutor:

> The lack of training in these legal questions is a big problem. It was even worse at the beginning of the judicialization process. All of these topics were new! When I went to school I took one human rights class that did not cover the debates with the depth required by these cases.[91]

Given these gaps in traditional legal education, a judge explained that the main contribution of the seminars organized by human rights NGOs was to expand their knowledge of relevant sources of law:

> The biggest contribution of these seminars organized by human rights NGOs is that they connect us with debates and questions that have already been answered in other countries. This makes our job much easier and enriches our decisions.... Without the diffusion of this information we would have encountered insurmountable obstacles to bring down amnesty laws or to properly characterize the nature of crimes that were committed decades ago.[92]

Another prosecutor was even more conclusive about the effect of pedagogical interventions. They exposed judicial actors to alternative, but unknown sources of legal authority, which nurtured a new professional duty to interpret the law differently in human rights cases, following the precepts of international law:

> Due to the training we received in law school, we did not see these cases as special cases that involved gross human rights violations. Instead we approached them as normal cases, applying the conventional standards of criminal law. This whole process has involved first and foremost an intellectual journey. We had to attend seminars both here and abroad in order to understand new legal paradigms, the use of international instruments and above all, understand that we had to invoke customary law as a source of law already in place at the time when the crimes were committed. We had to fight against the legality principle, and we had to know how to do it correctly in order to respect due process.... Without the training offered by NGOs and by some universities it would have been impossible to achieve these results. *We were blinded by the rules of conventional criminal law.* If you had conducted this interview 10 years ago I would be talking about statutes of limitations! Now we can talk about crimes against humanity, we can see the importance of the Inter-American Court.[93]

[91] Interview, Ayacucho, 1 May 2010.
[92] Interview, Lima, 23 March 2010.
[93] Interview, Ayacucho, 3 May 2010.

These testimonies are some examples of the broad consensus I found among judges and prosecutors with respect to the legal preference change that constituted a necessary condition for transitional justice. Broadening the normative and jurisprudential foundations of judicial decision making was crucial in order for them to overcome the legal prejudices that stood in the way of criminal prosecutions and punishments. Forging a new consensus about the validity of certain instruments, and providing judicial actors with the tools needed to articulate sophisticated constitutional arguments, made justice possible in the Peruvian case.

These pedagogical interventions were indeed necessary because the old formalist legal orthodoxy exerted a powerful constraining force even among the few existing committed members of the judiciary. Before NGOs reached out to judges and prosecutors, those who were predisposed to support the victims felt ill equipped when they sought to translate personal or ideological commitments into legal language. Previously we saw an example of this in the testimony of a lawyer who recalled that judges and prosecutors approached him at the start of the judicialization process in order to seek advice on how to frame arrest warrants and indictments. Similarly, the words of a judge who strongly supports the human rights cause are illustrative of the extent to which committed judicial actors like him were indeed constrained by their deficient technical capabilities:

> I remember the decisive impact that my contacts with human rights NGOs had when I was investigating these crimes. Had I not attended the seminars they organized at the time, I would have never been able to hand down an arrest warrant. They opened the jurisprudential doors I needed by making me familiar with questions of constitutional law and human rights law, and with international legal instruments and their applicability in a domestic setting. I have attended many of these courses, first as a student and now as a lecturer.[94]

More important perhaps is the fact that the typical judicial actor was not ideologically predisposed to rule in favor of the victims. In the terms of the theory developed in Chapter 2, most Peruvian judges and prosecutors were indifferent. As such, they were geared toward reproducing behavioral routines that allowed them to dispose of inconvenient cases quickly. For example, the prosecutors who responded to the survey revealed fairly centrist tendencies: The mean score for ideological self-placement in a 1 to 10 scale was 4.3. Moreover, the way judicial actors presented their views

[94] Interview, Lima, 19 March 2010.

about the internal armed conflict and their opinion of NGOs made it clear that their pro–transitional justice behavior was not driven by an ideological commitment that led them to look for sources of law that would rationalize a preexisting position. In interviews, judges and prosecutors often accused human rights NGOs of being too leftist, and many even referred to members of the military with pity and admiration as "brave" and "inexperienced" "young soldiers" (*soldaditos*) who selflessly combated the terrorist threat.

As a result, litigants could not rely on instant support based on political affinity. Instead, as argued in Chapter 2, they had to provide judicial actors with professional motivations compatible with the values underpinning international human rights law, hoping that they would trigger effective action. In other words, they had to convince judges of their professional duty to abide by international human rights law actively. In several of the testimonies quoted, members of the judicial community refer to the diffusion of new legal standards by NGOs as revolutionary because it manufactured deep awareness of the existence of alternative sources of legal authority that they had to acknowledge and try to reconcile with the domestic legal order. The space for the legal rationale sustaining impunity thus progressively narrowed, as it became inconsistent with this newly discovered professional imperative. Others also emphasized the intellectual appeal of the novel issues discussed in the seminars as one of the main reasons behind their willingness to incorporate experimental ideas in their rulings. Some interviewees even admitted that the experience had sparked an academic interest in these matters, leading them to pursue further studies.

In addition to supporting the idea that legal preferences play an important role in judicial decision making, the development of this allegiance to an international source of legal authority as a primary motivation for championing victims' cause also suggests that by forging a consensus around the legitimacy of alternative legal standards, NGOs transformed the judiciary's identity. This in turn gave judicial actors the reasons to defy powerful political players. In Peru, transforming legal preferences thus enabled courts to ignite proceedings in the early 2000s, but also led them to defend them later in the decade when the balance of power shifted against the human rights agenda. For example, the resistance to Presidential Decree 1097 was an instance in which this new identity was forcefully displayed. The following interview data shed light on the thought processes whereby the diffusion of new technical capabilities enabled the enactment of this new logic of behavioral appropriateness.

Engaging judicial actors in strictly legal terms, making available an argumentative infrastructure to justify deviations from standard praxis, led to a sense of professional empowerment. Judicial actors now had the tools to innovate in order to reconcile the demands of different sources of law. This was risky because it would naturally set limits to the prerogatives of the other branches of government. The testimony of a judge who in the midst of Fujimori's dictatorship refused to apply an amnesty law passed by congress is instructive. Her action contravened all standards of professional behavior as judges understood them at the time:

> The idea that laws had to be in harmony with the principles established in international treaties was not something internalized among us. Moreover, it was a law passed by Congress. Although judges are allowed to apply decentralized judicial review, in 1995 I only knew of one example in Peru and it wasn't even by a criminal court. My colleagues told me that I was mad; how could I declare a law unconstitutional! It was a valid piece of legislation. We weren't supposed to meddle in political affairs.... I didn't know how to back my decision to declare the inapplicability of the amnesty; it was something radically new!

She went on to explain how the intervention of human rights lawyers provided her with the legal tools she lacked, and without which she could not have acted as she did:[95]

> My contacts with a well-known human rights lawyer proved crucial. He gave me the legal instruments I needed to show that I was acting correctly, as mandated by the law, and that I wasn't circumventing the amnesty because I was against the military or because it was a crazy idea of mine. I felt extremely constrained by the information I had before I visited this lawyer. In fact when I entered his office I was shocked by the size of his book collection on human rights law.

In the interview, she also recognized the empowering aspect of this intervention given the political context in which she handed down that decision: "Knowing about these issues gives us power, power to decide. It allows us to act following our convictions, despite political pressures to the contrary. I cannot let them intimidate me because I have the legal tools with which to justify the correctness of my actions."[96]

The idea that expanding the sources of law that are known and seen as legitimate is empowering vis-à-vis external pressures was a recurrent

[95] Congress then passed a second amnesty and declared that it could not be subject to judicial review.

[96] Interview, Lima, 26 March 2010.

theme in other interviews. A prosecutor who participated in oral trials at the National Criminal Court stated:

> These doctrinal and jurisprudential sources empower prosecutors, especially when we have to present politically sensitive charges. International law and the legal human rights discourse become our best allies, our biggest sources of legitimacy and personal security.[97]

Another prosecutor referred to knowledge as an insurance policy against malicious prosecution charges:

> Getting to know other judicialization experiences and their respective jurisprudential developments reduces our uncertainty when we decide on a case. If others used this or that interpretation or instrument, then we know that we can also do it without running the risk of being accused of malicious prosecution. Better understanding these new and complex issues protects us and empowers us.[98]

Finally, a National Criminal Court judge succinctly echoed this consensus about the empowering effect of adequate technical capabilities when she explained that before receiving specialized training by NGOs, entering the human rights legal world felt like jumping "into a void".[99]

When judicial actors enter politically inhospitable territories or when they seek to pursue their personal or professional commitments, it is important for them to know how to legitimize their actions in the language of the law. Critics of the legal model of judicial decision making have argued that the law is epiphenomenal because its use constitutes an ex post rationalization of political or ideological decisions (Segal and Spaeth 1993). By contrast, the preceding testimonies of committed and converted judicial actors show that when the law to be applied is unknown or contravenes established standards of judicial praxis, this process is not so straightforward. But litigant groups can expand the possibilities for assertive behavior by transforming the ways judges and prosecutors perceive the reach of their formal prerogatives. Legal preferences put limits on what judges and prosecutors think is acceptable professional behavior, even when those limits severely constrain their policy preferences. The consequences of their actions in transitional justice processes are so far-reaching, both politically and legally, that the epistemic and social support offered by human rights activists is crucial.

[97] Interview, Lima, 22 April 2010.
[98] Interview, Ayacucho, 2 May 2010.
[99] Interview, Lima, 6 May 2010.

Human rights activists were able to diffuse a new legal orthodoxy in part because of their correct analysis of the problem of legal preferences. By taking seriously the technical and cultural underpinnings of judicial decision making, they activated a process of ideational transformation that modified judicial actors' sense of possibility and obligation vis-à-vis cases of state repression. The renewed sense of possibility was crucial among committed judges and prosecutors, whereas modifying the perception of what was mandatory under a previously ignored source of legal authority played a key role in the conversion of indifferent ones. In the next three sections I further explore the reasons behind litigants' pedagogical success.

The Timing of Pedagogical Interventions

In Chapter 3 we saw that during the 1990s, Argentine human rights activists had a hard time expanding the reach of their pedagogical efforts beyond certain actors and provinces. This was the case in part because they were not the first movers in the game to colonize the judiciary. By the time they launched these initiatives, the anti–transitional justice coalition had already taken control of key courts. Their Peruvian counterparts, by contrast, launched their strategies to craft a friendly and receptive judiciary before the anti–transitional justice coalition began exerting pressures on judicial actors. The proportion of unpersuadable judicial actors was therefore lower. This, of course, reflected the presence of a friendly environment following the collapse of Fujimori's regime in 2000, and further underscores the causal alchemy outlined in Chapter 2. Indeed, it illustrates how the interaction between litigants' own choices and the surrounding political climate conditions the successful deployment of strategies of institutional transformation.

As we saw, when the political environment changed, this first mover advantage proved crucial in restricting the damage caused by García's backlash. The extent to which early legal preference change was responsible for the limited impact of subsequent intimidation tactics is further revealed by the choices made by the proimpunity coalition once it became apparent that judicial actors in key courts would not cave in to external threats. Military actors reached the conclusion that instead of seeking to instill fear, they ought to fight in the legal and evidentiary terrain by imitating NGOs' softer pedagogical approach. To this end, in 2010 the armed forces attempted to approach the prosecutors amicably. With the help of the nation's chief prosecutor, a recalcitrant actor allied to President García, they organized a lecture series that included the following talks: "Basic and Conceptual Features about Peruvian National Identity"; "Analysis of the Social and Political Situation in Regions under the State of Emergency, and Other Related Topics" (referring to the regions in which the Shining Path is still active); "Problems Faced by the Peruvian Armed Forces as a Result of Their Involvement in Areas under the State of Emergency"; and "The Organizational Structure of the Army and the Chain of Command: Planning Operations."[100]

These titles clearly reveal the two main pedagogical goals. First, the military intended to make prosecutors sympathetic to the current challenges faced by the institution. In particular, they wanted to call attention to their patriotic involvement in an endless combat against insurgent groups, with precarious training and equipment. Second, the seminar sought to explain their vision of military command structures during the internal armed conflict, arguing that high commanders had no control over the actions of their subordinates. If prosecutors accepted this interpretation of military structures, they would have to circumscribe their accusations to those materially or directly responsible for the crimes, and abstain from pressing charges against those suspected of designing the antiterrorist insurgency and of giving orders to the rank and file. Doing so would have almost certainly led to impunity: With little access to military records about who was deployed in each combat area, as has been the case in Peru since the onset of the judicialization process, it is almost impossible to identify the direct perpetrators. This is indeed why human rights litigants all along focused their accusations on those in command of the military apparatus.

The following testimonies from interviews with the prosecutors who attended the events reveal that these efforts proved futile because human rights NGOs had already won the battle for their hearts and minds. Litigants' pedagogical interventions successfully molded a new legal consensus, which became internalized as the appropriate normative and doctrinal foundation for their professional undertakings. In the words of one of them: "We won't cease in our efforts to achieve justice. The arguments they tried to convey to us clearly do not persuade us and we won't use them."[101] Another participant said she told the military officers that "we have lived through decades of a bloody conflict. You talk about pacification and reconciliation, but that cannot happen without justice because

[100] The program is on file with the author.

[101] Interview, Ayacucho, 4 May 2010.

the nation's scars are still bleeding."[102] In other words, the legal arguments diffused in this particular venue did not resonate with their professional goals or with their view about the historical need for a successful judicialization process. It certainly did not help that among the lecturers there were two officials who were under investigation for human rights crimes. This obviously undermined the legitimacy of the message. Moreover, this lecture series was a stand-alone program. NGOs were quick to denounce the military for using the academic event to try to intimidate the prosecutors. Not surprisingly, the military responded that they were merely replicating the same strategies that the NGOs had deployed in the past. But the controversy became so public that it led the National Criminal Court to ban all future contacts outside the courtroom between judges and prosecutors and the parties in the case.

In sum, human rights NGOs understood much earlier than their rivals how judicial actors think, and engaged them in precisely those terms. Litigants were smart to frame the question of transitional justice as a legal question – as opposed to coercively seeking to induce strategic behavior – and tried to persuade judges and prosecutors of the validity of their international legal arguments. Their temporal advantage made counterdiffusion more difficult and undermined the effectiveness of intimidation tactics.

The Appeal of Pedagogical Interventions

One of the central challenges faced by human rights litigants who seek to transform a hegemonic legal orthodoxy is to make jurisprudential innovations look legitimate in the eyes of judicial actors. In line with my sociological institutionalist approach, judges and prosecutors must be persuaded that when they invoke international legal instruments, or when they modify evidentiary standards in order to take into account the special nature of human rights cases, they are not violating acceptable standards of professional behavior. Making an authoritative case in favor of the values underlying the new orthodoxy is crucial given the experimental nature of antiimpunity doctrines. As I suggested in Chapter 2, litigants are more likely to succeed when others speak for them. In particular, they must enlist prestigious law professors as well as local and foreign judicial actors who can establish a more horizontal, peer-to-peer connection with the target population.

102 Interview, Lima, 22 April 2010.

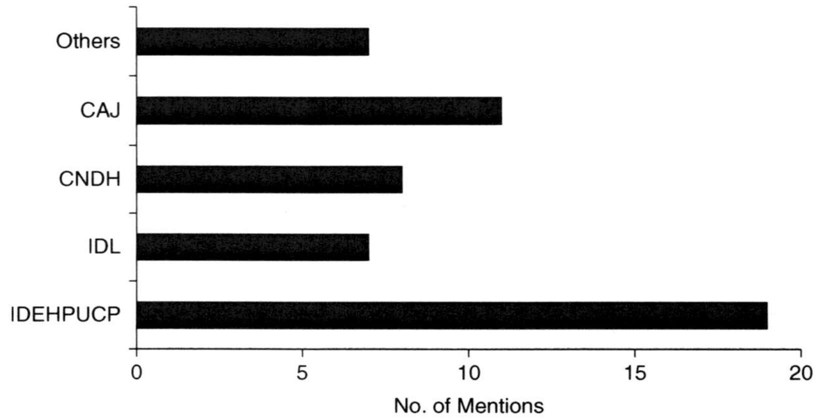

Figure 4.5. Organizations Providing Training Courses for Prosecutors.
Source: Original survey. Targeted universe: all prosecutors involved in human rights cases. Anonymous survey administered online. Link to survey sent via email by chief prosecutor on behalf of the author. Response rate: 43.5 percent. Question: "Please name up to four institutions in charge of organizing the courses you attended." IDL: Instituto de Defensa Legal; CNDH: Coordinadora Nacional de Derechos Humanos; IDEHPUCP: Instituto de Democracia y Derechos Humanos; CAJ: Comsión Andina de Juristas.

A careful analysis of the speaker series in the various seminar programs I had access to reveals that like Argentina's CELS in the 1990s, Peruvian human rights activists followed this approach. They themselves do not appear in those records, despite the fact that they were the organizers. Instead, NGOs left instruction in the hands of well-known academics. In addition, they counted on an important ally in the academic world to take on the challenge of training judges and prosecutors on their behalf: the Institute for Democracy and Human Rights at the Catholic University of Peru (IDEHPUCP). In the online survey of prosecutors reported earlier, the institute received the highest number of mentions when respondents were asked to name the organizations that had provided the training (Figure 4.5). This partnership guaranteed the neutrality of the message and helped lure indifferent judges to these informal spaces of academic exchange. As one of the parties in the criminal investigations and trials, NGOs could not run the risk of appearing to be trying to exert undue influence on the arbiters. After 2006, when the political environment shifted, this was especially important, as judicial actors needed reassurance that their attendance would not trigger suspicions. In the previous section, we saw that if these interventions become known and are criticized by proimpunity groups, problems may arise.

The strategy of disguising these interventions with an aura of neutrality is also clearly seen in the ways that NGOs approached the Supreme Court judges and prosecutors involved in the historic trial against Fujimori. Among them were highly respected experts in criminal law, a status that in principle means they constitute a "hard case" for my argument about persuasion. These individuals did not attend the seminars organized by the NGOs, as they probably had little patience for human rights activists trying to "teach" them international law. From activists' perspective, however, although many of these judicial actors were not foreign to the juridical issues at stake, they certainly did not have any experience in proceedings of the magnitude and complexity of the Fujimori case. It was not a given that they would be able to conduct their duties effectively in accordance with human rights standards. NGOs believed that these judges and prosecutors would need reassurance that the juridical innovations they were being asked to endorse during the trial constituted a legitimate way of interpreting the law. By opening informal channels of communication with the judges, and exposing them to similar experiences in other countries, litigants sought to convince them that they were not being asked to do anything out of the ordinary – and, most importantly, that it was possible to convict a powerful former president for crimes he had not directly perpetrated, but had nevertheless planned and endorsed. The challenge, of course, was to engage the judges and induce them to listen.

To this end, NGOs flew in a series of international observers (including human rights experts, international lawyers, and the Argentine judges of the historic 1985 trial against the military juntas) and organized meetings of them, the Supreme Court judges, and the prosecutor. A litigant described the purpose of this strategy:

> During the course of the [Fujimori] trial there was one non-legal strategy that was of paramount importance. We invited international experts to informally talk with the judges. The aim was to show the judges that what we were asking them to do was possible. "These Argentine judges did it; you can do it too." Our hidden message was: "Do not listen to us; listen to them." These experts were the true conveyor belts of our legal arguments and gave these Supreme Court judges the certainty that they needed to accept our theory about the crimes in question and the international jurisprudence we invoked. Although the three judges are experts in criminal law, they are not necessarily top-notch experts in international human rights law. I think that for them it was important to have this international support.[103]

[103] Interview, Lima, 21 April 2010.

In other words, the central concern of human rights NGOs was not simply to show judges that a well-organized and vocal civil society group was backing their efforts and would publicly defend them if necessary, but also to give them certainty about the legal tools they had to apply in order to issue a prison sentence. Their diagnosis was in fact correct, and their tactics effective in catching the attention of the judges. The Supreme Court judges I interviewed acknowledged that the trial, which involved extremely complex crimes and little direct evidence, was uncharted territory. External support was therefore much appreciated. As one of them explained in an interview:

> Both the meetings with international experts and the amicus curiae filed by international NGOs were important intellectual contributions. The meeting with the Argentine judges, for example, was a reassurance that we were on the right track. They shared their experience and the way in which they had applied the doctrines of criminal responsibility in joint criminal enterprises we were evaluating for our case.[104]

This strategy had similar effects on the prosecutor. He emphasized that informal contacts with international experts had reassured him of the fact that what he was doing was legally permissible:

> We needed an impartial, academic take on these matters. I had the pleasure of discussing many of the questions and doubts I naturally had with one of Roxin's former students who was invited by the NGOs to observe the trial. He helped me refine arguments that were not that clear in my head.[105]

It is striking how similar these statements are to those of committed judges in Argentina during the truth trials of the 1990s. Even these highly motivated judicial actors welcomed a type of external support that in a professional manner clarifies the available juridical options, provides them with authoritative legal tools, and becomes the intellectual anchor to justify courses of action compatible with their personal convictions.

The Content of Pedagogical Interventions

The creation of courts specialized in human rights cases allowed Peruvian NGOs to deploy relatively systematic pedagogical interventions, targeting

[104] Interview, Lima, 28 May 2010.

[105] Interview, Lima, 26 May 2010. Roxin is a famous jurist known for his work on criminal responsibility in crimes perpetrated via powerful state and nonstate actors.

an easily identifiable group of judicial actors. The content of their educational initiatives, however, varied significantly across legal issue areas. In particular, Peruvian activists carefully taught those principles of international human rights law that require the rejection of amnesties and statutes of limitations, but failed to pay enough attention to the diffusion of investigative protocols and evidentiary standards appropriate for human rights cases. The concomitant variation in the skills and ideas found among judges and prosecutors underscores the effectiveness of pedagogical interventions in manufacturing a consensus around certain issues, and the importance of legal preference change in achieving positive outcomes in human rights cases.

NGOs argued that in cases of state repression, direct incriminating evidence is usually rare, especially in cases of forced disappearances. Moreover, they insisted that in Peru, the quality of witness testimonies was jeopardized by the fact that many direct witnesses had died, and those who were still alive were extremely poor and uneducated. Consequently, NGOs warned judicial actors that they should not expect to base convictions on "smoking guns." Evidentiary standards had to be relaxed and adapted to the historical circumstances of the crimes in question. Human rights activists were therefore disappointed to see that in high-profile cases such as *Matero*, *Pomatanta,* and *Los Laureles*, the National Criminal Court failed to apply this progressive criterion and voted to acquit some or all of the accused as a result of the absence of direct evidence (Rivera 2010). These and other acquittals decided by various courts reflect the poor diffusion of alternative evidentiary standards. As shown in Table 4.4, human rights NGOs were less effective in persuading judicial actors about this second set of legal arguments. Prosecutors' level of agreement with the statement that after attending the seminars they were more likely to accept indirect evidence is lower than that of their responses to the other questions, such as the one about changes in the rate of citation of international legal instruments: an average of 2.55 in the 4-point agreement scale, versus an average of 3.75.

One of the reasons for this gap is the prevalent perception among judicial actors that the indirect evidence presented to them is of low quality. Proving that forced disappearances actually took place despite the usual official silence is not hard since victim groups have been decrying the loss of their loved ones for decades. By contrast, establishing individual criminal responsibility beyond reasonable doubt for state crimes that took place in the distant past is a daunting task. The available documents and testimonies are not enough to persuade them to sentence an individual to years in prison. As a Peruvian judge who participated in various oral trials stated in an interview:

> Although I am aware that the nature of these crimes demands a special treatment of the evidence, if I am not convinced that this or that person participated in the crime in question I cannot send him to jail and then be able to sleep at night. I hate it when this happens because I know I am not offering the victims the kind of justice they deserve.[106]

In line with her colleague, another judge explained:

> We do not demand direct proof in all cases. We understand that due to the passage of time and the patterns of behavior that one observes in these crimes, it is necessary to work with indirect evidence. But that evidence needs to be based on factual certainties. In the emblematic *Castillo Páez* case I had direct evidence and on that basis I interpreted the indirect evidence.... We often encounter contradictions in the testimonies of the victims or their relatives. Sometimes what they said in previous iterations of the investigations does not coincide with what they say in the oral trial. It is really hard to reconstruct what happened. True, our standards are high because we are not dealing with cases that are irrelevant for Peru's life as a nation, and on top of that, the liberty of the accused is at stake.[107]

In addition to the quality of the available indirect evidence, there is another reason why human rights litigants were less successful in diffusing their ideas on this particular issue area. The emphasis of the pedagogical interventions was primarily on diffusing knowledge about international human rights law, as opposed to techniques to evaluate evidence or skills to deal with other practical aspects of criminal investigations. This is consistent with the theory advanced in this book: Variation in the intensity of the interventions across issue areas should lead to variation in levels of persuasion across issue areas. For example, in 2009, five years after the launching of the first pedagogical interventions, the Institute for Democracy and Human Rights at the Catholic University of Peru organized a seminar attended by judges, prosecutors, and clerks. At the end of the seminar, a survey was distributed among 107 participants. One of the questions asked respondents to suggest topics for future seminars, i.e., topics that had not been sufficiently covered during that or prior academic events. Figure 4.6 shows the ranking of topics as a percentage of total suggestions.

The gray bars indicate topics related to questions about how to conduct criminal investigations in order to establish individual responsibility,

[106] Interview, Lima, 6 May 2010.
[107] Interview, Lima, 17 May 2010.

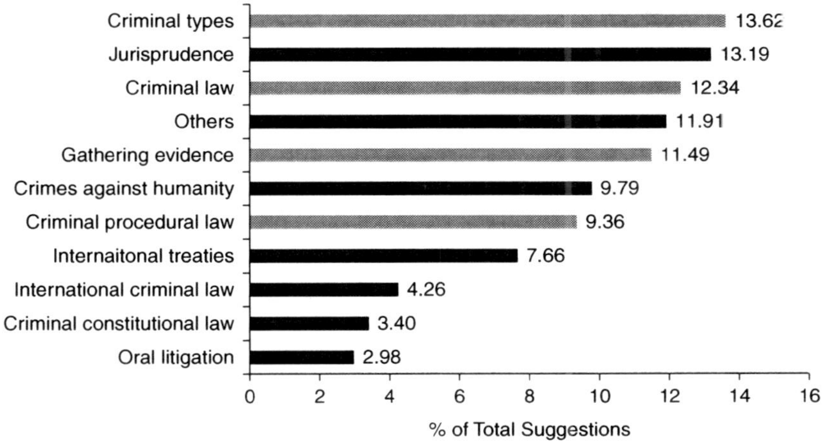

Figure 4.6. Topics Suggested by Judges and Prosecutors for Future Seminars (2009). *Source:* IDEHPUCP.

including the production of evidence, the use of domestic criminal definitions, criminal procedural law, and criminal law. Although not perfect, there is an identifiable pattern: Questions about constitutional law and international law, i.e., the legal framework needed to rescind amnesties or ignore statutes of limitations, rank at the bottom of the list. This suggests that judges and prosecutors already felt competent in those areas extensively covered by the seminars. As we saw in previous sections, this is reflected in the consensus surrounding these issues found in the rulings handed down by Peruvian courts. In a written evaluation of the results of the survey, the organizers concluded that something had to be done about this gap in technical knowledge. Since the judicialization process had already left behind debates about amnesties and statutes of limitations, it seemed urgent to address another set of legal preferences that hampered further victories: "We must highlight that among the five most voted topics, [there are] topics related to the gathering of evidence and the conduct of investigations.... [This] represents the most relevant novelty, which requires special attention in view of the design of future training activities."[108]

Echoing this report, a provincial prosecutor expressed frustration with the fact that the amount and variety of courses being offered had diminished in recent years. In particular, she emphasized the lack of training in

[108] IDEHPUCP, mimeo. On file with the author.

practical aspects of criminal investigations. In her view, better skills were desperately needed in order to empower them further vis-à-vis a hostile political class:

> We need more and better training. Defendants are all the time trying new arguments to stop these prosecutions, to invalidate pieces of evidence, etc. What do I do, for example, if after 3 decades the medical and psychological reports do not find evidence of torture? What other kind of evidence can I look for? How do I use it and what importance can I give to it? We need help! These are really tough questions and we are not trained to answer them. We always have to grapple with these issues and hand down decisions in a context of fear. We need better training to back the choices we make, often against powerful people.... We are afraid that we may end up being accused of malicious prosecution.[109]

In many ways this frustration is a consequence of litigants' own mistakes when designing pedagogical interventions, but also reflects the new inability of NGOs to deepen the process of legal preference change in the second half of the 2000s. An unfavorable political environment now constrained their capacity to continue with the institutional transformation ignited after the democratic transition. This issue is the focus of the following section.

The Limits of Persuasion: Recalcitrant Judges in High Courts

Although the backlash after 2006 was not fully effective in stopping the judicialization process, it clearly took its toll as it allowed for the resurgence of some judicial blockages and undermined the process of institutional change. As already noted, García's anti–transitional justice policies made the job of committed judges and prosecutors more difficult, slowing the progress of several important cases. Although it is hard to establish empirically, it is also likely that some indifferent judicial actors were deterred from pushing the investigations forward, others coerced into handing down acquittals, and yet others persuaded of the virtues of an alternative narrative of the internal armed conflict. Evidence of this is perhaps the fact that after a new president took office in 2011, one not fully committed to transitional justice but certainly not openly hostile to it, the conviction rate at the National Criminal Court increased (see Table 4.1). Finally, the shift in the balance of power was also accompanied by this court's ban on informal contacts between judicial actors and the parties in the cases, enacted

[109] Interview, Ayacucho, 4 May 2010.

after the controversy elicited by the military's own pedagogical intervention. Although further technical training was clearly needed, NGOs could not address these deficits as effectively as they had before the backlash. As one lawyer admitted, the strategies deployed "between 2001 and 2006 are impossible to imagine in this context."[110]

The most palpable effect of the backlash, however, was the empowerment of recalcitrant judges in the late 2000s and early 2010s. During these years, the terms of friendly judges appointed to seats in the Constitutional Court in the immediate aftermath of the transition began to expire, leading to the appointment of hostile replacements. Moreover, recalcitrant judges in the Supreme Court became increasingly influential.[111] As suggested in Chapter 2, this kind of political environment is not propitious for the activation of strategies directed at influencing judicial nominations and removals. This final empirical section shows that NGOs' inability to stock these courts with their allies threatened the stability of jurisprudential outcomes. Some of the new key judicial players, many of whom had strong ties to both APRA and Fujimorismo, tried to overturn high-profile convictions and bring the judicialization process to a permanent halt. However, the evidence also suggests that the prevalence of a fairly strong consensus in the legal community about how to deal with human rights cases minimized the impact of these decisions and, crucially, tempered the recalcitrance of some of the new appointees.

The contrast between Peru and Argentina offers an instructive starting point for the analysis. In Argentina, recalcitrant judges were appointed by the dictatorship in the 1970s and the anti–transitional justice coalition in the early 1990s. These judges blocked the progress of human rights cases well into the 2000s when the political climate was decisively in favor of trials, until NGOs named and shamed them into resignation or impeachment. In Peru, by contrast, recalcitrant judges began to reach key positions in the judiciary once the judicialization process was in its advanced stages. In the case of the Constitutional Court, for example, the first two administrations after the transition had appointed judges with strong academic credentials, nonpartisan backgrounds, and a high level of

110 Interview, Lima, 14 April 2010.

111 Constitutional Court judges are chosen by congress with qualified majorities and serve for a five-year term. They cannot be reelected. Vacancies do not happen all at once. Typically judges are replaced in groups of two or three. In contrast, Supreme Court judges are chosen by the judicial council, which is made up of members of the Supreme Court, high-level prosecutors, academics, and members of lawyers' professional associations. Supreme Court judges have no term limits but must be ratified every seven years by the council.

commitment to punishing the wrongdoings of the Fujimori regime. This was in part because (a) a ruling by the Inter-American Court of Human Rights demanded that the judges sacked by Fujimori be reinstated, (b) some members of the political elite were truly committed to turning the page on the authoritarian past, and (c) high levels of political fragmentation in congress made it difficult to impose highly partisan nominees. As a result, human rights NGOs did not have to engage actively in replacement strategies. The situation changed dramatically when APRA and Fujimorismo became electorally stronger. But at this point lobbying for favorable judicial appointments was no longer feasible.

In the case of the Constitutional Court, the presence of new recalcitrant judges had important consequences for a series of decisions handed down from 2008 onward.[112] The departure of judges highly committed to the principles of international human rights law led to changes in the court's criteria on constitutional questions it had already settled under its previous composition.

In 2008, for example, the Constitutional Court refused to accept an appeal presented by the Institute of Legal Defense (ILD), one of the leading NGOs offering counsel to the victims of state repression. The appeal was filed on behalf of the victims of a massacre that took place in 1986, in which the police and the army killed hundreds of individuals convicted of terrorism. In *El Frontón*, the ILD objected to a ruling handed down by a lower court in the Lima circuit that accepted an interlocutory appeal invoking statutes of limitations. To do so, the judges had argued that this massacre was not a crime against humanity. In response to the appeal, the Constitutional Court decided that the ILD could not claim to be a legitimate representative of the victims and therefore lacked standing. Most importantly, it minimized the extent to which the lower court was required to apply the Constitutional Court's established criteria on the nature of conflict-era atrocities.[113]

A few years later, in 2013, the court ruled on a habeas corpus petition filed by military and police officers accused of planning and executing the aforementioned massacre. This time the constitutional judges fully reversed the criteria of the court regarding the nature of the crimes in El Frontón prison. In particular, as had their lower court counterparts, they rejected the idea that they constituted crimes against humanity. According to the majority, not all forms of state violence that took place

[112] For a critique of these decisions by a human rights organization see Justicia Viva (2009).

[113] 03173-2008-PHC/TC, ruling of 11 December 2008.

during the armed conflict were part of a systematic attack on civilians. In this case, state officials had simply responded to a mutiny organized by the inmates.[114] This decision invalidated an investigation initiated by another lower court, but requested further investigation into the massacre in order to comply with an Inter-American Court ruling that demanded that the Peruvian state satisfy victims' demands for truth and justice.[115] Although the case is still ongoing, the investigations are highly unlikely to succeed, since the only way to ignore statutes of limitations (they expired in 2006) is to characterize the events as a crime against humanity.

The Constitutional Court also tried to jeopardize the trial against the members of the Grupo Colina. In 2010, it handed down an important decision on a habeas corpus petition filed by the defense of Julio Salazar Monroe, the leader of Fujimori's paramilitary group. The court considered that the proceedings conducted by the criminal chamber of the anti-corruption circuit in Lima for his involvement in the *Barrios Altos*, *El Santa,* and *La Cantuta* massacres had taken too long. According to the constitutional judges, this violated the right of the accused to a fair and timely trial. The decision also imposed a strict sixty-day period for the lower court to terminate all proceedings and issue a sentence. Failing to do so would result in the indefinite suspension of the trial.[116] Although the trial was clearly taking too long (five years), this was in part a result of the complexity of the crimes in question, and of the delaying tactics deployed by the defendants themselves: requests to cancel hearings due to health problems, interlocutory appeals, recusals, habeas corpus petitions, and others. The Constitutional Court's failure to see this threatened the success of one of the most significant trials held during this period. The Lima criminal court made its ruling two months later, barely meeting the deadline.

In an interview with the judge who was president of the Constitutional Court when two of the rulings discussed were handed down, and who voted with the majority in all of them, he stated:

> Now the court is willing to defend the human rights of all the parties in the process; justice cannot come at all costs. Having the accused indefinitely in jail without certainty about their future is unacceptable.... This judicialization process cannot last forever. Our country needs social peace and reconciliation.[117]

114 01969-2011-PHC/TC, ruling of 3 May 2013.

115 I/A Court HR, Case of *Durand y Ugarte v. Peru*, ruling of 16 August 2000.

116 05230-2009-PHC/TC, ruling of 10 August 2010.

117 Interview, Lima, 12 March 2010.

During the interview the judge also criticized the NGOs and the judicialization process, adopting a similar rhetoric than that expounded by the party with which he had a long-term association, APRA. Referring to the ILD, he described it as an "enemy of the Court" because "now that we are no longer their puppets, they criticize us." His words made direct reference to the avalanche of antiimpunity rulings handed down by the Constitutional Court under its previous composition. According to the judge, the former justices had built very close political connections with human rights NGOs. In his view, this was enough to put into question the legitimacy and impartiality of that jurisprudence.

It is important to note that despite changes in the court's composition and these jurisprudential setbacks, crucial criteria on the treatment of amnesties and statutes of limitations in cases of crimes against humanity remained unchanged. This suggests that even those judges unsympathetic to human rights litigants were compelled to acknowledge the broad consensus around the belief that the state has an international responsibility to investigate this special category of crimes. In fact, the arguments expounded in the preceding decisions in *El Frontón* constituted an attempt to circumvent this consensus without questioning it, i.e., by challenging the criminal definition used to characterize the events. Two important decisions by the Constitutional Court under its new composition reflect the resilience of certain legal ideas diffused and defended by human rights NGOs regarding the treatment of crimes against humanity.

First, in *Accomarca*, a case involving a massacre that took place in the second half of the 1980s, the new constitutional justices unequivocally upheld the court's previous jurisprudence on the inapplicability of domestic legal instruments that could bar the progress of the case.[118] It did so with full knowledge of the fact that the president of the republic, and leader of the party with which several justices sympathized, was among the alleged perpetrators. Second, in March 2011, the Constitutional Court decisively put an end to the controversy ignited by García's Presidential Decree 1097, declaring it unconstitutional. For example, the decree instructed judges and prosecutors to apply statutes of limitations to cases of state repression because the international treaties that mandated otherwise were ratified after the perpetration of the crimes. The Constitutional Court emphatically disagreed. The decision made it clear that the nonapplicability

[118] 00218-2009-PHC/TC, ruling of 11 November 2010.

of statutory limitations was first and foremost required by customary, not positive law:

> It must be clear that the rule about the non-applicability of statutory limitations to crimes against humanity, and consequently, the duty to prosecute them irrespective of when they were perpetrated, is not part of the Peruvian legal framework due to the ratification of the Convention on the Non-Applicability of Statutory Limitations to War Crimes and Crimes against Humanity (November 9th 2003), but by virtue of a general imperative of international law that... does not arise from the Convention but is recognized in it.[119]

If the attempts by recalcitrant judges in the Constitutional Court to limit the judicialization process proved controversial, those by some members of the Supreme Court were scandalous. Judge Villa Stein led the offensive within the Supreme Court. His allegiance to Fujimorismo was unequivocal. For example, his son was a partner at the law firm that represented Fujimori in court. Moreover, during his first years in office, Villa Stein voted in favor of overturning a series of rulings against individuals accused of participating in the former president's corruption network.[120] In the early years of García's second administration Villa Stein was a rather marginal member of the Supreme Court, but he patiently courted the new president and eventually won him over. In fact, after a failed bid to become chief justice in 2006, in 2010 Villa Stein garnered the support of Aprista judges and succeeded in becoming the leader of the judicial branch.[121] This position allowed him to exert great influence not only over the court's composition, but also over its jurisprudence in human rights cases.[122]

In July 2012, the criminal chamber of the Supreme Court presided over by Villa Stein handed down a decision on a case involving the crimes perpetrated by the Grupo Colina in the early 1990s. The ruling significantly modified the decision issued by a criminal chamber of the anticorruption Lima circuit in 2010. In particular, it concluded that the massacres and forced disappearances in *Barrios Altos*, *La Cantuta*, *El Santa*, and *Yauri* were not crimes against humanity. These were not attacks against civilians, but against terrorist suspects. As a result, Villa Stein and his colleagues

[119] 00024-2010-PI/TC, ruling of 21 March 2011, paragraph 62.

[120] *Revista Domingo*, 29 July 2012.

[121] Any member of the Supreme Court can become chief justice for a two-year period. Usually those interested in the position publicly announce their bids. The winner is then decided by simple majority vote.

[122] The president of the Supreme Court sits in the judicial council, a body in charge of appointing and ratifying Supreme Court justices.

argued that the statutes of limitations for one of the charges, participation in a criminal association,[123] had expired. Moreover, they decided that the notion of command responsibility was not applicable. These moves enabled them to acquit a former chief of military intelligence and reduce the prison sentences of the other defendants by two to five years.[124]

The ruling had serious implications. It was the first time that a Peruvian court circumvented arguments derived from international law by questioning the use of "crimes against humanity" as a legal category to define conflict-era crimes. In fact, as we saw, the following year the Constitutional Court made a similar case in *El Frontón*. Most importantly, in 2009 Fujimori had been convicted for these same crimes, but in his case, the Supreme Court did characterize them as crimes against humanity. The existence of two Supreme Court rulings with contradictory interpretations of the same facts now gave Fujimori's defense an opportunity to appeal the conviction before the Constitutional Court.

Within a few hours, human rights NGOs and their allies in the press were already denouncing the ruling as an attempt to stop the judicialization process. After a careful reading of the four hundred–page decision, they realized that it was full of irregularities. For example, only two judges had signed the majority opinion about the nature of the crimes, whereas the minority opinion that appeared in the annex had the signatures of the other three![125] In other words, most of the judges in the criminal chamber disagreed with Villa Stein's opinion that these were not crimes against humanity. This rendered the decision to acquit one of the perpetrators and reduce the prison sentences of the rest simply illegal. In a rather inexplicable move, the chief justice had modified the ruling and then went on air vigorously defending a position the court had not actually taken.

In order to mitigate the damage, NGOs immediately took the case before the Inter-American Court of Human Rights. In view of Villa Stein's blatant misconduct and the court's previous jurisprudence in *Barrios Altos* and *La Cantuta*, it decided to condemn the actions of the Peruvian state and requested a new ruling. The Supreme Court found in this Inter-American ruling an opportunity to save face and ordered a review of Villa Stein's decision in order to fulfill Peru's international legal obligations.[126] A new panel

[123] The Spanish term used in Peru is *asociación para delinquir*.

[124] Suprema Corte de Justicia de la Nación, Sala Penal Permanente, *Recurso No. 4104-2010*, ruling of 20 July 2012. On file with the author.

[125] *La República*, 25 July 2012.

[126] Suprema Corte de Justicia de la Nación, Sala Penal Permanente, *Recurso No. 4104-2010*, ruling of 27 September 2012. On file with the author.

of judges took on the task and produced an impressive six hundred–page ruling that ratified the lower court's decision, conclusively endorsing the international legal argument against impunity and forcefully dismissing the view that these emblematic cases of state repression did not constitute crimes against humanity.[127] It is no surprise that the judge in charge of drafting the decision was formerly a lower court judge regularly targeted by NGOs during their pedagogical efforts. She was so committed to writing an authoritative response to Villa Stein that she requested a leave of absence in order to focus exclusively on the Grupo Colina case.

These examples of proimpunity rulings handed down by the Constitutional and Supreme Courts between 2008 and 2012 show that there was a group of judges within the Peruvian judiciary willing to go to great lengths to stop ongoing trials and minimize the impact of some convictions. The presence of equally determined proimpunity allies in the presidential palace and the congress clearly emboldened these recalcitrant judges. At the same time, the limited effectiveness of these moves, explained both by the presence of committed judges and the persistence of a robust consensus around certain legal doctrines regarding the use of international human rights law, reinforces the point that well-timed pedagogical interventions can build buffer zones in the judicial branch that diminish the firepower of subsequent backlashes. Looking ahead, however, NGOs' inability to launch ambitious personnel-changing strategies targeting the upper echelons of the judiciary could have serious consequences for the depth and stability of transitional justice victories. This is a problem their Argentine counterparts will not likely encounter in the years to come.

Conclusion

As in Chapter 3, the account of the Peruvian judicialization process presented here is one characterized by a battle over the hearts and minds of judicial actors, one in which pro- and anti-transitional justice groups sought to institutionalize their interests inside the judiciary. In particular, litigants' focus on reshaping legal preferences is the common denominator to both stories. In the aftermath of the 2000 democratic transition, human rights organizations, who housed highly professionalized teams of legal experts and had strong international connections, anticipated that even

[127] Suprema Corte de Justicia de la Nación, Sala Penal Permanente, *Recurso No. 4104-2010*, ruling of 20 March 2013. On file with the author.

if the political class coalesced behind their agenda, the historic technical deficiencies of the Peruvian judiciary – in particular, its poor performance during the internal armed conflict – would pose insurmountable obstacles for the progress of the investigations and trials. In so doing, they displayed an understanding of the foundations of judicial behavior similar to the one advanced by my sociological institutionalist approach. For them, legal knowledge, bureaucratic routines, and professional values mattered in judicial decision making processes. They consequently designed a pedagogical intervention that managed to convert indifferent and poorly trained judicial actors into effective and committed stewards of transitional justice. NGOs did not simply respond to perceived changes in the growing receptivity of the judiciary by filing suits, but instead engineered it.

The narrative underscores one of the main points advanced in this book: Because judiciaries are subject to pressures and lobbying tactics deployed by myriad outside forces, the institution's bias in favor of certain jurisprudential criteria, which may translate into systematic support for particular sociopolitical causes, is never the outcome of a conflict-free normative evolution. Despite the fact that the Peruvian state was intensely exposed to "norm-affirming events" at the international level, it took a strenuous effort on the part of human rights activists to entrench ideas about international human rights law inside the judicial branch. Several factors explain the success of the persuasion effort. First, the timing of the intervention was important. Peruvian activists enjoyed a first mover advantage in the game to control the judiciary. Second, the choice of the agents of diffusion was also important in order to endow the pedagogical interventions with an aura of neutrality and authority. The academic flair of the events organized by NGOs increased the appeal of the message, convincing judges of the professional imperative to rule in accordance with nondomestic legal standards. The ideas diffused in these settings were couched in highly technical terms, leading to a sense of empowerment among the judges and prosecutors who attended. They now had an authoritative legal infrastructure to defy impunity. Finally, the systematic nature of the efforts also explains success. The consensus among judicial actors vis-à-vis the new legal orthodoxy is broader and stronger around those issue areas that received a more central treatment in the seminars organized by the NGOs.

But unlike the Argentine case – where after the passage of amnesty laws, the trajectory was one of progressive erosion of the impunity regime via ever more ambitious strategies of judicial change – the Peruvian story is certainly more contorted. The shifting balance of power between the pro– and anti–transitional justice coalitions offers a different setting for the battle over the judiciary and helps illuminate important implications of the theory. In particular, the backlash after 2006 forcefully highlights the power of legal preference change. The hostility of the anti–transitional justice coalition after this date was tangible and observable, and clearly aimed at deterring further judicial action in cases of state repression. Some judicial actors were physically threatened and others suffered serious setbacks in their careers. The rules designed to insulate judicial actors from political pressures were thus manipulated during the García administration. Yet, the strong institutional commitment of a critical mass of judicial actors, manufactured during previous years, constituted a buffer zone protecting the interests of human rights activists. The damage of the backlash was contained, and the costs of a counterreformation were raised. It is certainly surprising how rekindled professional values neutralized strategic patterns of behavior, and allowed judges and prosecutors to prevail in outright interbranch confrontations.

Because of this shifting political environment, NGOs were unable to cement legal preference change via aggressive replacement strategies. The structural transformation of the judiciary in favor of transitional justice therefore proved more fragile than in Argentina. In the latter case, the combination of persuasion and personnel changes ultimately guaranteed the reliability of the judicial branch. In Peru, by contrast, the judicialization process came under fire when the political class managed to stock high courts with recalcitrant judges. Although, once again, the resilience of the consensus around certain jurisprudential standards and the ultimate failure of attempts to overturn key rulings are a testament to the effectiveness of changes in legal preferences, these developments challenge any teleological view of transitional justice processes.

5

Mexico

An Untamed Judiciary and the Failure of Criminal Prosecutions

In this final empirical chapter I analyze the failure of criminal prosecutions in Mexico. After the 2000 democratic transition, President Vicente Fox decided to give transitional justice a chance. He did so by declassifying military archives and, most importantly, by creating a Special Prosecutor's Office in charge of investigating the crimes perpetrated by the military during the country's "dirty war" against left-wing student movements and guerillas in the late 1960s and 1970s. Between 2001 and 2006 the special prosecutor prepared and filed numerous indictments against high-profile military officers and a former president, but his efforts were unsuccessful. Unlike in Argentina or Peru, none of the cases filed in Mexican criminal courts resulted in convictions. In fact, none of them reached the trial stage. All of the indictments were rejected on procedural grounds invoking statutes of limitations or remitted to military courts, where they were stalled indefinitely.

The argument put forward in this chapter suggests that this failure is due to the absence of a coordinated effort by civil society actors to take full advantage of the unprecedented window of opportunity opened up by President Fox's decision. The human rights movement remained divided and in general expressed a profound distrust of judicial institutions. In addition, most NGOs lacked professionalized legal teams with expertise in domestic and international litigation, and proficient in international human rights law. This led some victim organizations to disengage from the initiative completely, undermining its legitimacy. Others courted the prosecutor, but did so in ways that did not strengthen his capacity to file effective indictments, and presented charges that did not resonate with the facts of the cases. The few NGOs familiar with the discourse of international human rights law also failed to build a productive working relation with the prosecutor. Most importantly, none of the civil society actors involved in the process ever thought about launching a resocialization effort to make Mexican judicial actors more aware and accepting of international legal doctrines, instruments, and precedents, in order to replace legal preferences and judicial decision making routines conducive to impunity.

As a negative case, Mexico offers a plausible counterfactual to trace what happens when human rights organizations fail to understand the obstacles posed by formalistic legal preferences and lack adequate professional resources to design effective strategies of judicial change. In particular, it shows that the absence of pedagogical interventions resulted in investigations that were not planned according to the special protocols required by cases of state repression, indictments that did not introduce well-crafted arguments advocating an innovative treatment of the legality principle, and judicial decisions that remained highly formalistic and reticent to incorporate new paradigms of rights adjudication. The absence of resocialization efforts also meant that key Mexican judges and prosecutors were never persuaded of the historical significance of these human rights cases, or of their international obligation to take them seriously. Consequently, in addition to lacking technical capabilities, these judicial actors were not fully committed to the cause, and treated the cases as normal criminal suits, applying narrow readings of domestic law to dismiss them on technicalities.

The deep institutionalization of traditional legal preferences in the Mexican judiciary constituted a genuine blockage for the unraveling of a justice cascade grounded upon the acceptance of international human rights norms. The plausibility of the aforementioned counterfactual assumption, however, hinges upon the extent to which NGOs could have chosen to act differently had they possessed the professional resources to diagnose the problem of legal preferences correctly. To be sure, the political environment was not as friendly as the one in Argentina during the Kirchner era, but it was not significantly more hostile than the one in Peru under García or Argentina under Menem, where litigants achieved and defended important victories. The narrative that follows shows that regardless of the political blockages that indeed existed in the Mexican case, the failure of prosecutions cannot be exclusively explained by these limitations. I show that as in Peru, the creation of a special prosecutorial team led to extensive interactions between prosecutors and human rights NGOs, which afforded ample opportunities for litigants actually to deploy adequate pedagogical interventions. During these moments of choice, litigants did not see the need to do so and occasionally diffused legal ideas or doctrines not well suited to solve the cases at hand. This is most unfortunate since at critical stages of the judicialization process, several prosecutors were surprisingly open to persuasion.

I begin with an overview of the debates about transitional justice during the 2000 democratic transition, and document the outcome of the judicialization process, describing the legal arguments put forward by the prosecution and those used by judges to dismiss the indictments. I then proceed to explain this outcome. First, I contextualize it by outlining the characteristics of the political environment, and then explore the interactions between litigants and judicial actors. The analysis shows why international norms failed to become an ideational focal point capable of disrupting long-standing juridical practices not compatible with the cause of truth and justice.

The Failure of Mexico's Special Prosecutor

The Partido Revolucionario Institucional (PRI) governed Mexico autocratically for more than seventy years. The regime oscillated between periods of political stability and of great political unrest (B. Magaloni 2007; Greene 2007). As in most of Latin America, the late 1960s and 1970s were characterized by the expansion of student movements and armed organizations, leading the state to implement highly repressive policies. Beginning with the crushing of the railroad movement in 1959 (Alegre 2013), for the next two decades the PRI would systematically and violently silence the opposition.

The best-known episode of state repression during this period is perhaps the Tlatelolco massacre of 1968, in which student protesters were shot, killed, and imprisoned by the armed forces in Mexico City (Poniatowska 1971). Three years later, the paramilitary group Los Halcones disbanded the first massive march organized after Tlatelolco, once again killing and imprisoning students in what became known as the Corpus Christi massacre. Parallel to what was happening in the capital, toward the end of the 1960s, the government militarized the state of Guerrero in an attempt to deactivate left-wing organizations operating in some of Mexico's poorest rural areas. The violent repression, most famously in the village of Atoyac, convinced community leaders such as Lucio Cabañas and Genaro Vázquez to take up arms. In the following years, more than thirty guerrilla groups became active across the country, including the Liga Comunista 23 de Septiembre, Unión del Pueblo, and Fuerzas Armadas Revolucionarias del Pueblo. After the Corpus Christi massacre, many urban activists felt the regime left them no choice and joined these clandestine organizations.

Although the state publicly denied the existence of armed guerrillas, under Presidents Echeverría (1970–1976) and López Portillo

(1976–1982), the military carefully orchestrated a plan to exterminate them, marking the beginning of Mexico's "dirty war." The leaders of the Federal Security Office (Dirección Federal de Seguridad, DFS) put in practice the national security doctrine they had learned at the School of the Americas (Hellman 1983; Gill 2004) and adopted techniques of torture and disappearance similar to those used in the Southern Cone (Aguayo 2001). In the early 1970s a considerable portion of the army was stationed in Guerrero in full antiguerrilla mode (Sierra 2003). Around 1975, the DFS radicalized these practices by creating a special operations group called Brigada Blanca. The outcome of these efforts is less well known than the crimes perpetrated by other Latin American dictatorships, but equally disturbing. Thousands of activists were taken to the main clandestine detention center in Mexico City, the Campo Militar Número 1; held there illegally; and tortured (Vicente 2012). In addition, hundreds were disappeared, making the per capita rate of forced disappearances in Guerrero as high as the one in Argentina or Chile. The victims included not only members of the guerrillas, but their relatives and friends, who were illegally detained by the military to extract information. Some evidence even suggests that Mexican officers were the first in the region to implement the infamous "flights of death," drugging and throwing prisoners into the Pacific Ocean to make sure their bodies would never be found.[1]

The Mexican human rights movement began to take shape in response to these crimes (Saltalamacchia 2009). As in other countries, these organizations were led by the relatives of political prisoners or victims of forced disappearances. After carefully gathering information for several years, in 1977, some groups published a list with the names of three hundred political prisoners and demanded immediate action to end highly irregular proceedings. That same year, activists in Guerrero announced that since 1970 the military had forced 300 to disappear; Amnesty International indicated that the figure was higher, around 360. According to organizations such as Asociación de Familiares de Detenidos, Desaparecidos y Víctimas de Violaciones a los Derechos Humanos en Mexico (AFADEM); the Comité pro Defensa de Presos, Perseguidos, Desaparecidos y Exiliados Políticos de Mexico; or the Comité Nacional Independiente pro Defensa de Presos, Perseguidos, Desaparecidos y Exiliados Políticos, by the early 1980s the count had risen to between 500 and 1,200 forced disappearances (Castellanos 2007; Antillón 2008).

[1] *Proceso*, 7 November 2002.

Constant pressures by human rights groups put the issue of the dirty war on the public agenda despite the press's reluctance to inform the public about the crimes (Rodríguez Mungía 2007). The authorities denied the existence of clandestine detention camps and special anti-guerrilla forces and argued that the alleged disappeared people either had died in combat, been killed by other armed groups, or were simply fugitives (Castellanos 2007). In order to avert a legitimacy crisis, however, between 1977 and 1978 President López Portillo implemented a series of political reforms, including an amnesty for more than one thousand political prisoners, and lifted the ban on left-wing parties (Camp 2003). López Portillo's reforms, coupled with the success of state repression, gave opposition forces on the Left the incentive to invest in party building (Greene 2007). Former political prisoners as well as human rights activists joined new and old party organizations. For example, Rosario Ibarra, whose son disappeared in 1975 and led the most prominent human rights organization of the period, was the presidential candidate of the Partido Revolucionario de los Trabajadores (PRT) in the 1982 elections, thus initiating a long political career.

Although key activists and victims of repression transitioned into the world of partisan politics, in the late 1980s and early 1990s the number of human rights NGOs grew exponentially. As the country liberalized both politically and economically, the international community started to pay attention to the domestic human rights situation (Keck and Sikkink 1998). The negotiation of free trade agreements with North America and Europe and the outbreak of the Chiapas conflict made the state vulnerable to outside pressures and empowered local activists (Anaya 2012). In fact, the Mexican state slowly began to shift from denial to action, from a foreign policy that emphasized the principle of noninterference to a gradual understanding of the normative imperatives that result from belonging to the club of democratic nations (Treviño 2004). The creation and later empowerment of the National Human Rights Commission, the peace talks with Zapatismo, the authorization of official visits by the Inter-American Commission of Human Rights and Amnesty International, and the appointment of special prosecutors to investigate widely publicized massacres such as Aguas Blancas, all indicated that the PRI reluctantly began to recognize the importance of showing the world at least some willingness to improve its dark record of repression and impunity (Anaya 2012).

The transfer of power to Vicente Fox of the Partido Acción Nacional (PAN) in 2000 further highlighted this tension between Mexico's international aspirations and its domestic practices. The penetration and relative effectiveness of the human rights discourse as a force of political change during the 1990s were well understood by the incoming government. The country was now nominally democratic, but Fox had to validate these credentials by showing a deeper commitment to human rights and the rule of law than his predecessors (Covarrubias 2003; Anaya 2006). Against this backdrop, the question of how to deal with the legacies of state repression haunted the Fox administration from the electoral campaign forward. On the one hand, as the armed forces became suspected of campaigning for the regime, Fox approached them to secure their loyalty in the event of a PRI defeat.[2] On the other, Fox sought to attract votes from the Left, arguing that a divided opposition could result in another PRI victory. As part of these efforts, he courted the leaders of the 1968 movement, victims of state repression, and left-wing activists, praising their contributions to democratization beginning in the 1960s and 1970s, and managed to lure some of them into his camp.[3] The PAN candidate thus engaged in a difficult balancing act, trying to appease the military while giving hints that he would not turn a blind eye to the abuses of the seventy-year-old regime.

The debate about how to hold the autocrats accountable began in earnest between the July election and the official transfer of power. In September, officials of the Guerrero Human Rights Commission put the issue on the agenda when they demanded the creation of a truth commission to investigate the fate of those who had disappeared.[4] Weeks later, the Comité 68, an NGO founded to demand justice for the Tlatelolco massacre, asked the president-elect to open the military archives to establish what happened during the dirty war.[5] Although skeptical about the potential of these initiatives, Rosario Ibarra, now leader of the NGO Eureka, seconded the request.[6] In October, the commemoration of the thirty-second anniversary of Tlatelolco intensified these demands and put the question of human rights violations into sharper focus, leading Fox to announce that he would create a "transparency commission."[7] For the *New York Times* this pledge indicated that the PRI had surrendered not only the presidency, but also "control over the past."[8]

[2] *El Universal*, 26 January 2000.

[3] *El Universal*, 27 May 2000; 30 May 2000.

[4] *El Universal*, 10 September 2000.

[5] *El Universal*, 22 September 2000.

[6] *El Universal*, 23 September 2000; 18 October 2000.

[7] *El Universal*, 3 October 2000.

[8] *New York Times*, 19 October 2000.

After Fox took office it was clear that his administration had to address the question of state repression one way or another. Although the transition team that counseled the president-elect on "political issues" recommended against implementing a transitional justice policy,[9] not doing so would have been a breach of campaign promises, and out of sync with the narrative of change. The exact way in which the new democratic government would satisfy the victims, however, was unclear, in part because inside the cabinet there were groups advocating different approaches. Well-known human rights activists such as Jorge Castañeda (secretary of foreign affairs) and Mariclaire Acosta (special ambassador for human rights), who advocated the creation of a truth commission, coexisted alongside politicians such as Secretary of Interior Santiago Creel, who knew that given the size of the PRI's legislative delegation the administration could not afford to antagonize the old ruling party. At an early stage, the more progressive elements in the cabinet, whom Fox valued for their efforts to attract decisive votes from the Left, had the upper hand. Following their advice, the administration asked a group of academics to draft a proposal for the creation of a truth commission (Aguayo and Treviño 2007), but pointed out that it would not engage in a "witch hunt."[10]

This initiative quickly lost momentum when the president, under Creel's influence, decided he needed PRI votes to pass economic reforms through congress.[11] The human rights question was thus relegated to an issue of foreign, not domestic policy, of the present and not of the past. As posttransitional governments elsewhere in the region did (Alcañíz 2012), the PAN government sent signals abroad about its greater commitment to human rights by ratifying myriad treaties central to the transitional justice agenda, including the Rome Statute, the Convention on the Non-Applicability of Statutory Limitations to War Crimes and Crimes against Humanity, and the Inter-American Convention on Forced Disappearances. In addition, congress passed a law including the crime of "forced disappearance" in the federal criminal code.[12] But in line with the administration's appeasement strategy, all of these changes to the legal system indicated that the aforementioned laws and international instruments could not be applied retroactively.

[9] Fox organized his transition team into groups in charge of different issues including economic policy, foreign affairs, and political issues.

[10] *El Universal*, 7 December 2000.

[11] *El Universal*, 26 June 2001.

[12] *El Universal*, 22 December 2000.

Despite these efforts to exclude transitional justice from the agenda, the problem soon resurfaced. A member of the administration stated in an interview that "when they were about to bury the issue, something completely unexpected happened: the suspicious death of a famous human rights lawyer, Digna Ochoa."[13] Many suspected that Ochoa was murdered, in part because she had been the victim of numerous threats for her work in high-profile torture cases involving the military. My interviewee further explained that because of these suspicions, "from then on domestic and international pressures forced the president to pay attention to human rights.... [The incident] opened a window of opportunity to discuss the crimes of the past."[14]

As these pressures continued to mount, the head of the National Human Rights Commission released a report on the forced disappearances perpetrated during the "dirty war." He did so during a highly publicized ceremony attended by the president, the leaders of the major parties, members of the armed forces, and some civil society organizations. The report was the result of an investigation that officially began in the late 1980s when then President Salinas promised Rosario Ibarra that his administration would look into her son's disappearance. Not surprisingly, the files remained dormant for more than a decade. Finally, in November 2001, the human rights commissioner announced that 532 cases had been investigated, and that there was sufficient evidence of 275 disappearances to proceed legally. In addition, he gave the president a sealed envelope with the names of the alleged perpetrators. This was the first time that a Mexican official admitted the existence of these crimes and acknowledged the state's responsibility. One of the attendees described the ceremony as "shocking": "Seeing the faces of the military officers was amazing, especially when Soberanes [the commissioner] read a passage from the report about how a one year old girl was tortured in front of her mother, inside a military barrack."[15]

In addition to releasing the report, Soberanes proposed the appointment of a special prosecutor to investigate the crimes. He also recommended against the creation of a truth commission.[16] This move was likely the result of consultation with the president's staff. By now the minister of interior had come to terms with the idea that some form of transitional

[13] Mariclaire Acosta, interview, Mexico City, 19 July 2010.

[14] Ibid.

[15] Ibid.

[16] *El Universal*, 25 June 2001.

justice was inevitable and preferred the judicial path to a truth commission, an option still favored by other members of the cabinet and human rights organizations. The following day, President Fox signed a decree creating this new office and gave it a rather convoluted name, which foreshadowed the complicated task that lay ahead of whoever was put in charge: Special Prosecutor's Office for the Investigation of Events Probably Constitutive of Federal Crimes Perpetrated Directly or Indirectly by Public Servants against People Associated with Social and Political Movements of the Past (hereafter, FEMOSPP).[17]

In sum, when he took office, Fox began to feel the constraints imposed by the PRI's enduring institutional presence in congress and preferred not to antagonize the opposition by launching a thorough review of the past. Moreover, he feared an outright confrontation with the military, which many in the administration saw as one of the few potential anchors of presidential power in a state decisively infiltrated by the PRI. But the dynamics of the transition ultimately forced the PAN to offer a path to accountability for human rights crimes, one that opened an unprecedented window of opportunity for civil society organizations to advance their demands for truth and justice. Much as in Peru, the creation of the FEMOSPP gave human rights activists a demarcated group of judicial interlocutors that they could lobby and closely scrutinize in order to guarantee positive outcomes.

Before the 2000s, human rights NGOs had only made sporadic and limited efforts to bring the perpetrators to justice. Attempts to initiate judicial proceedings include six criminal suits filed during the 1990s demanding justice for the disappearance of Rosendo Radilla in 1974;[18] the Comité 68's petition before the Supreme Court to investigate the Tlatelolco massacre in 1998 (Comité 68 2008); and, in 2000, AFADEM's request for military courts to include forced disappearances among the charges brought against the former leaders of the DFS, who were under investigation for drug trafficking.[19] By the time President Fox decided to give truth and justice a chance, none of these attempts had yielded positive results. The FEMOSPP significantly differed from these prior efforts. Although the presidential decree specified that the prosecutor would only

[17] In Spanish, FEMOSPP stands for Fiscalía Especial para la Atención de Hechos Probablemente Constitutivos de Delitos Federales Cometidos Directa o Indirectamente por Servidores Públicos en contra de Personas Vinculadas con Movimientos Sociales y Políticos del Pasado.

[18] Tita Radilla, interview, Mexico City, 23 July 2010.

[19] *El Universal*, 2 September 2000; 14 September 2000; 22 September 2000.

have jurisdiction over federal crimes perpetrated against social and political groups, which effectively excluded crimes perpetrated by local security forces and those against nonactivists, it still left ample room for investigating a wide range of cases involving politicians and the army. In other words, the FEMOSPP had, for the first time, the opportunity systematically to expose the Mexican judiciary to cases of state repression, and put significant state resources behind the cause, thus offering the possibility to end the cycle of impunity.

A lot hinged on who would be appointed to lead the Special Prosecutor's Office, his/her competence in investigating complex crimes, and his/her ability and willingness to withstand political pressures. In this regard, the government's initial plan to appoint a prestigious human rights lawyer failed. At least twenty candidates declined the offer, fearing the insurmountable legal and political obstacles they would face, and others refused to take the job because the office was put under the orbit of the attorney general,[20] an active duty general who had served as chief prosecutor in military courts.[21] When in January 2002 the administration finally appointed Ignacio Carrillo Prieto, it was clear that this law professor from the Autonomous National University of Mexico was not the candidate supporters of the initiative had wanted. In fact, not only did he have no experience investigating complex human rights crimes (which in any case very few in Mexico could include in their resumes), but he also had no background in international human rights law.

Despite this significant shortcoming, the prospects were still somewhat encouraging. First, Carrillo Prieto's office was well funded. Aguayo and Treviño (2007) indicate that between 2004 and 2006, the FEMOSPP had an authorized budget of nearly U.S.$10 million. In fact, year after year the government accepted the prosecutor's requests for budgetary increases. As a result, Carillo Prieto was able to increase his staff quickly from around 40 in 2002 to 160 in 2003, including assistant prosecutors, researchers, and administrative staff. These figures compare favorably with the resources available to the Argentine truth commission, the Prosecutor's Office at the Special Court for Sierra Leone, the Serious Crimes Investigations Unit in East Timor, or the Special Prosecutor's Office in Ethiopia (Seils 2004).

Second, in addition to the availability of adequate financial and human resources to conduct his duties, Carrillo Prieto benefited from President

[20] The attorney general is known in Mexico as the Procurador General de la República, and his office as the Procuraduría General de la República, or PGR.

[21] *La Jornada*, 7 December 2001.

Fox's decision to open the military archives.[22] The Mexican military had kept detailed records of its clandestine activities during the dirty war. This provided both researchers and prosecutors in his office with a wealth of evidence not available to their counterparts in other Latin American countries.[23] These archives had yet to be organized, but they contained excellent evidence about the treatment of political prisoners, who participated in torture sessions, and the fate of the disappeared, which could prove crucial when filing indictments in criminal courts.

Third, Carrillo Prieto had an ambitious interpretation of his mandate. Early on, he announced that not only would he focus on filing criminal charges against the alleged perpetrators, but that his team would also produce a report similar to those drafted by truth commissions around the world. In other words, the Mexican Special Prosecutor's Office quickly acquired the potential to become a pathway to both truth and justice. To accomplish this task, Carrillo Prieto appointed a team of historians to help organize the archives, provide prosecutors with relevant evidence, and produce the materials to be included in the final report. These efforts could result in a definitive and much more authoritative account of the PRI's repressive strategy than the one released by the National Human Rights Commission in 2001.

Finally, Carrillo Prieto showed good instincts in terms of how to organize the investigations effectively. Although the presidential decree mandating the appointment of a special prosecutor was a direct response to the National Human Rights Commission's report on the forced disappearances perpetrated during the 1970s, it did not specify the crimes against social and political movements of the past on which the office should focus. Between the late 1960s and the 2000s, there were numerous episodes of state repression in addition to the dirty war. Selectivity was therefore essential in order to preclude the perils of overreach. In response to this challenge, the prosecutor prioritized crimes that others had investigated before and had received ample attention by historians, namely, the forced disappearances of the 1970s and the emblematic massacres of Tlatelolco (1968) and Corpus Christi (1971). This meant that his team would not have to start from scratch, improving the chances of filing indictments in a timely manner. In addition to the so-called investigation programs A and B dedicated to the forced disappearances and the two massacres, respectively, there was a small team in charge of investigating the assassination of

[22] *El Universal*, 28 December 2001.

[23] Director of the Historical Investigations Team, interview, Mexico City, 27 September 2010.

leftist activists post 1988, but it received few resources and often served as an aid to the other two teams.

How did the prosecutors proceed with the investigations and the indictments?[24] In relation to the forced disappearances perpetrated during the dirty war, the FEMOSPP filed around a dozen cases against the commanders of the DFS. With a few exceptions, the cases generally involved one victim. The prosecutors chose to focus on high-profile victims such as the relatives of famous human rights activists and the leaders of armed organizations. With regard to the legal strategy, they were convinced that because the crime of "forced disappearance" was added to the Mexican Criminal Code in 2001, it was not possible to use it in the indictments. Instead they decided to bring charges for "unlawful deprivation of liberty."[25] Unlike their counterparts in Argentina and Peru, who faced the same problem, Mexican prosecutors did not subsume the domestic criminal definition valid at the time of perpetration in broader categories derived from international criminal and human rights law in order to defy statutes of limitations and characterize the crimes in question adequately. What is interesting about this choice is that in the Mexican case, it was not even necessary to resort to this complicated legal argument in order to use the notion of "forced disappearance." In 2004 the Supreme Court ruled that this was a continuous crime. Accordingly, until the bodies were found it was lawful to use this criminal definition even for crimes perpetrated before 2001.[26] As we shall see, this aspect of the prosecution's strategy had severe negative consequences.

In the first case submitted to a federal district court in Monterrey involving the disappearance of Rosario Ibarra's son, the judge quickly

[24] In Mexico, it is incredibly hard to find copies of the rulings handed down by lower courts. Reflecting on this problem, Human Rights Watch suggests: "a culture of secrecy prevails, for the most part, in the work of Mexican judges. Part of the problem is that many judges still believe that access to information and transparency belong to common law judicial systems and are incompatible with Mexico's legal system" (2006: 48). As a result, most of the information on the rulings on FEMOSPP cases, their chronology and content, is from an unpublished manuscript written by Ignacio Carrillo Prieto, which he was kind enough to share with me (Carrillo Prieto 2009). I triangulated this information with data on the status of the FEMOSPP docket as of August 2010. I obtained this information from the Attorney General's Office after filing a public information request. Some judges did grant me access to the rulings, so I reference those in the footnotes when relevant.

[25] In Spanish, "privación ilegal de la libertad en su modalidad de plagio o secuestro."

[26] The Supreme Court argued that this reasoning applies even though the law ratifying the Inter-American Convention on Forced Disappearances includes a clause prohibiting the retroactive use of this international instrument by domestic courts. Suprema Corte de Justicia de la Nación, *Tesis Jurisprudencial 49/2004*, ruling of 29 June 2004. On file with the author.

issued a dismissal, arguing that statutes of limitations had expired. On behalf of Carrillo Prieto, the attorney general asked the Supreme Court to review this decision. In November 2003, the Supreme Court handed down a ruling indicating that as long as the victim was not released, the crime of "unlawful deprivation of liberty" was still in course, thus overturning the district court's criteria.[27] It is important to note that, as in the aforementioned 2004 ruling on the use of "forced disappearance," in this decision, the justices made no reference to international law. By not doing so, they briefly vindicated Carillo Prieto's strategy to keep his strategy strictly within domestic legal territory.

Following the Supreme Court's decision, the district judge issued arrest warrants against the former leaders of the DFS, Miguel Nazar Haro, Juventino Cisneros, and Luis De la Barreda. Although these were not convictions, they indicated the judge believed there was probable cause to merit further investigations and eventually a trial. Nazar Haro and Cisneros were captured in February and October 2004, respectively, whereas De la Barreda remained fugitive until June 2006.[28] When issuing these warrants, the judge reclassified the charges as "due process violations,"[29] because unlike "unlawful deprivation of liberty," which only applies to private citizens, it is a criminal definition that can be used against public servants. Another district judge in the state of Mexico made a similar move when issuing five additional warrants in a case involving the disappearance of Ignacio Salas Obregón, one of the founders of the Liga Comunista 23 de Septiembre.

In total, the FEMOSPP obtained nine indictments. In 2005, however, appeals judges dismissed most of them. Like the initial reflex reaction by the Monterrey judge in the Ibarra case, this was further indication that Mexican judges were predisposed to render extremely formalistic readings of the law and the evidence, devoid of all human rights criteria. In general, judges were not convinced that the prosecution had produced enough evidence of the direct participation of the defendants in the crime, which they deemed necessary in order to uphold the indictments.[30] Shockingly, several judges discarded evidence derived from documents

[27] Primera Sala de la Suprema Corte de Justicia de la Nación, *Recurso de apelación extraordinario 1/2003*, ruling of 5 November 2003. On file with the author.

[28] For an account of why and how De la Barreda managed to remain fugitive, as well as for the legal arguments used by defense lawyers see De la Barreda Solórzano (2008).

[29] In Spanish, "violación de garantías."

[30] Some of the cases took longer to reach the appeals stages because the police did not execute the warrants, and thus stalled the investigations.

that the defendants had themselves signed, authorizing the transfer of the detainees to different detention camps. This type of evidence of punishable involvement in the perpetration of the crime is as valuable as it is rare in cases of clandestine state repression. Some judges made the formalistic argument that the prosecution had not submitted original copies of the aforementioned documents, while others refused to admit the files as incriminating evidence because they argued that authorizing the transfer of prisoners was not necessarily indicative of participation in their disappearance.[31] Most of the remaining indictments were dismissed in 2006 after congress removed the crime of "due process violations" from the criminal code. Legislators argued that it was too vague, and thus did not offer defendants enough due process guarantees.[32]

The fate of these cases was in part a consequence of Carrillo Prieto's decision to leave aside the tools of international human rights law, especially the category of "forced disappearance." First, even if the behavior of congress was deliberately orchestrated to stop efforts at transitional justice, it is unlikely that legislators would have derogated the crime of "forced disappearance," making it a safer bet. Second, the reclassification of the crimes by district judges reflected the inadequacies of "unlawful deprivation of liberty" as the category used to describe what in fact were forced disappearances. Judges in these and other cases only had to resort to plain meaning interpretation to conclude, for example, that in the events in question no one had asked for ransom, one of the elements of the crime of "unlawful deprivation of liberty" according to the Mexican Criminal Code. Most importantly, these events involved public officials, who the code indicates cannot be responsible for "unlawful deprivation of liberty."[33] Interestingly, the FEMOSSP persisted with this strategy as late as 2006, when it brought the same charges against several former military officers for the disappearance of Rodolfo Reyes Crespo. The case obviously failed, since by this point, courts in several states had repeatedly put these legal questions to rest.

[31] See, for example, Decimosegundo Juzgado de Distrito de Procesos Penales Federales en el Distrito Federal, *Causa 53/2005*, ruling of 25 June 2005. On file with the author.

[32] The judges based their decision on the principle of retroactivity of the most favorable criminal law. It is important to note that there is no evidence that congress's behavior was aimed at stopping these specific cases, first because the reform was passed almost three years after the FEMOSPP filed the indictments, and second because it passed with strong support from the leftist Partido de la Revolución Democrática (PRD), which had legislators with a past in guerrilla and student organizations.

[33] See, for example, Tercer Tribunal Colegiado en Materia Penal del Segundo Circuito, *Amparo en Revisión 125/2005*, ruling of 10 November 2005. On file with the author.

The problems related to the absence of references to international human rights law in the indictments were also apparent in yet another case against the former DFS director Luis de la Barreda. This one involved two victims, José Olivares and Salvador Corral, whose bodies were found eleven days after being taken into custody by the military in 1974. There was evidence that they had been abducted in Guadalajara and Monterrey, respectively, and interrogated in Mexico City. Because the victims were not missing, the FEMOSPP could not bring charges for "forced disappearance," so it decided to file charges for "aggravated homicide." As had the judges mentioned previously, the district court found it hard to accept the idea that a high-ranking officer could be responsible for an assassination without having directly participated in it. Most importantly, the statutes of limitations for "aggravated homicide" had expired, so the court dismissed the case in July 2006. Had they been more familiar with international human rights law, the prosecutors could have proceeded as their counterparts in other Latin American countries did, by arguing that this crime was part of a broader, systematic set of criminal acts orchestrated by the military, and therefore classifiable as an international crime not subject to statutory limitations. This is especially true in this case, which involved two unrelated victims in two different states, thus providing a better perspective on the systematic nature of the repressive policy.[34]

Unfortunately for Carrillo Prieto and the victims, there were more controversial legal issues in addition to the question of statutes of limitations and how to define the crimes. In August 2005, the FEMOSPP filed charges against a retired general accusing him of disappearing Rosendo Radilla, the father of Tita Radilla, leader of AFADEM. Rosendo, a leftist activist in Guerrero, was detained at a military checkpoint in 1974 and never seen again. Although the district judge accepted the indictment and issued an arrest warrant, he transferred the case to a military court. He based his decision on Articles 37 and 57 of the Military Code of Justice,

[34] In order to put forward this argument, the prosecutors would have had to invoke customary international law. This would have been possible not only because Mexican diplomats had an active role in the drafting of several international human rights legal instruments since World War II, but also because in addition to the treaties ratified after the 2000 transition, Mexico has ratified several other conventions such as the International Covenant on Civil and Political Rights (1981), the American Convention on Human Rights (1981), the Convention against Torture and Other Cruel, Inhuman, or Degrading Treatment or Punishment (1986), and the Inter-American Convention to Prevent and Punish Torture (1987). See Valadés (2001) and Human Rights Watch (2003).

which indicate that only military courts have jurisdiction over crimes perpetrated by soldiers on active duty (Centro Agustin Pro et al. 2006).[35] A Guerrero appeals court found against an *amparo* filed by Tita Radilla and confirmed the lower court's decision. The special prosecutor never invoked long-standing international precedents on the inappropriateness of military jurisdiction for human rights trials in order to challenge these decisions. In fact, he did not even appeal the last ruling. As expected, the case was stalled indefinitely.

The attempt to prosecute high-ranking military officers for the forced disappearances documented in the report released by the National Human Rights Commission in 2001 was clearly a fiasco. The other set of cases, the Tlatelolco and Corpus Christi massacres, suffered a similar fate.

In 1998, the Comité 68 filed a case against the former presidents Díaz Ordáz and Echeverría and several high-ranking military officers, accusing them of having perpetrated the crime of genocide against the students who marched in Mexico City on 2 October 1968.[36] A few days later, the Attorney General's Office announced that it would not conduct an investigation because statutes of limitations had expired. After a series of appeals, in January 2002, the Supreme Court ruled that the case could not be dismissed without first conducting a thorough legal analysis and a preliminary investigation, and remitted it to the recently created FEMOSPP. Carrillo Prieto and his team decided to investigate the Corpus Christi massacre alongside the Tlatelolco case.

In July 2004, the FEMOSPP shocked Mexican public opinion when it took the latter case to court. The prosecutor charged the former president Echeverría, the former secretary of interior Moya Palencia, the former chief of the special operations group Los Halcones, and several others with the crime of genocide.[37] Following the argument put forward by the Comité 68 in 1998, Carillo Prieto indicated that the students attacked by the armed forces constituted a clearly defined "national group," making the notion of genocide, as defined by the Mexican Criminal Code at the time of perpetration, applicable to the case. As in the forced disappearance cases, the district judge's reflex reaction to the nine-thousand-page-long indictment was to conclude, in a matter of hours, that statutes of limitations had expired and that the treaties invoked by the FEMPOSPP could

[35] The judge read these articles in light of a narrow interpretation of Article 13 of the Mexican constitution, which includes a provision against the possibility of being tried in special courts.

[36] In 1968 Echeverría was the secretary of interior and Díaz Ordáz the president.

[37] The indictment included the cases of 25 students.

not be applied retroactively.[38] In response to this initial disappointing result, the FEMOSPP requested that the Supreme Court make use of its prerogative to consider high-profile cases, in order to settle the legal controversy. The justices agreed, and in February 2005, they handed down a decision.

Carrillo Prieto and the victims never anticipated that the Mexican Supreme Court would agree with the idea that the crime of genocide was subject to statutes of limitations. Unfortunately for them, the degree of formalism in the court's reasoning was rather extreme. The Supreme Court argued that Article 149 *bis* of the Federal Criminal Code, which incorporated the crime of genocide into the Mexican legal framework in 1967, was subject to the same procedural rules as others in the code. It forcefully dismissed the idea that criminal prosecutions could be governed by rules or values other than those expressly stated in Mexican constitutional norms. In an archetypal legal positivist move, the court made the following argument:

> The great danger of sacrificing individual rights in light of the alleged existence of the rights of humanity, a race, a nation, or other personified, diffuse and totalizing entity of this sort, is the reproduction of a totalitarian form of argumentation ... [which puts] aside positive legality in favor of a supposedly "superior legality" that embodies justice or some other value that a judge considers relevant in any particular moment.[39]

In line with the district judge, the court also indicated that although the Mexican Senate had ratified the Convention on the Non Applicability of Statutory Limitations to War Crimes and Crimes against Humanity in 2001, the ratification law prohibited judges from using the convention retroactively as per Article 14 of the Mexican constitution, which enshrines the principle of strict legality in criminal prosecutions.[40] These two sets

[38] The judge also dismissed evidence presented by the FEMOSPP showing that there had been prior attempts to investigate the crime in the 1970s. The prosecution argued that those periods during which authorities formally investigated the crime should not be counted toward the calculus of statutory limitations. The judge dismissed this claim because Carrillo Prieto did not submit the original copies of the relevant documents. *El Universal*, 23 February 2005.

[39] Primera Sala de la Suprema Corte De Justicia de la Nación, *Recurso De Apelación No. 1/2004-Ps*, ruling of 23 February 2005, p. 110. On file with the author.

[40] This argument contrasts sharply with the one put forward by the Argentine Supreme Court in a famous 2004 ruling. According to Argentine justices, invoking domestic legal provisions to limit the reach of this particular convention constitutes a violation of its spirit and, therefore, of the country's international obligations. See Corte Suprema de Justicia de la Nación Argentina, *Arancibia Clavel, Enrique Lautaro s/homicidio calificado y asociación ilícita y otros*, ruling of 24 August 2004, concurrent vote of Justice Carmen Argibay.

of arguments led the justices to conclude that statutes of limitations had expired. Interestingly, however, they argued that this only applied to nine of the eleven defendants. According to the judges, for Echeverría and Moya Palencia, statutes of limitations would run out in more than a year. The court reasoned that since in the case of genocide statutes of limitations apply after thirty years, and these two defendants benefited from immunity while serving as president and secretary of interior, respectively, between 1970 and 1976, they could still be prosecuted until December 2006. In other words, the justices did not completely put an end to the quest for justice, but in what amounts to an unequivocal expression of formalistic legal preferences, they traced an extremely narrow legal path for the prosecution, in strict accordance with the imperatives of domestic criminal law.

In addition to these arguments, the Supreme Court suggested that Carrillo Prieto's characterization of the student movement as a national group subject to an extermination attempt by the armed forces was not persuasive, and did not resonate with the facts of the case. In fact, the judges even recommended that the prosecutor file charges for aggravated homicide, instead of genocide. The lower court judge who later received the case concurred, ruled that the genocide charges did not match the facts of the case, and proceeded to dismiss it. After this resounding defeat, the FEMOSPP focused its efforts on the Tlatelolco massacre. Despite the lack of success of its legal strategy in the Corpus Christi case, in September 2005 the prosecutor filed very similar charges against eight former political and military leaders responsible for the 1968 crimes. In line with the aforementioned precedent, the district judge did not grant the arrest warrants, arguing that there was no evidence of genocide. This time the Supreme Court refused to hear the case because it had already dealt with the same legal issues in the February decision.

In June 2006, the case landed in an appeals court. To everyone's surprise a judge accepted the genocide charges and granted an arrest warrant against former president Echeverría. Carrillo Prieto and the victims were ecstatic; this was by far their most important achievement in the transitional justice process. They soon realized that their optimism was unfounded, as the case became immersed in a Kafkaesque back and forth between district and appeals courts. When the case was remitted to a district judge to proceed with the indictment, he concluded that statutes of limitations had expired, and overturned the arrest warrant. In line with the outcome of the previous appeal, another appeals court quickly reversed this decision. Finally, a year later, in July 2007, with Echeverría still under house arrest, a judge in Mexico City ruled that statutes of limitations had now effectively expired, as indicated in the Supreme Court's 2005 decision. He also argued that there was no evidence of Echeverría's direct participation in the crime.

In the Tlatelolco and Corpus Christi cases, judges based their decisions on extremely formalistic readings of the law. International human rights law was hardly part of the debate. Although the briefs submitted by the prosecution did mention international human rights treaties on genocide and crimes against humanity as well as international customary law,[41] the judges chose to ignore these arguments. It is also important to note that by sticking to the Comité 68's long-standing position that these crimes constituted genocide, the special prosecutor did not help his case, putting forward a legal argument that did not resonate with the facts. Although this had the potential to expand the terms of the debate to include innovative international legal arguments pertaining to the special status of state crimes, the prosecution's case bluntly applied a criminal definition that is extremely restrictive and hard to prove. It is not surprising that most judges did not take the idea of genocide very seriously, since it is well known that political groups do not enter the scope of this criminal definition. As a result, the case lacked the nuance of the arguments routinely put forward by Argentine or Peruvian litigants, in which criminal conduct is usually defined using ordinary, less controversial domestic definitions such as homicide, kidnapping, or torture, and then subsumed under international ones in order to overcome procedural obstacles such as statutes of limitations. Interestingly, the prosecution pursued the same legal strategy in both cases, even when Carrillo Prieto had concrete evidence of judges' predisposition to dismiss it and had been advised by the Supreme Court to file charges for aggravated homicide. This produced a stagnant debate and failed to expose judges to new ideas that could induce changes to the prevailing jurisprudential standards.

The creation of the Special Prosecutor's Office represented a unique opportunity to focus the attention of the Mexican federal judiciary on issues related to the investigation, prosecution, and punishment of grave human rights violations. Yet, the prosecutor and the victims were unable

[41] Before filing the indictment, Carrillo Prieto asked the National Institute for Criminal Sciences for an opinion. According to a human rights lawyer who reviewed the document, international human rights law was used but the quality of the argumentation was very low: "I think the problem was that the prosecutor confused elements of the crime of genocide with those of crimes against humanity. This led to numerous inconsistencies." Interview, Mexico City, 26 July 2010.

to develop a legal discourse that captured the specificities of these crimes, and failed to alter the decision making routines of federal judges, who proceeded to treat these suits as normal criminal cases. Not fully incorporating juridical ideas derived from the international human rights regime made the legal space afforded to the prosecutor and the victims extremely narrow and difficult to navigate. Confining the debate to domestic legal arguments created the perfect environment for indifferent judges instinctively to invoke procedural rules, technicalities, and traditional evidentiary standards to trace possible, but narrow paths to accountability. Because of its inability to find adequate and creative alternatives to the legal status quo, the FEMOSPP was shut down in November 2006. The cases were remitted to an ordinary division within the Attorney General's Office, where they died. What explains this outcome?

Mixed Signals from the Political Environment

Existing explanations for the failure of the FEMOSPP highlight the lack of support from President Fox, and the enduring power of the PRI and the armed forces as a primary causal factor (e.g. Aguayo and Treviño 2007; Dutrénit Bielous and Varela Petito 2010). My account departs from the view that the outcome was overdetermined by the characteristics of the political environment. While acknowledging the challenges faced by the prosecutor on this front, I argue that Carillo Prieto and the victims still had room to maneuver. Unlike their counterparts in Argentina during the 1990s or Peru in the late 2000s, human rights NGOs failed to motivate judges and prosecutors to overcome the limits imposed by powerful soldiers and politicians. As a result, Mexican judicial actors remained both ill equipped and unmoved to take cases of state repression seriously. Victims and their lawyers therefore failed to activate the autonomous professional logic that can insulate these highly political cases from outside pressures, and trigger an effective institutional commitment to truth and justice.

To be sure, the political environment showed some degree of hostility toward transitional justice. Upon the creation of the FEMOSPP, the secretary general of the PRI declared, "We are not afraid of law enforcement, our only demand is that legality is respected."[42] The party's attitude toward the process became increasingly belligerent, especially as the first indictment against Echeverría loomed on the horizon. For example, in July 2004, PRI party leaders accused President Fox of being stuck between the "grudges

[42] *El Universal*, 28 November 2001, my translation.

of the past and his lack of objectives and vision for the future." They also announced they would lead a campaign in defense of the "Mexican state and the armed forces," and appoint a legal team to show the "illegality" of the process, which "ignores the specific political, legal, and administrative conditions under which civilian and military authorities confronted crime in the 1970s."[43] In addition, according to the press, the PRI's congressional delegation blackmailed Fox by delaying the passing of a social security reform, hoping that the president would pressure judges to dismiss the indictments.[44]

The military was also nervous about the consequences of Carrillo Prieto's actions and behaved accordingly. When the special prosecutor took office:

> I immediately contacted the Secretary of Defense, General Clemente Vega García. I explained what my mission was, and he told me: "Very well. Now, tell us who will investigate and repair the damage made to those whose husbands and parents were killed by the guerrillas?" ... The relationship was very respectful, but always very tense.[45]

This quote reflects a common claim made by military officers across Latin America: Transitional justice processes are fundamentally unjust unless they also prosecute former leftist activists, against whom soldiers fought in order to preserve the interests of the fatherland. The secretary of defense was quite adamant about these ideas and occasionally even expressed them in public. In addition to asking the victims to learn to "forgive and pursue reconciliation,"[46] he adhered to his institutions' long-standing denial of the existence of special operation groups and clandestine detention centers during the 1970s.[47] Veteran organizations were also active in defense of their colleagues, especially in the wake of arrest warrants and indictments. When Nazar Haro was put under investigation, the Fraternity of Former Policemen expressed its "unconditional support" for the former head of the DFS and accused Carrillo Prieto of using the FEMOSPP for a personal vendetta.[48] Finally, the connections between the security forces and the defendants were also used to stall the proceedings. For example, there is some indication that police officers deliberately delayed the enforcement

[43] *El Universal*, 13 July 2004, my translation.

[44] *El Universal*, 27 July 2004.

[45] Ignacio Carrillo Prieto, interview, Mexico City, 21 July 2010.

[46] *La Jornada*, 1 July 2004, my translation.

[47] *El Universal*, 25 February 2004.

[48] *El Universal*, 7 February 2003, my translation. According to the Fraternity of Former Policemen, Carrillo Prieto had a cousin who had been a member of guerrilla organizations.

of arrest warrants, or overlooked leads about the whereabouts of fugitives. On one occasion, the special prosecutor announced that the person in charge of executing the arrest warrant against Luis de la Barreda was his attorney's relative, thus explaining why he had been able to escape from the authorities for almost three years.[49] More disturbing, however, was the assassination of a witness in Guerrero in November 2003, which some attributed to the military.[50]

These attacks against the FEMOSPP's legitimacy contrast with the much more cordial relationship between Carrillo Prieto and the president. After all, it was Fox who although at first hesitant, ended up proposing the creation of this office. From a political point of view, the appointment of a special prosecutor entailed high risks, in part because it could expose the protagonists of the old regime to criminal charges. The fact that the special prosecutor was finally appointed, thus offering victims an unprecedented opportunity to realize their goals of truth and justice, indicates some willingness on the side of the president to hold the autocrats accountable. Moreover, as we saw earlier, the Attorney General's Office accepted many of Carrillo Prieto's funding requests, giving the special prosecutor adequate resources to conduct his duties.[51] There is also evidence suggesting that both the president and the secretary of interior were in agreement with some of his boldest legal moves. For example, the press reported that Carrillo Prieto met with Vicente Fox and Santiago Creel immediately before filing charges against Echeverría for the 1971 massacre and they approved his plans. They probably did so knowing that an indictment had the potential to rattle the PRI establishment, as became clear later on.[52] Similarly, Fox welcomed the arrest of Nazar Haro in February 2004. On that occasion, he praised the FEMOSPP for doing "a good job" and was confident that this time there was "no possibility that this case can sidestep justice."[53] The president's expressions of support were very much in line with public opinion, which valued the effort undertaken by Carrillo Prieto. According to a poll commissioned by *El Universal*, 57 percent of respondents thought that finding the truth about Tlatelolco was important in order to identify the perpetrators or put an

[49] *El Universal*, 28 April 2005.

[50] *El Universal*, 30 November 2003.

[51] Carrillo Prieto acknowledged that his requests were usually approved by the attorney general, but insisted that these funds were not sufficient. Interview, Mexico City, 21 July 2010.

[52] *La Jornada*, 23 July 2004.

[53] *El Universal*, 21 February 2004, my translation.

end to impunity, and 44 percent supported the investigation regardless of its political consequences.[54]

The president's political support notwithstanding, some of his public statements added noise to the debate surrounding the FEMOSPP and raised doubts about its true potential. In particular, Fox seemed to agree with influential voices within the country's legal establishment who were skeptical about the possibility of indicting former military officers and politicians for crimes perpetrated in the distant past. When asked by the press in late 2001 and early 2002 about their views on the path to transitional justice proposed by the president, Diego Valadés, director of the Institute of Legal Research at the National Autonomous University of Mexico, the main hub of legal academics in the country, and Héctor Fix-Zamudio, one its most prestigious professors, both argued that statutes of limitations had expired.[55] The head of the National Human Rights Commission and some high-ranking officials in the Attorney General's Office expressed similar concerns.[56] The president echoed these views when he declared, "It is very likely that a good portion of those responsible will not end up in jail because the legal time frame to prosecute these crimes has passed."[57] Later on, he even proposed to reopen the debate about the truth commission if judges dismissed the cases on these grounds.[58]

The signals sent by the political environment surrounding the transitional justice process were therefore quite mixed. On the one hand, unlike in Argentina in the 1990s or Peru in the late 2000s, the victims and the prosecutor did not face a president whose agenda was unequivocally opposed to transitional justice. On the other, and as expected, the military and the PRI strongly opposed the process and tried to delegitimize it. This is no different from what we saw in the other case studies, when at different stages soldiers and politicians also sought to put an end to the investigations and trials often with similar rhetoric and tactics. When looking at Mexico from this comparative angle, we are thus able to see that the political blockages on the road to truth and justice, often cited as the primary reason for the failure of criminal prosecutions, were shared by successful

[54] Survey results were made available to the author by a journalist at *El Universal*. Another poll published in the daily *Reforma* indicated that 67 percent of respondents thought that it was necessary to investigate and punish "any illegal act committed by public officials, including former presidents." *Reforma*, 11 July 2002, my translation.

[55] *El Universal*, 30 November 2001; *Proceso*, 20 January 2002.

[56] *La Jornada*, 26 May 2004.

[57] *El Universal*, 11 November 2002, my translation.

[58] *El Universal*, 2 September 2003.

cases. Put another way, it is possible to imagine a more positive outcome given these conditions.

This, however, would have required the consolidation of an alternative discourse about the legal possibilities and imperatives to hold past criminals accountable. As we have seen, although the president backed the prosecutor and gave him the resources to act, he concurred with other voices in the debate, which doubted the availability of solid legal grounds to proceed with the investigations. Victims and their lawyers were unable to counter this climate of legal pessimism by putting forth a vision that expanded the space for judicial action and legitimized innovative patterns of behavior in the legal field. As I showed in previous chapters, when there is a disjuncture between what judges deem professionally appropriate and what powerful actors in the system want them to do, judicial actors can effectively challenge politicians and make very risky moves. By contrast, Mexican judges followed their established legal preferences, not only because this was safe given the aforementioned hostility, but also, as we shall see later on, because it was what they knew how to do or thought was the correct thing to do as professionals of the law.

Yet, we should not overstate the similarities of hostile contexts across countries. In Peru, the motivation and resources that judicial actors could marshal to withstand political pressures were for the most part manufactured during a prior period of great political tolerance for transitional justice. With regard to Argentina, the political environment in the 1990s certainly did not deter litigants from deploying pedagogical interventions.[59] But in contrast to Mexico, NGOs could draw upon past judicial victories (most notably the 1985 trial) as a testament of the judiciary's capacity to defy the limits of political possibility, and as an incentive to try to replicate those acts of courage. In this sense, both the political environment and history matter to explain the inability of Mexican NGOs to act strategically following the model outlined in Chapter 2.

Without denying the importance of these factors, which certainly conditioned the deployment of pedagogical interventions (and which made replacement strategies impossible), I will show the crucial explanatory role played by litigants' lack of understanding of the problem of legal preferences. The interactions between NGOs and judicial actors reveal this much. Unlike their counterparts in Argentina and Peru, Mexican

[59] Peruvian litigants also deployed pedagogical interventions when the political climate shifted against them. As we saw in Chapter 4, however, they stopped when the National Criminal Court banned these initiatives.

NGOs did not take advantage of these interactions to remove ideational blockages inside the judicial branch and alter deeply ingrained ritualistic patterns of decision making. This is in part because they themselves did not have professional legal teams capable of crafting such strategies. Instead of forcing the circulation of new ideas and new voices within the judicial establishment, their interactions with judges and prosecutors heightened the walls of the labyrinth, making it ever more complicated to find a way out. Consequently, the prosecutor's lack of knowledge of international human rights law and its use in domestic settings led him to make a series of mistakes. In addition, the absence of a resocialization of judges meant that even if the prosecutors had known how to implement a more adequate strategy, it is likely that the judiciary would have remained unresponsive. Judges were also foreign to this legal discourse, making them fundamentally incapable of conceiving alternative courses of action to those dictated by long-standing judicial routines. This suggests that even if they had operated in more favorable political conditions, litigants still would not have realized their goals because they never took seriously the need to engineer a shift in legal visions that widened the terms of the legal debate.

The Absence of Pedagogical Interventions and Support for the Prosecutor

Long-standing divisions within the human rights movement, deficits in legal professionalization, and diverging agendas shaped the reactions of NGOs to the creation of the FEMOSPP, their engagement with it, and ultimately their failure to launch efforts to shape judicial outcomes in their favor. In this section, I discuss the strategies of two sets of civil society actors, victim organizations and more professionalized NGOs founded in the 1990s, vis-à-vis the window of opportunity opened by President Fox when he appointed a special prosecutor. I do so by looking at the microdynamics of the relationship they established with the prosecutor and their inability to steer Carrillo Prieto's legal strategy in productive directions.

As argued in Chapter 2, effective judicial behavior in cases of state repression requires the close involvement of litigants with judges and prosecutors. Organized litigation groups are in an unparalleled position to provide judicial actors with social backing, supervision, and the technical resources they need in order to conduct their duties in highly idiosyncratic cases. The challenge faced by the FEMOSPP was unprecedented, and it was in desperate need of this type of support. According to Human Rights Watch's assessment of the capabilities of the FEMOSPP in 2003:

> Where we did find consensus, however, was in the belief that prosecutors will need to navigate uncharted legal terrain and develop novel arguments that are acceptable to Mexican courts – and that it will be difficult for the lawyers in the Special Prosecutor's Office to do so without the assistance of more experienced and influential jurists. In other words, in the prosecutions as in the investigations, it will be difficult for the Special Prosecutor's Office to go it alone. (Human Rights Watch 2003: 3)

There are two reasons why this was an accurate diagnosis. First and foremost, Mexican prosecutors have a notoriously poor record of successfully discharging cases into the judicial system. For example, in cases of complex criminality such as torture, human trafficking, or kidnappings, Mexican prosecutors have a dismal record. The data shown in Table 5.1 indicate that between 2005 and 2010 the number of such cases investigated by the authorities was extremely low. Moreover, during this period the percentage of investigations followed by indictments was also low: 5.46 percent in abuse of authority cases, 11.11 percent in torture cases, 14.29 percent in human trafficking cases, and 8.04 percent in kidnapping cases. When looking at the percentage of indictments in homicide cases investigated between 2006 and 2009 (Table 5.2), the performance is also alarmingly poor across all Mexican states. In other words, if left to its own devices the FEMOSPP was very unlikely to become a beacon of effectiveness, especially because its staff was recruited from the pool of existing prosecutors.

Second, Mexican prosecutors' failure to prosecute ordinary criminals successfully indicated that they would probably find it even more difficult to succeed in the investigation of cases of state repression perpetrated in the distant past. This was especially true given that the focus of the investigations was not on the direct perpetrators, but rather on those in command of the repressive apparatus. Building a case against indirect perpetrators normally requires the careful reconstruction of the chain of command, a heavy reliance on witness testimony, the ability to see connections between cases, the use of historical information to show systematic patterns of repression associated with military operations ordered from above, and skills to articulate complex theories of criminal liability convincingly. The FEMOSPP staff was never trained to adapt their investigative routines to this new type of case. In an interview, Carrillo Prieto explained how these shortcomings were reflected in the everyday behavior of his staff:

> They lacked knowledge of international and national law, in particular in the area of crimes against humanity. And they not only lacked substantive

Table 5.1. *Indictments in Cases of Abuse of Authority, Torture, Human Trafficking, and Unlawful Deprivation of Liberty (2005–2010)*

Crime	Abuse of Authority		Torture		Human Trafficking		Unlawful Deprivation of Liberty	
Year	Number of Cases Investigated	% Indicted	Number of Cases Investigated	% Indicted	Number of Cases Investigated	% Indicted	Number of Cases Investigated	% Indicted
2005	79	11.39%	1	0	0	0	34	17.65%
2006	460	5.86%	24	0	0	0	105	8.57%
2007	514	3.31%	7	0	0	0	142	4.93%
2008	738	4.07%	15	0	0	0	242	4.55%
2009	784	4.34%	12	0	4	0	350	5.71%
2010	449	3.79%	9	11.11%	7	14.29%	253	6.81%

Source: Attorney General's Office. I obtained this information via a public information request. I am thankful to Ximena Medellín for her help drafting the request.

Table 5.2. *Indictments in Homicide Cases by State (2006–2009)*

Year	2006		2007		2008		2009	
State	No. of Cases Investigated	No. of Indictments	No. of Cases Investigated	No. of Indictments	No. of Cases Investigated	No. of Indictments	No. of Cases Investigated	Number of Indictments
Aguascalientes	0	0	0	0	0	0	2	0
Baja California	15	3	11	3	19	3	17	3
Baja California Sur	3	1	5	1	3	3	0	1
Campeche	1	1	1	0	1	0	1	0
Chiapas	9	3	3	2	5	1	6	1
Chihuahua	7	1	11	1	14	3	51	6
Coahuila	4	0	5	1	11	3	17	6
Colima	0	0	1	0	1	0	4	2
Federal District	110	7	39	4	64	10	91	11
Durango	1	1	3	1	16	1	12	0
Guanajuato	3	2	3	0	3	0	3	0
Guerrero	4	0	7	1	8	3	10	1
Hidalgo	8	3	0	3	3	0	5	1
Jalisco	24	2	23	0	7	6	30	8
Mexico	20	3	17	2	18	1	28	4
Michoacan	8	1	10	2	14	2	17	7
Morelos	4	2	4	0	4	0	3	1

(*continued*)

Table 5.2 (*cont.*)

Year	2006		2007		2008		2009	
State	No. of Cases Investigated	No. of Indictments	No. of Cases Investigated	No. of Indictments	No. of Cases Investigated	No. of Indictments	No. of Cases Investigated	Number of Indictments
Nayarit	0	0	2	0	2	0	8	0
Nuevo Leon	6	0	6	0	8	2	3	0
Oaxaca	4	1	15	5	9	2	5	2
Puebla	10	3	7	0	5	0	11	0
Queretaro	2	0	1	1	2	0	2	0
Quintana Roo	2	0	3	1	5	1	2	0
San Luis Potosi	11	1	6	2	4	1	2	2
Sinaloa	5	0	19	1	22	3	10	6
Sonora	6	1	9	3	15	4	11	4
Tabasco	8	1	8	2	18	5	9	5
Tamaulipas	11	3	15	2	2	1	3	1
Tlaxcala	0	0	3	2	1	1	1	0
Veracruz	6	4	10	3	16	3	12	4
Yucatan	3	0	3	1	7	3	3	1
Zacatecas	1	0	3	0	1	0	4	0

Source: Attorney General's Office. I obtained this information via a public information request. I am thankful to Ximena Medellín for her help drafting the request.

> knowledge but also knowledge of criminal procedure.... These were extremely routine-minded prosecutors that had to be rattled. One had to constantly oversee what they were doing. For example, among those investigating the forced disappearances there was one who seemed to be in charge of checking the clock to see when statutes of limitations had to be applied. This is what they normally do in most cases, they wait for statutes of limitations to expire in order to get rid of them and wash their hands.... I did not have properly trained aides who could speed up the proceedings, with rigor and depth.[60]

One of the prosecutors in charge of investigating the forced disappearances made a similar point:

> There was never an effort to train us on how to investigate these crimes. This was indispensable. Everything was very technical. No one knew a thing about forensic anthropology or about military chains of command in order to know what to ask the experts, where to do the excavations when we searched for mass graves, or what documents we should request from the army.[61]

The testimonies of two human rights lawyers who witnessed the activities of the FEMOSPP also support the idea that prosecutors were ill equipped for the task at hand, especially when it came to organizing their work in an effective manner:

> During the first few years the investigations were focused on establishing if there had been disappearances or not. We think this was a waste of time, because in most cases the National Human Rights Commission had already established that.[62]

> They were put in charge of investigating highly complex crimes.... In Mexico, public prosecutors conceive of the investigative stages as a period during which others must bring the evidence to them. They do not actively seek it, which is highly problematic.... Although there were many pieces of evidence, there was no clear strategy about how to prioritize each one. They faced a sea of information, and in the absence of any criteria, it was very easy to get lost or end up using irrelevant evidence.[63]

Finally, one of the prosecutors, who had more than thirty years of experience investigating criminal cases, provided a personal example of how he approached the evidence-gathering process, and how he assessed the documents he was able to obtain:

> Many talked about the existence of the Batallón Olimpia, supposedly responsible for the Tlatelolco massacre. I requested information about this

[60] Interview, Mexico City, 21 July 2010.
[61] Interview, Mexico City, 28 July 2010.
[62] Interview, Mexico City, 28 August 2010.
[63] Interview, Mexico City, 9 August 2010.

> group and a list of its members. The army replied: "We never had a batallion with that name." They gave me the names of a bunch of people deployed as security during the Olympic Games, but nothing that suggested the existence of the Batallón Olimpia [NB: The massacre occurred the same year Mexico City hosted the Olympics]. And I think that is probably true.[64]

It is important to note the excessive formalism that guided his actions, taking at face value the army's denial of the existence of official documents ordering the creation of a clandestine paramilitary group. Human rights cases require a much less passive attitude, a special drive to look for information that will obviously not be voluntarily surrendered by the institutions under investigation. Knowledge of how to do this, what to look for and with what eyes, as well as the willingness to go that extra mile, must be conveyed by external forces capable of disrupting the routines that make judicial bureaucracies tick. But as this example suggests, in the Mexican case, these routines remained firmly in place.

The subsidiary role given to historians within the FEMOSPP also reflected a problematic conceptualization of the crimes in question and a poorly designed investigative strategy. Carrillo Prieto understood from the start that investigating cases of state repression perpetrated in the distant past required dealing with large quantities of complex historical material. To this end, he appointed a team of historians to organize the archives and produce a report on the crimes of the dirty war. The problem, however, was that he did not fully integrate the work of the prosecutors with that of the historians, leading to an unproductive and conflictive relationship that undermined the quality of the indictments. In a report published as early as 2004, Human Rights Watch already warned about the dangers of marginalizing the historians:

> The creation of the PIA [Program of Information and Analysis] held great promise, but it has not been allowed to fulfill its potential. As such, the opportunity has been missed to carry out a truly multidisciplinary investigation with analysis at its center. Instead, investigations are based on traditional lines of investigating the immediate facts around the results of the crime through the search for eye-witnesses and forensic evidence. An over reliance on such investigative techniques is fundamentally unsuited to establishing the criminal responsibility of those involved in planning and directing system crimes, such as patterns of forced disappearances and killings. The principal concern ... is that the SPO [Special Prosecutor's Office] has not fully grasped the true nature of system crime investigation. This seems to be confirmed by the fact that two of the field investigation

[64] Interview, Mexico City, 11 August 2010.

> units have increased staff by 300 and 600 percent, while the PIA, with an already insufficient staff, has effectively been cut in half since January 2004. The investigations of disappearances, especially in the state of Guerrero, should be based on the study of patterns of violations, and not on isolated incidents. If cases are presented on the basis of multiple incidents, the chances of securing a conviction will be generally increased.... It appears that there is an institutional failure in understanding the importance of this element of the investigation.... To date, the PIA has not been in a position to develop its own hypotheses about the context, structures, patterns, and practices of the relevant institutions because it spends most of its time responding to requests for information. Rather than playing a central role in carrying out detailed research and analysis, the PIA has been little more than an auxiliary arm of the investigative effort. (Seils 2004: I-26)

As a result of these organizational deficiencies, prosecutors were not able to take full advantage of historians' macroperspective on the dynamics of state repression. Instead of accumulating several cases to persuade courts of the systematic nature of the forced disappearances, they continued to see them as isolated events and filed charges accordingly. This perspective was entirely compatible with the choice of a purely domestic legal strategy. After all, prosecutors did not feel the need to prove that these violations were part of a broader repressive plan, and that they ought to be characterized as crimes against humanity. In fact, the FEMOSPP's legal team vehemently objected to this line of argument. In an interview published in April 2006 in *La Jornada*, the last director of the historical team recalled the internal fight following the circulation of a draft of the report on the crimes of the dirty war commissioned by Carrillo Prieto:

> At some point they asked me for a draft... so that other departments could review it. The prosecutors sent very reasonable comments aimed at improving its content. However, the head of the legal department wanted us to remove the entire chapter on war crimes, and requested changes in the terminology used throughout the document. Instead of "forced disappearances," they wanted "unlawful deprivation of liberty." ... They removed all the terms that they could not find in the criminal code.... The list of unreasonable changes was huge, and we felt that they began to treat us as the enemy.[65]

In line with the legal department's criteria, Carrillo Prieto heavily edited the report so that its language remained consistent with the juridical strategy followed in the indictments. Before it was officially released, however,

[65] *La Jornada*, 30 April 2006. This was also confirmed during a personal interview with José Sotelo, director of the Historical Investigations Team. Interview, Mexico City, 27 September 2010.

the original document was leaked to the press, embarrassing the special prosecutor, who dissipated precious political capital explaining that this was a preliminary version of the report. This decisively undermined the legitimacy of the truth-telling effort, to the point that the official version was never published. Because of this incident, Carrillo Prieto referred to the historians as the "enemy within."[66]

In sum, the marginalization of historians under Carrillo Prieto's leadership, which resulted from a narrow understanding of the requirements of complex human rights investigations, led to these tensions and compromised the effectiveness of the prosecutorial effort.

It was against this backdrop that human rights organizations interacted with the prosecutors. But despite these obvious shortcomings, activists never even considered putting forward a coordinated and comprehensive pedagogical strategy to support Carrillo Prieto and his staff. Some organizations chose to disengage and fiercely denounced the initiative as a farce, thus discrediting it and failing to exploit its potential. Others overcame their initial skepticism and approached the prosecutor and his collaborators, but their lack of adequate technical skills pushed the prosecutor's strategy in the wrong direction. Finally, those who had developed expertise in human rights law and strategic litigation during the 1990s for the most part remained on the sidelines, and only approached Carrillo Prieto when it was too late to exert any positive influence.

Victim Organizations

As discussed previously, after the first signs of regime liberalization in the late 1970s many human rights activists joined the ranks of left-wing parties. Rosario Ibarra, for example, was the presidential candidate of the PRT in 1982 and 1988 and served in both houses of congress as a representative of the Partido de la Revolución Democrática (PRD). The PRD also had strong ties to the Comité 68, as several members of the 1960s student movement later became prominent figures within the party. These strong political connections naturally shaped the focus of the Mexican human rights movement. Unlike victim organizations in Argentina or Peru, which never had such direct links to political parties, and to the extent that they did they harbored individuals with diverse partisan attachments, Mexican victim NGOs centered their efforts on publicly denouncing the crimes, scoring political points, and organizing protest activities, and

[66] Interview, Mexico City, 21 July 2010.

never invested in creating professionalized litigation teams. As a result, when the Comité 68 filed its famous genocide suit in 1998, or when AFADEM attempted to litigate the disappearance of Rosendo Radilla in the 1990s, they outsourced legal representation to nonspecialist lawyers. In other words, in Mexico there was no equivalent to Argentina's CELS or Peru's IDL.

When the government announced the appointment of a special prosecutor, the organization led by Rosario Ibarra and the Comité 68 immediately expressed their skepticism.[67] From the point of view afforded by their partisan lens, the prospects of a human rights agenda in the hands of a right-wing administration were not very encouraging, and at the end of the day, they preferred not to give the government a victory in this area. Ibarra's criticisms were particularly tough and constant throughout the process. As early as January 2002, for example, she declared that the FEMOSPP was "destined to fail."[68] She pointed out that the appointment of a special prosecutor reflected the president's "hypocrisy." In her opinion, there was no real political will to realize the goals of truth and justice. Unlike her counterparts elsewhere in Latin America, she completely dismissed the potential of court proceedings to encapsulate the issue of human rights violations within an autonomous legal domain. This intransigent position led to a total lack of engagement with the FEMOSPP, consistent with her organizations' historic disregard for litigation as a viable institutional strategy.

Although it initially shared Ibarra's position, the Comité 68 eventually realized the potential of the initiative and forged a close relationship with the prosecutor. In fact, ultimately these activists forcefully defended the idea of launching criminal investigations and opposed the creation of a toothless truth commission. Unfortunately, however, they saw litigation as another way to make political noise and publicize their demands and did not adequately vet the arguments they presented in court. Most notably, the choice of "genocide" as the main charge brought against the alleged perpetrators reflected not only the organization's discourse about the nature of 1968 massacre, but also its desire to make headlines. Accusing a former president of genocide was surely a way to draw public attention, more so than presenting charges that relied on less controversial criminal definitions. But the Comité 68 never dedicated serious efforts to assembling a team to analyze the legal viability of this strategy carefully. The

[67] *El Universal*, 28 November 2001.

[68] *El Universal*, 19 January 2002.

crime of genocide as understood both domestically and internationally is extremely restrictive, leaving crimes against political groups such as Tlatelolco outside its scope, and in addition, it is very hard to prove. These two features made it extremely unlikely that a domestic court would support their argument, and hand down a condemnatory ruling.

Raúl Álvarez Garín, the leader of the Comité 68, described in an interview how they prepared their litigation efforts during the 1990s. His testimony highlights the degree of amateurism in the organization's dealings with the legal aspects of the challenge:

> Our legal team was very informal.... We did not formally train ourselves in international human rights law or look for specialized lawyers. We began to read about these topics and talk about them in public. We had to learn from scratch as we went along.[69]

When I asked him whether they had considered alternatives to the genocide charges, he categorically replied, "It was a genocide!" This evidenced the organization's unwillingness to prioritize a viable legal strategy over one that semantically captured their political discourse about the massacre. He added that this was not the first time he was asked this question, and explained: "In order to support the idea we had to argue against a bunch of pseudoexperts who said it was not [a genocide]."[70] In the late 1990s, a lawyer with some background in international human rights law approached the organization and began helping them design the legal strategy, but his role was not to assess their legal position and make recommendations. Instead, he focused on translating their preexisting conceptualization of the 1968 massacre as genocide into a document they could present in court. The relationship worked precisely because the lawyer did not question their approach:

> I had always followed the activities of the movement, their civic struggle against impunity,... Around 1998 I approached them to offer my services as a lawyer.... Definitely, they already had a strategy. What they needed was to frame it using the correct terminology.[71]

When the Comité 68 decided to court Carrillo Prieto, its members pushed for him to replicate the 1998 legal strategy. As other organizations remained distant or openly critical of his work, the prosecutor welcomed the support offered by the former student activists. According to a human

[69] Interview, Mexico City, 21 July 2010.
[70] Ibid.
[71] Comité 68 lawyer, interview, Mexico City, 10 August 2010.

rights lawyer involved in the process, "The prosecutor wanted to legitimize himself."[72] In fact, during an interview, the prosecutor admitted that he was in dire need of social support, and after a series of meetings with the leaders of the movement he decided to endorse the genocide argument:

> When I was appointed I called Rosario Ibarra. She told me she did not want to meet with me because her organization had no trust in the initiative. I insisted several times but the answer was always "no." I needed this support, from a very pragmatic point of view, I needed it.... The relationship with the Comité 68 was very different. They tested me and when they understood that I was ready, that this was no joke, that I did not respond to any other interests, that the prosecutor was truly independent, they said "yes." And that is why we achieved what we achieved: Echeverria spent two years under house arrest.[73]

Carrillo Prieto also mentioned that human rights lawyers advised him against pursuing the genocide argument. A lawyer who at the time worked for the Comisión Mexicana, another human rights NGO (see later discussion), stated in an interview that she

> discussed this strategy with the lawyers of the Comité 68, and I told them that using the idea of genocide was counterproductive. We had a fight! Most lawyers in Mexico laughed at this strategy. But for them it was a victory that the prosecutor decided to go along with it.[74]

The prosecutor dismissed these warnings. He was in need of a social umbrella, and having little technical expertise on the subject, he decided to go along with arguments that had the greatest potential to strengthen his feeble ties with important allies in civil society.

What is indeed puzzling is that Carrillo Prieto did not modify the strategy once it was clear it was destined to fail. According to the Comité 68's lawyer, this would have implied a political defeat, which neither his organization nor the prosecutor were willing to accept:

> It would have implied a catastrophic defeat. Why? Because the FEMOSPP went for the most serious criminal category, for the harshest characterization of a criminal act available in our criminal system, and in international criminal law. How could we justify in the media having filed an indictment in terms of one of the most abhorrent crimes, the crime of genocide, and on

72 Interview, Mexico City, 2 September 2010.

73 Interview, Mexico City, 21 July 2010.

74 Interview, Mexico City, 28 August 2010. Other human rights lawyers I interviewed for this study also disagreed with the Comité 68's strategy.

> the other hand saying "I am sorry, I made a mistake, it's really an aggravated homicide"?[75]

This explanation was also mentioned in an interview with a Supreme Court judge who had the opportunity to talk to Carrillo Prieto after the court handed down its 2005 ruling on the Corpus Christi case. The prosecutor was under pressure from his allies to stick to the genocide charges:

> In the court there was a general consensus that there was a crime involved. The problem is that there wasn't a consensus about whether or not it was genocide. The prosecutor aimed too high. In one of the passages of the ruling the majority suggested that he could file homicide charges, given that they had one more year before the statutes of limitations ran out. A massacre is not necessarily a genocide.... [The prosecutor] would not do it, ... he was under pressure from human rights activists.[76]

Regarding the possibility of using a different criminal definition as suggested by the Supreme Court, the evidence indicates that in addition to these civil society pressures, the FEMOSPP did not have the necessary expertise to change course effectively. When I asked one of the prosecutors about his thoughts on this alternative approach, he deemed it plausible, but his answer also made it clear that formalistic legal preferences prevalent inside the FEMOSPP would have hampered the development of an adequate argument in support of the new strategy:

> We could have used "homicide." Statutes of limitations expire after 30 years for homicides. We would have had to make the appropriate calculations to see if statutes of limitations were still running. These were clearly not crimes exempted from statutory limitations.[77]

In other words, this prosecutor's cognitive schemes left no room for seeing beyond the problem of statutes of limitations. Neither he nor his colleagues entertained the idea of integrating the homicide charges, defined according to domestic law, with international criminal definitions that make it possible to disregard statutes of limitations. As we saw in previous chapters, judicial actors in other countries routinely followed this argumentative move. Indeed, the lack of legal imagination among Mexican judicial actors was pervasive.

By stubbornly prioritizing the movement's definition of the events over a more viable or appropriate legal one, the Comité 68 seriously undermined its own case. Somewhat ironically, if Rosario Ibarra delegitimized the

[75] Interview, Mexico City, 10 August 2010.
[76] Supreme Court judge, interview, Mexico City, 15 July 2010.
[77] Interview, Mexico City, 2 September 2010.

Special Prosecutor's Office by remaining on the sidelines, the Comité 68 jeopardized its effectiveness by closely engaging with it without adequate technical capabilities. In Argentina, for example, many victim organizations also believe that what happened in the 1970s constituted genocide, but at crucial stages of the judicialization process, their extremely seasoned lawyers vetted this political definition of the events, and did not file charges using this criminal category. The following quote from an interview with an Argentine human rights lawyer illustrates this tension between different approaches to litigation in cases of state repression, and suggests how the professionalization of legal teams, the missing element in the Comité 68's strategy, can make a difference:

> Our approach is technical, not political.... We should not confuse our work with political activism. Many organizations have militants, but that does not mean that they are good legal professionals.... The question of genocide is a hot topic. One of my clients wanted to file genocide charges, and we said no. We do use the notion of genocide in the briefs, but as a sociological construct, not as a legal one.... In another of our cases, the prosecutor filed genocide charges, but luckily our charges included other criminal categories, so the judges could dismiss the idea of genocide but use our arguments to still hand down a condemnatory ruling.

She then moved on to explain that although human rights trials require a high degree of legal innovation and experimentation, this must be done carefully and professionally. The legal norms invoked by litigants, whether domestic or international, must resonate with the facts of the case:

> It is absolutely true that at some point someone had to come up with, for example, the strange idea that these crimes are not subject to statutory limitations because of the precepts of international customary law. This sounded like a crazy idea at first. If you don't shake things up nothing ever happens. When you introduce new legal arguments you force the court to say something about it, and that stirs the discussion, it opens up the legal debate. I understand this, but one has to do this in a strategic way, following a legal logic, not a political one.[78]

It is important to end this discussion about the strategies followed by victim organizations by noting that the differences of opinion around whether to engage with the FEMOSPP and how generated tensions within the movement that made it more difficult for activists to coordinate their strategies with political allies on the Left. This would have allowed them to create a more favorable climate for the trials. If their legal strategies were in

[78] Interview, human rights lawyer, Buenos Aires, 26 November 2010.

some cases nonexistent and in others highly misguided, their nonjudicial ones suffered from a total lack of coordination. For example, Mexico City's major, a central figure in the PRD who counted Rosario Ibarra among his advisers, called for the closing of the Special Prosecutor's Office. In October 2003, he argued that putting an end to Carrillo Prieto's efforts would end false hopes with regard to the legal viability of the initiative.[79] PRD officials with strong links to the Comité 68 also put forward defeatist arguments. In a meeting with President Fox, former senator Martínez Della Rocca proposed a reform of Article 14 of the constitution in order to introduce exceptions to the legality principle.[80] Noting that this amounted to an outright capitulation, Álvarez Garín was quick to oppose his colleague's proposal: "It's like accepting that it will be impossible to punish the perpetrators."[81]

In addition to reinforcing dominant, orthodox views about the legal limits imposed by Mexican legislation on human rights investigations, the behavior of the Left in congress overlooked the negative consequences of its support for certain bills. This further illustrates the absence of a coordinated strategy of human rights activists' legal strategies and those of their political allies. For example, in 2003 a congressman from the Worker's Party introduced a bill to allow individuals older than seventy years old to remain at home while serving prison sentences. Rosario Ibarra, who belonged to the same party as the sponsor, tried in vain to introduce an amendment in the senate so that the reform did not apply to cases of genocide and forced disappearances. After the law was passed in 2004, judges across the country systematically sentenced defendants in human rights cases to house arrest. Another shocking example of this lack of coordination was the unanimous support offered by the Left to a bill sponsored by a PRI congressman, which proposed the elimination of the crime of "due process violations" from the criminal code. As we saw before, federal judges invoked this new legislation when in 2006 they shut down the forced disappearance cases filed by the FEMOSPP. No one on the Left foresaw the deadly effects that this change would have on human rights trials.

Second-Generation Human Rights NGOs

The 1990s saw the strengthening of Mexican civil society with the creation of numerous NGOs and think tanks dedicated to promoting and defending

[79] *El Universal*, 3 October 2003.
[80] *El Universal*, 23 May 2003.
[81] *El Universal*, 1 June 2003.

human rights. These organizations were nonpartisan and staffed with professional academics, individuals with long careers in domestic and international civil society, and lawyers. They were founded primarily to address present-day problems, and not to seek justice for dirty war era crimes. In fact, during the first half of the 1990s, these organizations allocated very few resources to public interest litigation. As a result, second-generation NGOs were initially not well suited to compensate for the historic deficits of victim organizations. In an interview, one of the founders of two of the most visible NGOs of the period, the Academia Nacional de Derechos Humanos and the Comisión Mexicana de Defensa y Promoción de los Derechos Humanos, recounted the story behind their creation. The passage is worth quoting at length:

> When we founded the Academia Nacional de Derechos Humanos, the idea was to defend human rights, but not to litigate. Causes, but no cases. This in part responded to the logic of the PRI regime. In that regime you did not litigate; you denounced, you negotiated, you talked. But eventually we realized that we had to find a way to take care of the cases that were brought to our attention. That is why we opened a legal aid office.... After Salinas's victory in 1988, the person appointed by the president as the mayor of Mexico City gave a public sector job to Nazar Haro. One of the lawyers at the Academia filed a suit against him for the crimes of the dirty war. This caused a lot of controversy, because for many members of the board of directors that was against our charter. Due to this episode I left the Academia and founded the Comisión Mexicana in 1990.... In the Comisión it took us many years to put together a legal team because there were no good lawyers available, especially lawyers that understood international human rights law.... I remember that at some point we received several torture cases in which the army was involved, and our lawyer told me: "There is nothing we can do." I fired her immediately! It took a long time to train lawyers that also had the courage to take on this kind of case. We had to nurture a new generation of lawyers. Human Rights Watch was very helpful. We also sent a young lawyer to Washington to receive training from CEJIL. It was a very intense process.[82]

This excerpt is very interesting because it points to two problems that put the Mexican human rights movement at a clear disadvantage with respect to its counterparts in Argentina and Peru. First, as in the case of victim organizations, for many of the new, nonpartisan civil society actors, the development of strong litigation teams was not an early priority, especially when it came to dealing with issues of transitional justice. Second, and

[82] Interview, Mexico City, 19 July 2010.

most importantly, those who were willing to take cases to court found it excruciatingly difficult to develop the necessary expertise. This activist's recollections suggest that the discourse and technical tools associated with international law were foreign not only to judicial actors, but also to those in a position to expand the repertoire of ideas debated in court via the use of strategic litigation. Some organizations, most notably the Comisión Mexicana and the Centro Prodh, founded by the Jesuits in the late 1980s, used their links with international NGOs such as Human Rights Watch and the Center for Justice and International Law, and their gradual involvement with the Inter-American Commission of Human Rights, to bridge this gap. But they were the exception, not the rule. This is how a former director of the Centro Prodh described this process:

> We began to realize that it was not enough to just denounce human rights violations. Now we had to combine this with legal work, taking on cases and actively participating in the investigation of certain crimes. This was part of a learning process. At first we gained expertise basically by experimenting with cases at the local level, but when we began to work at the international level with the Inter-American Commission, we started to have lots of interactions with Peruvian and Colombian litigants from whom we learnt a lot. This international venue made possible informal encounters and meetings during the Commission's periodic hearings.... We had to gradually learn what was being debated at the international level. We had two main convictions. First that the structure of the Mexican judicial system was extremely narrow, so that the potential for achieving things domestically was limited. And second, we had to train our staff. We established contacts with CEJIL, we offered seminars, workshops.[83]

In addition to the initial lack of interest in dirty war era cases and the difficulties in developing the necessary technical capabilities to conduct effective strategic litigation, there were other factors further down the line that pulled old and new NGOs apart. As some of the organizations created during the 1990s gained expertise in public interest litigation and in international human rights law, they became more open to accepting dirty war era cases. Their focus was still on contemporary rights violations by security forces, but some of the 1970s disappearance cases offered interesting avenues to test arguments against the use of military jurisdiction and other abusive practices.[84] This willingness notwithstanding, they found it very hard to build a cooperative relationship with victim organizations. These older NGOs did not share the same appreciation for the potential of

[83] Interview, Mexico City, 9 August 2010.
[84] Human rights lawyer, interview, Mexico City, 15 July 2010.

international human rights law and the Inter-American system of human rights. For traditional victim organizations such as the one led by Rosario Ibarra, this approach was too neoliberal, too right-wing. Moreover, some of the victims already had their own lawyers. As we saw, these were not human rights specialists. This exacerbated the trust issues between old and new NGOs.

One of the civil society veterans quoted earlier recalls the difficulties in making the first contacts with victim organizations:

> The victims already had their lawyers.... They had legal strategies that were aligned with their political strategies. They saw us with a lot of mistrust, as right-wing reformists.... It was only towards the end of the 1990s that AFADEM approached the Comisión Mexicana, and it was by accident. We sent a lawyer to a workshop in Geneva, where she met someone from Colombia's FEDEFAM [a victim organization]. This person put us in touch with AFADEM. We gradually gained their trust and began working together.[85]

As a result of these difficulties, in the early 2000s, when the FEMOSPP was created, NGOs with professional legal teams were only beginning to forge a working relationship with victims of the dirty war. The only meaningful connections were with some of those involved in AFADEM, whereas icons of the human rights movement remained out of reach. For example, in an interview conducted in 2010, Raúl Álvarez Garín still showed deep mistrust for the agenda promoted by second-generation human rights NGOs:

> Some NGOs may appear as neutral, but in reality they respond to international forces. The Catholic Church, the United States. Human Rights Watch plays a special role in the reorganization of the world.... When some organizations, like for example the Comisión Mexicana – which is highly dependent on Human Rights Watch – writes about the disappeared, it puts the word between inverted commas; and when they talk about genocide, they put it between inverted commas.[86]

The absence of deep links with victim organizations meant that for these professionalized NGOs, transitional justice remained peripheral to their agenda. Both the Comisión Mexicana and Centro Prodh took on a few of the forced disappearance cases, but working alongside the FEMOSPP was not an institutional priority. In the words of two seasoned human rights activists, "We were busy with all the other human rights problems in Mexico,"[87] "We did not seek these cases as part of an institutional

[85] Interview, Mexico City, 19 July 2010.
[86] Interview, Mexico City, 21 July 2010.
[87] Interview, Mexico City, 19 July 2010.

strategy."[88] As a result of this relative detachment during the first few years of existence of the Special Prosecutor's Office, their role as attorneys in the forced disappearance cases was subsidiary to that of nonspecialist lawyers hired by victim organizations. Because they worked more closely with the FEMOSPP, these nonspecialist lawyers had more impact in shaping Carrillo Prieto's legal strategy. This made it very difficult for those working for the more professionalized NGOs to disseminate an alternative legal discourse once they took charge of the cases.

For example, there is evidence to suggest that AFADEM's lawyers introduced or were at least in agreement with the idea of filing charges for "unlawful deprivation of liberty," instead of resorting to more appropriate human rights categories such as "forced disappearance." In January 2002, weeks after the president announced the creation of the FEMOSPP, one of AFADEM's lawyers told the press that they had presented the prosecutor with 150 cases of "unlawful deprivation of liberty."[89] A month later, he suggested the organization would file even more cases using this criminal definition.[90] As I argued previously, this had serious negative consequences for the fate of the forced disappearance cases. When the Comisión Mexicana and Centro Prodh began to approach the Special Prosecutor's Office, the legal strategy had already been decided, so they encountered a lot of resistance to their legal ideas, especially their preference for using argumentative techniques associated with international human rights law. Much as in the genocide cases, the FEMOSPP was reticent to try new arguments, refusing to admit the failure of its initial approach. This caused tensions in the relationship between second-generation NGOs and the prosecutors:

> What happened was that there were serious deficiencies in the way they defined the crimes in the first few indictments. After that it was really difficult to build a respectful working relationship with the prosecutors.... There was also resistance to the idea of filing charges for a multiplicity of crimes. We told them that if they did not want to use solely human rights categories such as torture, disappearance, extrajudicial execution, they could always present a multiplicity of charges and not just "unlawful deprivation of liberty."[91]

> It was always a complicated relationship, which became even more complicated as they years went by. The cases were not making enough progress, and the victims felt that they were back to square one, that the story was

[88] Interview, Mexico City, 9 August 2010.
[89] *El Universal*, 13 January 2002.
[90] *El Universal*, 7 February 2002.
[91] Human rights lawyer, interview, Mexico City, 2 September 2010.

> going nowhere. Another source of conflict was that most of these prosecutors only had experience investigating regular crimes. They did not have a methodology, or experience using specialized investigative protocols. In this sense one of the big issues was the question of how to define the crimes. Should we use "forced disappearance" or "unlawful deprivation of liberty"?... On several occasions we met with them but we always encountered a lot of resistance to our strategy.... According to them, the notion of "forced disappearance" did not exist when the crimes took place. From a legal point of view, they did not feel empathy with our arguments.[92]

The tensions became more acute in 2005 as the FEMOSPP prepared to file *Radilla*, a case in which the Comisión Mexicana was now deeply involved. As he had done in previous cases, Carrillo Prieto charged the defendants for the crime of "unlawful deprivation of liberty" instead of "forced disappearance." One of the lawyers recalled a conversation he had with the prosecutor after he heard about the terms of the indictment:

> We heard from the press that Carrillo Prieto had filed the case. I immediately called him to tell him that he had not chosen the right legal strategy, that he had all the necessary elements to file charges for "forced disappearance" and yet he used "unlawful deprivation of liberty." I even mentioned the Supreme Court's decision on this issue. He replied that he was under no obligation to inform us of his decisions because we were not part of the case. This was funny because when I made the call I was sitting in my office with the victims' daughter! ... He went on to tell me that he would not hear a law lecture from me; that the crime of forced disappearance did not exist when the events took place.[93]

This quote reflects the lack of a close working relationship between the NGO and the FEMOSPP: The lawyers found out about the indictment when it was a fait accompli. At this point in the process, and as a result of their initial disengagement, it was clear that they had not built a sufficiently strong relationship with the prosecutor. They could not persuade Carrillo Prieto to modify an approach that was initially supported by the lawyers working for victim organizations. Some of the prosecutors at the FEMOSPP made this quite clear during interviews, also suggesting that there had not been extensive discussions about the alternative legal strategy favored by the Comisión Mexicana:

> We never thought of using the idea of crimes against humanity. Our argument was that at the time of the events, those crimes were not considered crimes against humanity. We always sought to respect the nonretroactivity

[92] Human rights lawyer, interview, Mexico City, 9 August 2010.
[93] Human rights lawyer, interview, Mexico City, 20 July 2010.

> principle, which is a constitutional principle that we must abide by. This was not a matter of opinion.[94]

> Forced disappearances were not part of Mexican law. We could not talk about forced disappearances or even about homicides, because we did not have the bodies. These were kidnappings, unlawful deprivations of liberty.... When I was working there I never heard the argument about the possibility of using "forced disappearance".[95]

Second-generation human rights NGOs thus failed to engage with the FEMOSPP in a timely and comprehensive manner. As a result, they were unable to diffuse their expertise, providing prosecutors with better technical skills to deal with dirty war era cases or persuading them to adopt alternative legal strategies capable of introducing new ideas to a stagnant legal debate. When asked about the existence of efforts to enhance the prosecutor's technical capabilities, his knowledge of international human rights law and his investigative techniques, the human rights lawyers I interviewed for this study all admitted that they never planned this type of pedagogical intervention. With the benefit of hindsight, several human rights lawyers recognized that this was a fatal flaw in their approach to transitional justice. According to one of them, their initial conversations with the prosecutors should have alerted them to the magnitude of the problem:

> The discussions we had with the prosecutors reflected the dominant mindset within the FEMOSPP, and within the judiciary more generally. This was the mindset that prevailed in almost every court ruling. What we failed to put into perspective was that those very concrete discussions with the prosecutors in charge of the forced disappearance cases were indicative of a more general, problematic approach to the law and legal practice in Mexican judicial circles.[96]

One of his colleagues was even more conclusive, pointing out the negative consequences of failing to design a broader strategy to manufacture both technical capabilities and political will among the relevant judges and prosecutors:

> In Mexico we clearly need more training for the judges. We need to make them aware of other international experiences, of international law, of why they can say "x" or "z" based on international jurisprudence.... The cost of

94 FEMOSPP prosecutor, interview, Mexico City, 11 August 2010.

95 FEMOSPP prosecutor, interview, Mexico City, 27 September 2010. This prosecutor stopped working for the FEMOSPP in 2004, before the Supreme Court's ruling on the status of forced disappearances.

96 Interview, Mexico City, 9 August 2010.

> issuing an arrest warrant is much higher than saying "statutes of limitations have ran out." There isn't a coordinated civil society movement that helps the judges understand why they must take those risks. No one is standing in front of their offices, pressuring them. No one files quality amicus briefs explaining how they should proceed.... We have not been able to put together a movement that includes both academics and civil society. When the cases were filed there wasn't an articulated movement behind them.... We did not even consider the possibility of organizing seminars for the judges or the prosecutors. We did not even try to do that.[97]

Even Carrillo Prieto candidly admitted during an interview that the absence of adequate training and support from civil society was one of the decisive factors behind the failure of his mission:

> Despite all my academic qualifications, it seems that we needed more [training]. But even if we take responsibility for our personal shortcomings, the problem was also that we did not have the necessary social support. We did not receive enough support in part because of the fights [within the human rights movement].[98]

Summary

The analysis of the interactions between litigants and prosecutors in genocide and forced disappearance cases shows that the former indeed faced moments of choice. Despite the lack of an unequivocally supportive political environment, the creation of the Special Prosecutor's Office offered a space in which they could have adopted different strategies to steer the prosecutorial effort in a more effective direction. Moreover, the special prosecutor was indeed open to ideas from human rights activists. Unfortunately, those who had the expertise to provide adequate technical assistance initially turned their back to him and later failed to build a productive relationship. Victim organizations did court the prosecutor, but they were notoriously ill equipped to understand the legal issues at stake and the need to trigger a widespread transformation of legal preferences. This transformation was necessary in order to carve out creative argumentative paths in a highly formalistic terrain, and thus to catalyze successful investigations and indictments. Prosecutors themselves candidly admitted their lack of appropriate training to carry out this task and the difficulties of doing it without external support. In the end, deficient technical

[97] Interview, Mexico City, 28 August 2010.

[98] Interview, Mexico City, 21 July 2010.

capabilities and institutional goals divorced from the transitional justice cause proved fatal in a context in which the political environment sent mixed signals about its level of tolerance for human rights prosecutions. Without a counterhegemonic juridical discourse, prosecutors were left with very few resources to confront these challenges, and most importantly, with very few reasons to take risks. As we shall see, this argument also applies to the judges.

An Untamed Judiciary: The Persistence of Traditional Legal Preferences

Unlike in the cases of Argentina and Peru, where litigants successfully designed ambitious pedagogical interventions targeted at both judges and prosecutors, in Mexico litigants haphazardly and ineffectively engaged with prosecutors and made no attempts to build bridges with the judicial branch. The absence of efforts to approach the judges proved particularly problematic, because even if litigants had been able to expand the terms of the legal debate via a successful relationship with the FEMOSPP, the novel juridical arguments needed to win these cases would have still sounded too foreign in the ears of Mexican federal judges. The fact that the pedagogical interventions aimed at judges were not even attempted means that there are no traces of informal interactions in which we can look at the ideas that were circulated and judges' responses to them. Moreover, it is difficult to determine whether judges would have agreed to participate in these informal spaces of academic exchange. What we do know is that in their rulings judges invoked statutes of limitations and remitted several cases to military courts, contravening international legal standards for human rights prosecutions. To overcome these data limitations, I use interviews with key judicial actors to show that they perceived human rights cases through a highly formalistic legal cultural lens. I also offer some evidence of the more general problematic relationship between the Mexican bench and international human rights law to explore the barriers posed by existing legal preferences to the diffusion of new paradigms of rights adjudication.

During the PRI regime, the Mexican judiciary was an appendix of the executive branch. Presidents used their "metaconstitutional powers" (Weldon 1997) to capture the Supreme Court by constantly modifying its composition and prerogatives, and, in turn, the Supreme Court maintained a firm grip on the composition of lower courts by controlling appointments and removals (Ansolabehere 2007; B. Magaloni 2008).

This began to change in the 1990s. The fragmentation of power that preceded the democratic transition led the PRI in 1994 to pass an ambitious constitutional reform, which strengthened the autonomy of the Supreme Court and granted it the power to become an arbiter of political conflict in a more plural polity. In particular, the creation of two writs, the "constitutional controversy" and the "anticonstitutionality action," gave the Supreme Court original jurisdiction on matters raised by political actors such as legislatures, parties, and governors (Domingo 2000; Finkel 2003). This expansion of the court's review powers allowed it to become an arbiter of conflicts between the branches of the federal government, and between the federal government and the states, spheres in which the opposition was becoming increasingly salient (B. Magaloni 2003; Finkel 2008). A more plural environment, coupled with stronger constitutional prerogatives, thus allowed the Supreme Court to begin to put checks on politicians, to a degree not seen before in Mexico (Ríos Figueroa 2007). As Ansolabehere characterizes it, "The Supreme Court ceased being the court of the government and became instead a court of politicians" (2010: 79).

After the reforms were passed, the Supreme Court came to embrace its new role at the center of the political process, carefully managing its newly acquired visibility and distributing power among the relevant actors (Ansolabehere 2007; Staton 2010). This revolution in judicial power notwithstanding, the Mexican judiciary in general and the Supreme Court in particular have lagged behind regional trends in terms of the development of doctrines that expand citizens' rights, using constitutional interpretation to define their content in progressive ways. This is in part because the reforms increased access to the judiciary for politicians interested in limiting the prerogatives of their adversaries, but not for ordinary citizens seeking protection from the state (Sanchez et al. 2011). Although the Mexican Constitution, the child of the 1917 revolution, generously enumerates a series of citizen rights, enforcement by courts has been historically ineffective. Mexican legal scholars often take pride in their country's pioneering role in the development of the writ of *amparo*, a procedure to challenge state abusive practices in line with the spirit of the Magna Carta. However, the Mexican version of the *amparo* is a deficient instrument for citizens to seek redress for rights violations. According to Beatriz Magaloni, the *amparo* is governed by "very strict procedural rules and could only be initiated within a short period of time following the application of the challenged law" (2008: 189). Given these strict access rules, judges tend to dismiss the overwhelming majority of *amparo* suits on procedural grounds, rendering it toothless.[99] Indeed, although there is some evidence that the Mexican Supreme Court is beginning to take discussions about fundamental rights seriously in areas such as freedom of expression, freedom of association, or indigenous rights, up to 2007, the court had "developed a mere thirty-eight main doctrines or criterios, with respect to rights issues in twenty years" (Ansolabehere 2010: 79). Moreover, most of these doctrines arose from cases brought forward by politicians using constitutional controversies or anticonstitutionality actions, not by citizens via the writ of *amparo*.[100]

Apart from these access issues, the slow development of a rights-centered jurisprudence is often seen as the product of a rigid view of the constitution among judges. Judicial actors tend to emphasize procedural issues, and favor a mechanical, plain meaning interpretation of the constitutional text, without much consideration for how different articles may be read against each other, or interpreted in light of general principles of law, custom, or international law. The law is thus seen as a set of unequivocal, noncomplementary rules, and the role of judges remains focused on enforcing their hierarchical arrangement with no room for interpretation or integration (Caballero 2009). In a book written to argue against this form of legal praxis, a Supreme Court justice and his coauthor aptly describe how Mexican judges think:

> It has become clear that written law cannot cover all possible conflict scenarios: it does not have the capacity to formulate its commands in an unambiguous way and with a non-controversial, apprehensible meaning, all the time and without exceptions. If the law was characterized solely by a finite number of items and these were known alongside all their possible combinations, ... it would be possible to develop rules which could be applied to particular cases without requiring a choice. This would be an adequate world for a "mechanical" legal theory. However, reality and the limits of language have made clear, more or less explicitly, the need for an additional exercise of choice in the application of general rules to particular cases. (Silva Meza and Silva Garcia 2009: 198)

The following statement from an interview with a former Supreme Court judge is illustrative of this legal vision, which does not encourage judges to

[99] For a discussion of the access problems associated with the writ of *amparo* see Carbonell (2000).

[100] The Mexican Supreme Court has the prerogative to derive jurisprudential guidelines from its rulings on specific cases. These guidelines are at first considered *tesis aisladas*, or "isolated guidelines," but when invoked in five different decisions they become a *tesis jurisprudencial*, which is binding for lower courts.

think in terms of fundamental rights, and leads them to behave as arbiters of procedure and formal prerogatives, as well as enforcers of the literal meaning of the constitutional text:

> I would place myself closer to positivism, because I think that our role is to be arbiters. Our role is to read the Constitution, not to read ourselves in the Constitution. [Our role is] to read the Constitution, not to say what I would like the Constitution to say. This position, which is closer to positivism, saves us from all countermajoritarian objections because it reduces the court to a technical role, that is to say, we must establish what is technically correct given what the Constitution says. We are not here to say if a law is good or bad, if it is constitutional or not constitutional.[101]

The institutionalization of these legal preferences is the product of a highly formalistic legal education, which teaches lawyers to apply rules and not to argue rights (Adler Lomnitz and Salazar 2002). More important as a causal factor, however, is the legacy of authoritarian rule (B. Magaloni 2008; Sanchez et al. 2011). During the PRI regime, the role of Supreme Court jurisprudence was to generate strict rules guiding how the law should be applied in specific cases. This was intended to discipline lower courts, minimize their ability to interpret the law discretionally, and make them perfect agents of the regime. By promoting an extreme version of legal formalism, and ingraining rigid interpretative routines, the system thus reduced the power of the judiciary (A. L. Magaloni 2007). Despite the appointment of a more diverse set of judges to the Supreme Court since 1995, the judiciary continues to reproduce this decades-old formalistic vision. Lawyers from outside the "judicial family" rarely become judges or are promoted to federal courts, and the institution still does not reward innovative behavior in the development of jurisprudence. In many ways, these dynamics are an example of how external groups can entrench their interests in the judiciary overtime by promoting legal preferences that bias jurisprudential outcomes in their favor, a phenomenon discussed in Chapter 2. Reflecting on this issue and how difficult it is to disrupt the reproduction of traditional problem solving templates, a Supreme Court judge stated: "There is an institutional inertia that determines attitudes and ways of reading the Constitution and our main laws. It is hard to overcome this longstanding way of understanding the role of the judiciary in the context of the Mexican state, and its place with regards to the other branches."[102]

[101] Supreme Court judge, Interview, Mexico City, 27 July 2010.
[102] Email correspondence, Supreme Court judge.

It is through this legal cultural lens that Mexican judges approached the few dirty war era cases that made their way through the judicial system. These were cases that from the point of view of a strict reading of the constitution and domestic criminal law were clearly outside their scope, mainly because of the exhaustion or near-exhaustion of statutes of limitations. The absence of a robust rights-centered jurisprudence capable of integrating various bodies of law (in particular international law) to problematize these domestic procedural rules and adjudicate, enrich, and give content to constitutionally enshrined rights resulted in a very narrow chance of victory for the prosecution and the victims. In a report on the Mexican situation, Human Rights Watch pointed out the magnitude of the challenge, and the urgent need to engineer a shift in legal visions:

> When the Special Prosecutor's Office was created in 2001, it was already clear that it would face enormous legal hurdles. The most obvious of these was the problem of statutes of limitations.... Under the circumstances, the task of developing a viable legal strategy was far too ambitious and complex to leave entirely to the Special Prosecutor's Office. Forging viable legal strategies would entail breaking new ground within a criminal justice system that was poorly equipped to deal with crimes of this nature. And it wouldn't be enough merely to choose the legal arguments that were legally sound. Prosecutors would also need to convince judges that their novel legal arguments were consistent with Mexican law. They would need to impress upon judges the weight of Mexico's international obligations to prosecute human rights violations. In short, prosecuting these cases would require pushing Mexican criminal law in new directions. It would require overcoming the very legal doctrine and habits that had, for decades, served to perpetuate the culture of impunity. (Human Rights Watch 2006: 100–101)

At the root of the difficulties that the prosecution would encounter to get around the problem of statutes of limitations was the amount of attention Mexican judges historically paid to Article 14 of the constitution, which enshrines the legality principle. For example, there is evidence to suggest that this is by far the most heavily invoked article in Supreme Court decisions. The Supreme Court can extract guiding interpretive principles from its rulings on specific cases, and when these are invoked in five or more cases they become binding for lower courts. Figure 5.1 shows the number of these principles developed between 1917 and 2005 regarding the first 29 articles of the constitution, the ones that outline individual rights. Article 14 is by far the most regulated one, with a total of 444 binding interpretive guidelines. This certainly has had the effect of cementing formalistic rules of praxis across the judicial branch with regard to the enforcement of the nonretroactivity principle and of statutory limitations.

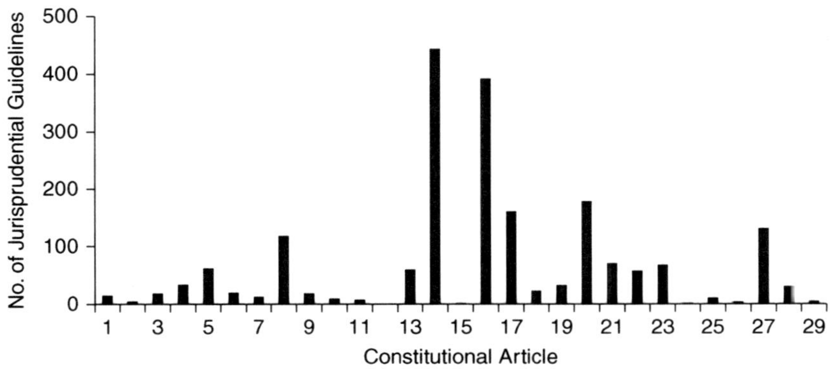

Figure 5.1. Number of Jurisprudential Guidelines for the Interpretation of Constitutional Articles 1–29 (1917–2005).
Source: Barrena (2007).

A rigid understanding of the legality principle fosters a form of legal reasoning that does not take into account contextual factors, which could in principle lead judges to consider substantive aspects of the case such as the nature of the crimes in question (e.g. whether or not they are crimes against humanity) in order to relax the prohibition against the retroactive use of the law or disregard statutes of limitations.

Circumventing this highly regulated environment would have required courts to alter their standards of adjudication and develop new doctrines applicable to a special category of crimes. International human rights law offered the avenues to disrupt this inertia, but these ideas were alien to most Mexican judges. A former Supreme Court justice, who was part of the more progressive wing of the court in the late 1990s and early 2000s, was highly critical of his colleagues' treatment of international law in dirty war cases. He attributed the observed jurisprudential patterns to sheer ignorance and stressed the importance of legal preferences in the failure of the transitional justice effort:

> Formalism would not have allowed these cases to go through, even if the entire political class had been behind the process. The judges were not ready to read rights such as the right to truth into the Constitution, or to limit the use of statutes of limitations.... The opposition to other ways of thinking about and reading the law has a lot to do with ignorance. The fact that the 2003 [supreme court] ruling on forced disappearances does not mention any international legal instruments, is the product of ignorance.... In Mexico we have members of the supreme court who are very formalistic

> and positivist. As long as that doesn't change, the judicial branch won't become a steward of rights.[103]

During an interview, another former Supreme Court judge, who belonged to the dominant conservative camp, expressed skepticism about some of the arguments derived from international human rights law pertaining to state crimes: "Do you remember Hitler and race, or Stalin and the proletariat? That kind of transpersonalism is very dangerous. The same could be said about humanity, what is humanity?" But as the interview went on, he acknowledged that he was only beginning to think seriously about these legal doctrines:

> You must remember that litigants are the unknown soldiers of jurisprudence.... The judge responds to whatever the litigants propose. In many ways we have not discussed international human rights law in this court because litigants have not invoked it.... It's possible that these ideas will be gradually adopted in order to strengthen our decisions, but we are in a very initial stage of the process. There is an awakening of Mexican lawyers to these issues. This includes myself, other judges, and the litigants.[104]

In line with this justice's view that new ideas about the law may gradually make their way through the judiciary, one of his colleagues in the Supreme Court pointed to the importance of resocializing judges in order to deinstitutionalize certain decision making routines, and open the judiciary to international human rights law. When asked why the court had not made any reference to international human rights law in the 2003 decision on forced disappearances, he responded:

> How interesting that you noticed that. In general Mexican lawyers do not cite that kind of thing.... Many judges do not know about these things because they have simply not encountered them before; that's it. This court should start doing it, but for the most part it doesn't know how to, which means we have to retrain our lawyers. We are starting to do this by sending clerks to spend some time at the Inter-American Court. It's a process that will take some time.[105]

Confronted with a similar question, a lower court judge who intervened in some of the forced disappearance cases also indicated that at the time the FEMOSPP filed the charges, Inter-American jurisprudence was not something judges like him were accustomed to paying attention to when writing their decisions. In fact, despite the 2001 reform of the Mexican Criminal

[103] Supreme Court judge, Interview, Mexico City, 3 September 2010.
[104] Supreme Court judge, Interview, Mexico City, 27 July 2010.
[105] Supreme Court judge, Interview, Mexico City, 15 July 2010.

Code, which incorporated the crime into domestic positive law, and the 2003 Supreme Court precedent on the topic, he made it quite clear that an indictment for the crime of "forced disappearance" following domestic and international precedents, instead of one for "unlawful deprivation of liberty," would have never led to a conviction. It was literally inconceivable given decision making routines prevalent at the time:

> I doubt that approach would have been promising. You can't apply criminal definitions retroactively.... At that time it wasn't obvious that Inter-American precedents were formally valid and mandatory for us to consider them. It wasn't something that was clear to us, or even relevant.... That is why I did not look to see what the [Inter-American Court] had said about these questions.[106]

The lack of diffusion of interpretative practices that take into account international human rights law is characteristic of the Mexican judiciary. For example, an extensive search of the use of Inter-American jurisprudence as a source of law in the decisions of the Mexican Supreme Court, the Argentine Supreme Court, and the Peruvian Constitutional Court shows that between 1994 and 2012 Mexican judges cited Inter-American precedents on only 54 occasions, contrasting sharply with the 459 citations found in Argentina and the 1,017 found in Peru (see Chapter 6). This is certainly a factor that limits the ability of the Mexican judiciary to think expansively about the content of the fundamental rights enshrined in the constitution. Although in the early 2000s the constitutionalization of international law was not as strong as in Argentina after the 1994 reform, Article 133 of the constitution had long incorporated international law into the domestic legal system. The problem was that Supreme Court precedents historically treated international law as infraconstitutional. In practice, this meant that judges did not feel the need to read the constitution in light of these alternative bodies of law, and applied its articles on the basis of plain meaning interpretation (Caballero 2009). As suggested by the testimonies of the judges quoted, these jurisprudential patterns are not merely a function of formal rules, i.e., the weak constitutionalization of international law, but reflect a deeply ingrained understanding of how the process of rights adjudication ought to work.

An example of the obstacles posed by this legal cultural lens on the penetration of international legal principles into local jurisprudence is the reaction of the judiciary to one of the first high-profile decisions handed

[106] District court judge, Interview, Mexico City, 18 August 2010.

down against Mexico by the Inter-American Court of Human Rights. The legal debate that followed the 2009 decision in *Radilla v. Mexico* is particularly relevant for our analysis, because this was a case filed by the Comisión Mexicana after domestic courts failed to investigate, prosecute, and punish those responsible for the forced disappearance of Rosendo Radilla.[107] At first, the Supreme Court was completely jolted outside its comfort zone by the ruling and responded in a highly formalistic fashion. Eventually, the more progressive wing of the court prevailed in the internal debate and produced a ruling that revolutionized Mexican jurisprudence. Yet as several sources pointed out during interviews, the effects of the ruling vis-à-vis greater judicial activism in the definition of the content of fundamental rights will be limited until the legal preferences of lower court judges are modified.

The *Radilla* ruling ordered the Mexican state to resume investigations in order to establish what happened to Rosendo Radilla; promote changes to the Military Code of Justice, excluding human rights crimes from its jurisdiction; and introduce changes to the legislation concerning the crime of forced disappearance. In *Radilla v. Mexico* the Inter-American Court also addressed the judicial branch, reminding it of its international obligations to abide by Inter-American jurisprudence and actively to review the "conventionality" of Mexican laws and state practices, i.e., the degree to which they are in line with the American Convention on Human Rights. Aware of the legal cultural barriers to initiating a productive dialogue between international and domestic jurisprudence, the Inter-American Court ordered the design of a pedagogical intervention to train Mexican judges in the use of Inter-American jurisprudence as a source of law. On this crucial point, the court decided that:

> the State shall implement, within a reasonable period of time and with the corresponding budgetary stipulation: a) Programs or permanent courses regarding the analysis of the jurisprudence of the Inter-American Human Rights Protection System in reference to the limits of military criminal jurisdiction, as well as the rights to judicial guarantees and judicial protection, as a way of preventing that cases of violations of human rights be investigated and prosecuted by that jurisdiction.... b) A training program on the due investigation and prosecution of events that constitute the forced disappearance of persons, addressed to agents of the Public Prosecutors' office of the Attorney General of the Republic and judges of the Judiciary of the Federation, who have jurisdiction in the investigation and prosecution

[107] Inter-American Court of Human Rights, *Radilla Pacheco v. Mexico*, ruling of 23 November 2009.

> of crimes such as the ones that occurred in the present case, in order to provide those officials with the legal, technical, and scientific elements necessary to comprehensively evaluate the phenomenon of forced disappearance. Specifically, in this type of cases the authorities in charge of the investigation shall be trained in the use of circumstantial evidence, indicia, and presumptions, the assessment of the systematic patterns that may lead to the facts under investigation and the location of persons who have suffered a forced disappearance.... Within the aforementioned programs, special reference shall be made to the present judgment and to the human rights international instruments to which Mexico is a party.[108]

Naturally, the ruling raised highly controversial issues, as Mexican judges were directly confronted with the need to clarify the status of Inter-American precedents in the domestic legal order, specify the reach of the court's decisions, and acknowledge their structural inability to deal with international sources of law. At the initiative of the chief justice, the Supreme Court began to debate its response, in what amounted to Mexican judges' first serious consideration of international human rights law and its relationship to judicial decision making. The court started to discuss the implications of *Radilla* in public plenary sessions held during 2010. Interestingly, the judges had a protracted debate about whether or not they should be hearing the case at all. In this sense, some argued that since the Inter-American Court had failed to notify the Supreme Court of the ruling formally, the debate was moot. This was an absurd argument that, on the one hand, reflected Mexican judges' fascination with procedure and technicalities, but, on the other, how unsettling and disconcerting the situation was for many of them.[109] According to a high-ranking clerk who had direct access to the internal deliberations:

> These arguments resulted from an extremely formalistic vision of the law, and to the lack of adequate information about the procedures of the Inter-American system. Of course the Inter-American Court won't notify the Mexican Supreme Court directly; it notifies the Mexican embassy! These procedures, or the idea that they had to discuss the implications of an international ruling against Mexico and comply with it, were not things that fell within their legal horizons.[110]

Eventually, a majority in the court agreed that it had an international responsibility to address the issues put forward by the Inter-American

[108] Ibid., paragraphs 347–348.

[109] Transcripts of the discussions are available at www.scjn.gob.mx/pleno/Paginas/ver_taquigraficas.aspx (last accessed 23 December 2014).

[110] Supreme Court clerk, Interview, Mexico City, 12 June 2014.

Court, even though it had not received a direct official notification of the ruling. The final decision on how to respond was nevertheless delayed.

In the meantime, two events generated the conditions for the Supreme Court to hand down a ruling that fully complied with the Inter-American Court's decision. First, the terms of a few conservative justices expired, and they were replaced by more progressive lawyers. Second, in 2011 congress amended Article 1 of the constitution to include unequivocal references to Mexico's obligations under international law and the importance of interpreting the constitution in accordance with human rights norms.[111] The amendment represented the most significant change to the Mexican legal order in decades. One month after this reform took effect, the Supreme Court handed down a ruling in response to *Radilla v. Mexico*, which further revolutionized the Mexican legal system by clarifying the implications of the amendments and the new spirit of the constitution.[112] A majority of judges decided to comply with the Inter-American Court's decision, limiting the reach of military jurisdiction in cases of human rights violations and, most importantly, establishing that Mexican judges have an obligation to check the compatibility of internal legislation with the American Convention on Human Rights. On this crucial point, a plurality of justices indicated that the jurisprudence of the Inter-American Court of Human Rights is mandatory, and should be taken into account during the review of conventionality. As one of the leading members of the conservative bloc expressed in an interview, "Sadly, here we lost."[113]

The ruling immediately sent shock waves throughout the judiciary, to the point that the Supreme Court formally inaugurated a new "jurisprudential period."[114] Two high-ranking clerks explained the motivation behind such

[111] The new version of Article 1 begins as follows: "In the United States of Mexico all persons shall enjoy the human rights recognized in the Constitution and in the international treaties to which Mexico is a party.... Human rights norms shall be interpreted in accordance with this Constitution and the relevant international treaties always providing people the greatest possible protections." The entire text of the constitution can be accessed at http://info4.juridicas.unam.mx/ijure/fed/9/default.htm?s=(last accessed 23 December 2014). My translation.

[112] Suprema Corte de Justicia de Mexico, *Expediente Varios 912/2010*, ruling of 14 July 2011.

[113] *Canal Judicial*, 8 November 2013. In a subsequent decision, the Supreme Court expanded the reach of this decision by establishing that the entire body of jurisprudence developed by the Inter-American Court is mandatory, i.e. not only the rulings against Mexico. In a concession to the more conservative camp, however, this second ruling also indicates that whenever there is a conflict between the constitution and a treaty, the former should prevail.

[114] Supreme Court jurisprudence is divided into periods, which coincide with important constitutional transformations. This ruling inaugurated the tenth period.

an ambitious ruling. The court wanted to manage the way international law entered the Mexican legal system, regulating the response of lower courts to the new legal paradigm:

> The Constitution had been radically transformed. It was necessary to build a narrative that explained these changes. The court had to participate in that process, showing that the reform had implications for its own decisions. Lower court judges were anxious to hear what these constitutional changes meant for them, what did it mean that they now had to defend human rights. This is what strengthened the position of the majority, because it was clear that things had changed, and the court could not remain silent.[115]

> The *Radilla* case and the issues raised by the Inter-American Court squared very well with the agenda of some of the justices, which included the question of diffuse judicial review, or the invocation of international law in order to give content to constitutional rights. ... Moreover, *Radilla* allowed the judges to position themselves as intermediaries between the Inter-American Court and Mexican judges, and thus contain the problem of international law. They were able to moderate the impact of the Inter-American Court, and explain the way in which Mexican judges should apply a part of the legal order over which Supreme Court judges have no control. It was a way of internalizing the external juridical problem.[116]

Yet, for many lower court judges, the majority's opinion was more unsettling than clarifying. The ruling not only ordered them to alter the way in which they treated cases involving the powerful armed forces, but also mandated a radical change to their decision making routines, especially with regard to the treatment of international human rights law. In other words, according to the Supreme Court, Mexican judges now had an international obligation to abandon their passive, formalistic role, and embrace a more activist and progressive position vis-à-vis domestic legislation. From one day to the next they became the guardians and architects of fundamental rights, as opposed to mere enforcers of written laws. In the process, they had to learn about new bodies of law and new argumentative techniques.

The doubts, fears, and resistance that these changes generated among lower court judges were a recurrent theme in my interviews with them and their clerks. The following quote from an interview with the judge who was put in charge of retraining Mexican judicial personnel as per the Inter-American Court's decision is illustrative. He vividly described the

115 Supreme Court clerk, Interview, Mexico City, 12 June 2014.
116 Supreme Court clerk, Interview, Mexico City, 16 June 2014.

reaction of Mexican judges when they were introduced to their new professional mission during a series of courses organized by the Judicial Academy:

> What prevails in the Mexican judiciary is an extreme form of positivism, which is a result of the type of legal education. The law is what its text says, and that's the end of it. There was only superficial knowledge of the Inter-American System of Human Rights.... What did we find [during the courses]? Well, people who were very perplexed. "What is this all about?" They had never thought about these issues before. They have developed patterns, routines, and when you start to suggest that there may be different points of view, well, people are surprised.... Some are also afraid. "What if we make a mistake? We may be held responsible." Others are worried about the consequences of this new vision. "What happens if we accept every suit for access to HIV medications?" Many judges come from a tradition in which what prevails is the reason of state, not individual rights.... Patterns of behavior are difficult to shake up.... We must intensify these courses, because we are not done yet. We are only beginning to remove certain inertias, generate some interest, show viability, but judges are still lacking a lot of tools.[117]

A Supreme Court clerk who participated in these training initiatives also referred to bureaucratic routines and the reproduction of legal preferences as a key obstacle to the effective penetration of new standards of adjudication:

> If some members of the Supreme Court were not fully aware of the implications of the ruling, you can only imagine the reaction among lower court judges! There was a lot of uncertainty, especially among federal judges. They are used to having clear instructions about how to act, with the jurisprudence clearly defined. They are creatures of habit.... Up to this point the Mexican judicial system did not reward innovation, creativity, or the horizontal development of jurisprudence.[118]

The *Radilla v. Mexico* case is clearly a success story in terms of the capacity of international law and international litigation to bring about changes in domestic legal structures, in ways that make them more effective in the protection of human rights. In addition to the Supreme Court's decision, *Radilla* generated changes in domestic military justice legislation and led congress to repeal a reservation against the retroactive use of the Inter-American Convention on Forced Disappearances, which had been adopted when the treaty was originally ratified.[119] From an analytical

[117] Appeals court judge, Interview, Mexico City, 22 May 2013.

[118] Supreme Court clerk, Interview, Mexico City, 27 November 2012.

[119] Despite these efforts to comply with its international obligations, at the time of writing Mexico is yet to establish what happened to Rosendo Radilla and bring the perpetrators to

perspective, the impact of this international ruling is in line with the idea that international pressure and norm diffusion can indeed change states' human rights practices (Sikkink 2011). Moreover, the 2011 constitutional change, which preceded the ambitious ruling by the Supreme Court, also highlights the role of formal legal changes as triggers of effective judicial responses to rights violations (Skaar 2011).

But this example also points to legal preferences as a crucial blockage for the enforcement of human rights and the expansion of the justice cascade. Not only did the international system shine a bright spotlight on the deficiencies of judicial behavior in the defense of fundamental rights, but the political system also opened up the formal legal space for a more adequate jurisprudential evolution. Yet, legal preferences mediated the ability of lower courts to understand these signals and operationalize the change they promoted. This clearly reinforces the broader points made by the sociological institutionalist theory of judicial decision making developed in this book: Jurisprudential outcomes reflect the internalization of norms and standards of professional conduct. With regard to the argument about formal institutional change, the reaction of Mexican judges to the ongoing legal transformations suggests that alterations to the formal rules of the game are inert unless they are accompanied by changes in informal practices that uphold or undermine the spirit of those reforms. If the legal preferences of Mexican judges remain unchanged, greater constitutional protections will not automatically benefit litigants seeking redress for the state's abusive practices. In terms of the pressures and signals from abroad, this example shows that the impact of international norms is decisively tempered by the behavior of domestic judges, who must come to know, understand, and endorse them. In other words, the evidence highlights a missing link in the diffusion stream. Lack of knowledge and aversion to international human rights law defined the initial reaction of the Mexican Supreme Court to the Inter-American Court's ruling, as well as that of lower courts once the Supreme Court's ruling had been handed down. As the last set of excerpts suggests, a deeper process of norm diffusion and internalization will require efforts by domestic judicial and civil society actors to transform the legal preferences of Mexican judges.

justice. Although immediately after the Inter-American Court handed down its decision prosecutors ordered new excavations to find the remains of the disappeared, the case has not made any significant progress.

Conclusion

As I write this concluding section, Mexico is immersed in a deep human rights crisis. The war against drug cartels has led to more than twenty thousand forced disappearances, many at the hands of security officers, and the discovery of mass graves frequently makes headlines. For many years after the escalation of drug related violence in the mid-2000s, these crimes did not trigger significant reactions from civil society. Moreover, no serious judicialization effort is under way. Conditions, however, may be changing. Following the brutal disappearance of forty-three students in the state of Guerrero in September 2014, citizens took the streets in an unprecedented wave of protests.

Despite the hope inspired by these popular reactions, recent events make it patently clear that the ruthlessness of state repression still haunts Mexican rural communities and their youth. Two of these students were relatives of Lucio Cabañas, the founder of the Liga Comunista 23 de Septiembre, whose members, as we have seen, were also victims of the crime of forced disappearance in the 1970s. Moreover, the organization that the forty-three students belonged to has participated in almost every episode of popular unrest in the country since the 1920s, including the dirty war. If Mexico's more distant past remains "unmastered" it is unlikely that this cycle of impunity will ever end. Mexican security officers may continue to anticipate no consequences for behaving lawlessly because no one has ever been punished for using state resources to plan and execute massive human rights violations, frequently against the same groups.

One of the implications of the failure of transitional justice efforts analyzed in this chapter is that human rights norms have not been effectively communicated within Mexico, first triggering a deterrence effect and eventually resocializing security forces into institutions respectful of domestic and international law.[120] Even if these long-term aspirations are deemed too idealistic, it is still possible to see how the failure of human rights prosecutions constitutes bad news for those who hope to bring about justice for more recent crimes, and in the process strengthen the rule of law. The evidence presented here suggests that Mexican judges and prosecutors are structurally incapable of effectively investigating, prosecuting, and punishing complex forms of criminality. They lack the technical capabilities to process these cases using internationally recognized standards to gather

[120] See Sikkink and Walling (2007) and Kim and Sikkink (2010) for statistical analyses showing the positive rule of law consequences of human rights trials.

and evaluate the evidence and to define the crimes in ways that adequately capture their significance and facilitate their punishment. Moreover, ideas related to the international responsibility of the state to address human rights crimes via the judiciary remain too foreign to them, as the doctrines, instruments, and precedents of international human rights law have not fully penetrated their cognitive maps. More importantly, traditional legal preferences lead judicial actors to be uncommitted to solving human rights crimes, perpetuating a bureaucratic culture that puts a premium on the use of technicalities to dismiss cases and lighten the docket. These behavioral patterns severely constrain the power of the judiciary to become a guarantor and architect of the content of fundamental rights.

The story of human rights trials in Mexico strengthens the argument put forward in this book, suggesting the importance of litigation groups as an exogenous force that must alter routine practices and established legal preferences in order to make the judiciary a hospitable arena for the investigation and punishment of cases of state repression perpetrated in the distant past. Unlike their counterparts in Argentina and Peru, Mexican litigants did not design appropriate strategies to transform the judiciary and realize its potential as a vehicle for truth and justice. Mexico thus offers a plausible counterfactual to trace what happens when human rights organizations choose to remain on the sidelines, do not dedicate enough resources to engage with judicial actors, or engage with them without the adequate tools. The behavior of Mexican NGOs in the early 2000s illustrates all three possibilities. As we saw in previous chapters, international legal ideas help expand the sphere of victims' rights and overcome obstacles associated with the investigation and punishment of complex and distant state crimes. Moreover, once their precepts are internalized, they have the potential to create an institutional commitment against impunity, even in the face of political and military actors seeking to put an end to the trials. The lack of a pedagogical effort along the lines of those deployed in Argentina or Peru meant that NGOs failed to become the conveyor belts of international human rights law. They failed to make these legal ideas the new focal point of the juridical debate, widening the narrow space for judicial action afforded by domestic criminal law.

The pervasiveness of a legal cultural blockage that hinders changes in the judicial imagination is one of the key components of my explanation for the failure of prosecutions in Mexico. Litigants' lack of professional resources to diagnose the problem correctly and influence changes in the way judicial actors think about the law and their professional mission is the other. It is important to note, however, that the political environment also played its part in narrowing the space for the activation of strategies of judicial change. Although clear moments of choice existed, the hostility of important members of the political class, and poorly coordinated strategies with others, further complicated the challenge faced by the NGOs. As shown in previous chapters, pedagogical interventions can be deployed effectively even in the face of political opposition, when replacement strategies are unthinkable. This is of particular importance in the Mexican case, because as the recommendations of the Inter-American Court in *Radilla* implicitly suggest, nurturing a judiciary capable of adequately processing rights claims in line with international human rights norms requires far-reaching changes in who the judges are, their educational and professional backgrounds, and how they understand their job. In this sense, breaking with formalistic bureaucratic inertias, which in Mexico are deeply ingrained, will most certainly necessitate a profound generational change in the judicial community. This is not something the Mexican NGOs could trigger, or count on, when they demanded justice for the crimes of the dirty war.

6

Comparative Perspectives on the Problem of Legal Preferences

Solving the Problem of Legal Preferences

The preceding chapters told the story of resourceful individuals and organizations that sought to transform judiciaries into institutions capable of coping with difficult, idiosyncratic, and politically sensitive cases. To varying degrees, they strengthened judges' and prosecutors' technical capabilities, expanded their legal horizons, and cemented their commitment to truth and justice, motivating them to withstand pressures and fulfill the state's responsibility to punish the perpetrators of horrendous crimes. The formal and informal tactics of legal contention deployed by several NGOs grounded the elusive but powerful norms developed in the international arena to describe, condemn, and prevent state abuses in the practices of those in charge of interpreting and enforcing the law at the domestic level.

Enhancing judiciaries' ability to cope with these cases requires the interruption of long-standing bureaucratic inertia and the transformation of traditional legal preferences. A crucial dimension of this process is the diffusion of alternative legal knowledge to dismiss amnesties, overcome statutes of limitations, and investigate chains of command. More importantly, transforming judiciaries into suitable arenas for the advancement of the human rights cause involves ingraining a discourse, a conceptual system that motivates judges and prosecutors to capture the essence of these crimes adequately, revealing them as what they truly are, certainly not ordinary crimes. The shift in legal visions away from a narrow focus on domestic law and formalistic practices nurtures an allegiance to a juridical lexicon that is more sensitive to the nature and historical significance of mass atrocities. In this sense, persuading judges to use certain techniques of legal argumentation, such as the double characterization of the facts of a case as a homicide and a crime against humanity, not only leads, from a technical point of view, to the expansion of the sphere of victims' rights, but is also an act of semantic justice.

Human rights litigants' ability to engineer this type of judicial change is grounded first and foremost in their capacity to diagnose the problem posed by traditional legal preferences correctly. The sociological institutionalist approach to judicial decision making developed in this book suggests that judicial actors' thought processes and rulings are mediated by a cultural lens that fixes their problem solving templates, behavioral routines, and professional values. To understand jurisprudential patterns and their implications for the distribution of power in politics and society, we must therefore look at the dynamics behind the production and reproduction of hegemonic legal preferences, not just the strategic environment confronted by individual judges or prosecutors when making specific substantive choices. In this sense, impunity is not just the product of the absence of political will among the ruling class or the lack of personal commitment among certain judges; it is also sanctioned by a structurally biased tradition of legal interpretation, one that is inherently conservative and incapable of, first, acknowledging the solutions afforded by international human rights law and, second, reconciling them with the domestic legal order. It follows that the radical shift in jurisprudence demanded by human rights prosecutions needs an exogenous force that redefines norms of professional behavior in accordance with shifting socially and politically constructed ideas about what constitutes appropriate praxis in the legal field.

Litigants' choice of pedagogical interventions as the main tactic of legal contention vis-à-vis committed and indifferent judges and prosecutors reflects their awareness of the ideational/cultural infrastructure that underpins judicial decision making. Put another way, their plan of action "imagines" the ontology of the judicial world in terms surprisingly similar to those of my sociological institutionalist framework. In the Peruvian case discussed in Chapter 4, the judiciary was not necessarily favorably predisposed to support NGOs. Moreover, judges and prosecutors were unfamiliar with the international legal case against impunity. But key members of the judicial community became effective agents of transitional justice after human rights litigants managed to transform their legal preferences. The ambitious pedagogical interventions designed by NGOs presented to judicial actors a set of juridical principles, precedents, and doctrines that emphasized their duty to become enforcers of Peru's international obligations. Pedagogical efforts filled gaps in legal knowledge, sparked curiosity to find out more about the imperatives of the new orthodoxy, and engendered a new logic of behavioral appropriateness.

In Argentina, as shown in Chapter 3, during the early 1990s NGOs also built bridges with judges, prosecutors, and clerks working in the capital city and some provinces, with the intention of diffusing the principles of international human rights law. Some of the judicial actors incorporated in these networks had already shown commitment to the cause during the previous decade. This normative commitment notwithstanding, prior to these diffusion efforts they felt ill equipped to act in defense of the victims. Established legal preferences did not allow them to see viable pathways to truth and justice and engage in juridical experimentation. By diffusing the idea of a right to truth, and offering guidance on how to proceed with highly idiosyncratic cases, litigants manufactured a plausible legal framework for judges and prosecutors to break with past routines.

Both cases show the importance of using pedagogical interventions to encapsulate decision making in a logic that prioritizes legal considerations. This is crucial in order to convert and motivate indifferent judges and prosecutors. Via pedagogical interventions and targeted diffusion strategies, litigants move to the fore the professional duty to enforce the rule of law, thus putting limits on the possibility of turning a blind eye to uncomfortable cases or dismissing them on the basis of technicalities. Greater awareness of the historical significance of the crimes and the international legal obligations to punish them, constant exposure to evidence that resonates with innovative criminal definitions, and feelings of discomfort regarding the contradictions in the legal order or the disjuncture between evidence about individual criminal responsibility and the impossibility of punishing the perpetrators, all contributed to manufacturing professional motivations to rebel against the status quo.

As part of the diffusion effort, litigants in Argentina and Peru had to pay special attention to judicial actors' concern for maintaining the legal legitimacy of their decisions. Endowing pedagogical interventions with an aura of authority was of paramount importance in order to undermine traditional legal preferences successfully. To this end, litigants made sure that the agents of diffusion who spoke on their behalf were respected legal experts and practitioners. In Argentina, for example, organizations such as the CEJIL, as well as prestigious intellectuals, became key allies in the diffusion process. Peruvian litigants followed a similar strategy. In fact, NGOs relied on their academic partners to host most of the seminars attended by judges and prosecutors. In the trial of Fujimori, activists also succeeded in reassuring high-ranking members of the judiciary that a condemnatory ruling would not contravene acceptable standards of behavior by enabling contacts between local judicial actors and high-profile international experts. Finally, litigants in both countries understood that to ease qualms about the perils of juridical experimentation, they had to use the informal contacts afforded by pedagogical interventions to expose judicial actors to jurisprudence that exemplified how others had dealt with similar problems. In other words, they were aware of the fact that judges think and act on the basis of formulas, templates, and precedents.

The shortcomings of the diffusion effort in both countries further highlight the importance of legal preferences and their transformation to the outcome of the judicialization process. Peruvian judges and prosecutors responded favorably to victims' requests in those areas in which persuasion mechanisms were better orchestrated, but did not endorse NGOs' arguments where the imperatives of the old legal orthodoxy were not fully challenged via informal diffusion channels. They were persuaded of the nonapplicability of amnesties and statues of limitations, but were not fully convinced that they could lower the standards for evaluating evidence. In fact, some prosecutors expressed their frustration with the lack of adequate training in the type of skills needed to carry out these investigations and build solid cases against the defendants. Similarly, in Argentina diffusion efforts in several jurisdictions forged a strong consensus around the need to reopen the investigations and trials. As a result, in the 2000s, key aspects of the new legal orthodoxy were no longer in question. However, the geographical bias of the pedagogical interventions organized in the 1990s negatively affected the progress of cases in the interior of the country, even in the presence of a favorable political environment after Kirchner's inauguration. In particular, my sources pointed to the lack of adequate training as one of the reasons why formalistic bureaucratic inertia persisted, leading judges and prosecutors in those jurisdictions to conduct deficient investigations and delay decisions.

Subscribing to a particular legal orthodoxy and the techniques of interpretation and investigation sanctioned by it can turn members of the judicial community into actors willing and able to perpetuate or defy impunity, regardless of the power and preferences of politicians and the military. Because of the crucial role played by legal preferences, the political environment does not fully determine the outcome of human rights prosecutions. In this sense, the sociological approach to judicial behavior anchored in the notion of legal preferences offers important explanatory advantages over accounts that see judges and prosecutors as interest maximizers, always conscious of their status as the least dangerous branch and consequently wary of external political constraints. By not paying enough attention to the ways in which organizational cultures shape the cognitive maps and professional commitments of members of the judiciary as a group, rationalist accounts provide few tools to identify the limits of individual instrumental reasoning in highly bureaucratic environments.

Organizational dynamics can certainly narrow the vision of its members, because internal socialization processes define the set of conceivable or known courses of action that are factored in when making choices. For example, it cannot be assumed that judges who refrain from questioning amnesties do so because they are always fearful of potential retaliation. Given the predominance of certain legal cultures, it is possible that defying an amnesty law is not even considered as a viable option and that upholding it reflects bureaucratic reflexes. In addition to a narrower field of vision, organizations such as judiciaries can nurture specific institutional preferences, which dictate logics of behavioral appropriateness capable of trumping a rational logic of consequences. The methodological individualism of strategic approaches abstracts judicial actors from their professional environment, and instills in them individual preferences such as tenure stability or the desire to elicit compliance with their decisions. But this fails to see the collective dimension of the judicial world, which creates its own goals and shared norms, motivating the defense of certain positions and making available a whole array of resources to resist external attacks.

In Chapters 3 and 4 we clearly saw this logic of appropriateness at work. First, I showed that the logic of consequences cannot explain why Argentine judges took bold steps to undermine the impunity regime in the late 1990s and early 2000s, when both their superiors in the judiciary and two successive presidential administrations opposed reopening the prosecutions. Moreover, if strategic behavior were characteristic of judiciaries in processes of transitional justice, judges and prosecutors would not have resisted unequivocal calls for justice in the 2000s. Second, I also showed that the logic of consequences cannot explain why Peruvian judicial actors decisively departed from the preferences of the García administration, often risking their job security and personal integrity. Judges and prosecutors acted on the basis of what they thought was legally appropriate given the evidence and legal arguments at stake. On several occasions, these ideas served as a catalyst of collective responses to political affronts against transitional justice.

In addition to motivating principled behavior and the open defiance of presidents and the military, the logic of appropriateness dictated by legal preferences also defined judges' ability and willingness to become involved in transitional justice struggles in contexts in which doing so did not necessarily pose personal or professional risks. Both in Peru and in Argentina, litigants had to put the possibility of defying amnesties and statutes of limitations on the map. They could not wait for a favorable political climate to whip judges into changing deeply ingrained legal cultures, which made certain jurisprudential outcomes literally "unthinkable." Moreover, judges and prosecutors had to be persuaded of the validity and applicability of international legal doctrines and instruments before they decided to act in favor of the victims. In other words, judges' legal knowledge and received understandings of legal praxis mattered greatly.

Even though the political environment did not necessarily induce strategic behavior, it did affect the judicialization process where it mattered the most: It shaped litigants' ability to engage in strategies of judicial change with the goal of altering the profile of dominant legal preferences. In the early 1990s in Argentina, the anti–transitional justice coalition in power successfully colonized key courts. When human rights NGOs launched their attempt to diffuse a new legal orthodoxy, many courts were therefore out of reach. The recalcitrant judges strategically placed by Menem in the Supreme Court and the Court of Cassation remained influential players in determining the scope and progress of the trials even after the demise of the political coalition that appointed them. But a favorable shift in the balance of power in the 2000s allowed NGOs to activate the second mechanism of institutional change identified by the theory, seeking to remove from the bench those judicial actors who systematically stalled the trials. These tactics, coupled with the process of normative diffusion of the previous decade, cemented a new sense of institutional mission among the members of the federal judiciary, and strongly shaped the long-term propensity of the judicial corporation to act in defense of victims' interests.

In the Peruvian case, the political environment also played a role. At the onset of the judicialization process, recalcitrant judges made up a smaller portion of the judiciary. Moreover, politicians' support for their cause allowed litigants to engage in aggressive pedagogical interventions from the start. This not only expanded the reach of their initiatives. It was also crucial later in the decade when the balance of power turned against them, as the early emergence of judicial buffers minimized the effects of President García's backlash. The impossibility of furthering the pedagogical effort and combining it with replacement strategies, however, meant that at the end of the period under study, Peruvian NGOs stood on much weaker ground than their Argentine counterparts. Emboldened by a hostile political environment, Peruvian recalcitrant judges reached influential positions in high courts, and managed to put crucial judicial victories in jeopardy.

Comparative Perspectives on the Problem of Legal Preferences

Successful human rights prosecutions and trials require the removal of judicial blockages. As argued in this book, these take the form of formalistic and positivist legal preferences. On this point, the case study of Mexico in Chapter 5 offered interesting insights into the obstacles posed by these informal norms of juridical praxis and litigants' inability to dismantle them. Like Argentina and Peru, Mexico had a vocal human rights movement, but one that did not invest resources in recruiting professionalized litigation teams. This was especially true in the case of victim organizations. The absence of strong ties between these activists and the second-generation NGOs that eventually developed expertise in international law further conspired against civil society's capacity to diagnose the problem posed by traditional legal preferences. In fact, despite the creation of the FEMOSPP, which gave activists the chance to interact face to face with judicial actors, human rights groups did not design effective pedagogical strategies to expand the terms of the legal debate and equip prosecutors with the skills to conduct effective investigations. In the absence of serious resocialization efforts or exogenous disruptive forces, judicial actors continued to ignore, and consequently failed to understand and internalize, new standards of juridical interpretation. Prosecutors replicated long-standing bureaucratic routines, showing no capacity to imagine alternative pathways to truth and justice. In addition, judges showed indifference, tracing possible but extremely narrow paths to accountability, and not deviating an inch from the written letter of domestic positive law. The difficulties of the Mexican judiciary in responding to rulings handed down by the Inter-American Court on dirty war cases also evidenced the persistence of informal legal cultures that hamper a more effective treatment of state abusive practices.

The lack of penetration of international human rights law into the cognitive maps and decision making routines of judicial actors is also pervasive in other countries where progress in transitional justice has been limited. In fact, the general use of international law in domestic jurisprudence maps well onto different countries' record with human rights trials, suggesting that structurally shifting the judiciary's legal vision away from a narrow focus on domestic law is an important precondition for successful prosecutions. Figure 6.1 shows the number of yearly citations of all the rulings handed down by the Inter-American Court of Human Rights (some of which are related to transitional justice processes) in the jurisprudence of twelve Latin American high courts between 1994 and 2012.

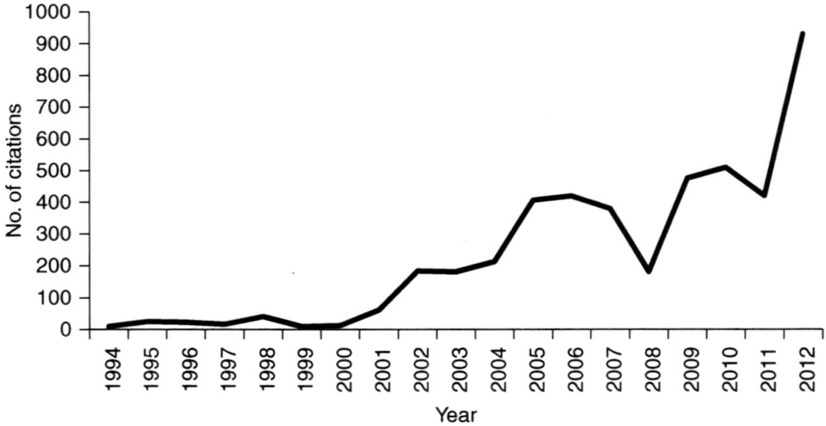

Figure 6.1. Number of Citations of Inter-American Court of Human Rights Rulings in the Jurisprudence of Twelve Latin American High Courts (1994–2012).
Note: The database includes the jurisprudence of the Supreme Courts of Argentina, Brazil, Chile, Costa Rica, El Salvador, Mexico, Paraguay and Uruguay, and of the Constitutional Courts of Colombia, Ecuador, Guatemala and Peru. I thank Santiago Basabe and Sandra Botero for sharing with me their data on Ecuador and Colombia, respectively.

The trend is clear: The use of international precedents is a relatively recent phenomenon in the region, which happens to coincide with the explosion of human rights prosecutions and trials in Latin America after 2000. The inroads made by alternative sources of law reflect a slowly changing culture of legal interpretation in which substantive debates about the content of fundamental rights begin to take a more prominent role. However, not all countries are included in this trend. Peru and Argentina are second and fourth in the ranking, with 1,017 and 459 citations each, whereas Mexico, together with Brazil and Uruguay, are at the bottom with 54, 40, and 21 citations, respectively.[1] Not surprisingly, Argentina and Peru have an outstanding record of bringing perpetrators to justice. By contrast, Mexico, Brazil, and Uruguay lag behind the move to greater criminal accountability. Judicial actors in these countries have not reached a consensus on the legality of antiimpunity doctrines grounded in international law, especially those developed by the Inter-American Court regarding states'

[1] The first and third in the ranking are Colombia and Costa Rica with 1,292 and 851 citations each.

responsibility to investigate serious human rights violations. As a result, the validity of amnesties and the applicability of statutes of limitations are still contentious issues.

A brief look at the judicialization process in Brazil and Uruguay suggests that in line with my argument, traditional legal preferences constitute important blockages on the road to truth and justice. Judicial actors in both countries lack the technical capabilities and the professional values to commit themselves to highly demanding and complex cases. As in Mexico, no human rights trials have been held in Brazil and the investigations that began in 2008 have made little progress. Although a few courts have shown some receptiveness to the innovative arguments put forward by a specialized group of prosecutors, the Supreme Court still holds the upper hand in the appeals process and is yet to issue a definitive ruling on the validity of the 1979 amnesty law. Uruguay is an intermediate case because some courts have handed down convictions, but the jurisprudential development is still deficient. Despite a Supreme Court ruling against the amnesty, the reach of this decision remains contested, and judges still enforce statutes of limitations in a way that jeopardizes the long-term viability of the judicialization process.

Both countries share important common characteristics that increase the attractiveness of the comparison. First, the military exerted great power and influence over democratic transitions, which affected the ability of civil society organizations to lobby for justice during the first decade and a half of the new democracies. Second, victim organizations in Brazil and Uruguay are weaker than those in Argentina or Peru. Although demands for justice resurfaced in the 2000s, only Uruguayan activists have recently invested in the development of professionalized legal teams. Third, the judicialization process unraveled at a time when left-wing parties were in power. Although their support has not been as strong as that of the Kirchner administrations in Argentina, they have occasionally shown commitment to the cause, adding to the momentum gained by prosecutorial efforts. Finally, despite this increasingly favorable context, the judicial branch remains a key source of opposition. In particular, Supreme Courts have shown no willingness to endorse legal arguments that can sustain the process over time. In both countries, isolated victories were the result of the commitment of a handful of judicial actors, who modified traditional legal preferences without external pedagogical support from civil society. As argued in Chapter 2, comprehensive programs of criminal prosecutions require much more than these spontaneous islands of commitment; they require widespread changes in the institutional goals of the judiciary, changes that more often than not must be manufactured from outside.

Brazil: No Trials and the Resilience of the Amnesty Law

During the 1990s, the Brazilian state began to implement an ambitious reparations program for the victims of the dictatorship. Although immediately after the 1985 democratic transition civil society remained fragmented and "did not successfully pressure the judiciary to investigate past crimes" (Abrão and Torelly 2012: 172), this and other memory policies eventually emboldened activists to step up demands for criminal accountability. In particular, they allowed victim organizations to document the crimes extensively, and thus provided the "factual basis for legal initiatives" (Abrão and Torelly 2012: 168). In addition, the human rights movement gradually expanded beyond a few victim relatives and activists attached to labor unions.

As part of this growing interest in criminal trials, prosecutors began filing cases in 2008. Their efforts, however, proved futile. Judges made formalistic interpretations of the legality principle, rejected extemporaneous criminal definitions as contrary to the nonretroactivity principle, and invoked the amnesty law, statutes of limitations, and the rules against double jeopardy to dismiss them all on procedural grounds. In 2010, a ruling by the Supreme Court reaffirmed the validity of the amnesty, further blocking the progress of these cases. The initial wave of Brazilian jurisprudence on mass atrocities thus perfectly enforced the standards enshrined by the positivist legal orthodoxy.

The debate was jump-started by President Lula Da Silva's 2010 proposal to create a truth commission, and by the Inter-American Court's decision in *Gomes Lund v. Brazil* (2010), which declared the illegality of the amnesty under international law. In response to this ruling, the prosecutor general created a specialized division to process dictatorship-era crimes and staffed it with the few committed prosecutors working on the cases since 2008, who proceeded to open around three hundred investigations. Although Brazilian prosecutors proved far more creative in crafting innovative arguments and knowledgeable of international criminal law than their Mexican counterparts, the judiciary's response remained the same: The cases that were eventually filed in court were summarily dismissed (Ministério Publico Federal 2013). A ruling by an appeals court in Rio de Janeiro in 2014 constitutes a major exception: For the first time judges recognized "crimes against humanity" as a valid criminal definition, thus overcoming some of the limits imposed by the amnesty law. At the time of writing, however, the case is still awaiting a final decision by the Supreme Court. In fact, the Supreme Court is yet to rule in a number of special writs known as Allegations of Breach of Fundamental Precept, in which the prosecutor general and the Brazilian Bar Association asked the judges to change their 2010 criteria on the amnesty in accordance with the Inter-American Court's ruling, and to exclude serious human rights violations from the reach of the impunity law.

Traditional legal preferences, and the absence of civil society efforts to deinstitutionalize them, played a key role in this story. Although occasionally respectful of due process, the judiciary was highly complicit with the dictatorship (Pereira 2005). In fact, this influence continued after the democratic transition. For example, it was not until 2003 that the last Supreme Court judge appointed by the dictatorship left the bench. This "enabled the survival of a conservative mentality in the Brazilian legal system" (Abrão and Torelly 2012: 174), which made it difficult for the institution to prioritize human rights cases and modify its interpretative routines when courts were suddenly confronted with the problem of the past. In addition to the entrenchment of recalcitrant positions, Matthew Taylor points to the prevalence of a highly formalistic legal culture: "Despite an extensive catalogue of individual rights in the 1988 constitution, protection of individual rights is almost always the exception" (Taylor 2008: 37). The author attributes this conservatism to judges' career incentives to avoid jurisprudential innovations that could upset their superiors in the judicial hierarchy, and to a legalistic education that leads them to focus "on the law as is written" (Taylor 2008: 35). When confronted with the figures reported in Figure 6.1 and asked to reflect on his country's position in the citations ranking, a Brazilian federal prosecutor also referred to traditional legal preferences as a core obstacle to the development of rights jurisprudence. In the case of lower courts, he argued, these preferences engender bureaucratic indifference toward transitional justice:

> The judiciary lacks knowledge of the jurisprudence of the Inter-American Court.... Judges are very traditional and avoid innovation.... They only pay attention to what is written in the criminal code.... In Brazil judges enjoy strong judicial independence, so it's not that they act in this way due to fear. It is simply easier to follow what the Supreme Court said [in the 2010 ruling], because it is a way of getting rid of these cases. It is difficult to find judges who are interested in international law, who are worried about this issue and willing to innovate.[2]

[2] Telephone interview, 1 September 2015.

Those judges who eventually reach the Supreme Court almost invariably hold these "well-established legal views" (Brinks 2011: 141). For example, during the public debate triggered by the prosecutors' attempt to circumvent the 2010 ruling on the amnesty with the argument that continuous crimes such as forced disappearances should be excluded from its reach, a Supreme Court judge made it crystal clear that prosecutors' innovative doctrines are unlikely to change the mainstream opinion of the court: "Let's wait for this issue to make it to the Supreme Court.... In the meantime we should let people debate and have fun."[3] A comment to the press by one of his colleagues, who suggested that these ideas jeopardize legal security, further foreshadows the likely content of future jurisprudence on the matter.

The contrast between the behavior of the judges and that of the prosecutors put in charge of the investigations is most revealing about the importance of shifting legal visions. The presence of islands of commitment to the human rights cause in the Ministério Publico Federal partly explains the large number of investigations launched in Brazil and the continuity of the effort despite judicial resistance. The roots of this commitment can be found in the linkages established between these Brazilian prosecutors and civil society actors, which helped broaden their value and legal horizons. Brazilian prosecutors are in a much better position to innovate and champion emerging social demands because their constitutional mandate is one that includes the defense of human rights (Hoffmann and Bentes 2008). They are formally assigned the role of what in other countries is known as the ombudsman, which leads them to maintain permanent contact with members of civil society, including victims of state repression. This is how the prosecutor who pioneered the investigations in 2008 explained his personal journey:

> The prosecutors are closer to the people [than the judges]. Understanding their demands led us to change our conservative traditions. We are not only a criminal agency; we are also a human rights agency.... My process is a good example of how things can change. Until 2007 I was among those who said that we had an amnesty law and that statutes of limitations would be a difficult barrier. What made me change my mind was the decision of the Inter-American Court in *Almonacid v. Chile*. When I came across this decision, in which for the first time the court said that we experienced crimes against humanity in South America ... I could see that the situation here in Brazil was the same.... [When] you become familiar with this legal background you get more convinced and more committed to apply this

[3] *Periodismo Humano*, 21 March 2012.

> law, and recognize that international human rights law is binding.... This decision made a difference because it gave me parameters that I could use internally.... In 2007 we could also, for the first time, identify the remains of a disappeared person. That day I remember one of my colleagues said: "Now we have the element of a crime, we have a body! We know it was a crime. We have to move forward."[4]

This fascinating quote crystallizes key aspects of my argument. First, it shows that contact with the victims was important in motivating prosecutors to act in groundbreaking ways. Although Brazilian NGOs never invested in the development of professionalized legal teams capable of deploying pedagogical interventions to diffuse new paradigms of rights adjudication inside the judicial community, their official interactions with the prosecutors seem to have instilled a sense of historical urgency regarding the need to come to terms with the country's past. As in other countries, familiarity with the evidence and the victims' suffering played a role in modifying the allegiances of indifferent judicial actors. Second, despite prosecutors' institutional permeability to these bottom-up pressures, commitment to human rights was ultimately mediated by the acquisition of new technical knowledge and the subsequent erosion of their blind allegiance to domestic sources of law. This change in legal preferences led the interviewee to see the legal possibilities afforded by the cases and his institutional responsibility in a different light. Evidentiary questions, especially whether the facts resonated with international criminal definitions, also played an important role in his conversion.

Unfortunately for the victims, because of the absence of more ambitious efforts to promote this type of ideational change, this prosecutor is an exception to the rule. One of his colleagues describes his experience in similar terms, and points out that for the cases to make any significant progress in the future, there must be a disruption of received legal opinions across a wider pool of judicial actors, followed by a broader institutional commitment to the cause of truth and justice:

> Before 2008 this was not a topic that was debated in Brazil. I had never heard that it was possible to move forward with these investigations. Studying in Argentina helped me because the arguments they use over there are very solid.... We face a lot of obstacles, even among the prosecutors.... In 2008 there were around six prosecutors that saw the possibility of punishing the perpetrators. Now there are new prosecutors who had to pass entrance examinations that require this type of knowledge. As a result, they are more favorable to transitional justice. But we haven't made a lot of progress.... It

[4] Telephone interview, 5 August 2015.

> is still a question of personal commitment, a commitment to study these topics in depth. The majority is simply not interested.[5]

This overview of the Brazilian judicialization process thus points to legal preferences as a crucial block to the progress of human rights prosecutions. It also shows that commitment to human rights cases among a handful of prosecutors was underpinned by a prior transformation of received formalistic and positivistic legal routines. Interestingly, the positive impact and limitations of this spontaneous transformation highlight the importance of engineering more widespread ideational changes in order to guarantee stable jurisprudential outcomes in favor of the victims of state repression.

It is important to conclude by noting that other factors also shaped the outcome of the judicialization process. For one, the Brazilian military has remained a politically influential voice ever since the democratic transition, and that may in part explain the reluctance or inability of civil society to fight harder to promote criminal prosecutions (Lessa et al. 2014). Moreover, the Supreme Court continues to be a crucial political hurdle. Supreme Court judges are probably aware that their next decision on the amnesty will be a leading case that clarifies the status of the American Convention on Human Rights in the Brazilian legal order. In this sense, ruling against the amnesty may well run contrary to their legal preferences. But the judges are also likely to take into account political factors when they finally hand down that ruling. In particular, they will probably consider the fact that given the country's current crisis, such a decision could add fire to a precarious political situation and therefore decide to delay it.[6] Although the Supreme Court has historically been autonomous vis-à-vis politics, it remains what Kapiszewski (2012) calls a "statesman court," i.e., one that prefers to be seen as a policy partner and not a court that is willing to jeopardize governability.

Uruguay: Limited Justice and the Enduring Problem of Statutes of Limitations

The situation in Uruguay is not as bleak, but traditional legal preferences still compromise the viability of human rights trials. Four years after the 1985 democratic transition, Uruguay held a referendum on the validity of the amnesty law, and proimpunity forces won the popular vote. This demoralized victim groups, leading them to "drop the demand of justice"

[5] Telephone interview, 1 September 2015.

[6] At the time of writing, President Dilma Rousseff is being threatened with impeachment as a result of a series of corruption scandals.

(Lessa 2013: 141). As in Brazil, calls for criminal accountability regained momentum after 2000, following the revival of civil society (Sikkink 2005). The number of NGOs pushing for justice expanded greatly, and in the 2010s, several of them formed the Observatorio Luz Ibarburu. Thanks to the financial support of the Open Society Foundation, this umbrella organization is now able to provide legal support to the victims and supervise the judicialization process. As a result, in recent years Uruguay has finally witnessed the creation of a professional group of lawyers similar to the ones housed by Argentine and Peruvian NGOs since the late 1980s.

Parallel to these developments, the political environment became progressively less hostile to the cause despite the enduring presence of a powerful and influential military opposed to criminal accountability. President Batlle (2000–2005) contributed to this thawing by appointing a Peace Commission tasked with producing a report about the crimes of the dictatorship. After the leftist Frente Amplio won the presidency in 2005, and in response to growing civil society pressures, Presidents Tabaré Vázquez (2005–2010) and José Mujica (2010–2015) opened further avenues for justice. In particular, since the amnesty law gave the executive the prerogative to decide whether specific cases fell within its reach, they both used it to allow the judiciary to investigate (Skaar 2011). In one of these cases, the Supreme Court concluded that the amnesty was contrary to the separation of powers principle and international human rights law (Lessa 2013). Although the ruling did not have *erga omnes* effects, it did improve the general prospects for justice.

The combination of more professionalized civil society demands and a more favorable political environment breathed new air into the judicialization process. Compared to Brazil, the change in the balance of power played a far more important role in reinvigorating the quest for justice. This was due largely to the fact that the amnesty afforded the Uruguayan executive greater control over the possibility of launching investigations. As a result, between 2000 and 2013, 201 new cases were filed in lower courts. It is noteworthy that after a concerted effort by the human rights NGOs who later formed the Observatorio Luz Ibarburu, in 2012 alone the courts received an impressive number of cases (ninety-three).

Of all the cases filed since the 1980s, 71 have been shelved, 163 are in the investigation phase, and 6 have resulted in condemnatory rulings.[7] Compared to Mexico and Brazil, Uruguay is therefore a more successful

[7] These and other statistics can be found on the Website of the Observatorio Luz Ibarburu: www.observatorioluzibarburu.org (last accessed 3 September 2015).

case, but it is still one of limited justice. In this sense, the absence of active efforts to trigger a profound resocialization of the judiciary into new traditions of legal interpretation and progressive institutional goals remains a major obstacle to a more effective prosecutorial wave. For example, in 2012 courts made reference to formalistic arguments related to the lack of direct evidence to hand down acquittals in three cases. Even the few condemnatory rulings are highly problematic because they narrowly focus on domestic law as a legal source. For example, most judges defined the crimes as "specially aggravated homicides," a definition found in the Uruguayan criminal code, and refused to apply the notion of crimes against humanity. Although this domestic criminal definition has longer statutes of limitations and therefore allows judges to hand down prison sentences, the tendency to reject international legal categories jeopardizes the long-term viability of the judicialization process. As a judge explained in an interview:

> In the jurisprudence one cannot see that what happened in Uruguay was a dictatorship. When you say that this was a crime against humanity, you are also saying that the state attacked its own citizens. If you read the rulings, however, it seems as though they were ordinary homicides.[8]

But in addition to this semantic and conceptual problem, the refusal to define the crimes as crimes against humanity implies that statutes of limitations can still be applied. For example, as a result of the passage of time, torture cases can no longer be tried. Moreover, as the years pass, statutes of limitations will also run out for "specially aggravated homicides."

The Supreme Court has used plain formalistic language to reject the validity of innovative criminal definitions, suggesting that these interpretive instincts are pervasive throughout the judiciary despite the constitutional status of international law (Lessa 2013):

> Because the notion of forced disappearance constitutes a crime defined only recently, it is inapplicable.... The constitutional status of the principle of formal legality implies that the only source of criminal law in this nation's system are the bodies authorized by the constitution, and the only criminal law is the one that they create.... This means that doctrine, jurisprudence or national or international customary practices cannot authorize the punitive power of the state.... The retroactive use of criminal norms is inadmissible. (Suprema Corte de Justicia de la Nación, *Sentencia No. 1501*, ruling of 6 May 2011)

The Supreme Court further constrained the terms of the legal debate in a landmark ruling handed down in 2013, in which it declared the

[8] Telephone interview, 7 July 2015.

unconstitutionality of key provisions of a law passed by congress to comply with the Inter-American Court's decision in *Gelman v. Uruguay* (2011). The judges rejected congress's claims that the crimes perpetrated during the dictatorship constitute crimes against humanity and that statutes of limitations were interrupted during the time the amnesty law was in force. In other words, following a traditional legal approach, judges drew a narrow path to justice, one that relied exclusively on orthodox readings of domestic legislation. They thus limited the scope of the proceedings and the possibilities of seeing a greater number of condemnatory rulings. This is similar to what happened in Mexico.

The positions taken by the Supreme Court in these and other cases generated tensions with the progressive Mujica administration, which at some point even debated the possibility of proposing reforms to reduce the power of the highest court in the land.[9] Most notably, in one of its many attempts to halt the judicialization process, the Supreme Court used its ability to control judicial careers to move Mariana Mota, a committed judge who oversaw more than fifty human rights criminal cases, to a civil court. This was not the first time the Supreme Court tried to undermine the progress of human rights cases in this fashion. The same occurred in the late 1990s and early 2000s, when it successfully deactivated attempts by individual judges to accelerate the judicialization process (Skaar 2011). But in Mota's case the government repudiated the court's decision, to the point that it included the episode in a report on the country's human rights situation submitted to the United Nations.[10] What this example of interbranch confrontation suggests is that despite changing political circumstances, Supreme Court judges are willing to go to great lengths to preserve a pyramidal decision making structure, one that does not challenge its conservative preferences on matters of great legal and political importance.[11]

Following the example set by the Supreme Court, most Uruguayan judicial actors have shown a great degree of indifference to human rights cases. This is reflected in the slow pace of the investigations and in the jurisprudence of appeals courts, which block the introduction of international legal ideas to the debate. The few positive outcomes are the result of the obstinacy of a handful of independent-minded judges, a situation similar to that in Brazil, where committed prosecutors managed to find creative ways to keep

[9] *El País*, 17 September 2013.

[10] *El País*, 18 February 2014.

[11] The judges were probably emboldened by the failure of a second attempt to nullify the amnesty law via a referendum in 2009.

the cases alive despite general resistance from the judicial community. As Daniel Brinks suggests, the top-down control of Uruguayan judges' careers generates negative incentives for innovation, "maintaining a generally conservative judiciary that is cautious, resistant to change, and very orthodox in its interpretation of the laws" (2008: 198–199). The testimony of one of the few committed judges further illustrates how the internal reproduction of these legal preferences constitutes a major problem:

> At first I didn't know in detail what happened during the dictatorship.... I began working like in any other criminal case, but soon realized that because of the obstacles posed by the state and the defendants I had to proceed differently.... This attitude has not become a general one among my colleagues.... Unlike in Argentina with the case of CELS, we don't have an organization dedicated to training judges.... We need a lot more specific training in human rights: how to evaluate the evidence, how to interrogate witnesses.... There isn't even a minority committed to these issues.... This is due in part to the way judges are trained.... They do not have the tools to protect human rights and act independently [of the Supreme Court].... [We must rethink] how judges are trained. Do we want judges that always defend the status quo? ... The culture of fear is deeply engrained; it is not even a conscious process, but it suppresses dissidence. We have professionals trained in replicating what the books say, but not in taking risks and challenging the books.[12]

Like the Brazilian prosecutors quoted previously, this judge highlights the importance of transforming skills and the ways judges read the law. She admits that her professional routines and legal knowledge had to change in order for her to conduct her duties more effectively in human rights cases. However, this is not something most of her colleagues can see or are willing to do. Professional socialization nurtures bureaucratic reflexes, which in Uruguay lead judges submissively to uphold the status quo. In the absence of ambitious efforts to redefine institutional priorities and circulate new ideas in the judicial branch, the success of the judicialization process will continue to hinge on spontaneous but extremely volatile and fragile commitments by those willing to defy the judicial establishment.

Legal Preferences and Judicial Independence

One of the central tenets of my sociological approach to judicial decision making suggests that legal preferences reflect the institutionalization of interests in the form of ideas that stabilize jurisprudential outcomes. The

[12] Telephone interview, 7 July 2015.

law and the discourses used to justify different ways of interpreting it are therefore political constructs, carefully and patiently developed by groups that hope to benefit from them. The arguments put forward in court to support or undermine impunity are no exception. The empirical analysis presented in this book looked at how pro– and anti–transitional justice coalitions competed for control over the normative allegiances of members of the judicial community, promoting the production and reproduction of professional cultures, values, and unconscious routines of praxis. The case studies portrayed judicial actors as socially embedded creatures, anchored in organizational environments governed by these informal rules and expectations, and surrounded by social forces trying to influence who they are and how they think. This framework has important implications for how we think about the idea of judicial independence, and the relative importance of formal versus informal rules in shaping the motivations and power of judges and prosecutors.

Judicial independence is often equated to freedom from interference with courts' decision making processes (e.g. Ferejohn 1998; Domingo 1999; Cameron 2002; Ríos Figueroa and Staton 2014); impartiality in courts' adjudication criteria (e.g. Shapiro 1981; Fiss 1993); respect for the legitimacy of courts' decisions by other political actors (e.g. Verner 1984); and the absence of the politicization of the judiciary (e.g. Dodson 2002). Larkins's definition of judicial independence is representative of the way some scholars understand the term: "Judicial independence refers to the existence of judges who are not manipulated for political gain, who are impartial toward the parties of a dispute, and who form a judicial branch which has the power as an institution to regulate the legality of government behavior, enact 'neutral' justice, and determine significant constitutional and legal values" (1996: 611). In the 1990s, and inspired by these ideals, international organizations spent millions of dollars in the developing world to strengthen the independence of judiciaries via formal institutional changes (Hammergren 1998, 2007; Carothers 1999; Salas 2001; Sarles 2001; Finkel 2008). Reforms included the constitutionalization of judicial review and human rights, the creation of judicial councils to depoliticize the process of appointing and removing judges, and the establishment of judicial academies (Finkel 2008: 9–10). The reforms sought to insulate judicial actors from political pressures, enhance their ability to hold elected officials accountable and defend individual and collective rights, professionalize personnel, secure their impartiality, reduce their caseloads, and expedite procedures.

By paying more attention to the double social embeddedness of judicial actors (in judicial organizations and the wider sociopolitical environment) it is possible to see the sociological deficits in both the concept of judicial independence and the causal assumptions linking formal changes to greater judicial power. This embeddedness constantly exposes courts to the risk of falling prey to external attempts to manipulate their formal prerogatives, composition, and institutional safeguards and, most importantly, the informal norms that endow actual judicial behavior with a clear political purpose. First, too much is at stake in contemporary judicial dockets for formal parchment barriers fully to deter politicians, NGOs, trade unions, businessmen, or military officers from trying to use multiple tactics to influence jurisprudence that affects their long-term interests. Moreover, as we saw in some of the case studies, judicial reform initiatives often present unparalleled opportunities for elites to craft courts that reliably favor their goals (Hirschl 2004; Finkel 2008).

Second, despite these shenanigans, robust formal institutions may well facilitate changes in the extent of autonomous judicial intervention in sensitive areas, enabling judges to set strict constitutional boundaries for the exercise of political power. But the content and effectiveness of these transformations are ultimately a function of the meaning judges ascribe to their new prerogatives. The reproduction of certain legal preferences by the judicial bureaucracy, and the promotion of others by sociopolitical groups can severely constrain the capacity of judges and prosecutors to develop jurisprudence that checks presidents, legislators, or the military (Hilbink 2012). Formal rules designed to insulate judges and prosecutors from external pressures can be rendered ineffective if informal behavioral norms deprive these actors of the motivations and skills to subject government policies to strong constitutionality tests (Couso 2010). As several of the case studies in the book indicate, formal institutional changes such as the constitutionalization of human rights treaties do not produce the desired effects in the absence of deeper cultural transformations that redefine perceptions about the possibilities for assertive behavior and provide principled reasons for taking risks.

In other words, regardless of the spirit and letter of the formal rules that govern how the bench is populated and how judges should behave, the notions of independence and impartiality only make sense in a world in which judges are other-worldly figures, fully abstracted from the social and political arenas. But this is precisely the world that appoints them, regulates the rules that frame their actions, denounces them, and interacts with them inside and outside the courtroom. If we take seriously the idea that the human resources and ideational makeup of courts are always the product of these interactions, struggles, and institutional choices, we might conclude that in complex, pluralistic societies it is hard to conceive of an insulated, politically neutral judicial branch. There is a deeper sociological sense in which impartiality or independence is more often than not an illusion: a valid normative aspiration, but a problematic concept to describe and analyze empirical reality.

Once we accept that courts are the product of sociopolitical struggles constitutive of their personnel, their ideologies, and their ideas about correct legal praxis, the focus of the analysis shifts from questions about the extent to which they can be independent, or the conditions that may foster impartiality, to the study of the origins and consequences of built-in biases that affect how judicial actors distribute power. In the human rights cases studied in this book, the outcomes were not the result of neutral and impartial decision making. Both pro– and anti–transitional justice rulings resulted from the predominance of legal cultures that favored the interests of those who, coming from the social and political world, and in alliance with members of the bench, actively engineered them. One should expect trade unions to try similar things when it comes to labor courts, religious groups to seek to influence the way family court judges think about important issues such as abortion, and political parties try to stock courts in charge of investigating corruption. The legal criteria that are systematically used in rulings on these various topics are most certainly not borne out of endogenous institutional dynamics or purely technical considerations, but out of virulent struggles to tame the bench.

The present study thus constitutes a call to think less about the formal architecture of courts, and the changes that are needed for courts to become stewards of impartial arbitration, and to pay more attention to the processes that lead to the consolidation of hegemonic legal discourses, and the implications of such transformations for the rights of individuals and groups. How courts think and whom they are willing to stand up for are the outcome of the interactions between judicial institutions and the nonjudicial world. We cannot fully understand the political impact of courts if we do not study the broader social and historical processes that craft courts' interests and identities, as well as their structural biases when deciding what power arrangements to endow with the legitimacy of authoritative constitutional interpretations.

BIBLIOGRAPHY

Abrão, Paulo, and Marcelo Torelly. 2012. "Resistance to Change: Brazil's Persistent Amnesty and Its Alternatives for Truth and Justice." In *Amnesty in the Age of Human Rights Accountability*, ed. Francesca Lessa and Leigh Payne. New York, NY: Cambridge University Press.

Abregú, Martín, and Christian Courtis, eds. 1997. *La aplicación de los tratados sobre derechos humanor por los tribunales locales.* Buenos Aires, Argentina: CELS.

Abuelas de Plaza de Mayo. 2007. *La historia de Abuelas: 30 años de búsqueda.* Buenos Aires, Argentina: Asociación Abuelas de Plaza de Mayo.

2009. *El papel del sistema de justicia frente a las violaciones masivas a los derechos humanos. problemáticas actuales.* Buenos Aires, Argentina: Asociación Abuelas de Plaza de Mayo.

Acharya, Amitav. 2004. "How Ideas Spread: Whose Norms Matter? Norm Localization and Institutional Change in Asian Regionalism." *International Organization* 58(2): 239–275.

Acuña, Carlos, and Catalina Smulovitz. 1995. "Militares en la transición Argentina: Del gobierno a la subordinación constitucional." In *Historizar el pasado vivo en América Latina*, ed. Anne Pérotin-Dumon. Buenos Aires, Argentina: Nueva Visión.

1997. "Guarding the Guardians in Argentina: Some Lessons about the Risks and Benefits of Empowering the Courts." In *Transitional Justice and the Rule of Law in New Democracies*, ed. A. J. McAdams. Notre Dame, IN: Notre Dame University Press.

ADC (Asociación por los Derechos Civiles). 2008. *La Corte Suprema y los derechos.* Buenos Aires, Argentina: Siglo XXI Editores.

Adler Lomnitz, Larissa, and Rodrigo Salazar. 2002. "Cultural Elements in the Practice of Law in Mexico: Informal Networks in a Formal System." In *Global Prescriptions: The Production, Exportation and Importation of a New Legal Orthodoxy*, ed. Yves Dezalay and Bryant Garth. Ann Arbor, MI: University of Michigan Press.

Aguayo, Sergio. 2001. *La Charola: Una historia de los servicios de inteligencia en Mexico.* Mexico D.F., Mexico: Grijalbo.

Aguayo, Servio, and Javier Treviño. 2007. "Fox y el pasado: Anatomía de una capitulación." *Foro Internacional* 47(4): 709–739.

Alcañíz, Isabella. 2012. "Democratization and Multilateral Security." *World Politics* 64(2): 306–340.

Alegre, Robert. 2013. *Railroad Radicals in Mexico: Gender, Class and Memory*. Lincoln, NB: University of Nebraska Press.

Alivizatos, Nicos C., and P. Nikiforos Diamandouros. 1997. "Politics and the Judiciary in the Greek Transition to Democracy." In *Transitional Justice and the Rule of Law in New Democracies*, ed. A. J. McAdams. Notre Dame, IN: Notre Dame University Press.

Ambos, Kai. 2009. "The Legal Framework of Transitional Justice: A Systematic Study with a Special Focus on the Role of the ICC." In *Building a Future on Peace and Justice: Studies on Transitional Justice, Peace and Development*, ed. Kai Ambos, Judith Large, and Marieke Wierda. Berlin, Germany: Springer.

Ambos, Kai, Judith Large, and Marieke Wierda, eds. 2009. *Building a Future on Peace and Justice: Studies on Transitional Justice, Peace and Development*. Berlin, Germany: Springer.

Amnesty International. 2001. *Universal Jurisdiction: The Duty of States to Enact and Implement Legislation*. London, UK: Amnesty International.

2009. "International Report: Regional Overview: Americas." www.amnesty.org/en/library/info/POL10/033/2009/en (last accessed 11 June 2012).

Anaya, Alejandro. 2006. "Hacia una nueva política exterior mexicana en materia de derechos humanos: Entrevista con Juan José Camacho." *Revista Iberoamericana de Derechos Humanos* 2: 187–203.

2012. *El país bajo presión: Debatiendo el paper del escrutinio internacional de derechos humanos sobre México*. Mexico D.F., Mexico: CIDE.

Ansolabehere, Karina. 2007. *La política desde la justicia: Cortes Supremas, gobierno y democracia en Argentina y México*. Mexico D.F., Mexico: FLACSO-Fontamara.

2010. "More Power, More Rights? The Supreme Court and Society in Mexico." In *Cultures of Legality: Judicialization and Political Activism in Latin America*, ed. Javier Couso, Alexandra Huneeus, and Rachel Sieder. New York, NY: Cambridge University Press.

Antillón, Ximena. 2008. *La desaparición forzada de Rosendo Radilla en Atoyac de Álvarez. Informe de Afectación Psicosocial*. Mexico D.F., Mexico: Comisión Mexicana de Defensa y Protección de los Derechos Humanos.

Aponte, Alejandro. 2010. "El Sistema Interamericano de Derechos Humanos y el Derecho Internacional Humanitario: Una relación problemática." In *Sistema Interamericano de Protección de los Derechos Humanos y Derecho Penal Internacional*, ed. Kai Ambos. Montevideo, Uruguay: Fundación Konrad Adenauer.

APRODEH (Asociación pro Derechos Humanos). 2008. *Podrán matar las flores, Peru nunca las cantutas: Los familiares del caso La Cantuta: Actores en el proceso de búsqueda de verdad y justicia*. Lima, Peru: APRODEH.

Baglini, Raúl and Hipólito Orlandi. 1993. *Juicio a la corte: Texto y fundamentos del pedido de juicio político promovido a los jueces de la Corte Suprema de Justicia de la Nación por Diputados Nacionales de la Unión Cívica Radical*. Buenos Aires, Argentina: R. Baglini.

Baird, Vanessa A. 2007. *Answering the Call of the Court: How Justices and Litigants Set the Supreme Court Agenda*. Charlottesville, VA: University of Virginia Press.

Barnett, Michael N., and Martha Finnemore. 2004. *Rules for the World: International Organizations in Global Politics*. Ithaca, NY: Cornell University Press.

Barrena, Guadalupe. 2007. "Oportunidades y retos para el litigio estratégico en México." In *El litigio estratégico en México*, ed. Alto Comisionado de las Naciones Unidas para los Derechos Humanos. Mexico D.F., Mexico: OACNUDH.

Bassiouni, M. Cherif. 1986. *International Criminal Law*. Dobbs Ferry, NY: Transnational.

1996. "International Crimes: 'Jus Cogens' and 'Obligatio Erga Omnes'." *Law and Contemporary Problems* 59(4): 63–74.

2002. *Post-Conflict Justice*. Ardsley, NY: Transnational.

2003. *Introduction to International Criminal Law*. Ardsley, NY: Transnational.

2011. *Crimes against Humanity: Historical Evolution and Contemporary Application*. New York, NY: Cambridge University Press.

Baum, Lawrence. 1994. "What Judges Want: Judges' Goals and Judicial Behavior" *Political Research Quarterly* 47: 749–768.

2006. *Judges and Their Audiences: A Perspective on Judicial Behavior*. Princeton, NJ: Princeton University Press.

Beissinger, Mark R. 2002. *Nationalist Mobilization and the Collapse of the Soviet State*. New York, NY: Cambridge University Press.

Bergara, Mario, Barak Richman, and Pablo T. Spiller. 2003. "Modeling Supreme Court Strategic Decision Making: The Congressional Constraint." *Legislative Studies Quarterly* 28(2): 247–280.

Berman, Sheri. 1998. *The Social Democratic Movement: Ideas and Politics in the Making of Interwar Europe*. Cambridge, MA: Harvard University Press.

Bierbrauer, Gunter. 1994. "Toward an Understanding of Legal Culture: Variations in Individualism and Collectivism between Kurds, Lebanese and Germans." *Law and Society Review* 28(2): 243–264.

Bimbi, Bruno. 2010. *Matrimonio igualitario*. Buenos Aires, Argentina: Grupo Editorial Planeta.

Bourdieu, Pierre. 1977. *Outline of a Theory of Practice*. New York, NY: Cambridge University Press.

1984. *Distinction: A Social Critique of the Judgement of Taste*. Cambridge, MA: Harvard University Press.

1986. "The Force of Law: Toward a Sociology of the Juridical Field." *Hastings Law Journal* 38: 805.

Bourdieu, Pierre, and Jean-Claude Passeron. 1977. *Reproduction in Education, Culture and Society*. London: Sage.

Bourdieu, Pierre, and Loïc J. D. Wacquant. 1992. *An Invitation to Reflexive Sociology*. Chicago, IL: University of Chicago Press.

Brinks, Daniel. 2008. *The Judicial Response to Police Killings in Latin America: Inequality and the Rule of Law*. New York, NY: Cambridge University Press.

2011. "Faithful Servants of the Regime: The Brazilian Constitutional Court's Role under the 1988 Constitution." In *Courts in Latin America*, ed. Gretchen Helmke and Julio Ríos Figueroa. New York, NY: Cambridge University Press.

Brinks, Daniel M., and Michael Coppedge. 2006. "Diffusion Is No Illusion: Neighbor Emulation in the Third Wave of Democracy." *Comparative Political Studies* 39(4) (May 1): 463–489.

Brysk, Alison. 1990. *The Political Impact of Argentina's Human Rights Movement: Social Movements, Transition and Democratization*. Stanford, CA: Stanford University Press.

1994. *The Politics of Human Rights in Argentina: Protest, Change, and Democratization*. Stanford, CA: Stanford University Press.

2005. *Human Rights and Private Wrongs: Constructing Global Civil Society*. New York, NY: Routledge.

Bunce, Valerie, and Sharon Wolchik. 2011. *Defeating Authoritarian Leaders in Postcommunist Countries*. New York, NY: Cambridge University Press.

Burstein, Paul. 1991. "Legal Mobilization as a Social Movement Tactic: The Struggle for Equal Employment Opportunity." *American Journal of Sociology* 96(5): 1201–1225.

Burt, Jo-Marie. 2007. *Political Violence and the Authoritarian State in Peru: Silencing Civil Society*. New York, NY: Palgrave Macmillan.

2009. "Guilty as Charged: The Trial of Former Peruvian President Alberto Fujimori for Human Rights Violations." *International Journal of Transitional Justice* 3(3): 384–405.

Bybee, Keith. 2010. *All Judges Are Political - Except When They Are Not: Acceptable Hypocrisies and the Rule of Law*. Palo Alto, CA: Stanford University Press.

Caballero, José Luis. 2009. *La incorporación de los tratados internacionales sobre derechos humanos en España y México*. Mexico D.F., Mexico: Editorial Porrúa.

Cameron, Charles M. 2002. "Judicial Independence: How Can You Tell It When You See It?" In *Judicial Independence at the Crossroads: An Interdisciplinary Approach*, ed. Stephen Burbank and Barry Friedman. Thousand Oaks, CA: Sage.

Camp, Roderic. 2003. *Politics in Mexico: The Democratic Transformation*. Oxford, UK: Oxford University Press.

Carbonell, Miguel. 2000. *Constitución, reforma constitucional y fuentes del derecho en México*. Mexico D.F., Mexico: Porrúa.

Cardenas, Sonia. 2007. *Conflict and Compliance: State Responses to International Human Rights Pressures*. Philadelphia, PA: University of Pennsylvania Press.

Carothers, Thomas. 1999. *Aiding Democracy Abroad: The Learning Curve*. Washington, DC: Carnegie Endowment for International Peace.

Carrillo Prieto, Ignacio. 2009. *La fiscalía especial para movimientos sociales y políticos del pasado*. Mimeo.

Carrió, Alejandro. 1996. *La Corte Suprema y su independencia: Un análisis a través de la historia*. Buenos Aires: Abeledo-Perrot.

Carrión, Julio, ed. 2006. *The Fujimori Legacy: The Rise of Electoral Authoritarianism in Peru*. University Park, PA: Pennsylvania State University Press.

Cassel, Douglass. 1996. "Lessons from the Americas: Guidelines for International Response to Amnesties for Atrocities." *Law and Contemporary Problems* 59: 197–224.

Castellanos, Laura. 2007. *México armado 1943–1981*. Mexico D.F., Mexico: Ediciones Era.

CEJIL. 2011. "Condena contra militares guatemaltecos en el caso de la masacre de las dos erres representa un avance para la justicia." http://cejil.org/comunicados/condena-contra-militares-guatemaltecos-en-el-caso-de-la-masacre-de-las-dos-erres-represe (last accessed 11 June 2012).

CELS (Centro de Estudios Legales y Sociales).1995a. *Informe anual sobre la situación de los derechos humanos en la Argentina*. Buenos Aires, Argentina: Centro de Estudios Legales y Sociales.

1995b. *Informe sobre la situación de los derechos humanos en la Argentina*. Buenos Aires, Argentina: Centro de Estudios Legales y Sociales.

1998. *Informe sobre la situación de los derechos humanos en Argentina*. Buenos Aires, Argentina: Centro de Estudios Legales y Sociales.

1999 *Derechos humanos en Argentina. Informe anual*. Buenos Aires, Argentina: Centro de Estudios Legales y Sociales/EUDEBA.

2000. *La situación de los derechos humanos en Argentina. Informe anual*. Buenos Aires, Argentina: Centro de Estudios Legales y Sociales.

2001. *La situación de los derechos humanos en Argentina. Informe anual*. Buenos Aires, Argentina: Centro de Estudios Legales y Sociales.

2008a. *Derechos humanos en Argentina. Informe anual*. Buenos Aires, Argentina: Centro de Estudios Legales y Sociales.

2008b. *La lucha por el derecho: Litigio estratégico y derechos humanos*. Buenos Aires, Argentina: Siglo Veintiuno.

2010. *Derechos humanos en Argentina. Informe anual*. Buenos Aires, Argentina: Siglo XXI Editores.

2011. *Derechos humanos en Argentina. Informe anual*. Buenos Aires, Argentina: Siglo XXI Editores.

Centro Agustín Pro et al. 2006. *Esclarecimiento y sanción de los delitos del pasado durante el sexenio 2000–2006*. Mexico D.F., Mexico.

Centro de Estudios Legales y Sociales et al. 2002. "Una Corte Para La Democracia." www.adc.org.ar/2013/wp-content/uploads/2014/04/Una-Corte-para-la-Democracia-I.pdf (last accessed 11 February 2015).

Chávez, Rebecca Bill. 2003. "The Construction of the Rule of Law in Argentina: A Tale of Two Provinces." *Comparative Politics* 35(4): 417–437.

2004. *The Rule of Law in Nascent Democracies: Judicial Politics in Argentina*. Stanford, CA: Stanford University Press.

Chávez, Rebecca Bill, John Ferejohn, and Barry R. Weingast. 2011. "A Theory of the Politically Independent Judiciary: A Comparative Study of the United States and Argentina." In *Courts in Latin America*, ed. Gretchen Helmke and Julio Ríos Figueroa. New York, NY: Cambridge University Press.

Checkel, Jeffrey. 1997. "International Norms and Domestic Politics: Bridging the Rationalist-Constructivist Divide." *European Journal of International Relations* 3(4): 473–495.

2005. "International Institutions and Socialization in Europe: Introduction and Framework." *International Organization* 59(4): 801–826.

Cichowski, Rachel A. 2007. *The European Court and Civil Society: Litigation, Mobilization and Governance*. New York, NY: Cambridge University Press.

Clayton, Cornell W. 1992. *The Politics of Justice: The Attorney General and the Making of Legal Policy*. Armonk, NY: M. E. Sharpe.

Clayton, Cornell W., and Howard Gillman. 1999. *Supreme Court Decision-Making: New Institutionalist Approaches*. Chicago, IL: University of Chicago Press.

Cohen, Stanley. 1995. "State Crimes of Previous Regimes: Knowledge, Accountability and the Policing of the Past." *Law and Social Inquiry* 20(1): 7–50.

Collins, Cath. 2010. *Post-Transitional Justice: Human Rights Trials in Chile and El Salvador*. University Park, PA: Pennsylvania State University Press.

Comisión de la Verdad y Reconciliación. 2003. *Informe final*. Lima, Peru: Comisión de la Verdad y Reconciliación.

Comité 68. 2008. *México: Genocidio y delitos de lesa humanidad. Documentos básicos 1968–2008*. Mexico D.F., Mexico: Comité 68 pro Libertades Democráticas A.C.

CONADEP (Comisión Nacional sobre la Desaparición de Personas). 1984. *Nunca Más: Informe de la Comisión Nacional sobre la Desaparición de Personas*. Buenos Aires: EUDEBA.

Conaghan, Catherine M. 1998. "The Permanent Coup: Peru's Road to Presidential Reelection." *LASA Forum* 29 1: 5–9.

2002. "Cashing in on Authoritarianism: Media Collusion in Fujimori's Peru." *Harvard International Journal of Press/Politics* 7(1): 115–125.

Conaghan, Catherine M., and Carlos Basombrío Iglesias. 1996. "Public Life in the Time of Alberto Fujimori." *Woodrow Wilson International Center for Scholars, Latin American Program, Working Paper Series*. Working Paper No. 219.

Cortell, Andrew, and James Davis. 2000. "Understanding the Domestic Impact of International Norms: A Research Agenda." *International Studies Review* 2(1): 65–87.

Cotler, Julio, and Romeo Grompone. 2000. *El Fujimorismo: Ascenso y Caída de un Régimen Autoritario*. Lima, Peru: Instituto de Estudios Peruanos.

Couso, Javier. 2007. "The Role of Chile's Legal Complex in the Configuration of a Moderate State." In *Fighting for Political Freedom: Comparative Studies of the Legal Complex and Political Liberalism*, ed. Terence C. Halliday, Lucien Karpik, and Malcolm M. Feeley. Portland, OR: Hart.

2010. "The Transformation of Constitutional Discourse and the Judicialization of Politics in Latin America." In *Cultures of Legality: Judicialization and Political Activism in Latin America*, ed. Javier Couso, Alexandra Huneeus, and Rachel Sieder. New York, NY: Cambridge University Press.

Couso, Javier, and Lisa Hilbink. 2011. "From Quietism to Incipient Activism The Institutional and Ideological Roots of Rights Adjudication in Chile." In *Courts in Latin America*, ed. Gretchen Helmke and Julio Ríos Figueroa. New York, NY: Cambridge University Press.

Covarrubias, Ana. 2003. "La política mexicana hacia Cuba durante el gobierno de Salinas de Gortari." *Foro Internacional* 34(4): 652–682.

Cuneo. Andrés. 1980. "La Corte Suprema de Chile, sus percepciones acerca del derecho, su rol en el sistema legal, y la relación de éste con el sistema político." In *La administración de justicia en América Latina*, ed. Universidad de Costa Rica. San José, Costa Rica: Universidad de Costa Rica.

Dargent, Eduardo. 2009. "Determinants of Judicial Independence: Lessons from Three 'Cases' of Constitutional Courts in Peru (1982–2007)." *Journal of Latin American Studies* 41(02): 251–278.

De la Barreda Solórzano, Luis. 2008. *El pequeño inquisidor*. Mexico D.F., Mexico: Océano.

De la Jara, Ernesto. 2001. *Memoria y batallas en nombre de los inocentes, Perú 1992–2001*. Lima, Peru: Instituto de Defensa Legal.

Defensoría del Pueblo. 2001. *Aministías vs. Derechos Humanos: Buscando Justicia*. Lima, Peru: Defensoría del Pueblo.

Deitelhoff, Nicole. 2009. "The Discursive Process of Legalization: Charting Islands of Persuasion in the ICC Case." *International Organization* 63(01): 33–65.

Dezalay, Yves, and Bryant G. Garth. 1998. "Argentine Law at the Periphery and Law in Dependencies: Political and Economic Crisis and the Instrumentalization and Fragmentation of Law." American Bar Foundation. Working Papers. No. 9708.

DiMaggio, Paul, and Walter Powell, eds. 1991. *The New Institutionalism in Organizational Analysis*. Chicago, IL: University of Chicago Press.

Dodson, Michael. 2002. "Assessing Judicial Reform in Latin America." *Latin American Research Review* 37(2): 200–220.

Domingo, Pilar. 1999. "Judicial Independence and Judicial Reform in Latin America." In *The Self-Restraining State: Power and Accountability in New Democracies*, ed. Andreas Schedler, Larry Jay Diamond, and Marc F. Plattner. Boulder, CO: Lynne Rienner.

2000. "Judicial Independence: The Politics of the Supreme Court in Mexico." *Journal of Latin American Studies* 32(3): 705–735.

Domingo, Pilar, and Rachel Sieder, eds. 2001. *Rule of Law in Latin America: The International Promotion of Judicial Reform*. London: Institute of Latin American Studies.

Dondé, Javier. 2010. "El concepto de impunidad: Amnistía y otras formas estudiadas por la Corte Interamericana de Derechos Humanos." In *Sistema Interamericano de Protección de los Derechos Humanos y Derecho Penal Internacional*, ed. Kai Ambos. Montevideo, Uruguay: Fundación Konrad Adenauer.

Donnelly, Jack. 1986. "International Human Rights: A Regime Analysis." *International Organization* 40(03): 599–642.

DPLF (Due Process of Law Foundation). 2010. *Digesto de jurisprudencia latinoamérica sobre crímenes de derecho internacional*. Washington, DC: DPLF.

Dutrenit Bielous, Silvia, and Gonzalo Varela Petito. 2010. *Tramitando el pasado: Violaciones de los derechos humanos y agendas gubernamentales en casos latinoamericanos*. Mexico D.F., Mexico: Flacso México/Clacso.

Eliaschev, Pepe. 2011. *Los hombres del juicio*. Buenos Aires, Argentina: Sudamericana.

Elster, Jon. 2004. *Closing the Books: Transitional Justice in Historical Perspective*. New York, NY: Cambridge University Press.

2006. *Retribution and Reparation in the Transition to Democracy*. New York, NY: Cambridge University Press.

Epp, Charles R. 1998. *The Rights Revolution: Lawyers, Activists, and Supreme Courts in Comparative Perspective*. Chicago, IL: University of Chicago Press.

2009. *Making Rights Real: Activists, Bureaucrats, and the Creation of the Legalistic State*. Chicago, IL: University of Chicago Press.

Epstein, Lee, and Jack Knight. 1998. *The Choices Justices Make*. Washington, DC: CQ Press.

2013. "Reconsidering Judicial Preferences." *Annual Review of Political Science* 16: 11–31.

Epstein, Lee, Jack Knight, and Andrew D. Martin. 2001a. "The Supreme Court as a Strategic National Policymaker." *Emory Law Journal* 50: 583–612.

Epstein, Lee, Jack Knight, and Olga Shvetsova. 2001b. "The Role of Constitutional Courts in the Establishment and Maintenance of Democratic Systems of Government." *Law & Society Review* 35(1): 117–164.

Espinoza, Julio. 2010. "La actividad probatoria en procesos por violaciones de derechos humanos: El juicio contra Alberto Fujimori." In *Judicialización de violaciones de derechos humanos: Aportes sustantivos y procesales*, ed. Víctor Quinteros. Lima, Peru: Instituto de Derechos Humanos de la Pontificia Universidad Católica del Perú.

Evans, Rebecca. 2007. "Treating Poorly Healed Wounds: Partisan Choices and Human Rights Policies in Latin America." *Human Rights Review* 8(3): 249–276.

Ferejohn, J. 1998. "Independent Judges, Dependent Judiciary: Explaining Judicial Independence." *Southern California. Law Review* 72: 353.

Ferejohn, J. A., and B. R. Weingast. 1992. "A Positive Theory of Statutory Interpretation." *International Review of Law and Economics* 12(2): 263–279.

Fernández Meijide, Graciela. 2009. *La historia íntima de los derechos humanos en la Argentina: A Pablo*. Buenos Aires, Argentina: Editorial Sudamericana.

Ferreira Rubio, Delia, and Mateo Goretti. 1998. "When the President Governs Alone: The Decretazo in Argentina, 1989–93." In *Executive Decree Authority*, ed. John Carey and Matthew Soberg Shugart. New York, NY: Cambridge University Press.

Filippini, Leonardo. 2006. "El Derecho Internacional de los Derechos Humanos no es un préstamo." *Revista Jurídica de la Universidad de Palermo* 7(2): 191–202.

2007. "Argentina." In *Víctimas sin mordaza: El impacto del Sistema Interamericano en la jusiticia transicional en latinoamérica: Los casos de Argentina, Guatemala, El Salvador y Perú*, ed. Fundación para el Debido Proceso Legal. Washington, D.C.: Fundación para el Debido Proceso Legal.

Finkel, Jodi. 2003. "Supreme Court Decisions on Electoral Rules after Mexico's 1994 Judicial Reform: An Empowered Court." *Journal of Latin American Studies* 35(04): 777–799.

2004. "Judicial Reform in Argentina in the 1990s: How Electoral Incentives Shape Institutional Change." *Latin American Research Review* 39(3): 56–80.

2008. *Judicial Reform as Political Insurance*. Notre Dame, IN: University of Notre Dame Press.

Finnemore, Martha. 1993. "International Organizations as Teachers of Norms: The United Nations Educational, Scientific, and Cultural Organization and Science Policy." *International Organization* 47(4): 565–597.

1996. *National Interests in International Society*. Cornell Studies in Political Economy. Ithaca, NY: Cornell University Press.

Fiss, O. M. 1993. "The Limits of Judicial Independence." *University of Miami Inter-American Law Review* 25(1): 57–76.

Friedman, Barry. 2006. "Taking Law Seriously." *Perspectives on Politics* 4(2): 261–276.

García Iommi, Lucrecia. 2012. *Thinking Institutions in 3-D*. Ph.D. Dissertation. Department of Political Science, University of Notre Dame.

García Villegas, Mauricio, and Rodrigo Uprimny. 2004. *Corte Constitucional y emancipación social en Colombia*. Bogotá, Colombia: Editorial Norma.

Gargarella, Roberto, Pilar Domingo, and Theunis Roux, eds. 2006. *Courts and Social Transformation in New Democracies: An Institutional Voice for the Poor?* Burlington, VT: Ashgate.

Garro, Alejandro Miguel, and Enrique Dahl. 1987a. "Argentine Judgment on Human Rights Violations by Former Military Leaders." *International Legal Materials* 26: 317–372.

1987b. "Legal Accountability for Human Rights Violations in Argentina: One Step Forward and Two Steps Backward." *Human Rights Law Journal* 8: 283–344.

Gauri, Varun, and Daniel M. Brinks. 2008. *Courting Social Justice: Judicial Enforcement of Social and Economic Rights in the Developing World*. New York, NY: Cambridge University Press.

George, Alexander L., and Andrew Bennett. 2004. *Case Studies and Theory Development in the Social Sciences*. Cambridge, MA: MIT Press.

Gheciu, Alexandra. 2005. "Security Institutions as Agents of Socialization? NATO and the New Europe." *International Organization* 59(4): 973–1012.

Gibson, James L., and Gregory A. Caldeira. 2009. *Citizens, Courts, and Confirmations: Positivity Theory and the Judgments of the American People*. Princeton, NJ: Princeton University Press.

Giddens, Anthony. 1979. *Central Problems in Social Theory: Action, Structure and Contradiction in Social Analysis*. London, UK: Macmillan.

1984. *The Constitution of Society: Outline of the Theory of Structuration*. Berkeley, CA: University of California Press.

Gill, Lesley. 2004. *The School of the Americas: Military Training and Political Violence in the Americas*. Durham, NC: Duke University Press.

Gillman, Howard. 1993. *The Constitution Besieged: The Rise and Demise of Lochner Era Police Powers Jurisprudence*. Durham, NC: Duke University Press.

1999. "The Court as an Idea, Not a Building (or a Game): Interpretive Institutionalism and the Analysis of Supreme Court Decision-Making." In *Supreme Court Decision-Making: New Institutionalist Approaches*, ed. Cornell W. Clayton and Howard Gillman. Chicago, IL: University of Chicago Press.

2002. "How Political Parties Can Use the Courts to Advance Their Agendas: Federal Courts in the United States, 1875–1891." *American Political Science Review* 96(3): 511–524.

2008. "Courts and the Politics of Partisan Coalitions." In *The Oxford Handbook of Law and Politics*, ed. Keith E. Whittington, R. Daniel Kelemen, and Gregory A. Caldeira. New York, NY: Oxford University Press.

Ginsburg, Tom. 2003. *Judicial Review in New Democracies: Constitutional Courts in Asian Cases*. New York, NY: Cambridge University Press.

2008. "The Global Spread of Constitutional Review." In *The Oxford Handbook of Law and Politics*, ed. Keith E. Whittington, R. Daniel Kelemen, and Gregory A. Caldeira. New York, NY: Oxford University Press.

Glasius, Marlies. 2005. *The International Criminal Court: A Global Civil Society Achievement*. Hoboken: Taylor & Francis.

Glendon, Mary A. 2008. "The Forgotten Crucible: The Latin American Influence on the Universal Human Rights Idea." *Harvard Human Rights Journal* 16: 27.

Goffman, Erving. 1974. *Frame Analysis*. Cambridge, MA: Harvard University Press.

Goldman, Robert. 2009. "History and Action: The Inter-American Human Rights System and the Role of the Inter-American Commission on Human Rights." *Human Rights Quarterly* 31(4): 856–887.

Goodman, Ryan, and Derek Jinks. 2013. *Socializing States: Promoting Human Rights through International Law*. Oxford: Oxford University Press.

Graham, Randal. 2009. "What Judges Want: Judicial Self-Interest and Statutory Interpretation." *Statute Law Review* 30(1): 38–72.

Greene, Kenneth. 2007. *Why Dominant Parties Lose: Mexico's Democratization in Comparative Perspective*. New York, NY: Cambridge University Press.

Guzmán Dálbora, José Luis. 2010. "El principio de legalidad penal en la jurisprudencia de la Corte Interamericana de Derechos Humanos." In *Sistema Interamericano de Protección de los Derechos Humanos y Derecho Penal Internacional*, ed. Kai Ambos. Montevideo, Uruguay: Fundación Konrad Adenauer.

Haas, Peter M. 1992. "Knowledge, Power, and International Policy Coordination. Special Issue." *International Organization* 46(1)

Hall, Peter A. 2003. "Aligning Ontology and Methodology in Comparative Research." In *Comparative Historical Analysis in the Social Sciences*, ed. James Mahoney and Dietrich Rueschemeyer. New York, NY: Cambridge University Press.

Hall, Peter A., and Rosemary C. R. Taylor. 1996. "Political Science and the Three New Institutionalisms." *Political Studies* 44(5): 936–957.

Halliday, Terence C., Lucien Karpik, and Malcolm M. Feeley, eds. 2007. *Fighting for Political Freedom: Comparative Studies of the Legal Complex and Political Liberalism*. Portland, OR: Hart.

Hammergren, Linn A. 1998. *The Politics of Justice and Justice Reform in Latin America: The Peruvian Case in Comparative Perspective*. Boulder, CO: Westview Press.

2007. *Envisioning Reform: Improving Judicial Performance in Latin America*. University Park, PA: Pennsylvania State University Press.

Hattam, Victoria Charlotte. 1993. *Labor Visions and State Power: The Origins of Business Unionism in the United States*. Princeton, NJ: Princeton University Press.

Hayner, Priscilla. 2002. *Unspeakable Truths: Facing the Challenge of Truth Commissions*. New York, NY: Routledge.

Hellman, Judith. 1983. *Mexico in Crisis*. New York, NY: Holmes and Meier.

Helmke, Gretchen. 2005. *Courts under Constraints: Judges, Generals, and Presidents in Argentina*. New York, NY: Cambridge University Press.

Helmke, Gretchen, and Levitsky. 2006. "Introduction." In *Informal Institutions and Democracy: Lessons from Latin America*, ed. Gretchen Helmke and Steven Levitsky. Baltimore, MD: Johns Hopkins University Press.

Helmke, Gretchen, and Frances Rosenbluth. 2009. "Regimes and the Rule of Law: Judicial Independence in Comparative Perspective." *Annual Review of Political Science* 12: 345–366.

Helmke, Gretchen, and Jeffrey K. Staton. 2011. "The Puzzling Judicial Politics of Latin America: A Theory of Litigation, Judicial Decisions and Interbranch Conflict." In *Courts in Latin America*, ed. Gretchen Helmke and Julio Ríos Figueroa. New York, NY: Cambridge University Press.

Hilbink, Lisa. 2007a. *Judges beyond Politics in Democracy and Dictatorship: Lessons from Chile*. New York, NY: Cambridge University Press.

2007b. "Politicizing Law to Liberalize Politics: Anti-Francoist Judges and Prosecutors in Spain's Democratic Transition." In *Fighting for Political Freedom: Comparative*

Studies of the Legal Complex and Political Liberalism, ed. Terence C. Halliday, Lucien Karpik, and Malcolm M. Feeley. Portland, OR: Hart.

2012. "The Origins of Positive Judicial Independence." *World Politics* 64(4): 587–621.

Hirschl, Ran. 2004. *Towards Juristocracy: The Origins and Consequences of the New Constitutionalism*. Cambridge, MA: Harvard University Press.

Hoffmann, Florian F., and Fernando R. Bentes. 2008. "Accountability for Social and Economic Rights in Brazil." In *Courting Social Justice: Judicial Enforcement of Social and Economic Rights in the Developing World*, ed. Varun Gauri and Daniel Brinks. New York, NY: Cambridge University Press.

Human Rights Watch. 2003. *Justice in Jeopardy: Why Mexico's First Real Effort to Address Past Abuses Risks Becoming Its Latest Failure*. Washington, DC: Human Rights Watch.

2006. *Lost in Transition: Bold Ambitions, Limited Results for Human Rights under Fox*. Washington, DC: Human Rights Watch.

2009. "Presunción Fundada." www.hrw.org/en/reports/2005/12/20/presunci-n-fundada (last accessed 11 June 2012).

Humphrey, John. 1984. *Human Rights and the United Nations: A Great Adventure*. Dobbs Ferry, NY: Transnational.

Huneeus, Alexandra. 2010a. "Rejecting the Inter-American Court: Judicialization, National Courts and Regional Human Rights." In *Cultures of Legality: Judicialization and Political Activism in Latin America*, ed. Javier Couso, Alexandra Huneeus, and Rachel Sieder. New York, NY: Cambridge University Press.

2010b. "Judging from a Guilty Conscience: The Chilean Judiciary's Human Rights Turn." *Law & Social Inquiry* 35(1): 99–135.

Huntington, Samuel P. 1991. *The Third Wave: Democratization in the Late Twentieth Century*. Norman, OK: University of Oklahoma Press.

Iaryczower, Matías, Pablo T. Spiller, and Mariano Tommasi. 2002. "Judicial Independence in Unstable Environments, Argentina 1935–1998." *American Journal of Political Science* 46(4): 699–716.

Ingram, Matthew. 2012. "Crafting Courts in New Democracies: Ideology and Judicial Council Reforms in Three Mexican States." *Comparative Politics* 44(4): 439–458.

Jelin, Elizabeth. 1994. "The Politics of Memory: The Human Rights Movements and the Construction of Democracy in Argentina." *Latin American Perspectives* 21(2): 38–58.

Johnson, Timothy R., Paul J. Wahlbeck, and James F. Spriggs. 2006. "The Influence of Oral Arguments on the U.S. Supreme Court." *American Political Science Review* 100(1): 99–113.

Justicia Viva. 2006. *Cambios en el sistema de justicia: Entre la expectativa y la incertidumbre*. Lima, Peru: Consorcio Justicia Viva.

2009. *Balance 2008 del Tribunal Constitucional Peruano: El TC que se nos fue y el TC que viene*. Lima, Peru: Consorcio Justicia Viva.

Kahn, Ronald. 1999. "Institutionalized Norms and Supreme Court Decision Making: The Rehnquist Court on Privacy and Religion." In *Supreme Court Decision Making: New Institutionalist Approaches*, ed. Cornell Clayton and Howard Gillman. Chicago, IL: University of Chicago Press.

Kapiszewski, Diana. 2012. *High Courts and Economic Governance in Argentina and Brazil*. New York, NY: Cambridge University Press.

Kapiszewski, Diana, and Matthew M. Taylor. 2008. "Doing Courts Justice? Studying Judicial Politics in Latin America." *Perspectives on Politics* 6(04): 741–767.

Kastellec, Jonathan. 2011. "Hierarchical and Collegial Politics in the US Courts of Appeals." *Journal of Politics* 73(2): 345–361.

Karl, Terry Lynn. 2007. "Panel: The Justice Cascade in Latin America." *Santa Clara Journal of International Law* 5(2): 345–362.

Karl, Terry Lynn, and Philippe C. Schmitter. 1991. "Modes of Transition in Latin America, Southern and Eastern Europe." *International Social Science Journal* 128(2): 267–282.

Keck, Margaret E., and Kathryn Sikkink. 1998. *Activists beyond Borders: Advocacy Networks in International Politics*. Ithaca, NY: Cornell University Press.

Kim, Hun Joon. 2012. "Structural Determinants of Human Rights Prosecutions after Democratic Transitions." *Journal of Peace Research* 49(2): 305–320.

Kim, Hun Joon, and Kathryh Sikkink. 2010. "Explaining the Deterrence Effect of Human Rights Prosecutions for Transitional Countries." *International Studies Quarterly* 54(4): 939–963.

Kok, Ruth A. 2007. *Statutory Limitations in International Criminal Law*. New York, NY: Cambridge University Press.

Kopstein, Jeffrey, and David Reilly. 2000. "Geographic Diffusion and the Transformation of the Post-Communist World." *World Politics* 53(1): 1–37.

Larkins, Christopher. 1996. "Judicial Independence and Democratization: A Theoretical and Conceptual Analysis." *American Journal of Comparative Law* 44(4): 605–626.

Lax, Jeffrey. 2011. "The New Judicial Politics of Legal Doctrine." *Annual Review of Political Science* 14: 131–157.

Legro, Jeffrey. 1997. "Which Norms Matter? Revisiting the Failure of Internationalism." *International Organization* 51(1): 31–63.

Lessa, Francesca. 2013. *Against Impunity: Memory and Transitional Justice in Argentina and Uruguay*. London: Palgrave Macmillan.

Lessa, Francesca, Tricia Olsen, Leigh Payne, Gabriel Pereira, and Andrew Reiter. 2014. "Overcoming Impunity: Pathways to Accountability in Latin America." *International Journal of Transitional Justice*, 8: 75–98.

Lessa, Francesca, and Leigh Payne, eds. 2012. *Amnesty in the Age of Human Rights Accountability*. New York, NY: Cambridge University Press.

Levitsky, Steven. 2003. *Transforming Labor-Based Parties in Latin America: Argentine Peronism in Comparative Perspective*. New York, NY: Cambridge University Press.

2005. "Argentina: Democratic Survival amidst Economic Failure." In *The Third Wave of Democratization in Latin America: Advances and Setbacks*, ed. Frances Hagopian and Scott Mainwaring. New York, NY: Cambridge University Press.

Levitsky, Steven, and Lucan Way. 2010. *Competitive Authoritarianism: Hybrid Regimes after the Cold War*. New York, NY: Cambridge University Press.

Linz, Juan J., and Alfred Stepan. 1996. *Problems of Democratic Transition and Consolidation: Southern Europe, South America, and Post-Communist Europe*. Baltimore, MD: Johns Hopkins University Press.

Llanos, Mariana, and Constanza Figueroa Schibber. 2008. "La participación de la presidencia y el senado en el nombramiento del Poder Judicial." *Desarrollo Económico* 47(188): 607–637.

López Medina, Diego Eduardo. 2004. *Teoría impura del derecho: La transformación de la cultura jurídica jatinoamerica*. Bogotá, Colombia: Legis.

Lovatón, David. 2003. "Cambios en el sistema de justicia y sociedad civil en Perú (1990–2002), informe de Perú." In *Justicia y sociedad civil: El papel de la sociedad civil en la reforma judicial: Estudios de casos en Argentina, Chile, Colombia y Perú*, ed. Luis Pásara. Buenos Aires, Argentina: CEJA.

Lutz, Ellen L., and Kathryn Sikkink. 2000. "International Human Rights Law and Practice in Latin America." *International Organization* 54(3): 633–659.

2001. "The Justice Cascade: The Evolution and Impact of Foreign Human Rights Trials in Latin America." *Chicago Journal of International Law* 2: 1–33.

Magaloni, Ana Laura. 2007. "¿Por qué la Suprema Corte no ha sido un instrumento para la defensa de los derechos fundamentales?" Serie Documentos de Trabajo, Centro de Investigación y Docencia Económicas.

Magaloni, Beatriz. 2003. "Authoritarianism, Democracy and the Supreme Court: Horizontal Exchange and the Rule of Law in Mexico." In *Democratic Accountability in Latin America*, ed. Scott Mainwaring and Christopher Welna. New York, NY: Oxford University Press.

2007. *Voting for Autocracy*. New York, NY: Cambridge University Press.

2008. "Enforcing Autocratic Political Order and the Role of Courts: The Case of Mexico." In *Rule by Law: The Politics of Courts in Authoritarian Regimes*, ed. Tom Ginsburg and Tamir Moustafa. New York, NY: Cambridge University Press.

Mahoney, James, and Gary Goertz. 2004. "The Possibility Principle: Choosing Negative Cases in Comparative Research." *American Political Science Review* 98(4): 653–669.

Mainwaring, Scott, and Aníbal Pérez-Liñán. 2013. *Democracies and Dictatorships in Latin America: Emergence, Survival and Fall*. New York, NY: Cambridge University Press.

Malarino, Ezequiel. 2010. "Activismo judicial, punitivización y nacionalización. Tendencias antidemocráticas y antiliberales de la Corte Interamericana de Derechos Humanos." In *Sistema Interamericano de Protección de los Derechos*

Humanos y Derecho Penal Internacional, ed. Kai Ambos. Montevideo, Uruguay: Fundación Konrad Adenauer.

Mallinder, Louise. 2009. "Exploring the Practice of States in Introducing Amnesties." In *Building a Future on Peace and Justice: Studies on Transitional Justice, Peace and Development*, ed. Kai Ambos, Judith Large, and Marieke Wierda. Berlin, Germany: Springer.

Manzetti, Luigi. 1993. *Institutions, Parties, and Coalitions in Argentine Politics*. Pittsburgh, PA: University of Pittsburgh Press.

March, James G., and Johan P. Olsen. 1984. "The New Institutionalism: Organizatio nal Factors in Political Life." *American Political Science Review* 78(3): 734–749.

McAdam, Doug. 1982. *Political Process and the Development of Black Insurgency, 1930–1970*. Chicago, IL: University of Chicago Press.

McCann, Michael W. 1994. *Rights at Work: Pay Equity Reform and the Politics of Legal Mobilization*. Chicago, IL: University of Chicago Press.

McGuire, James W. 1997. *Peronism without Perón: Unions, Parties, and Democracy in Argentina*. Stanford, CA: Stanford University Press.

Meléndez, Carlos, and Carlos León. 2009. "Perú 2008: El juego de ajedrez de la gobernabilidad en partidas simultáneas." *Revista de Ciencia Política* 29(2): 591–609.

2010. "Perú 2009: Los legados del autoritarismo." *Revista de Ciencia Política* 30(2): 451–477.

Méndez, Juan. 1997. "In Defense of Transitional Justice." In *Transitional Justice and the Rule of Law in New Democracies*, ed. A. J. McAdams. Notre Dame, IN: Notre Dame University Press.

Meron, Theodor. 2000. "The Humanization of Humanitarian Law." *American Journal of International Law* 94(2) (April 1): 239–278.

Mettraux, Guénaël. 2009. *The Law of Command Responsibility*. New York, NY: Oxford University Press.

Mignone, Emilio Fermín. 1991. *Derechos humanos y sociedad: El caso argentino*. Buenos Aires, Argentina: Centro de Estudios Legales y Sociales/Ediciones del Pensamiento Nacional.

Ministério Publico Federal. 2013. *Grupo de Trabalho Justiça de Transição: Atividades de Persecução Penal Desenvolvidas Pelo Ministério Publico Federal 2011/2013*. Brsilia, Brazil: MPF, Série Relatórios de Actuação.

Modolell González, Juan Luis. 2010. "El crímen de desaparición forzada de personas en la jurisprudencia de la Corte Interamericana de Derechos Humanos." In *Sistema Interamericano de Protección de los derechos humanos y Derecho Penal Internacional*, ed. Kai Ambos. Montevideo, Uruguay: Fundación Konrad Adenauer.

Morales Solá, Joaquín. 1990. *Asalto a la ilusión: Historia secreta del poder en la Argentina desde 1983*. Buenos Aires, Argentina: Editorial Planeta.

Moustafa, Tamir. 2007. *The Struggle for Constitutional Power: Law, Politics, and Economic Development in Egypt*. New York, NY: Cambridge University Press.

Murillo, María Victoria. 2001. *Labor Unions, Partisan Coalitions and Market Reforms in Latin America*. New York, NY: Cambridge University Press.

Nalepa, Monika. 2010. *Skeletons in the Closet: Transitional Justice in Post-Communist Europe*. New York, NY: Cambridge University Press.

Nino, Carlos Santiago. 1996. *Radical Evil on Trial*. New Haven, CT: Yale University Press.

Nobles, Melissa. 2010. "The Prosecution of Human Rights Violations." *Annual Review of Political Science* 13: 165–182.

Norden, Deborah L. 1996. *Military Rebellion in Argentina: Between Coups and Consolidation*. Lincoln, NA: University of Nebraska Press.

Novaro, Marcos. 2009. *Argentina en el fin de siglo: Democracia, mercado y nación (1983–2001)*. Buenos Aires, Argentina: Paidós.

Novkov, Julie. 2008. "Law and Political Ideologies." In *The Oxford Handbook of Law and Politics*, ed. Keith E. Whittington, R. Daniel Kelemen, and Gregory A. Caldeira. New York, NY: Oxford University Press.

Nunes, Rodrigo M. 2010. "Ideational Origins of Progressive Judicial Activism: The Colombian Constitutional Court and the Right to Health." *Latin American Politics and Society* 52(3): 67–97.

O'Donnell, Guillermo. 1988. *Bureaucratic Authoritarianism: Argentina, 1966–1973, in Comparative Perspective*. Berkeley, CA: University of California Press.

2010. *Democracy, Agency, and the State: Theory with Comparative Intent*. Oxford, UK: Oxford University Press.

O'Donnell, Guillermo A., and Philippe C. Schmitter. 1986. *Transitions from Authoritarian Rule: Tentative Conclusions about Uncertain Democracies*. Baltimore, MD: Johns Hopkins University Press.

Olásolo Alonso, Héctor. 2010. *Estudios de Derecho Penal Internacional*. Mexico D.F., Mexico: Instituto Nacional de Ciencias Penales.

Olsen, Tricia, Leigh Payne and Andrew Reitner. 2010. *Transitional Justice in Balance*. Washington, DC: United States Institute for Peace.

Orentlicher, Diane F. 1991. "Settling Accounts: The Duty to Prosecute Human Rights Violations of a Prior Regime." *Yale Law Journal* 100: 2537–2618.

Orren, Karen. 1991. *Belated Feudalism: Labor, the Law and Liberal Development in the United States*. New York, NY: Cambridge University Press.

Osiel, Mark. 1986. "The Making of Human Rights Policy in Argentina: The Impact of Ideas and Interests on a Legal Conflict." *Journal of Latin American Studies* 18(01): 135–180.

2000. "Why Prosecute: Critics of Punishment for Mass Atrocity." *Human Rights Quarterly* 22: 118–147.

Oyhanarte, Julio. 1972. "Historia del Poder Judicial." *Todo Es Historia* 61.

Panfichi, Aldo, ed. 2009. *La ciencia política en el Perú de hoy*. Lima, Peru: PUCP-CISEPA.

Parenti, Pablo. 2010. "La inaplicabilidad de las normas de prescripción en la jurisprudencia de la Corte Interamericana de Derechos Humanos." In *Sistema*

Interamericano de Protección de los derechos humanos y Derecho Penal Internacional, ed. Kai Ambos. Montevideo, Uruguay: Fundación Konrad Adenauer.

Pásara, Luis. 2010. *Tres claves de la justicia en el Perú: Jueces, justicia y poder en el Perú; La enseñanza del derecho; Los abogados en la administración de justicia.* Lima, Peru: Fondo Editorial de la Pontificia Universidad Católica del Perú.

Patterson, James. 2001. *Brown v. Board of Education: A Civil Rights Milestone and Its Troubled Legacy*. New York, NY: Oxford University Press.

Payne, Leigh. 2008. *Unsettling Accounts: Neither Truth nor Reconciliation in Confessions of State Violence*. Durham, NC: Duke University Press.

Pereira, Anthony. 2005. *Political (In)justice: Authoritarianism and the Rule of Law in Brazil, Chile, and Argentina*. Pittsburgh, PA: University of Pittsburgh Press.

Pérez Perdomo, Rogelio. 2006. *Latin American Lawyers: A Historical Introduction*. Stanford, CA: Stanford University Press.

Pérez-Liñán, Aníbal, and Andrea Castagnola. 2009. "Presidential Control of High Courts in Latin America: A Long-Term View (1904–2006)." *Journal of Politics in Latin America* 1(2): 87–114.

Peterson, M. J. 1992. "Whalers, Cetologists, Environmentalists, and the International Management of Whaling." *International Organization* 46(1): 147–186.

Pevehouse, Jon. 2002. "Democracy from the Outside-In?: International Organizations and Democratization." *International Organization* 56(3): 515–549.

Pickerill, Mitchell, and Cornell Clayton. 2004. "The Rehnquist Court and the Political Dynamics of Federalism." *Perspectives on Politics* 2(2): 233–248.

Pion-Berlin, David. 1994. "To Prosecute or to Pardon? Human Rights Decisions in the Latin American Southern Cone." *Human Rights Quarterly* 16(1): 105–130.

1995. "To Prosecute or to Pardon?" In *Transitional Justice: How Emerging Democracies Reckon with Former Regimes*, ed. Neil Kritz. Washington, DC: United States Institute of Peace Press.

1997. *Through Corridors of Power: Institutions and Civil-military Relations in Argentina*. University Park, PA: Pennsylvania State University Press.

2004. "The Pinochet Case and Human Rights Progress in Chile: Was Europe a Catalyst, Cause or Inconsequential?" *Journal of Latin American Studies* 36(03): 479–505.

Poniatowska, Elena. 1971. *La noche de Tlatelolco: Testimonios de historia oral*. Mexico D.F., Mexico: Biblioteca Era.

Prusak, Christina. 2010. "The Trial of Alberto Fujimori: Navigating the Show Trial Dilemma in Pursuit of Transitional Justice." *NYU Law Review* 85: 867–2209.

Quinteros, Víctor, ed. 2010. *Judicialización de violaciones de derechos humanos: Aportes sustantivos y procesales*. Lima, Peru: IDEHPUCP.

Ratner, Steven, and Jason Abrams. 1997. *Accountability for Human Rights Atrocities in International Law: Beyond the Nuremberg Legacy*. New York, NY: Oxford University Press.

Ríos Figueroa, Julio. 2007. "Fragmentation of Power and the Emergence of an Effective Judiciary in Mexico, 1994–2002." *Latin American Politics and Society* 49(1): 31–57.

2011. "Institutions of Constitutional Justice in Latin America." In *Courts in Latin America*, ed. Gretchen Helmke and Julio Ríos Figueroa. New York, NY: Cambridge University Press.

Ríos Figueroa, Julio, and Jeffrey Staton. 2014. "An Evaluation of Cross-National Measures of Judicial Independence." *Journal of Law, Economics and Organization* 30(1): 104–137.

Ríos Figueroa, Julio, and Matthew Taylor. 2006. "Institutional Determinants of the Judicialisation of Policy in Brazil and Mexico." *Journal of Latin American Studies* 38(04): 739–766.

Risse-Kappen, Thomas, Steve C. Ropp, and Kathryn Sikkink, eds. 1999. *The Power of Human Rights: International Norms and Domestic Change*. New York, NY: Cambridge University Press.

Risse-Kappen, Thomas, and Kathryn Sikkink. 1999. "The Socialization of International Human Rights Norms into Domestic Practices: Introduction." In *The Power of Human Rights: International Norms and Domestic Change*, ed. Thomas Risse-Kappen, Steve C. Ropp, and Kathryn Sikkink. New York, NY: Cambridge University Press.

Rivera, Carlos. 2010. *"El estado del proceso de judicialización de graves violaciones a los derechos humanos en el Perú"*. Mimeo.

Rodríguez Garavito, César. 2009. *La globalización del estado de derecho: El neoconstitucionalismo, el neoliberalismo y la transformación institucional en América Latina*. Bogotá, Colombia: Ediciones Uniandes/Facultad de Derecho.

2011a. "Latin American Constitutionalism: Social and Economic Rights: Beyond the Courtroom: The Impact of Judicial Activism on Socioeconomic Rights in Latin America." *Texas Law Review* 89: 1669–1977.

2011b. "Toward a Sociology of the Global Rule of Law Field: Neoliberalism, Neoconstitutionalism, and the Contest over Judicial Reform in Latin America." In *Lawyers and the Rule of Law in an Era of Globalization*, ed. Yves Dezalay and Bryant G. Garth. New York, NY: Routledge.

Rodríguez Mungía, Jacinto. 2007. *La otra guerra secreta: Los archivos prohibidos de la prensa y el poder*. Mexico D.F., Mexico: Debolsillo.

Rodríguez Raga, Juan Carlos. 2011. "Strategic Deference in the Colombian Constitutional Court, 1992–2006." In *Courts in Latin America*, ed. Gretchen Helmke and Julio Ríos Figueroa. New York, NY: Cambridge University Press.

Roehrig, Terence. 2009. "Executive Leadership and the Continuing Quest for Justice in Argentina." *Human Rights Quarterly* 31(3): 721–747.

Roht-Arriaza, Naomi. 2005. *The Pinochet Effect: Transnational Justice in the Age of Human Rights*. Philadelphia, PA: University of Pennsylvania Press.

2006. "The New Landscape of Transitional Justice." In *Transitional Justice in the Twenty-First Century: Beyond Truth versus Justice*, ed. Naomi Roht-Arriaza and Javier Mariezcurrena. New York, NY: Cambridge University Press.

2015. "After Amnesties Are Gone: Latin American National Courts and the New Contours of the Fight against Impunity," in *Human Rights Quarterly* 37(2): 341–382.

Romero, Luis Alberto. 2002. *A History of Argentina in the Twentieth Century*. University Park, PA: Pennsylvania State University Press.

Rosenberg, Gerald. 1991. *The Hollow Hope: Can Courts Bring About Social Change?* Chicago, IL: University of Chicago Press.

Roxin, Claus. 2006. "El dominio de organización como forma independiente de autoría mediata." *Revista de Estudios de la Justicia* (7): 11–22.

Ruibal, Alba. 2009. "Self-Restraint in Search of Legitimacy: The Reform of the Argentine Supreme Court." *Latin American Politics and Society* 51(3): 59–86.

Salas, Luis. 2001. "From Law and Development to Rule of Law: New and Old Issues in Justice Reform in Latin America." In *The Rule of Law in Latin America: The International Promotion of Judicial Reform*, ed. Rachel Sieder and Pilar Domingo. London, UK: Institute of Latin American Studies, University of London.

Saltalamacchia, Natalia. 2009. "1968 y los derechos humanos en México." *Foreign Affairs: Latinoamérica* 9(1): 133–142.

Sanchez, Arianna, Beatriz Magaloni and Eric Magar. 2011. "Legalist versus Interpretativist: The Supreme Court and the Democratic Transition in Mexico." In *Courts in Latin America*, ed. Gretchen Helmke and Julio Ríos Figueroa. New York, NY: Cambridge University Press.

Sancinetti, Marcelo. 1987. *Derechos humanos en la Argentina postdictatorial: Juicio a los ex comandantes, punto final, obedencia debida, apéndice documental*. Buenos Aires, Argentina: Lerner Editores Asociados.

Sarles, Margaret. 2001. "USAID's Support of Justice Reform in Latin America." In *The Rule of Law in Latin America: The International Promotion of Judicial Reform*, ed. Rachel Sieder and Pilar Domingo. London, UK: Institute of Latin American Studies, University of London.

Schauer, Frederick. 2008. "Formalism: Legal, Constitutional, Judicial." In *The Oxford Handbook of Law and Politics*, ed. Keith E. Whittington, R. Daniel Kelemen, and Gregory A. Caldeira. New York, NY: Oxford University Press.

Scheb, John M., and William Lyons. 2000. "The Myth of Legality and Public Evaluation of the Supreme Court." *Social Science Quarterly* 81(4): 928–940.

Scribner, Druscilla. 2011. "Courts, Power and Rights in Argentina and Chile." In *Courts in Latin America*, ed. Gretchen Helmke and Julio Ríos Figueroa. New York, NY: Cambridge University Press.

Segal, Jeffrey Allan, and Harold J. Spaeth. 1993. *The Supreme Court and the Attitudinal Model*. New York, NY: Cambridge University Press.

Seils, Peter. 2004. "Promised Unfulfilled? The Special Prosecutor's Office in Mexico." Occasional Papers Series. Internacional Center for Transitional Justice.

Shapiro, Martin M. 1981. *Courts: A Comparative and Political Analysis*. Chicago, IL: University of Chicago Press.

Shor, Eran. 2008. "Conflict, Terrorism and the Socialization of Human Rights Norms: The Spiral Model Revisited." *Social Problems* 55(1): 117–138.

Sieder, Rachel, Line Schjolden, and Alan Angell, eds. 2005. *The Judicialization of Politics in Latin America*. New York, NY: Palgrave Macmillan.

Sierra, Jorge Luis. 2003. *El enemigo interno: Contrainsurgencia y fuerzas armadas en Mexico*. Mexico D.F., Mexico: Universidad Iberoamericana.

Sikkink, Kathryn. 1993. "Human Rights, Principled Issue-Networks, and Sovereignty in Latin America." *International Organization* 47(3): 411–441.

2005. "The Transnational Dimension of the Judicialization of Politics in Latin America." In *The Judicialization of Politics in Latin America*, ed. Rachel Sieder, Line Schjolden, and Alan Angell. New York, NY: Palgrave Macmillan.

2011. *The Justice Cascade: How Human Rights Prosecutions Are Changing World Politics*. New York, NY: W. W. Norton & Co.

Sikkink, Kathryn, and Carrie Booth Walling. 2007. "The Impact of Human Rights Trials in Latin America." *Journal of Peace Research* 44(4): 427–445.

Silva Meza, Juan N., and Fernando Silva García. 2009. *Derechos fundamentales: Bases para la reconstrucción de la jurisprudencia constitucional*. Mexico D.F., Mexico: Porrúa.

Simmons, Beth A. 2009. *Mobilizing for Human Rights: International Law in Domestic Politics*. New York, NY: Cambridge University Press.

Skaar, Elin. 2011. *Judicial Independence and Human Rights in Latin America: Violations, Politics, and Prosecution*. Basingstoke: Palgrave Macmillan.

Smith, Rogers. 1988. "Political Jurisprudence, the 'New Institutionalism' and the Future of Public Law." *American Political Science Review* 82(1): 89–108.

2008. "Historical Institutionalism and the Study of Law." In *The Oxford Handbook of Law and Politics*, ed. Keith E. Whittington, R. Daniel Kelemen, and Gregory A. Caldeira. New York, NY: Oxford University Press.

Smulovitz, Catalina. 1995. "Constitución y Poder Judicial en la nueva democracia Argentina: La experiencia de las instituciones." In *La nueva matriz política argentina*, ed. Carlos Acuña. Buenos Aires, Argentina: Ediciones Nueva Visión.

2002. "The Discovery of Law: Political Consequences in the Argentine Case." In *Global Prescriptions: The Production, Exportation, and Importation of a New Legal Orthodoxy*, ed. Yves Dezalay and Bryant G. Garth. Ann Arbor, MI: University of Michigan Press.

Spiller, Pablo T., and Mariano Tommasi. 2009. *The Institutional Foundations of Public Policy in Argentina: A Transaction Costs Approach*. New York, NY: Cambridge University Press.

Staton, Jeffrey K. 2004. "Judicial Policy Implementation in Mexico City and Mérida." *Comparative Politics* 37(1): 41–60.

2010. *Judicial Power and Strategic Communication in Mexico*. New York, NY: Cambridge University Press.

Steinmo, Sven, Kathleen Ann Thelen, and Frank Longstreth, eds. 1992. *Structuring Politics: Historical Institutionalism in Comparative Analysis*. New York, NY: Cambridge University Press.

Stern, Steve J. 1998. *Shining and Other Paths: War and Society in Peru, 1980–1995*. Durham, NC: Duke University Press.

Stinchcombe, Arthur L. 1997. "On the Virtues of the Old Institutionalism." *Annual Review of Sociology* 23(1): 1–18.

Stone, Alec. 1992. *The Birth of Judicial Politics in France*. New York, NY: Oxford University Press.

Stone Sweet, Alec. 2000. *Governing with Judges: Constitutional Politics in Europe*. New York, NY: Oxford University Press.

Struett, Michael J. 2008. *The Politics of Constructing the International Criminal Court: NGOs, Discourse, and Agency*. New York, NY: Palgrave Macmillan.

Tanaka, Martín. 1998. *El espejismos de la democracia: El colapso del sistema de partidos en el Perú, 1980–1995, en perspectiva comparada*. Lima, Peru: Instituto de Estudios Peruanos.

2005. *Democracia sin partidos, Perú, 2000–2005: Los problemas de representación y las propuestas de reforma política*. Lima, Peru: Instituto de Estudios Peruanos.

2006. "From Crisis to Collapse of the Party Systems and Dilemmas of Democratic Representation: Peru and Venezuela." In *The Crisis of Democratic Representation in the Andes*, ed. Scott Mainwaring, Ana María Bejarano, and Eduardo Pizarro Leongómez. Stanford, CA: Stanford University Press.

Tate, C. Neal, and Torbjörn Vallinder, eds. 1995. *The Global Expansion of Judicial Power*. New York, NY: New York University Press.

Taylor, Matthew. 2008. *Judging Policy: Courts and Policy Reform in Democratic Brazil*. Palo Alto, CA: Stanford University Press.

Teitel, Ruti G. 1997. "Transitional Jurisprudence: The Role of Law in Political Transformation." *Yale Law Journal* 106(7): 2009–2080.

2000. *Transitional Justice*. Oxford, UK: Oxford University Press.

2003. "Transitional Justice Genealogy." *Harvard Human Rights Journal* 16: 69–94.

2014. *Globalizing Transitional Justice*. New York, NY: Oxford University Press.

Thelen, Kathleen. 1999. "Historical Institutionalism in Comparative Politics." *Annual Review of Political Science* 2(1): 369–404.

Treviño, Javier. 2004. "Las ONG de derechos humanos y la redefinición de la soberanía del Estado Mexicano." *Foro Internacional* 44(3): 509–539.

Tushnet, Mark. 1994. *Making Civil Rights Law: Thurgood Marshall and the Supreme Court, 1936–1961*. New York, NY: Oxford University Press.

2004. *The NAACP's Legal Strategy against Segregated Education, 1925–1950*. Chapel Hill, NC: University of North Carolina Press.

United Nations. 2010. "World Drug Report 2010." www.unodc.org/unodc/en/data-and-analysis/WDR-2010.html (last accessed 11 June 2012).

Uprimny, Rodrigo. 2004. "The Constitutional Court and the Control of Extraordinary Powers in Colombia." In *Democratization and the Judiciary: The Accountability Function of Courts in New Democracies* ed. Siri Gloppen, Roberto Gargarella, and Elin Skaar. Portland, OR: Frank Cass.

Valadés, Diego. 2001. "La obre es una república: La tradición internacionalista mexicana." *Anuario Mexicano de Derecho Internacional* 1: 9–15.

Valladares, Jorge. 2010. "Unidad de los grupos parlamentarios en el congreso de la república 2006–2007." In *Estudios sobre el congreso peruano: Grupos parlamentarios, disciplina partidaria y desempeño profesional*, ed. Jorge Valladares. Lima, Peru: IDEA.

Van Der Voort, Karlijn, and Marten Zwanenburg. 2001. "From Raison d'Etat to Etat de Droit International – Amnesties and the French Implementation of the Rome Statute." *International Criminal Law Review* 1: 315–342.

Vanberg, Georg. 2001. "Legislative-Judicial Relations: A Game-Theoretic Approach to Constitutional Review." *American Journal of Political Science* 45(2): 346–361.

2005. *The Politics of Constitutional Review in Germany*. New York, NY: Cambridge University Press.

Vargas, Luis. 2010. "Tratamiento de la prueba en el delito de desaparición forzada: Especial referencia a la prueba indiciaria." In *Judicialización de violaciones de derechos humanos: Aportes sustantivos y procesales*, ed. Víctor Quinteros. Lima, Peru: Instituto de Derechos Humanos de la Pontificia Universidad Católica del Perú.

Vecchioli, Virginia. 2010. "*Derechos Humanos y Compromiso Militante: Un Recorrido por la Constitución de Esta Causa a Través del Activismo de los Profesionales del Derecho*." Mimeo.

2011. "Human Rights and the Rule of Law in Argentina: Transnational Advocacy Networks and the Transformation of the National Legal Field." In *Lawyers and the Rule of Law in an Era of Globalization*, ed. Yves Dezalay and Bryant G. Garth. London, UK: Routledge.

Verbitsky, Horacio. 1993. *Hacer la corte: La construcción de un poder absoluto sin justicia ni control*. Buenos Aires, Argentina: Planeta.

2003. *Civiles y militares: Memoria secreta de la transición*. Editorial Sudamericana.

Verner, Joel G. 1984. "The Independence of Supreme Courts in Latin America: A Review of the Literature." *Journal of Latin American Studies* 16(2): 463–506.

Vicente, Camilo. 2012. "La conspiración de las ratas: La construcción del enemigo político en México, 1970–1980." *Naveg@mérica* 9: 1–21.

Villarán, Susana. 2007. "Perú." In *Víctimas sin mordaza: El impacto del Sistema Interamericano en la jusiticia transicional en latinoamérica: Los casos de*

Argentina, Guatemala, El Salvador y Perú, ed. Fundación para el Debido Proceso Legal. Washington, D.C.: Fundación para el Debido Proceso Legal

Wasby, Stephen L. 1983. "Interest Groups and Litigation." *Policy Studies Journal* 11(4): 657–670.

Wasserstrom, Richard. 1968. "Lawyers and Revolution." *University of Pittsburgh Law Review*, 30: 125–133.

Weldon, Jeffrey. 1997. "The Political Sources of Presidencialismo in Mexico." In *Presidentialism and Democracy in Latin America*, ed. Scott Mainwaring and Mathew Shugart. New York, NY: Cambridge University Press.

Whittington, Keith E. 2000. "Once More unto the Breach: Post-Behavioralist Approaches to Judicial Politics." *Law and Social Inquiry* 25(2): 601–634.

Wilson, Bruce M., and Juan Carlos Rodríguez Cordero. 2006. "Legal Opportunity Structures and Social Movements: The Effects of Institutional Change on Costa Rican Politics." *Comparative Political Studies* 39(3): 325–351.

Woods, Patricia J. 2008. *Judicial Power and National Politics: Courts and Gender in the Religious-Secular Conflict in Israel.* Albany, NY: SUNY Press.

Woods, Patricia J., and Lisa Hilbink. 2009. "Comparative Sources of Judicial Empowerment: Ideas and Interests." *Political Research Quarterly* 62(4): 745–752.

Yacobucci, Guillermo J. 2005. "Hacia una nueva legalidad penal (a propósito del fallo 'Espósito' de la Corte Suprema de Justicia de la Nación.)" *La Ley* C (1).

Youngers, Coletta. 2003. *Violencia política y sociedad civil en el Perú: Historia de la Coordinadora Nacional de Derechos Humanos*. Lima, Peru: Instituto de Estudios Peruanos.

Zalaquett, José. 1992. "Balancing Ethical Imperatives and Political Constraints: The Dilemma of New Democracies Confronting Past Human Rights Violations." *Hastings Law Journal* 43(6): 1425–1438.

1995. "Confronting Human Rights Violations Committed by Former Governments: Principles Applicable and Political Constraints." In *Transitional Justice: How Emerging Democracies Reckon with Former Regimes*, ed. Neil Kritz. Washington, DC: United States Institute of Peace Press.

INDEX

Books in the Series

China and Islam: The Prophet, the Party, and Law
Matthew S. Erie

Diversity in Practice: Race, Gender, and Class in Legal and Professional Careers
Edited by Spencer Headworth and Robert Nelson

Diseases of the Will
Mariana Valverde

The Politics of Truth and Reconciliation in South Africa: Legitimizing the Post-Apartheid State
Richard A. Wilson

Modernism and the Grounds of Law
Peter Fitzpatrick

Unemployment and Government: Genealogies of the Social
William Walters

Autonomy and Ethnicity: Negotiating Competing Claims in Multi-Ethnic States
Yash Ghai

Constituting Democracy: Law, Globalism and South Africa's Political Reconstruction
Heinz Klug

The Ritual of Rights in Japan: Law, Society, and Health Policy
Eric A. Feldman

The Invention of the Passport: Surveillance, Citizenship and the State
John Torpey

Governing Morals: A Social History of Moral Regulation
Alan Hunt

The Colonies of Law: Colonialism, Zionism and Law in Early Mandate Palestine
Ronen Shamir

Law and Nature
David Delaney

Social Citizenship and Workfare in the United States and Western Europe: The Paradox of Inclusion
Joel F. Handler

Law, Anthropology and the Constitution of the Social: Making Persons and Things
Edited by Alain Pottage and Martha Mundy

Judicial Review and Bureaucratic Impact: International and Interdisciplinary Perspectives
Edited by Marc Hertogh and Simon Halliday

Immigrants at the Margins: Law, Race, and Exclusion in Southern Europe
Kitty Calavita

Lawyers and Regulation: The Politics of the Administrative Process
Patrick Schmidt

Law and Globalization from Below: Toward a Cosmopolitan Legality
Edited by Boaventura de Sousa Santos and Cesar A. Rodriguez-Garavito

Public Accountability: Designs, Dilemmas and Experiences
Edited by Michael W. Dowdle

Law, Violence and Sovereignty among West Bank Palestinians
Tobias Kelly

Legal Reform and Administrative Detention Powers in China
Sarah Biddulph

The Practice of Human Rights: Tracking Law Between the Global and the Local
Edited by Mark Goodale and Sally Engle Merry

Judges Beyond Politics in Democracy and Dictatorship: Lessons from Chile
Lisa Hilbink

Paths to International Justice: Social and Legal Perspectives
Edited by Marie-Bénédicte Dembour and Tobias Kelly

Law and Society in Vietnam: The Transition from Socialism in Comparative Perspective
Mark Sidel

Constitutionalizing Economic Globalization: Investment Rules and Democracy's Promise
David Schneiderman

The New World Trade Organization KnowledgeAgreements: 2nd Edition
Christopher Arup

Justice and Reconciliation in Post-Apartheid South Africa
Edited by François du Bois and Antje du Bois-Pedain

Militarization and Violence against Women in Conflict Zones in the Middle East: A Palestinian Case-Study
Nadera Shalhoub-Kevorkian

Child Pornography and Sexual Grooming: Legal and Societal Responses
Suzanne Ost

Darfur and the Crime of Genocide
John Hagan and Wenona Rymond-Richmond

Fictions of Justice: The International Criminal Court and the Challenge of Legal Pluralism in Sub-Saharan Africa
Kamari Maxine Clarke

Conducting Law and Society Research: Reflections on Methods and Practices
Simon Halliday and Patrick Schmidt

Planted Flags: Trees, Land, and Law in Israel/Palestine
Irus Braverman

Culture under Cross-Examination: International Justice and the Special Court for Sierra Leone
Tim Kelsall

Cultures of Legality: Judicialization and Political Activism in Latin America
Javier Couso, Alexandra Huneeus, Rachel Sieder

Courting Democracy in Bosnia and Herzegovina: The Hague Tribunal's Impact in a Postwar State
Lara J. Nettelfield

The Gacaca Courts and Post-Genocide Justice and Reconciliation in Rwanda: Justice without Lawyers
Phil Clark

Law, Society, and History: Themes in the Legal Sociology and Legal History of Lawrence M. Friedman
Robert W. Gordon and Morton J. Horwitz

After Abu Ghraib: Exploring Human Rights in America and the Middle East
Shadi Mokhtari

Adjudication in Religious Family Laws: Cultural Accommodation: Legal Pluralism, and Gender Equality in India
Gopika Solanki

Water On Tap: Rights and Regulation in the Transnational Governance of Urban Water Services
Bronwen Morgan

Elements of Moral Cognition: Rawls' Linguistic Analogy and the Cognitive Science of Moral and Legal Judgment
John Mikhail

A Sociology of Constitutions: Constitutions and State Legitimacy in Historical-Sociological Perspective
Chris Thornhill

Mitigation and Aggravation at Sentencing
Edited by Julian Roberts

Institutional Inequality and the Mobilization of the Family and Medical Leave Act: Rights on Leave
Catherine R. Albiston

Authoritarian Rule of Law: Legislation, Discourse and Legitimacy in Singapore
Jothie Rajah

Law and Development and the Global Discourses of Legal Transfers
Edited by John Gillespie and Pip Nicholson

Law against the State: Ethnographic Forays into Law's Transformations
Edited by Julia Eckert, Brian Donahoe, Christian Strümpell and Zerrin Özlem Biner

Transnational Legal Process and State Change
Edited by Gregory C. Shaffer

Legal Mobilization under Authoritarianism: The Case of Post-Colonial Hong Kong
Edited by Waikeung Tam

Complementarity in the Line of Fire: The Catalysing Effect of the International Criminal Court in Uganda and Sudan
Sarah M. H. Nouwen

Political and Legal Transformations of an Indonesian Polity: The Nagari from Colonisation to Decentralisation
Franz von Benda-Beckmann and Keebet von Benda-Beckmann

Pakistan's Experience with Formal Law: An Alien Justice
Osama Siddique

Human Rights under State-Enforced Religious Family Laws in Israel, Egypt, and India
Yüksel Sezgin

Why Prison?
Edited by David Scott

Law's Fragile State: Colonial, Authoritarian, and Humanitarian Legacies in Sudan
Mark Fathi Massoud

Rights for Others: The Slow Home-Coming of Human Rights in the Netherlands
Barbara Oomen

European States and their Muslim Citizens: The Impact of Institutions on Perceptions and Boundaries
Edited by John R. Bowen, Christophe Bertossi, Jan Willem Duyvendak and Mona Lena Krook

Environmental Litigation in China
Rachel E. Stern

Indigeneity and Legal Pluralism in India: Claims, Histories, Meanings
Pooja Parmar

Paper Tiger: Law, Bureaucracy and the Developmental State in Himalayan India
Nayanika Mathur

Contractual Knowledge: One Hundred Years of Legal Experimentation in Global Markets
Edited by Grégoire Mallard and Jérôme Sgard

Religion, Law and Society
Russell Sandberg

The Experiences of Face Veil Wearers in Europe and the Law
Edited by Eva Brems

The Contentious History of the International Bill of Human Rights
Christopher N. J. Roberts

Transnational Legal Orders
Edited by Terence C. Halliday and Gregory Shaffer

Lost in China?, Law, Culture and Society in Post-1997 Hong Kong
Carol A. G. Jones

Security Theology, Surveillance and the Politics of Fear
Nadera Shalhoub-Kevorkian

Opposing the Rule of Law: How Myanmar's Courts Make Law and Order
Nick Cheesman

The Ironies of Colonial Governance: Law, Custom and Justice in Colonial India
James Jaffe

The Clinic and the Court: Law, Medicine and Anthropology
Edited by Tobias Kelly, Ian Harper and Akshay Khanna

A World of Indicators: The Making of Government Knowledge Through Quantification
Edited by Richard Rottenburg, Sally E. Merry, Sung-Joon Park and Johanna Mugler

Contesting Immigration Policy in Court: Legal Activism and its Radiating Effects in the United States and France
Leila Kawar

The Quiet Power of Indicators: Measuring Governance, Corruption, and Rule of Law
Edited by Sally Engle Merry, Kevin Davis, and Benedict Kingsbury

Investing in Authoritarian Rule: Punishment and Patronage in Rwanda's Gacaca Courts for Genocide Crimes
Anuradha Chakravarty

Iraq and the Crimes of Aggressive War: The Legal Cynicism of Criminal Militarism
John Hagan, Joshua Kaiser, and Anna Hanson

Culture in the Domains of Law
Edited by René Provost

A Sociology of Transnational Constitutions: Social Foundations of the Post-National Legal Structure
Chris Thornhill

Shifting Legal Visions: Judicial Change and Human Rights Trials in Latin America
Ezequiel A. González Ocantos

The Demographic Transformations of Citizenship
Heli Askola

Criminal Defense in China: The Politics of Lawyers at Work
Sida Liu and Terence C. Halliday

Contesting Economic and Social Rights in Ireland: Constitution, State and Society, 1848–2016
Thomas Murray

Buried in the Heart: Women, Complex Victimhood and the War in Northern Uganda
Erin Baines

Palaces of Hope: The Anthropology of Global Organizations
Edited by Ronald Niezen and Maria Sapignoli

CPSIA information can be obtained
at www.ICGtesting.com
Printed in the USA
LVOW10*2136120717
541124LV00009B/211/P